The Empire of Civilization

The Empire of Civilization: The Evolution of an Imperial Idea

Brett Bowden

The University of Chicago Press :: Chicago and London

Brett Bowden is senior lecturer in politics at the University of New South
Wales at the Australian Defence Force Academy, Canberra. He is the coedi-
tor of *Terror: From Tyrannicide to Terrorism*, *The Role of International
Law in Rebuilding Societies after Conflict*, and *Global Standards of Market
Civilization*.

The University of Chicago Press, Chicago 60637
The University of Chicago Press, Ltd., London
© 2009 by The University of Chicago
All rights reserved. Published 2009
Printed in the United States of America

18 17 16 15 14 13 12 11 10 09   1 2 3 4 5

ISBN-13: 978-0-226-06814-5 (cloth)

ISBN-10: 0-226-06814-5 (cloth)

Library of Congress Cataloging-in-Publication Data

Bowden, Brett, 1968–
    The empire of civilization : the evolution of an imperial idea /
Brett Bowden.
        p. cm.
    Includes bibliographical references and index.
    ISBN-13: 978-0-226-06814-5 (cloth : alk. paper)
    ISBN-10: 0-226-06814-5 (cloth : alk. paper) 1. Civilization—
Philosophy. 2. Civilization—History. 3. Imperialism. 4. International
relations—Philosophy. 5. Philosophy, European. 6. Europe—Territorial
expansion. I. Title.
    CB19.B598 2009
    303.48'201—dc22

                                                        2008029873

♾ The paper used in this publication meets the minimum requirements of
the American National Standard for Information Sciences—Permanence
of Paper for Printed Library Materials, ANSI Z39.48-1992.

In memory of my Nan, Pearl Bowden, 1906–2007.

A most remarkable and inspiring woman.

Contents

Preface and Acknowledgments

This book was prompted by an article I read about the need for new standards of civilization to better order our world. With the best of intentions, the article outlined a range of perceived benefits for the global human condition, but it gave little consideration to the possible downsides of such a course of action. This oversight and the proposal more generally were particularly disconcerting given that the language of civilization comes with so much baggage. Soon after the publication of the article came the atrocities of September 11, 2001, and the subsequent launch of the global war on terror—a war that the most powerful man in the world, United States President George W. Bush, sees as a "fight for civilization." This characterization is cause for even greater concern, and not just because the language of civilization comes with baggage; it is cause for concern because the actions that all too often follow the language of civilization are anything but civilized. These two not unrelated developments—one born of the world of academia and ideas, the other straight out of the "real world" of global politics—led me to recall Albert Camus's warning in *The Plague* that the "evil that is in the world always comes out of ignorance, and good intentions may do as much harm as malevolence, if they lack understanding." With that thought in mind, this book is about advancing understanding. It is about having a better understanding of the language of civilization and about having a better understanding of the actions that tend to follow the language of civilization. To a certain degree, it is about advancing self-understanding.

In seeking understanding, this book engages with a wide range of interrelated ideas and events across a vast expanse of time and space, from the eleventh-century Crusades to the discovery of the New World to the global war on terror. It cautiously navigates this long, winding, and sometimes treacherous path because Johann Gottfried Herder was never more right than when he suggested that the present is pregnant with the past. In order that we are able to understand and make sense of the present, we must have an adequate understanding of our history, which in turn offers the hope of being better prepared for what the future might hold in store. The ongoing relevance of the past to the present and the prospects for the future were made painfully clear to me on Wednesday, February 13, 2008, when the newly elected prime minister of Australia, Kevin Rudd, officially apologized on behalf of the parliament and the government to indigenous Australians over the past practice of removing Aboriginal children, the so-called stolen generations, from their parents. Such policies and practices were in large part directed by the kind of thinking about civilization that is outlined in this book.

In seeking to enhance my own understanding of how our world works, and in attempting to relay this to a wider audience via this book, I have been fortunate to benefit from the wisdom and generosity of a good many people. First and foremost, I am grateful to Barry Hindess, who engaged with the project at length and in depth from day one. In addition to his expansive knowledge, probing questions, and wise counsel, I am also grateful for his friendship. Early drafts of the manuscript were read in their entirety by Pal Ahluwalia, David Armitage, John M. Hobson, Paul Keal, Leonard Seabrooke, and Andrew Schuller. Many thanks go to them for their thoughtful comments and insightful suggestions, all of which helped to make this a more polished book than it would otherwise have been. Thanks also goes to Ali Aslan, Maria Bargh, Bruce Buchan, Federico Dalpane, Chris Hobson, Cindy O'Hagan, Tim Rowse, Michael Schiavone, and Nicholas Wheeler, who engaged with various sections of the manuscript, or engaged me in conversation, or both, and offered much helpful advice. I must also acknowledge the invaluable part played by a number of institutions which provided the necessary space, resources, and collegial environment to undertake the research and writing of this book: the Political Science Program and the Regulatory Institutions Network in the Research School of Social Sciences at the Australian National University, the Centre for the History of European Discourses at the University of Queensland, and the School of Humanities and Social Sciences at the University of New South Wales at the Australian Defence Force Academy.

I owe a considerable debt of gratitude to Andrew Schuller, who, despite claiming to be retired, generously gave his time and energy in helping me to find the right publisher for the book—thank you kindly. Once that was achieved, David Pervin at the University of Chicago Press has been the consummate professional to work with, and I thank him for his commitment to the book and his wise counsel and steady hand in guiding me and the book through to publication. Thanks to all of the team at the University of Chicago Press who have had a hand in the publication of this book. I am also grateful to the anonymous reviewers who engaged with the book in depth and at length and offered a range of helpful comments and constructive criticisms; it is a better book for it.

On a more personal note, I am most grateful for the ongoing support and friendship, manifested in a variety of pleasant and surprising ways, which has helped to make the preparation of this book a more enjoyable and shared experience. Heartfelt thanks to distant friends, Jane Morrison and family, Sarah Nwangwa, Kim Stepien, and Emily Trudeau. Closer to home I am fortunate to have such good friends as Victoria Bickford, Sharon Hicks, and Brendon McKinley. I would particularly like to thank Jacob Ramsay for his friendship and good conversation—long may it last.

This book and much more would not be possible without the endless encouragement and generous support of my parents, Allan and Miriam Bowden. It is a debt I am unlikely to ever be able to repay in full. Thanks Mum and Dad. Finally, I am most fortunate to have a loving and understanding partner, Gerda Roelvink, who shares with me both the highs and the lows of such a process. And I am grateful that she shares hers with me. Thank you Gerda for your boundless encouragement and support at every turn, it is greatly appreciated, if not always acknowledged.

Thanks kindly to you all for your individual and collective generosity and support, it is much appreciated. Without it the book would have suffered accordingly. Naturally, whatever faults remain are of my own making or a result of my own shortcomings or stubbornness.

A Note on Spelling

The variations in the spelling of *civilization* (or *civilisa-tion*) in the texts cited in this book have caused more than a little angst during the writing process. When not using direct quotations, I have generally followed the *Oxford English Dictionary* by using *civilization*, the spelling that it uses in the first instance, while *civilisation* is offered as an alternative spelling. The exception to this guiding principle occurs in discussions of the French origins of the word and concept of *civilisation* in chapter 2, wherein the French spelling is of some etymological significance in its own right. When quoting passages directly from a source, I have followed the spelling of *civilization/civilisation* verbatim; the fact that a number of the texts cited use both spellings should account for any apparent inconsistencies.

1

Introduction: Guizot's Question: Universal Civilization?

Civilization as threat, civilization as threatened: these are just two of many contradictory themes that have gained urgency in recent years. In the clash of opposites, civilization is both threatening and threatened, persecutor and persecuted.   **Jean Starobinski,** *Blessings in Disguise; or, The Morality of Evil*

: : :

Guizot's Question

In the early nineteenth century, the distinguished French historian François Guizot asked "whether it is an universal fact, whether there is an universal civilization of the human species, a destiny of humanity; whether the nations have handed down from age to age, something which has never been lost, which must increase, form a larger and larger mass, and thus pass on to the end of time?" To this question he immediately responded: "For my own part, I am convinced that there is, in reality, a general destiny of humanity, a transmission of the aggregate of civilization; and, consequently, an universal history of civilization to be written."[1]

In essence, this book is an exploration of the ongoing attempt to write that universal history of civilization and the consequences that flow from it. Or to put it slightly differently, this book examines the concerted attempt to inculcate "civilization" in all corners of the globe, what I have termed expanding the empire of civilization. It is a story about the crafting of universal teleological history, or History, and the influence this has had on the classification and treatment of certain peoples thanks to their temporal and geographic positioning in history. In order to undertake such a task, this is a necessarily interdisciplinary project, encompassing a number of fields of the social sciences and humanities, including anthropology and ethnology, political theory and the history of political thought, the philosophy of history, international politics, international law, and world history.

In a vein similar to that of Guizot, the prominent American commentator and scholar Robert Wright has more recently claimed that the closer one examines "the drift of biological evolution and, especially, the drift of human history, the more there seems to be a point to it all." Moreover, he claims that the study of cultural evolution enables us to explain and "define the arrow of the history of life, from the primordial soup to the World Wide Web." Building on these bold claims, Wright further contends that "Globalization . . . has been in the cards not just since the invention of the telegraph or the steamship, or even the written word or the wheel, but since the invention of life."[2]

The object of my exercise here is less ambitious, the size of my canvas and the scope of my enquiry pale in comparison to Wright's. The primordial soup and the vast majority of the subsequent thirteen billion–odd years of history will go unexamined, as will any attempt to rationalize them—but they are related in some small way. For my part, I contend that the evolutionary logic that Guizot, Wright, and other thinkers and chroniclers throughout history see as a natural and inevitable turn of events is anything but. Rather, this book outlines how a concerted effort has been made and continues to be undertaken to impose a particular ideological rationale on the passage of history. By peering into some of the more recent reaches of human history, it seeks to explain the logic underpinning certain trends and events that are transpiring in the present era. Or to put it another way, I argue that certain forces are at work in world politics striving to impose a purposefully charted "directionality" on our world's near-term history and future—at least as far as political, economic, legal, social, and cultural organization are concerned. In short, the book details how significant forces acting within and upon the international states system have a clear-cut vision of the form of international society they envisage for the future and are taking certain steps to see that it is realized. That is to say that the dominant architects of international society continue to be informed and influenced by a faith in the Enlightenment ideal of progress and humankind's universal linear march toward modernity, a modernity that is universally liberal democratic, market capitalist, and cosmopolitan in appearance. In making this case, the book necessarily engages with both the practical realm of international affairs and the owl-of-Minerva-like scribes who undertake to theorize and rationalize the construction process.

This is still a rather large and ambitious project, but that is not sufficient reason not to undertake it; it just makes it all the more interesting, thought provoking, challenging, and, ultimately, necessary. What makes it necessary is that the world-shaping ideas and events explored herein are too rarely thought about or examined together as part and parcel of a larger process. Some are studied as stand-alone concepts or events; some go largely ignored. Occasionally links are made between two or more of them, but rarely are they drawn together in an endeavor to fashion a coherent and comprehensive theory that seeks to explain the course of world politics and history.[3] In this respect I take my lead, in part at least (and despite having some serious misgivings about many of the positions he has taken over the years), from Samuel Huntington, who made some pertinent points in the preface to *The Soldier and the State*. Writing around fifty years ago, Huntington posited that "understanding requires theory; theory requires abstraction; and abstraction requires the simplification and ordering of reality." Yet "no theory can explain all the facts." He noted that the "real world is one of blends, irrationalities, and incongruities: actual personalities, institutions, and beliefs do not fit into neat logical categories. Yet neat logical categories are necessary" if we are to "think profitably" about the world in which we live and "derive from it lessons for broader application and use." Huntington thus concluded that we are "forced to generalize about phenomena which never quite operate according to the laws of human reason. One measure of a theory is the degree to which it encompasses and explains all the relevant facts. Another measure, and the more important one, is the degree to which it encompasses and explains those facts better than any other theory."[4] While this book is unlikely to satisfy all in its endeavor to explain a broad range of ideas and events across equally expansive time and space, I believe that it accounts for those events as effectively as any other theory, or the absence of theory.

Two attempts at grand theory that have captured imaginations in recent times are Francis Fukuyama's *The End of History and the Last Man* and Huntington's *The Clash of Civilizations and the Remaking of World Order*.[5] Both of these works have their share of admirers and critics, and both purport to be expounding premonitions of the future of world politics. If one is a fan or is won over by the picture presented in either of these works, then it is likely that they will be skeptical or unconvinced by the other, for they are generally thought of as competing or incompatible accounts of the future of world politics. Neither of the works is discussed at length here, partly because they are known to many and partly because they have been discussed, analyzed, and broken down *ad nauseam* in a multitude of forums. That should not be taken to imply that either is irrelevant or anachronistic. Particularly in the volatile world order since September 11, 2001, both continue to figure prominently in theoretical and practical discussions of world politics and in influential policy circles. While I engage with neither of the books or theories at length, their respective topics are germane to considerable portions of this book. The point to be made about these two particular works here is that they are not necessarily competing theories of world politics. Rather, they can be thought of as two sides of the same coin. By that I mean that the pursuit of one of these visions potentially begets the other; an attempt to impose Fukuyama's liberal democratic master plan across the globe will almost inevitably result in confrontations between Western civilization and the peoples on which it is imposing this plan. At the same time, should confrontations and wars break out between different civilizations for one reason or another (possibly between the "West and the rest"[6]), then this too might well lead to the victor imposing their will, values, and institutions and systems on the vanquished. I trust that this reading of Fukuyama's and Huntington's respective arguments and their relation to each other will be detectable in the chapters that follow, although it is not essential to the general aim and arguments of this book that the reader be necessarily convinced by this point of view. It might also be the case that Fukuyama, Huntington, and, consequently, the juxtaposing of their theories herein are all off the mark, with a more accurate theoretical picture of the future of world politics still in the pipeline.

The working subtitle of this book was originally "Uniform, Not Universal." It is an idea that borrows a little from another of Huntington's claims: that the West and its values and systems are "unique, not universal." He first made this argument in *Foreign Affairs* and then restated it in the expanded account of his "clash of civilizations" thesis.[7] This argument cuts two ways: the rest of the world is similarly unique, made up of numerous cultures and ways of life and, just as importantly, numerous ways of organizing society, including the realms of politics, economics, and systems of law, not to overlook community and family. The uniform-not-universal idea highlights that any concerted effort to write a universal history of civilization promotes the creation of an international society of reasonably uniform states based on an ideal type or model. While once it was the European imperial powers that were held up as the model, today it is the modern liberal democratic Western state—warts and all—which all other states and societies are encouraged to emulate. As Richard Shweder describes it, at present the "gold standard for defining progress is often, if only implicitly, the United States—our wealth and free enterprise, our democratic form of government, our dedication to work, and our ideas about gender, sexuality, marriage, and the family."[8] Instead of a cooperative, peaceful, and supposedly cosmopolitan world, the result of this neoimperial exercsie is the further erosion of cultural pluralism and heightened intercivilizational tensions. Or to put it differently, what is being promoted is an empire of civilization that is more *uniform* than *universal*;[9] the consequence of which is an almost inevitable backlash against such an imposition—as the world now increasingly bears witness.

The Power of Ideas

In order to explain the range of interrelated events across time and space with which this book engages, there are a number of ideas or concepts that are integral to its general argument. At any given point, one or more of them is either running through the heart of it or very close to the surface. Not by coincidence, these concepts are all long-standing ideas that, for one reason or another, have largely been out of fashion in scholarly and popular circles for a generation or two. Recent dramatic events, however, such as the demise of communism and the rise of the international terrorist threat have seen new life breathed into each of them; returning them one after the other to center stage. Each of these ideas or concepts has a part to play in driving history "forward" along a path that is thought to be a universal history of human progress and civilization.

The power of ideas is not to be underestimated—ideas do matter, both "good" and "bad" ideas.[10] John Maynard Keynes was on the mark when he proclaimed that the "ideas of economists and political philosophers, both when they are right and when they are wrong, are more powerful than is commonly understood." As he added:

> Indeed the world is ruled by little else. Practical men, who believe themselves to be quite exempt from any intellectual influences, are usually the slaves of some defunct economist. Madmen in authority, who hear voices in the air, are distilling their frenzy

from some academic scribbler of a few years back. I am sure that the power of vested interests is vastly exaggerated compared with the gradual encroachment of ideas. Not, indeed, immediately, but after a certain interval; for in the field of economic and political philosophy there are not many who are influenced by new theories after they are twenty-five or thirty years of age, so that the ideas which civil servants and politicians and even agitators apply to current events are not likely to be the newest. But, soon or late, it is ideas, not vested interests, which are dangerous for good or evil.[11]

Whether it is ideas associated with Marxism-Leninism, responsible for the deaths of untold millions in revolutions gone awry, or expansionist liberalism in the guise of colonialism, the consequences of ideas and the musings of "academic scribblers" reverberate well beyond the realm of purely abstract theory or the ivory tower—they have a very real impact on actions and outcomes.

The most significant of the recently revived concepts explored in this book is the idea and ideal of civilization. The concept of civilization is an ever-present theme that affects in one way or another virtually every aspect of the book. This book is in essence something of a genealogy of civilization and an explication of the transmission and deployment of ideas and concepts across time and space. It is about the power and persistence of ideas—the power of the idea of civilization, the power of civilization and associated and antithetical concepts to be utilized or manipulated to explain, rationalize, and justify decisions and actions that shape the course of history. The significance of the idea of civilization further stems from the fact that it is intrinsically related to the other revived concepts, or, perhaps more accurately, it is the root from which these concepts spring forth—which in part explains their near simultaneous resurrection.

The second concept is the idea of progress. Some version of the idea of progress has been with us for centuries. But the notion that has recently been revived takes the general principle of progress a step further. It is best identified as the "end of History" thesis, the basic argument of which is that human history has a purpose or *telos*, that history is a story of linear progress toward a certain point or end. The third concept to resurface is the idea that the world can be divided and classified into states and societies of varying shades or degrees of civilization, which is to say that the contemporary world effectively still consists of "civilized" and "uncivilized" societies. Closely related to this concept is the increasing number of both implicit and explicit calls for the reinvigoration and enforcement of twenty-first-century "standards of civilization" in international society. Finally, as history foretells, the escalating push for renewed standards of civilization is accompanied by equally loud calls for the return of a "new imperialism" to deal with the threats posed by today's uncivilized states and societies. In this regard, Naeem Inayatullah and David Blaney poignantly highlight that the seemingly "competing impulses to divide and separate or unify and homogenize seem to go hand in hand."[12] Another way to explain the revival of these interrelated ideas and concepts is to see the ideal of civilization, and ultimately progress toward universal civilization, as representing an end, while the standard of civilization and concomitant imperial civilizing missions constitute a means to that end.

I have characterized the reemergence of these ideas as a revival. Given a short-term view of history, this is correct. Through a longer-term perspective that accounts for centuries as opposed to decades, however, it appears to be more of a perpetuation than a resurrection. That is to say, the postcolonial moment and the demands of political correctness represent more of a blip on history's radar screen (granted, a significant blip), than an altogether about-face or sea change in the nature of European/Western and Nonwestern relations.

In exploring the power of ideas and the political deployment of concepts, this study draws heavily, but not exclusively on the Western tradition of social, political, and legal thought. While other traditions of thought are not unimportant, this branch of the history of ideas and thought has been most influential on the "madmen" and powerbrokers that have done most to shape the landmark events and the general passage of world history. In delving into this body of work, some of it the so-called canon of Western thought, this book adopts a methodological approach that is influenced by or is perhaps best associated with the Cambridge School approach to the history of ideas and political thought.[13] The Cambridge School approach to textual research and analysis is particularly relevant to a study such as this because of the emphasis and significance it places on the language of political thought and the relationship between thought and action. It is also relevant here because of the significant consideration this methodological approach gives to both biography (experience) and contextualism (the study of texts in context). That is, it recognizes that texts and experiences or actions are best understood in context and through having a broader understanding of that context. More generally, the Cambridge School "method should be seen as essentially archaeological, concerned as it is

with elucidating the concepts through which human collectivities organize and constitute themselves and the meaningful shift(s) in such understandings."[14] As Duncan Bell has recently argued, the Cambridge
School "approach has much to offer the theorist of international politics, especially through its focus on the historicity of conceptual change
and its understanding of how political legitimacy is embedded in and
constrained by the set of political vocabularies available at any given
time" (328). And as Ken Booth has lamented, "it is vital that students of
IR [international relations] give language more attention than hitherto,
as words shape as well as reflect reality."[15]

As is demonstrated throughout this book, *civilization* is one of those
words; it is a concept that is used to both describe and shape reality. It
is what Quentin Skinner, considered a pioneer of the Cambridge School
method, calls an "evaluative-descriptive" term, a concept "which perform[s]
evaluative as well as descriptive functions in natural languages."[16] The
"special characteristic" of such concepts is that "they have a standard application to perform one of two contrasting ranges of speech-acts. They
are available, that is, to perform such acts as commending (and expressing and soliciting approval) or else of condemning (and expressing and
soliciting disapproval) of any action or state of affairs they are used to
describe."[17] As will become increasingly evident below, *civilization* is
a term of considerable power that is used both to commend and condemn.

The explicit link between language and action, or political thought
and political practice and outcomes, is captured in Skinner's assertion
that "to make a statement *is* to perform an action."[18] He goes on to explain, the "fact that a knowledge of the context of any given text does
help in understanding it reflects the fact, surely undeniable, that for the
performance of any action—and the making of statements is surely to
be appraised as a *performance*—it will always be possible at least in
principle to discover a set of conditions either such that the action (the
statement made) might have been different or might not have occurred
in their absence, or even such that the occurrence of the action might
have been predicted from their presence." Skinner concludes that there
"seems no question that for every statement there must be *some* explanatory context, for every action *some* set of antecedent causal conditions" (43; emphasis in original).

J. G. A. Pocock, another founding father of the Cambridge School,
is particularly instructive for the exercise undertaken herein. He writes
of "the functions within a political society of what may be called its
language (or languages) of politics." He further notes, "Any stable and

articulate society possesses concepts with which to discuss its political affairs."[19] The argument herein is that civilization is one of these key concepts, but it is not used only in shaping domestic political affairs, it is a concept that has also long been employed to describe and shape relationships in international political affairs. According to Pocock, the "business of the historian of thought is to study the emergence and roles of the organizing concepts employed by society." He acknowledges that this is no straightforward task, for there "is a gap between thinking and experience; but it is the business of the historian of political ideas to inhabit that gap and try to understand its significance." Pocock insists that "the knowledge that this role has necessary limitations need not deter" one from undertaking such challenging exercises (198–99).

Particularly relevant to the aims and objectives of this book is Pocock's observation that "the practical and the theoretical are not separable" (197). In light of this, it is worth emphasizing that this book is both an exercise in the history of ideas, through a reading of the historical political thought of civilization, *and* an attempt to explain contemporary policy making as it relates to this history of thought and the actions that accompanied it. The connections between ideas and outcomes will not always be straightforward or obvious, but as Pocock highlights, to "deny that concepts may be isolated and shown to play a determining role in politics is not to deny that they play any role whatever" (193). That is, while at times there might be only circumstantial evidence of causal links between thought and action, that does not necessarily mean that ideas have not been influential in making policy and pursuing outcomes.

As noted, an appreciation of ideas in context is an important consideration in the methodology of the Cambridge School. In this regard, similar to Skinner, Pocock makes the point that "much (though not all) political thinking does take shape in an immediate practical context" (194). He goes on to stress that it "is of some importance to be able to interpret thought by placing it in the tradition of discourse to which it rightfully belongs; and this is for two reasons." First, "it enables us to interpret thought as social behaviour, to observe the mind acting with relation to its society, that society's traditions and its fellow-inhabitants of that society." And second, "it is of assistance in rendering thought intelligible to be able to identify the concepts which the thinker was handling and the language in which he was communicating with his fellow-men; what he was talking about and what he was taken to mean" (200).

In a similar vein of thought, John Dunn, the third significant figure identified with the emergence of the Cambridge School, asserts that "the connection between an adequate philosophical account of the notions held by an individual in the past and an accurate historical account of these notions is an intimate one; that both historical specificity and philosophical delicacy are more likely to be attained if they are pursued together, than if one is deserted for the other at an early stage of the investigation."[20] Similar to Skinner, Dunn makes the point that "few branches of the history of ideas have been written as the history of an *activity*" (87; emphasis in original). In doing so, he is emphasizing that there is an inherently strong connection between ideas and actions. He goes on to note that "language is not . . . a repository of formal truths donated by God to Adam but simply the tool which human beings use in their struggle to make sense of their experiences," adding that "talking and thinking" should be "considered seriously as social activities" (88). Further, in relation to the importance of context, Dunn argues that if "we are to understand the criteria of truth or falsehood implicit in a complex intellectual architectonic, we have to understand the structures of biographical or social experience which made these criteria seem self-evident. To abstract an argument from the context of truth-criteria which it was devised to meet is to convert it into a different argument" (96). In essence, Dunn contends that the history of political thought is concerned with at least two things: "the set of argued propositions in the past which discuss how the political world is and ought to be and what should constitute the criteria for proper action within it; the set of activities in which men were engaged in when they enunciated these propositions" (92). A key point here in relation to the link between ideas and actions is that we must keep in mind that people such as John Locke and James and John Stuart Mill were more than just men of ideas, they also occupied prominent hands-on roles in the extension of civilization through the colonial enterprise.

In essence, the Cambridge School approach to the history of ideas can be summarized as "rooted in the role of language in the establishment, communication, and reproduction of political legitimacy. In particular, it concentrates on the role of politico-moral concepts," concepts such as civilization, "through which we order social and political life and by which we are in turn ordered, and the manner in which such concepts are manipulated and embedded in the discursive construction of world politics."[21] But as Bell argues, the Cambridge School approach alone "is not enough to answer the inevitable, timeless problems of interpretation . . . and the intellectual historian should always remain open to divergent methodological perspectives, to the plurality of reading strategies" (334). As such, the methodology employed in this book also has some similarities with the German mode of inquiry known as *Begriffsgeschichte*, the history of concepts, or conceptual history, which is described as "more a procedure than a definite method."[22] There is more to this procedure than just etymological explorations or revealing the meaning or noting the changes in meaning of a concept. To undertake a conceptual history is "to trace the thread of life and language that connects past and present. . . . The aim is not to restore the past but to remember it and to retrace the path to the present."[23] These two methodological approaches should not be seen as incompatible or in conflict, for, as Melvin Richter argues, the Cambridge School, the work of Pocock and Skinner in particular, and *Begriffsgeschichte* share "a common concern with political language treated historically, and the insistence on both sides that political thought and behaviour, now and in the past, cannot be understood without reference to the distinctive vocabularies used by agents in given contexts."[24]

Skinner has actually acknowledged the complementary attributes of the two approaches and praised the work of Reinhart Koselleck, a leading architect and practitioner of *Begriffsgeschichte*.[25] Skinner writes that he has "not only been innocent of any desire to question Koselleck's methodological assumptions, but that [he has] . . . even attempted to write some conceptual histories."[26] More importantly for my purposes here, Skinner recognizes "that if we are interested in mapping the rise and fall of particular normative vocabularies, we shall have to devote ourselves to examining the *longue durée*." And this is precisely the kind of large-scale exercise that is undertaken in this book in exploring the concept of civilization and its use. Skinner goes on to note that his "own research-programme might even be regarded as an aspect of the vastly more ambitious one pursued by Koselleck." He adds that "Koselleck is interested in nothing less than the entire process of conceptual change;" whereas he is "chiefly interested in one of the means by which it takes place." He concludes that the "two programmes do not strike . . . [him] as necessarily incompatible" (71–72).

Ultimately, in seeking to "to trace the thread of life and language that connects past and present," the aim herein is to better understand the past so that we may better understand the present and, in doing so, avoid replicating the mistakes or indiscretions of the past. As Terence Ball, James Farr, and Russell L. Hanson write in respect to ideas and actions, "remembering [and acknowledging] our past enables us to have a clearer—and perchance a more critical—perspective on our present."[27] In this general regard, this book is not just about drawing parallels between past and present, and it is not about drawing the unsustainable conclusion that just because in the past the adoption of certain ideas or language has led to certain outcomes, therefore the same outcomes will inevitably be replicated in the present and into the future if similar ideas and language are adopted. International politics is too complex to be simply written off as what Martin Wight has termed "the realm of recurrence and repetition."[28] Rather, in highlighting the power of ideas and in giving examples of past relationships between thought and action, specifically in regard to the concept of civilization, this book warns of possible outcomes or consequences associated with certain conceptual and language choices. As Skinner poignantly notes, history and the understanding of history are important not so much "because crude 'lessons' can be picked out of them, but because the history itself provides a lesson in self-knowledge."[29]

The aim here is to generate a wider and deeper self-knowledge and understanding in order to circumvent what Ball, Farr, and Hanson describe as the "Little wonder" that there are concerted "attempts to control the past [and through it the present] by rewriting history or, failing that, by obliterating memory altogether." As they further warn, people "adrift in the present and cut off" from the past and the understanding that might be gleaned from it "become more manipulable and pliable subjects." Furthermore, if "we are to remain lost" and blinded in the present then we are obliged to "retrace our steps."[30] In respect to the revived deployment of the evaluative-descriptive concept civilization (and its antitheses, barbarism and savagery), the potential consequences of which have largely been overlooked in contemporary thought and practice, this book seeks to remove a blindfold and shine a light.

Book Structure

The book is arranged in three parts. Part 1 is about ideas and concepts; it lays the foundation for parts 2 and 3, which are about the application and consequences of those ideas. Part 1 comprises chapters 2 though 4. Chapter 2 outlines the Enlightenment origins of the ideal of civilization and its sociopolitical character. Chapter 3 explores the intimate relationship between the ideal of civilization and the idea of progress, while chapter 4 outlines the proposed destination that the universal history of civilization is progressing toward. Chapter 5, the first chapter in part 2, gives an account of the classical standard of civilization in international law and explains why it is a direct result of the ideas explored in part 1. The second chapter in part 2, chapter 6, explains how the standard of civilization goes hand-in-hand with centuries of European "civilizing missions" in the non-European world that evolved into full-blown colonialism. Part 3 is something of a contemporary account of part 2, albeit in a more compressed time frame. Chapter 7 outlines the more recent division of our world into its "civilized" and "uncivilized" spheres and what are effectively standards of civilization for the late twentieth and early twenty-first centuries. Chapter 8 brings part 3 to a close with an account of the growing calls for a "new imperialism" to deal with the problems that result from the divisions identified in the preceding chapter. A concluding chapter recounts the overall argument of the book and highlights some of the consequences of the events outlined, while pointing to some possible alternative ways forward.

Wolf Schäfer recently made the point that for a long time it was very much the case that "Sociologists, anthropologists and historians have learned to avoid civilization, and instead, analyze everything with culture" as a point of reference. In fact, it would be fair to say that a generation of social and behavioural scientists have hesitated to use the concept of civilization as a tool of social analysis; it was more the case that "Culture is 'in' and civilization is 'out.'"[31] In his highly regarded *Keywords*, Raymond Williams suggests that "culture is one of the two or three most complicated words in the English language."[32] While this may well be the case, it is not unreasonable to add that *civilization*, a word with which *culture* shares a close but complicated relationship, is one of the other words that fall into this category. So long as *civilization* was out of fashion, this point was largely inconsequential for social scientific study; but *civilization* is now back, and how.

One of the reasons why the concept of civilization is so complicated is the fact that the term *civilization* and its plural have been applied to so many arenas of analysis. The concept has been loaded with so much meaning and so much social analysis falls under the umbrella of civilization that it often lacks any specific or readily graspable meaning. But as chapter 2 outlines in detail, its greatest complexity derives from the fact that, apart from its many descriptive uses, *civilization* also has an inherent value-laden or normative quality. This characteristic is evident in the French linguist Jean Starobinski's assertion that "traditionally the contrary of civilization was barbarity. Nations not as directly identifiable as France with the spirit of civilization were accordingly not exempt— particularly in times of international crisis—from suspicion of barbarity."[33] As will be seen in later chapters, little has changed; the "global war on terror" represents a time of crisis and, as such, similar judgments are handed down against states or groups that are deemed deficient in the "spirit of civilization." In order to analyze the normative dimension of civilization, or civilization as ideal, chapter 2 first explores the term's etymological origins and eighteenth-century French and British Enlightenment origins and meanings. These closely related definitions are contrasted with the German concept of *Kultur*, which has a quite distinct meaning from the term *Zivilisation*. In essence, the chapter outlines how some measure of social cooperation and a capacity for sociopolitical organization or self-government among any given people have long been considered key characteristics or requirements of civilization.

The idea of progress is intimately related to the ideal of civilization and is another key theme running through the book. Chapter 3 delves into the nature of the relationship between these two concepts. To do so, it necessarily engages with early works of anthropology and ethnology—or the science of races, as it was sometimes known—as well as some of the more well-known thinkers on the philosophy of history and modernization theory. The idea of progress has two related components. The first is that the human species universally progresses, albeit at different rates and to different degrees, from an original primitive or childlike condition, referred to as savagery, through to barbarism, and culminates at the apex of progress in the status of civilization. The second component of the idea of progress holds that human experience, both individual and collective, is cumulative and future-directed, or teleological, with the specific objective being the ongoing improvement of the individual, the society in which the individual lives, and the world in which the society must survive. Indicative of this line of thinking are Friedrich von Schiller's thoughts on the significance of the discovery of the Americas. He stated: "A wise hand seems to have preserved these savage tribes until such time as we have progressed sufficiently in our own civilization to make useful application of this discovery, and from this mirror to recover the lost beginning of our own race." But like so many other commentators on the discovery of the indigenous peoples of the New World and elsewhere, he adds, "But how embarrassing and dismal is the picture of our own childhood presented in these peoples!" For they represent the "barbarous remains of the centuries of antiquity and the middle ages!"[34] As chapters 5 and 6 outline, if these "savages" were ever going to "catch up" to the civilized or at least approach civilization, then European "civilizing missions" were the answer.

For some thinkers, it seems logical that what follows from the general idea of progress is the notion that progress is directed in a particular direction, or that history is moving forward along a particular path toward a specific end. History, in this conception, is not merely a catalog of events but a universal or all-encompassing teleological history, a cumulative and collective history of civilization, that is—History. Chapter 4 outlines the end that the prophets of History see progress, and history, heading toward. On the whole this end is one that remains deeply influenced by Immanuel Kant's idea of "perpetual peace" among an international society of republican states, or an *ius cosmopoliticum*. For the latter-day heirs of Kant, the member states of today's proposed cooperative, interdependent, peaceful international society are required to be governed according to the principles of liberal democracy combined with a market economy. Despite the many criticisms leveled against Fukuyama's "end of history" thesis from a wide range of viewpoints, there remains a widely held belief that liberal democracy and a market economy represent the best way to govern any given society. Just as significantly, there is an equally widely held view that liberal democracies do not fight one another. And as liberal democracy is considered to be a universally applicable governing principle, it is argued that the wider democracy spreads, the greater the chances of realizing a peaceful world order.

Chapter 5 outlines the foundations and evolution of the classical standard of civilization in international law, one of the key tools in shaping an international society of largely uniform states which adopt the same "operating system." While there were obviously rules of engagement governing interactions between the nations of Europe, along with another set for their relations with the peoples and civilizations that bordered (Western) Europe, it was not until the Spanish "discovery" of the New World that an incipient law of nations really started to take shape. Such a legal code was necessary to regulate the burgeoning contact between the "civilized" states of Europe and the "uncivilized" Amerindians and other native peoples; at stake was no less than the legal standing between the respective peoples. As the jurist James Lorimer explains, "Till there were two nations, international law could not have been; when there were two nations, it could not but have been."[35] In documenting the evolution of international law, the chapter takes as its starting point Pope Innocent IV's thirteenth-century commentary on Pope Innocent III's decretal *Quod super his*, in which he begins to articulate the nature of papal-infidel or civilized-uncivilized relations. Innocent IV is significant for the influence he was to have on jurisprudential successors like Franciscus de Vitoria, whom the Spanish relied upon for their legal justification for conquering and occupying the Americas. Along with Hugo Grotius, Vitoria is widely recognized as a founding father of modern international law, a system of law that is inextricably linked to "civilized" Europe's case for conquering and subjecting "uncivilized" native peoples. This history is hard to escape from, even down to this day, for Article 38.1(c) of the Statute of the International Court of Justice still reads, "The Court, whose function is to decide in accordance with international law such disputes as are submitted to it, shall apply: . . . the general principles of law recognized by *civilized nations*."[36]

The standard of civilization is essentially a means to distinguish between "civilized" and "uncivilized" nations or peoples in order to determine membership in the international society of states. Membership in international society confers full sovereignty upon a state, thus entitling it to full recognition and protection under international law. The general test of whether a nation was deemed civilized revolved around its degree of sociopolitical organization and capacity for self-government in accordance with accepted European standards. By the nineteenth century, a civilized state required (*a*) basic institutions of government and public bureaucracy, (*b*) the organizational capacity for self-defense, (*c*) a published legal code and adherence to the rule of law, and (*d*) recognition of international law and norms, including those on the conduct of war and diplomatic exchange. If a nation could meet these requirements, it was generally deemed to be a legitimate sovereign state entitled to full recognition as an international personality. In essence, a government had to be sufficiently stable to allow it to enter into reciprocally binding commitments under international law and possess the will and capacity to guarantee the life, liberty, and property of members of foreign civilized states living and operating within its borders.

Norbert Elias made the pertinent point in *The Civilizing Process* that "it is not a little characteristic of the structure of Western society that the watchword of its colonizing movement is 'civilization.'"[37] Indeed, as this book continuously highlights, many unsavory acts have been carried out down through the past five hundred plus years in the name of civilization. Chapter 6 catalogs some of the crimes of colonialism and articulates how the standard of civilization and concomitant civilizing missions are implicated in the exploitation and extinguishing of countless peoples and cultures deemed to be inferior to the self-appointed standard-bearers of civilization. The justifications for these offenses were often couched in terms of the self-appointed duty of "civilized" European nations to bring the blessings of civilization to the "savage" and "barbarian" hordes; that is, the "white man's burden" or the "burden of civilization." The general aim of these often violent and overly zealous "civilizing missions" was to ameliorate—if it was thought possible, depending on the depth of native peoples' crudity—the state of the "uncivilized" through tutelage, training, and conversion to Christianity. The chapter explores how such missions were first undertaken in

Europe and then exported to the Americas, honed further again in the "scramble for Africa," and finally came full circle with the United States of America's arrival as a formal imperial power in the late nineteenth century.

Huntington argued in the late 1960s that the "most important political distinction among countries concerns not their form of government but their degree of government."[38] During the era of the classical standard of civilization, which is effectively the colonial era, this may well have been so, but it is no longer necessarily the case. Chapter 7 opens the final section of the book, which, while engaging with more recent developments in world politics, demonstrates that the same set of ideas and concepts—civilization, progress, universality, and modernity—remain both salient and powerful when it comes to explaining and justifying policy making and decision making. It begins by assessing the various arguments put forward by proponents of standards of civilization for the contemporary era, both theoretical and functional. Some of the cases for a resurrected standard of civilization are implied, others explicit, but, to varying degrees, they generally advocate a standard that incorporates the values of human rights and liberal democracy. The more ambitious accounts claim that modernity—or more specifically, Western modernity and all of its inherent values—is a condition to which all societies should aspire if they are to be admitted into contemporary international society and afforded all its rights and privileges.

As in the era of the classical standard, contemporary standards of civilization—albeit more political than legal in the late twentieth and early twenty-first centuries—arise out of the division of our world into states and societies of various shades of civilization. During the Cold War, this division lay largely beneath the surface of international affairs, the world instead being divided between East and West. However, in the post–Cold War world and in the wake of September 11, 2001, and the ongoing terrorist threat, the division between the "civilized" and the "new barbarians" has become far more pronounced. Hence, the chapter also assesses the work of a number of prominent commentators who have clearly spelled out where the dividing line runs as it demarcates the civilized world from the cacophony of quasi, collapsing, and rogue states and other international actors. At times the terminology used to describe these different states and groups differs from that of the earlier era of "savages," "barbarians," and the "civilized," while at times it closely reflects it; either way the descriptive-evaluative effect remains much the same as it was in the past.

Similar too are the consequences that follow from such divides and the subsequent efforts to enforce new standards of civilization. These consequences are laid bare in chapter 8 through analyses of the ever more common and ever more intense calls for the revival of a "new imperialism" to deal with the potential problems—real or imagined—that uncivilized or rogue states and nonstate actors pose to the broader international society of states. With the end of the Cold War, the new imperialism on many peoples' lips is "humanitarian imperialism," the sort of long-term nation-building exercise that is perceived as the natural next step that should follow humanitarian interventions in collapsing or failed states. There are even calls from some for greater economic imperialism, that is, the kind of supposedly legitimate imperial exercise that is associated with interventions by international financial institutions such as the International Monetary Fund and the World Bank in states with economies on the brink of ruin. Unavoidably, the chapter also explores the allegations—and more than a few boastful claims—that, as the lone superpower, the United States is on the brink of or has evolved into a modern imperial power. The final issue addressed in the chapter is that of the imperial urgency that has been aroused by the threat of terrorism and rogue actors in the wake of September 11 and subsequent terrorist attacks on Western targets around the world.

Chapter 9 recaps and reiterates the book's core claims and arguments. By the time the reader reaches this point, I trust that they will be convinced that the account of the general aims of the Enlightenment and its liberal descendants as outlined herein is an accurate one. The following passage from John Gray is noted again in chapter 4, but it is worth highlighting twice, for it summarizes those aims as well as any other and better than most. He writes:

> The core project of the Enlightenment was the displacement of local, customary or traditional moralities, and of all forms of transcendental faith, by a critical or rational morality, which was projected as the basis of a universal civilization. Whether it was conceived in utilitarian or contractarian, rights-based or duty-based terms, this morality would be secular and humanist, and it would set universal standards for the assessment of human institutions. The core project of the Enlightenment was the construction of such a critical morality, rationally binding on all human beings, and, as a corollary, the creation of a universal civilization.[39]

What follows is a step-by-step account of how the project of creating a universal empire of civilization or, more accurately, a uniform empire of civilization has been pursued down through the centuries and continues to be pursued into the twenty-first century. It is a story about the crafting of teleological History and the influence and effect it has on peoples who are swept up or swept aside in the process. As is detailed throughout this book, some of the driving forces behind this project are the ideal of civilization and the idea of progress, powerful and influential ideas that have captured imaginations and influenced the thinking of powerful people down through the centuries and literally across the globe.

Part One: Civilization, Progress, and History: Universals All?

What contrasting pictures! Who would suppose that the refined European of the eighteenth century is only a more advanced brother of the Red Indian and of the Celt? All these skills, artistic instincts, experiences, all these creations of reason have been implanted and developed in man in a matter of a few thousand years; all these marvels of invention, these tremendous works of industry have been called forth from him. What brought them to life? What elicited them? What conditions of life did man traverse in ascending from that extreme to this, from the unsociable life of the cave dweller to the life of the thinker, of the civilized man of the world? Universal world-history answers these questions.

Friedrich von Schiller, "The Nature and Value of Universal History," 1789

2

The Ideal of Civilization: Its Origins, Meanings, and Implications

It is never a waste of time to study the history of a word.

Lucien Febvre, *A New Kind of History*

Civilization is a fact like any other—a fact susceptible, like any other, of being studied, described, narrated.   **François Guizot, *The History of Civilization in Europe***

: : :

"Civilization" Revived

The terms *civilization* and *civilizations* have recently regained some of their lost prominence as tools for describing and explaining how our world works. As will become apparent, the term *civilization* and its plural continue to be interpreted and applied in a variety of manners and different contexts. In response to this revival and as an explanatory tool itself, this study also makes extensive use of the idea of civilization in order to explain certain processes in history and world politics. As will be explained, this includes the idea of civilization as both a process and a destination or state of being; it also includes the ideal of civilization as a comparative benchmark that manifests itself in a "standard of civilization." As the idea of civilization is both a key concept and a broader theme running through the heart of this book, this chapter gives a comprehensive overview of the evolutionary origins and contested meanings of the term *civilization* and its plural.[1] In undertaking this etymological exploration early on, my intention is to lay the foundation upon which the rest of the book is built. It is further intended to illuminate and aid in navigating the key issues addressed in this study.

The first task is to review the circumstances under which the word *civilization*, or its linguistic equivalents, entered into French, English, and German usage. These three languages are the most significant for a number of reasons, not the least of which is the fact that they are the three languages that dominated European diplomacy in the eighteenth and nineteenth centuries, when both the word and ideal of civilization entered into European thought. French was likely the most widely spoken language in Western Europe at the time, while English was the language of the dominant power of the era, and German was used widely because of the vast web of diplomatic relations that linked the various Germanic provinces. Furthermore, French is important because it is the language in which the word *civilization* is first known to have appeared. The next significant development was when *civilization* appeared shortly thereafter in English usage. Whether it was received from the French or came into being independently is unclear, but it carried much the same meanings as it did in French. Perhaps most interesting, though, is the somewhat complicated translation of the word and idea of *civilization* into German, in which *Zivilisation* stands for something quite different and is altogether subordinate or, by some accounts, antithetical to the German concept of *Kultur*.

As seen in following chapters, the Spanish discovery of the New World also played a significant role in shaping the events that led to the birth of the ideal of civilization. However, I think it is fair to say that the Spanish, and the Portuguese, were considered by other European powers to be a declining imperial force by the time of the arrival of the word *civilization*, a time when much of the Americas had already won their independence. That is not to say that French and English second-wave imperialism did not learn many lessons from first-wave Spanish imperialism, two phases of European imperialism that Anthony Pagden describes as "distinct, but [with] interdependent histories."[2] As in German, so too in Dutch and Italian the word *civilization* was confronted by local terms that served a similar purpose, yet did not quite mesh with the ideals of civilization. In the Netherlands the noun *beschaving*, based on the verb *bechaven*, meaning to refine, polish, or civilize, was widely used, while in Italy the word *civilità*, as found in Dante, had long been entrenched in the language.[3] The significance of *civilization* as both a word and an ideal and the key role the three prominent Western European languages played in shaping both have been captured in a rather effusive statement by the French linguist Émile Benveniste: "The whole history of modern thought and the principal intellectual achievements in the western world are connected with the creation and handling of a few dozen essential words which are all the common possession of the western European languages." *Civilization* is one of those words.[4]

For much of the twentieth century, a century in which two World Wars, the Great Depression, and the Holocaust all served to undermine the very *idea* of civilization, it seemed as though it was more the case that it *was* one of those words. Despite this, the middle years of the century did produce a number of comprehensive studies of the rise and fall of major civilizations by noted historians, sociologists, and anthropologists. The 1980s also saw the publication of a major study on the "standard of civilization" in international society,[5] but this too was a largely historical study and by century's end these styles of investigations had become scarce in mainstream fields of inquiry.

A contemporary work that has captured imaginations and helped revive what might loosely be called "civilization studies" as a legitimate or worthwhile field of study is Samuel Huntington's "clash of civilizations" thesis.[6] The airing of this thesis and the post–Cold War international political climate into which it was born, along with the subsequent rise of the threat of fundamentalist terrorism, has generated extensive and ongoing debates that have helped to again popularize the term *civilization(s)*, nowhere more so than in the realm of world politics. Despite being one of the more notable contributors to this revival, Huntington offers only the briefest history and definition of the term, stating that the "idea of civilization was developed by eighteenth-century French thinkers as the opposite of 'barbarism.'" Simply put, "To be civilized was good, to be uncivilized was bad." Huntington acknowledges that out of its origins evolved a distinction between the usage of *civilization* in the singular and "civilizations in the plural," the latter being the concern of his book. But this development is oversimplified to the point that the arrival of the latter merely marks the "renunciation of a civilization defined as an ideal, or rather as the ideal."[7] The study of the plural variant, or "civilizations as fact," however, is not as readily divorced from a concern with "civilization as ideal" as Huntington suggests. As Quentin Skinner notes, it is at once both a descriptive and an evaluative term.[8] Or as Fernand Braudel suggests, the triumph of one over the other "does not spell disaster" for it because they are necessarily tied together in "dialogue."[9] In contrast to Huntington, it is the study of *civilization* that is the greater concern of this book, but, as noted, this concern cannot arbitrarily exclude discussions of *civilizations*, for the two concepts are closely linked. The nature of the dialogue between the singular and the plural begins to reveal itself as soon as one starts to explore the origins of the word *civilization*.

French Origins of Civilisation

The French historian François Guizot's declaration that "civilization is a fact like any other,"[10] susceptible to detailed study, is a little misleading in that it makes the task sound considerably more straightforward than it actually is. Even in Guizot's own use of the term, in fact since its very inception, the word *civilization* has been imbued with a plurality of meanings. Some render it a "fact" amenable to measurement, while others refer to it as a not so readily quantifiable "ideal."

The word *civilisation* has its foundations in the French language, deriving from words such as *civil* (thirteenth century) and *civilité* (fourteenth century), all of which in turn derive from the Latin *civitas*. Prior to the appearance of *civilisation*, words such as *poli* or *polite*, *police* (which broadly meant law and order, including government and administration), *civilizé*, and *civilité* had all been in wide use, but, in Benveniste's view, none of these adequately met the evolving and expanding demands on the language. Upon the appearance of the verb *civiliser* sometime in the sixteenth century, which provided the basis for the noun, the coining of *civilisation* was only a matter of time, for *civilisation* was a neologism whose time had come. As Benveniste states it, "*civilité*, a static term, was no longer sufficient," requiring the coining of a term "which had to be called *civilisation* in order to define together both its direction and continuity."[11] But in its first-known recorded usage, the word *civilisation* held a quite different meaning to that with which it is generally associated today. For some time *civiliser* had been used in jurisprudence to describe the transformation of a criminal matter into a civil one, hence *civilisation* was defined in the Trévoux *Dictionnaire universel* of 1743 as a "Term of jurisprudence. An act of justice or judgement that renders a criminal trial civil. *Civilisation* is accomplished by converting informations (*informations*) into inquests (*enquêtes*) or by other means."[12] But *civilisation*'s life as a term of jurisprudence was a rather brief and sparing one once it was appropriated by thinkers who imbued it with the meanings we associate with it today, meanings which were to catch on quickly and gain wide acceptance in intellectual and popular thought.

Just when the written word *civilisation* first appeared in its more contemporary sense is open to conjecture. Despite his extensive enquiries, the French historian Lucien Febvre admits that he has no accurate idea as to "who was the first to use it or at least to have it printed." But he offers that he has "not been able to find the word *civilisation* used in any French text published prior to the year 1766," when it appeared in a posthumous publication by M. Boulanger titled *Antiquité dévoilée par ses usages*.[13] The passage in which it appeared reads: "When a savage people has become civilized, we must not put an end to the act of *civilisation* by giving it rigid and irrevocable laws; we must make it look upon the legislation given to it as a form of *continuous civilisation*."[14] From this early passage it is evident that *civilisation* is used to represent both an ongoing process and a state of being that is an advance on the condition of "savagery."

Claims to uncertainty aside, Benveniste and Jean Starobinski independently argue that *civilisation* first appeared in written form in its nonjuridical sense ten years earlier than Febvre believed.[15] Dated 1756 but not published until 1757, *civilisation* appears three times (on pages 136, 176, and 237) in Victor de Riquetti, marquis de Mirabeau's (1715–1789) treatise on population, *L'Ami des hommes ou Traité de la population*. Perhaps somewhat curiously, Voltaire makes no use of what one would think would be a highly useful word (*civilization*) in a prominent work of the same year, his *Essay on the Customs and Spirit of Nations*.[16] Reflecting Mirabeau's usage of the term, the 1771 edition of the Trévoux *Dictionnaire universel* included for the first time both the jurisprudential and newer meaning of *civilisation*. The entry reads: "The *ami des hommes* [Mirabeau] *used this word for sociabilité*. See that word. Religion is undeniably the first and most useful brake on humanity; it is the first source of civilization. It preaches to us and continually recalls us to confraternity, to soften our hearts."[17]

Starobinski argues that the authors of the Trévoux *Dictionnaire* chose their example carefully, for Mirabeau's usage of *civilisation* provided a "welcome" contradistinction to the Enlightenment philosophes and encyclopedists' advocacy of reason and the sciences. Rather than singing the praises of reason, virtue, and morality as the successors of religion and the true path to human perfectibility, Mirabeau argued that "religion was 'the principal source' of civilization." Thus, as Starobinski states it, "the word civilization first appeared in a eulogy of religion, which was praised not only as a repressive force (a 'brake') but also as unifying and moderating influence ('confraternity')."[18] For Benveniste, though, "*civilisation* is one of those words which show a new vision of the world," one that is "an optimistic and resolutely nontheological interpretation of its evolution." In this regard, he refers to "the very novelty of the notion and the changes in the traditional concept of man and society that it implies."[19]

Starobinski notes that, once coined, the term *civilisation* was rapidly adopted into common usage because it encapsulated a broad range of terms that were already in use to describe a preexisting concept, one that included notions such as advancements in comfort, increased material possessions and personal luxuries, improved education techniques, "cultivation of the arts and sciences," and the expansion "of commerce and industry."[20] Thus, as *civilisation* became increasingly common in French vocabulary, so too it was defined in greater detail in French dictionaries. This development can be seen in Snetlage's *Nouveau Dictionnaire français contenant de nouvelles créations du peuple français* of 1795, which defined *civilisation* thus: "This word, which was used only in a technical sense to say that a criminal case was made civil, is used to express the action of civilizing or the tendency of a people to polish or rather to correct its mores and customs by bringing into civil society a luminous, active, loving morality abounding in good works. (Every citizen of Europe is today embarked upon this last combat of civilization. Civilization of mores.)"[21] Building on Boulanger's account of *civilisation*, we see in this definition a hint of the notion that the condition of civilization is the preserve of the peoples of Europe (albeit to varying degrees), while its opposites, savagery, barbarism, or the state of nature lay beyond Europe's borders.

As seen in these early appearances of *civilisation*, from the very outset it was a term imbued with a plurality of meanings. Serving as something of a "synthetic" or "unifying concept," *civilisation* was used to describe both a process through which individual human beings and nations became civilized and the cumulative outcome of that process. As Starobinski states, the "crucial point is that the use of the term, *civilization*, to describe both the fundamental process of history and the end result of that process established an antithesis between civilization and a hypothetical primordial state (whether it be called nature, savagery, or barbarism)."[22] Thus, it was used both to describe and to evaluate, or to pass judgment in the very act of describing. In order to explore further the nature of the relationship between the state of civilization and its alternatives (be they antithetical or otherwise), it is helpful to first understand the plurality of meanings attributed to *civilization*.

Apart from the distinction between civilization as process and civilization as the end condition resulting from that process, further distinctions have been drawn between what is characterized as civilization as *fact* and civilization as *value* or *ideal*. In the former sense, it is said to be largely a "descriptive and neutral" term used to identify what are thought to be quantifiable values held in common by a distinct group of peoples, that is, a specific civilization such as that of ancient Greece or contemporary Western civilization. In the latter sense, civilization is a "normative concept on the basis of which it was possible to discriminate the civilized from the uncivilized, the barbarian, and the incompletely civilized."[23] Following a similar line of thought, Febvre notes that the "same word [civilization] is used to designate two different concepts." What is elsewhere described as civilization as "fact" is referred to by Febvre as its "ethnographic" usage.

> In the first case civilization simply refers to all the features that can be observed in the collective life of one human group, embracing their material, intellectual, moral and political life and, there is unfortunately no other word for it, their social life. It has been suggested that this should be called the "ethnographical" conception of civilization. It does not imply any value judgement on the detail or the overall pattern of the facets examined. Neither does it have any bearing on the individual in the group taken separately, or their personal reactions or individual behaviour. It is above all a conception which refers to a group.[24]

But even this definition is more than just descriptive; it too has an (unacknowledged) normative-evaluative component. *Civilization* is not usually used to describe the collective life of just any group, as *culture* sometimes is; rather, it is reserved for collectives that demonstrate a degree of urbanization and organization. This normative assumption is evident in that Febvre's ethnographic markers all relate, either directly or indirectly, to a group's sociopolitical organization.

Immediately following the "ethnographic" account of civilization, Febvre gives a definition of civilization as an ideal or value.

> In the second case, when we are talking about the progress, failures, greatness and weakness of civilization we do have a value judgement in mind. We have the idea that the civilization we are talking about—ours—is itself something great and beautiful; something too which is nobler, more comfortable and better, both morally and materially speaking, than anything outside it— savagery, barbarity or semi-civilization. Finally, we are confident

> that such civilization, in which we participate, which we propa-
> gate, benefit from and popularize, bestows on us all a certain
> value, prestige, and dignity. For it is a collective asset enjoyed by
> all civilized societies. It is also an individual privilege which each
> of us proudly boasts that he possesses. (220)

From these accounts it is evident that the former usage is used to describe distinctive *civilizations* across time and place, while the latter signifies a benchmark or *the civilization*—that is, it represents the *ideal of civilization*—which all other societies or collectives are compared to and measured against. While the former have been the subject of much comparative historical analysis, which in itself is an unavoidably evaluative exercise, it is the conception of civilization as normative ideal that is more the concern herein.

The reason for focusing on the value-laden nature of civilization begins to reveal itself when looking into further accounts of civilization, such as Comte de Volney's, published in 1803 after his travels in the United States in the late 1790s. Reflecting the general principles of social contract theory, but just as importantly for the purposes here, the criteria of requiring a capacity for self-government, Volney wrote: "By *civilisation* we should understand an assembly of the men in a town, that is to say in an enclosure of dwellings equipped with a common defence system to protect themselves from pillage from outside and disorder within. . . . The assembly implied the concepts of voluntary consent by the members, maintenance of their right to security, personal freedom and property: . . . thus *civilisation* is nothing other than a social condition for the preservation and protection of persons and property etc."[25]

As becomes increasingly evident, the demand for a nation or people to have the capacity to organize into a cooperative society with a capacity for self-government is central to the ideal of civilization. But the identification of different collectives as civilizations on the basis of their capacity for social cooperation and self-government has really only served to distinguish them from other human collectives. Importantly, I demonstrate in following chapters that it is not just about a people organizing and governing in any fashion that counts. Rather, it is governing in accordance with certain standards—first set by Europe and later by the West more generally—that determines a society's approximation to the idealized "standard of civilization." This factor becomes increasingly apparent when exploring the English language origins and evolution of the word *civilization*.

English Origins of Civilization

According to the *Oxford English Dictionary*, the word *civilization* first appeared in English in 1772, some fifteen years after its initial appearance in a French text. The reference it cites is a passage in James Boswell's *Life of Johnson* that reads: "On Monday, March 23, [1772,] I found him [Dr. Samuel Johnson] busy, preparing a fourth edition of his folio Dictionary. . . . He would not admit *civilization*, but only *civility*. With great deference to him, I thought *civilization*, from to *civilize*, better in the sense opposed to *barbarity*, than *civility*; as it is better to have a distinct word for each sense, than one word with two senses, which *civility* is, in his way of using it."[26] The entry in Boswell's diary is much in keeping with *civilization*'s French foundations; it also gives a good indication of at least one sense in which the term entered into English usage. But as the context in which Boswell uses it hints at, it appears as though the word had already been in use for some time prior—and indeed it had. The honor of first recorded English usage of *civilization* is in fact thought to go to the Scottish Enlightenment thinker Adam Ferguson, who used *civilization* in his *Essay on the History of Civil Society*, first published in 1767.[27] There is good reason, however, to believe that Ferguson actually used the term some years prior to 1767, as is indicated in a letter of April 12, 1759, from David Hume to Adam Smith in which he makes reference to a "treatise on Refinement" by "our friend Ferguson."[28] If Ferguson also used the word *civilization* in this earlier draft of his *Essay* manuscript, then there is cause to believe that *civilization* was in use in English, albeit rarely, no more than three years after its first recorded use in French.[29] As to whether Ferguson began using *civilization* independently of the French, assuming that he was indeed the first to use and record it, which cannot be guaranteed, or had picked it up from the French remains open to speculation.

While the word *civilization* appears in Ferguson's *Essay* only eight times (on pages 1, 75, 90, 203, 232, 243, 244, and 249), the work itself has been described as "a history of civilization."[30] At its core it is an investigation into the progress of humankind and society from a state of "rudeness" to a "refined" or "polished" state. This theme is established on the very first page of the *Essay*, where Ferguson writes, "Not only the individual advances from infancy to manhood, but the species itself from rudeness to civilization."[31] As Duncan Forbes states it in his introduction to the 1966 edition of the *Essay*, what Ferguson was looking for was a "true criterion of civilization."[32] And as Ferguson clearly states in his later *Principles of Moral and Political Science*, that criterion was some degree of sociopolitical organization. For he writes in the *Principles* that "success of commercial arts . . . requires a certain order to be preserved by those who practice them, and implies a certain security of the person and property, to which we give the name civilization, although this distinction, both in the nature of the thing, and derivation of the word, belongs rather to the effects of law and political establishment, on the forms of society, than to any state merely of lucrative possession or wealth."[33] From these passages alone, and from the general theme of Ferguson's *Essay* in particular (also from his *Principles*), it is apparent that, like the French, he too uses the term *civilization* to describe both a process and a condition. As becomes evident below, Ferguson's line of thought on the criteria of civilization contains elements that social and political thinkers had been pursuing as early as the ancient Greeks.

As indicated by both Volney's and Ferguson's respective accounts of civilization, it becomes increasingly the case that sociopolitical and legal organization is inherently and inextricably linked to the ideal of civilization. An example of this is John Stuart Mill's essay of 1836 titled "Civilization," which is also an indicator of the general acceptance and widespread use of the term in English around eighty years after it was introduced. At the beginning of his essay, Mill, like others before him, notes that the "word civilization . . . is a word of double meaning," sometimes standing "for *human improvement* in general, and sometimes for *certain kinds* of improvement in particular."[34] For the purposes of his essay, however, Mill is referring to civilization as ideal condition, or what he calls "civilization in the narrow sense: not that in which it is synonymous with improvement, but that in which it is the direct converse or contrary of rudeness or barbarism." And he is not talking here just about the condition of the individual, but "the best characteristics of Man and Society" (51–52).

The importance of society to the qualification for civilization is expressed in Mill's recipe, in which he lists the "ingredients of civilization." Following Montesquieu to some degree, he states that whereas

> a savage tribe consists of a handful of individuals, wandering or thinly scattered over a vast tract of country: a dense population, therefore, dwelling in fixed habitations, and largely collected together in towns and villages, we term civilized. In savage life there is no commerce, no manufactures, no agriculture, or next to none; a country in the fruits of agriculture, commerce, and manufactures, we call civilized. In savage communities each per-

son shifts for himself; except in war (and even then very imperfectly) we seldom see any joint operations carried on by the union of many; nor do savages find much pleasure in each other's society. Wherever, therefore, we find human beings acting together for common purposes in large bodies, and enjoying the pleasures of social intercourse, we term them civilized. (52)

The presence, or otherwise, of the institutions of society that facilitate governance in accordance with established (Western) European traditions was widely believed to be a hallmark of the makings of or potential for civilization. Mill was representative of this belief in his assertion that "in savage life there is little or no law, or administration of justice; no systematic employment of the collective strength of society, to protect individuals against injury from one another." Despite the fact that similar institutions performed similar functions in the non-European world, the absence of institutions that resembled those of the "civilized" nations of Europe meant that much of the world beyond its borders was deemed by "civilized" Europe to fall short of meeting Mill's necessary "ingredients of civilization." As Mill stated, "We accordingly call a people civilized, where the arrangements of society, for protecting the persons and property of its members, are sufficiently perfect to maintain peace among them" (52–53).

The requirement of a capacity for sociopolitical organization and the role of society are reaffirmed in Mill's declaration: "There is not a more accurate test of the progress of civilization than the progress of the power of co-operation." For it was widely held that "only civilized beings . . . can combine," and "none but civilized nations have ever been capable of forming an alliance." Savages, on the other hand, are characterized by "incapacity of organised combination." The reasoning behind this belief was that combination requires compromise: "it is the sacrifice of some portion of individual will, for a common purpose." As such it was thought that "the whole course of advancing civilization is a series of such training" (55–56). But as becomes increasingly evident, there was a prevailing view among the self-declared civilized societies of Europe that savages and barbarians lacked the discipline and predilection for compromise and cooperation among themselves. Rather, savages and barbarians were seen as trapped in a "state of nature" in which "every one trusts his own strength or cunning, and where that fails . . . is without resource" (52). There were, of course, thinkers like Edmund Burke who recognized the value and achievements of non-European civilizations.[35] But for others like James and J. S. Mill, the only way the "uncivilized" could hope to rise to some degree of civilization—if it was thought possible at all—was under the guiding hand of civilized Europeans who would instill the necessary discipline and training that made society possible.

In essence, for Mill, civilization was marked by "sufficient knowledge of the arts of life," "diffusion of property and intelligence," "sufficient security of property and person," and "power of co-operation" in society so as to "render the progressive increase of wealth and population possible."[36] But the maintenance of civilization did not come cheaply. Adam Smith, for example, argued that an increase in wealth and population was in fact a prerequisite for the discharge of the "first duty of the sovereign" of civilized societies; that of protecting the society from external "violence and injustice." According to Smith, it was "only by means of a standing army . . . that the civilization of any country can be perpetuated," an exercise that becomes increasingly expensive the larger society grows and the more "society advances in civilization."[37] Smith also maintained that it was "only by means of a well regulated standing army . . . that a barbarous country can be suddenly and tolerably civilized" (296). In summary, much of British thinking is neatly captured by Herbert Spencer's claim: "We may consider it [civilization] as progress towards that constitution of man and society required for the complete manifestation of every one's individuality."[38]

German Kultur *versus* Zivilisation

While the evolution of the word *civilization* ran along roughly parallel lines in French and English thought, in German the term *Zivilisation* stood for something quite different and was altogether subordinate to the concept of *Kultur*. While still useful, *Zivilisation* is a term of "second rank" that deals only with superficialities, such as external appearances. *Kultur,* on the other hand, is a term that is representative of Germany's self-understanding of national pride and sense of achievement—its sense of being. Furthermore, the French and English conceptions of civilization generally refer to political, social, economic, religious, scientific, and or moral issues, while the German term *Kultur* is essentially reserved for expounding intellectual, artistic, and religious facts or values. Moreover, *Kultur* is inclined to include a distinct divide between these more valued concerns on the one side and subordinate political, social, and economic issues on the other.[39]

Some of the reasons behind the distinctions between the French and English concept of civilization and its German counterpart *Kultur* have been set out by Norbert Elias in *The Civilizing Process*. Elias maintains that the differences are attributable to the contrasting roles played by the respective intellectual classes that gave birth to and shaped the meanings of the concepts. In France, the concept of *civilisation*—and French civilization itself—was born at court and in Paris cafés, where it took shape amidst ongoing intellectual exchanges between a politicized and politically engaged French intelligentsia. In contrast, German *Kultur* was generated by a more widely dispersed, less interactive middle-class German intelligentsia that Elias describes as "far removed from political activity, scarcely thinking in political terms and only tentatively in national ones, whose legitimation consists primarily in its intellectual, scientific or artistic *accomplishments*."[40] Given the late development and tenuous unity of the German state, the intellectual middle-class was highly individualized and said to be "floating in the air to some extent," distinctly different from the "closed circle" or "society" that was the French court. The space it occupied was *das rein Geistige* (the purely spiritual), where a preoccupation with scholarship and the development of the mind or intellect (*Bildung*)[41] was both a refuge and source of pride. Politics, commerce, and the economy were peripheral concerns in which there was little scope or prospect for engagement.[42]

Counterpoised to this "floating" intelligentsia was the class equivalent of French intellectuals, an upper-class German courtly aristocracy that produced and accomplished little or nothing in terms of *Kultur*, but which played a significant early role in shaping the national self-image. Elias explains that at the heart of the tensions between middle-class German intellectuals and the courtly aristocracy were "pairs of opposites such as 'depth' and 'superficiality,' 'honesty' and 'falsity,' 'outward politeness' and 'true virtue' . . . from which, among other things, the antithesis between *Zivilisation* and *Kultur* grew up" (26–27). Hence, it is also the bedrock on which the antithetical relationship between French *civilisation* and German *Kultur* is based. Given the nature of the intellectual class's relationship with the courtly elite, there were considerable obstacles to the intelligentsia's rise "from being a second-rank class to being the bearer of German national consciousness." Nevertheless, despite the relatively late unification of the German state making this transition even more drawn out, the intelligentsia ultimately rose, albeit conditionally, to an influential class that transformed "the antithesis between *Kultur* and *Zivilisation*" from being a "*primarily social antithesis*" to a "*primarily national one*" (27; emphasis in original). To put it another way, given the changing role and status of the German intelligentsia, the "specific social characteristics" that are its hallmark "gradually become national characteristics" (29–30). And as I shall show, they are characteristics that were incongruous with the ideas and values inherent in the French/English concept of civilization that were thought to be universal, particularly by the French.[43]

In effect, *Kultur* and *civilisation* were said to be squared off against each other as Counter-Enlightenment versus Enlightenment, the "authentic" *Kultur* of Germany versus the "artificial" cosmopolitan *civilisation* of which France was representative.[44] Indeed, Oswald Spengler writes of an "opposition" between the "conceptions of culture-man and civilization-man." He considered that "every Culture has *its own* Civilization" and that "Civilization is the inevitable *destiny* of the Culture." With this in mind, he suggested that "the 'Decline of the West' comprises nothing less than the problem of *Civilization*." Spengler further contended that "civilizations are the most external and artificial states of which a species of developed humanity is capable. They are a conclusion, the thing-become succeeding the thing-becoming, death following life. . . . *Pure* Civilization, as a historical process, consists in a progressive exhaustion of forms that have become inorganic or dead."[45] As Jeffrey Herf notes, however, while "Spengler juxtaposed German *Kultur* and Western *Zivilisation*," unlike others "he sought to reconcile *Kultur* with twentieth-century German nationalism."[46]

Adam Kuper describes this general oppositional scenario in terms of the forces of civilization engaged in a "struggle to overcome the resistance of traditional cultures, with their superstitions, irrational prejudices, and fearful loyalties to cynical rulers," who in turn saw their "defining enemy" as "rational, scientific universal civilization." He contends that "German intellectuals . . . were provoked to stand up for national tradition against cosmopolitan civilization; for spiritual values against materialism; for the arts and crafts against science and technology; for individual genius and self-expression against stifling bureaucracy; for the emotions, even for the darkest forces within us, against desiccated reason: in short, for *Kultur* against *Civilization*."[47]

But perhaps this is all a bit of an overstatement, for it does not take into account the many advancements made in Germany in fields of study such as philosophy, the sciences, and technological innovation. A classic case in point is the pioneering work of the naturalist Alexander von Humboldt (1769–1859), a virtual "renaissance man" of science whose five-volume *Cosmos*, among other publications, contributed significantly to the advancement of scientific enquiry.[48] It also fails to explain the perfectionist philosophy of G. W. F. Hegel, whose interpretation of history and its ultimate purpose does not fit with the more pessimistic perspective offered by Kuper. In fact, during a series of lectures that Hegel gave at the University of Berlin during the winter of 1830–31, he used the terms *Kultur* and *Zivilisation* virtually interchangeably.[49] And Hegel was by no means alone in his thinking; the possibility that *Kultur* and *Zivilisation* were not always directly opposed to one another in the minds of all German intellectuals can also be found in the following passage from Sigmund Freud on what constitutes human culture or civilization:

> Human culture—I mean by that all those respects in which human life has raised itself above animal conditions and in which it differs from the life of the beasts, and I disdain to separate culture and civilization—presents, as is well known, two aspects to the observer. It includes on the one hand all the knowledge and power that men have acquired in order to master the forces of nature and win resources from her for the satisfaction of human needs; and on the other hand it includes all the necessary arrangements whereby men's relations to each other, and in particular the distribution of the attainable riches, may be regulated. The two tendencies of culture are not independent of each other . . . because the mutual relations of men are profoundly influenced by the measure of instinctual satisfaction that the existing resources make possible.[50]

Nevertheless, there were points of differentiation between *Kultur* and *Zivilisation* in the thought of many intellectuals. In the *Communist Manifesto* Karl Marx and Friedrich Engels effectively prioritize *Kultur* over civilization, arguing that "there is too much civilisation, too much means of subsistence, too much industry, too much commerce."[51] Similar sentiments were later expressed by Thomas Mann, the German Nobel Laureate in Literature of 1929 for whom "culture equals true spirituality, while civilization means mechanization."[52] This line of thinking can also be traced through the respective works of the sociologists Ferdinand Tönnies and Alfred Weber, who saw civilization as little more than the collective practical and technical know-how with which to manage the challenges of nature. *Kultur*, on the other hand, they saw as "a set of normative principles, values and ideals—in a word, the spirit."[53] This particular tension between the two ideals also helps to explain the German historian Wilhelm Mommsen's statement: "It is man's duty today to see that civilization does not destroy culture, nor technology the human being."[54] A further incompatibility arises when recalling that in at least one sense, civilization is said to explicitly relate to an evolutionary process. *Kultur* on the other hand "has a different relation to motion," encapsulating instead the best of the uniquely human endeavors such as the fine arts, literature, painting and poetry , and religious or philosophical thinking—all of which are thought to capture the unique collective identity of a people. Or as Elias further explains it, the "concept of *Kultur* delimits" and "places special stress on national differences and the particular identity of groups," whereas "the concept of civilization plays down the national differences between peoples."[55] It should be noted that while the French/English concept of civilization might play down certain (but not all) differences between the "civilized" peoples of Western Europe in particular, that courtesy is not extended to non-European peoples who were often thought to be "beyond the pale of civilization."

Starobinski insists that the tension between civilization and *Kultur* has been "vehemently express[ed]" by Friedrich Nietzsche, for whom civilization "is nothing but discipline, repression, diminution of the individual; by contrast, culture can go hand in hand with social decadence because it is the fruition of individual energy."[56] The unfathomable depth of this divide is captured in Nietzsche's commentary *Kultur contra Zivilisation* (Culture versus Civilization), as follows: "The highpoints of Culture and of Civilization are remote from one another: one should not be misled about the abysmal antagonism between Culture and Civilization. The greatest moment of Culture was always, morally speaking, a time of corruption; and time and again they were epochs of wilfully and forcefully domesticating men like animals (so-called 'Civilization'). These are times of intolerance for the most spirited and hardiest of natures. Civilization is altogether something different than Culture will allow: it is perhaps its inverse."[57]

According to Nietzsche then, not only are civilization and its objectives at odds with the aims and ideals of *Kultur*, but there is an antagonism between them that has the potential to manifest itself in means beyond the realm of theoretical ideology. In the absolute extreme case— in a somewhat overstated manifestation of this antithesis—Kuper asserts that the "First World War was fought behind the rival banners of Western Civilization and German *Kultur*."[58] This is an oversimplification of what was a complex series of events that led to the outbreak of the First World War, but nevertheless, it gives a vivid indication of the extent of the at times irreconcilable differences that are said to exist between the two concepts.

While the forces of civilization might have won the Great War, this has not always been the outcome, for similar arguments to Kuper's have been made in connection with other conflicts in Europe's history. In speaking of a time long before the word *civilization* had come into being, the German historian G. Kuhn characterized the victory of the barbarian hordes of Germany over the armies of Imperial Rome as "the victory of peasants over warriors, of country over town, of culture over civilization."[59] But according to Victor Hugo, even when the "barbarism" of German *Kultur* defeated the "light" that was French civilization; it still lost out because of what it was not. Addressing the French National Assembly in 1871 following defeat in the Franco-Prussian War at the hands of Germany, Hugo proclaimed:

> And while the victorious nation, Germany, the slave horde, will bend its brow beneath its heavy helmet, France, the sublime vanquished nation, will wear the crown of a sovereign people.
>
> And civilization, once again set face to face with barbarism, will seek its way between these two nations, one of which has been the light of Europe, and the other of which will be the night.[60]

The key point here is Hugo's proclamation that, despite its defeat, the French nation was still considered superior to a less than unified Germany precisely because, unlike Germany up to that point, it was, and had long been, a sovereign, centrally and self-governed nation. As reinforced throughout this study, a nation's capacity for sociopolitical organization and self-government, and hence its claims to sovereignty, has a significant bearing on whether it is deemed to meet the requisite "standard of civilization." It also becomes evident in chapter 4 that German critiques of the French/English account of civilization and its claims to universality, as couched in terms of *Kultur*, have much in common with what might be called contemporary "cultural" critiques of cosmopolitanism and its claims to universality. Finally, in regard to the tensions between *Kultur* and civilization, it is an overstatement to say that German intellectuals across the board perceived the aims and objectives of the two ideals as perpetually at odds or antithetical to one another. While the tensions between *Kultur* and civilization are very real, Braudel suggests that perhaps the greater threat to the ideal of civilization is posed by ethnographers and anthropologists working on civilizations rather than the "perfectly defensible persistence of German thinkers."[61]

What Civilization *Means and Its Implications*

As noted, *civilization* and its plural are interrelated terms and subjects of study that have been examined both independently and with reference to one another. An initial concern with the concept of civilization gave way to detailed studies of civilizations in the nineteenth and twentieth centuries, in large part instigated by the foundation and development of the fields of anthropology and ethnography. Such a shift led to claims that a broader concern with the normative-evaluative aspects of civilization had "lost some of its cachet."[62] The result of this shift was a preoccupation with narrow definitions such as that offered by Émile Durkheim and Marcel Mauss, who state that a "civilization constitutes a kind of moral milieu encompassing a certain number of nations, each national culture being only a particular form of the whole."[63]

One of the leading and most influential exponents of the comparative study of civilizations was the historian Arnold Toynbee. In his *Study of History* and related works, however, he did not completely set aside the ideal of civilization, for he stated that "Civilizations have come and gone, but Civilization (with a big 'C') has succeeded" or endured.[64] Toynbee also sought to articulate a link between "civilizations in the plural and civilization in the singular," noting that the former refers to "particular historical exemplifications of the abstract idea of civilization." This abstract idea of civilization is defined in "spiritual terms" which "equate civilization with a state of society in which there is a minority of the population, however small, that is free from the task, not merely of producing food, but of engaging in any other of the economic activities—e.g. industry and trade—that have to be carried on to keep the life of the society going on the material plane at the civilizational level."[65]

Toynbee's line of argument concerning the organization of society as marked by the specialization of skills, the move toward elite professions, and the effective use of leisure time is one that has long been held in connection with the advancement of civilization (and civilized society). It is found in the work of Thomas Hobbes, for instance, for although his life and work preceded the term *civilization*, Robert Kraynak argues that "the primary theme of Hobbes' studies in civil history is the distinction between barbarism and civilization." Hobbes is said to equate the "*political* characteristics" of "'commonwealths,' 'cities,' or 'polities'" with their "*civilized* qualities," such as "'civil society' or 'civil life,'" to the extent that "he regards civilization as a condition which combined a certain level of political development and a certain manner of living."[66] This is suggested in Hobbes's assertion that the "procuring of the necessities of life . . . was impossible, till the erecting of great Commonwealths," which are "the mother of *Peace*, and *Leasure*," which is, in turn, "the mother of *Philosophy*. . . . Where first were great and flourishing *Cities*, there was first the study of *Philosophy*."[67] That is to say, "Wherever government is sufficiently strong and well-established to provide peace and leisure, men began to cultivate the finer things in life," the very things that are said to be the outward expression of civilization. In "contrast, savagery or barbarism has been a condition where political authority was developed insufficiently or non-existent." Kraynak concludes that by Hobbes's account, "civilization has been distinguished from barbarism by the power and sufficiency of political authority, the enjoyment of leisure, and the development of philosophy or the arts and sciences."[68] But, it is the first of these hallmarks of civilization, the presence of increasingly complex sociopolitical organization, that, in the first instance at least, is the prerequisite and facilitator of the latter qualities.

Some semblance of this general line of argument has been made time and again throughout history, its influence ebbing and flowing with the times. One of the earliest to do so was Aristotle in the *Politics*, in which he posited that "society [meaning the *polis* or state] . . . contains in itself . . . the end and perfection of government: first founded that we might live, but continued that we may live happily."[69] On this point, Kraynak argues that for "Aristotle and other classical philosophers the good life is the end or purpose of civilization."[70] While Aristotle's conception of society might differ from contemporary usage, what this is in effect saying is that the realization of the good life is the purpose of government. Furthermore, it is only by living in society with others that this might be achieved, for Aristotle insists, "whosoever is . . . unfit for society, must be either inferior or superior to man." He further singles out "the man in Homer, who is reviled for being 'without society, without law, without family,'"[71] for, in effect, the absence of at least the first two of these institutions means he is without civilization. Instead, he is either savage or barbaric, or a god. Such accounts of the relationship between civilization, society, and government fit with Anthony Pagden's claim that the "philosophical history of civilization was, then, a history of progressive complexity and progressive refinement which followed from the free expression of those faculties which men possess only as members of a community."[72]

In a 1940 lecture titled "What 'Civilization' Means," R. G. Collingwood spoke of three elements of civilization: economic civilization, social civilization, and legal civilization. The realm of economic civilization is marked not simply by the pursuit of riches—which might in fact be inimical to economic civilization—but by "the civilized pursuit of wealth." The pursuit of wealth is in turn carried out in two ways: through "civilized exchange" and "civilized production." The former means that exchange is carried out justly and fairly in the absence of domination, such as master-slave relationships (which puts him at odds with Aristotle), in accordance with the principles of *laissez-faire* economics. The latter, "Civilized production is scientific production." It is production that is carried out "intelligently" such that "productive industry [is] controlled by an understanding of natural laws." That is to say, it is a mode of production that employs the practice of "natural science . . . wherein, by means of experiment and observation, men find out how to use the forces of nature to the advancement of their own welfare."[73]

The second of Collingwood's three elements of civilization is "social civilization": it is the forum in which humankind's sociability is thought to be satisfied by "the idea of joint action," or what we might call community. It bears the name "civilization" because it is said to have been "civilized" to the point wherein its members refrain from the threat and use of both physical and moral force to induce fellow members to do "what [they] want them to do," instead employing methods of persuasion to win them over. Completing Collingwood's tripartite definition of civilization is the legal component. The final mark of civilization is "a society governed by law," and not so much by criminal law but by civil law in particular, "the law in which claims are adjusted between its members." Furthermore, while military and ecclesiastical law may well have their respective places in such a society, those places are subordinate to the role played by civil law. Moreover, a "society thus governed by civil law is one in which there is no arbitrary power; no executive, however constituted, able to override the law and no judicature able to defy it" (502–11; quote at 510). For Collingwood, then, "Civilization is *something which happens to a community*. . . . Civilization is a *process of approximation to an ideal state*" (283; emphasis in original). In essence, what Collingwood is arguing is that civilized society—and thus civilization itself—is guided by and operates according to the principles of the rule of law.

When we combine the collective criteria of Collingwood's tripartite components of civilization—economic civilization, social civilization, and legal civilization—they amount to what I would call sociopolitical civilization, or the capacity of a collective to organize and govern itself under some system of laws or constitution. Not too far removed from Collingwood's concern with the elimination of physical and moral force via "social civilization" are the more recent accounts of civilized society that address issues relating to the historical and ongoing endeavor to manage violence, if only by removing it from the public sphere. Such a concern is extended in Zygmunt Bauman's account of civilization to the more general issue of producing readily governable subjects. The "concept of *civilization*," he argues, "entered learned discourse in the West as the name of a conscious proselytizing crusade waged by men of knowledge and aimed at extirpating the vestiges of wild cultures."[74]

The nature of the "proselytizing crusade" in the name of civilization is one of the central concerns of this book. Its rationale or driving force is not too difficult to determine when one considers Starobinski's assertion that, "taken as a value, civilization constitutes a political and moral norm. It is the criterion against which barbarity, or non-civilization, is judged and condemned."[75] A similar point is made by Pagden, who states that civilization "describes a state, social, political, cultural, aesthetic even moral and physical—which is held to be the optimum condition for all mankind, and this involves the implicit claim that only the civilized can know what it is to be civilized."[76] Out of this implicit claim and the judgments passed in its name, the notion of the "burden of civilization" was born.

The argument that only the civilized know what it means to be civilized is an important one, for, as Starobinski notes, the "historical moment in which the word *civilization* appears marks the advent of self-reflection, the emergence of a consciousness that thinks it understands the nature of its own activity." More specifically, it marks "the moment that Western civilization becomes aware of itself reflectively, it sees itself as one civilization among others. Having achieved self-consciousness, civilization immediately discovers civilizations."[77] But as Elias notes, it is not a case of Western civilization being just one among equals, for the very concept of civilization "expresses the self-consciousness of the West. . . . It sums up everything in which Western society of the last two or three centuries believes itself superior to earlier societies or 'more primitive' contemporary ones." Elias further explains that in using the term *civilization*, "Western society seeks to describe what constitutes its special character and what it is proud of: the level of *its* technology, the nature of *its* manners, the development of *its* scientific knowledge or view of the world, and much more."[78] Again, it is not too difficult to see how the harbingers of civilization might gravitate toward a (well-meaning) "proselytizing crusade" driven, at least in part, by a deeply held belief in the "burden of civilization." That is not to deny that the same era produced outspoken critics who denounced such a crusade as distinctly uncivilized; apart from Burke, there are the underlying messages of H. G. Wells's *War of the Worlds* and *The Island of Dr. Moreau*[79] and George Orwell's essay "Shooting an Elephant."

The issue is not only the denial of the value and achievements of other civilizations,[80] but the implication that they are in near irreversible decline. From this perspective, their contribution to "big C" Civilization (if any is acknowledged) is seen as largely limited to the past, out of which comes the further implication that if anything of value is to be retrieved, it cannot be done without the assistance of a more civilized tutor. Such thinking is only too evident, for example, in Ferdinand Schiller's mistaken claim that "the peoples of India appear to care very little for history and have never troubled to compile it."[81] Hence, the British took it upon themselves to compile such uneven accounts as that which was prepared by James Mill and published as *The History of British India* in 1817. Despite never having visited India, Mill's *History*, an attack on William Robertson's *Historical Disquisition* of 1791, relayed to European audiences an equally mistaken image of Indian civilization as eternally backward and undeveloped.

Returning to the meaning of civilization, perhaps the best way to summarize it is to follow the lead of Guizot, who claimed not so much to define but rather to describe civilization. For Guizot, "the first fact comprised in the word civilization . . . is the fact of progress, of development; it presents at once the idea of a people marching onward, not to change its place, but to change its condition; of a people whose culture is conditioning itself, and ameliorating itself. The idea of progress, of development, appears to me the fundamental idea contained in the word, *civilization*."[82] The progress or development referred to here concerns "the perfecting of civil life, the development of society, properly so called, of the relations of men among themselves." Yet according to Guizot, "instinct" tells us "that the word, civilization, comprehends something more extensive, more complex, something superior to the simple perfection of the social relations, of social power and happiness" (17). That is, *civilization* means something more than just the sociopolitical organization and government of members or citizens of society. This something more is the realm of humankind's general moral progress, that is, "the development of the individual, internal life, the development of man himself, of his faculties, his sentiments, his ideas." As with Aristotle, Hobbes, and others, sociopolitical organization or the government of society is only the first part of the puzzle, for out of this development, "Letters, sciences, the arts, display all their splendour." Guizot concludes his description of civilization with the declaration: "Wherever mankind beholds these great signs, these signs glorified by human nature, wherever it sees created these treasures of sublime enjoyment, it there recognizes and names civilization." For Guizot, and others, "two facts" are integral elements to the "great fact" that is civilization: "the development of social activity, and that of individual activity; the progress of society and the progress of humanity." Wherever these "two symptoms" are present, "mankind with loud applause proclaims civilization" (18).

Following this proclamation, it was another French historian, Febvre, who stated that the word (and idea of) "*Civilisation* was born at the right time." "Above all," he added, "it was born at a time when, emerging from the entire *Encyclopédie*, the great concept of rational and experimental science was beginning to make itself felt, constituting a whole in its methods and procedures."[83] The air of enthusiasm surrounding the newly born concept of civilization and the general atmosphere it engendered at the time is captured by Febvre in an unidentified citation he quotes from the work of Albert Counson: "Civilisation is inspired by a new philosophy of nature and of man. Its philosophy of nature is evolution. Its philosophy of man is perfectibility."[84]

While this might sound innocuous enough, Starobinski goes to some length in highlighting the dangers associated with this philosophy, in particular, and the deification of civilization, more generally. In a passage worth quoting at some length, he argues that

> because of the connection with the ideas of perfectibility and
> progress, the word *civilization* denoted more than just a com-
> plex process of refinement and mores, social organization, tech-
> nical progress, and advancing knowledge; it took on a sacred
> aura, owing to which it could sometimes reinforce traditional
> religious values and at other times supplant them. The history of
> the word *civilization* thus leads to this crucial observation: once
> a notion takes on a sacred authority and thereby acquires the
> power to mobilize, it quickly stirs up conflict between political
> groups or rival schools of thought claiming to be its champions

and defenders and as such insisting on the exclusive right to propagate the new idea.[85]

Starobinski goes on to highlight some of the consequences of this situation, one of which is his prescient warning that a "term fraught with sacred content demonizes its antonym." He continues:

> Once the word *civilization* ceases to denote a fact subject to judgement and becomes an incontestable value, it enters the verbal arsenal of praise and blame. Evaluating the defects and merits of the civilization is no longer the issue. Civilization itself becomes the crucial criterion: judgement is now made in the name of civilization. One has to take its side, adopt its cause. For those who answer its call it becomes ground for praise. Or, conversely, it can serve as a basis for denunciation: all that is not civilization, all that resists or threatens civilization, is monstrous, absolute evil. As rhetoric heats up it becomes legitimate to ask for the supreme sacrifice in the name of civilization. This means that the service or defence of civilization can in certain circumstances justify the recourse to violence. Civilization's enemies, the barbarians, if they cannot be educated or converted, must be prevented from doing harm. (29–30; emphasis in original)

This is one of the key issues this book addresses: the sometimes extreme measures that have been and continue to be taken by the "civilized" peoples or states of the world against the "uncivilized" in the name of civilization. As Starobinski notes, in one of the more extreme cases, the consequences of the demands of civilization manifest themselves in a "justification for colonization" (18), as is explored in this book more generally and in part 2 in particular. And as is addressed in part 3, one requires little imagination to recognize how relevant this warning is to the present era, given the foreign policy goals and the general direction that some Western leaders are hotly pursuing in the wake of the global war on terror(ism) and its perceived associates. But before we get to that, Starobinski makes the point that the "word *civilization*, which denotes a process, entered the history of ideas at the same time as the modern sense of the word *progress*. The two words were destined to maintain a most intimate relationship" (4; emphasis in original). It is that topic, the idea of progress and its relation to the ideal of civilization, that I turn to in the following chapter.

3 Civilization and the Idea of Progress

We may therefore acquiesce in the pleasing conclusion that every age of the world has increased and still increases the real wealth, the happiness, the knowledge, and perhaps the virtue, of the human race.

Edward Gibbon, *The Decline and Fall of the Roman Empire*

Modern science . . . claims to be proving, by the most careful and exhaustive study of man and his works, that our race began its existence on earth at the bottom of the scale, instead of at the top, and has been gradually working upward; that human powers have had a history of development; that all the elements of culture—as the arts of life, art, science, language, religion, philosophy—have been wrought out by slow and painful efforts, in the conflict between the soul and mind of man on the one hand, and external nature on the other—a conflict in which man has, in favoured races and under exceptional conditions of endowment and circumstance, been triumphantly the victor, and is still going on to new conquests.

William Dwight Whitney, *Oriental and Linguistic Studies*

: : :

Introduction

Despite Jean Starobinski's claims about the interrelated emergence in the history of ideas of the concepts civilization and progress, it is also the case that variations on the idea of progress predate the appearance of the word and ideal of civilization by many centuries. As Joel Colton notes, when "flexibly interpreted," the idea of progress has not merely a 250 year-old but a twenty-five hundred year-old ancestry.[1] Robert Nisbet agrees, arguing that J. B. Bury, among others, was mistaken in his classic study when he claimed "that speculative Greek minds never hit on the idea of Progress."[2] That said, in terms of the uniquely *modern* idea of progress that Starobinski has in mind when making his remark, it is both more common and more convincing to conceive of its emergence as related to advancements in the sciences, the development of the scientific method, and the faith in reason that mark the dawning of the Enlightenment in the seventeenth and eighteenth centuries. Indeed, it is not uncommon for the idea of progress to be characterized as one of the defining aspects of the Enlightenment.

This account, however, fails to fully satisfy, for the key turning point in the story of the emergence of the idea of progress is an event that predates the foundations of the Enlightenment. Ronald Meek has asked the question: "What was it which gave unity to the ideas about the structure and development of society generated in Europe during that incredible century between the English and French revolutions—the century traditionally described as the Enlightenment?" His answer fits neatly with the points made above that it was a common concern to apply recently acquired scientific methods to the study of humans and human society.[3] But this is only part of the story. Beate Jahn accepts Meek's answer, in part, but argues that the underlying answer is "the discovery of the American Indian" and the New World in 1492.[4] As Tzvetan Todorov explains, "the discovery of America, or of the Americans, is certainly the most astonishing encounter of our [European] history. We do not have the same sense of radical difference in the 'discovery' of other continents and of other peoples."[5] A pointer to the logic behind this argument is to be found in John Locke's famous declaration that "in the beginning all the World was *America*."[6] This claim suggests that the "discovery" of the Amerindians of the New World went some way toward providing the missing link or the starting point or original condition of the species prior to any evolutionary improvements. Or, as Adam Ferguson would later state, "It is in their [American savages] present condition, that we are to behold, as in a mirror, the features of our own progenitors; and from thence we are to draw our conclusions with respect to the influence of situations, in which, we have reason to believe, our fathers were placed."[7] More than just providing an opportunity for the application of scientific methods, the equating of Amerindians "with man in the state of nature led to a redefinition of history along a linear time scale providing a secular *telos* as the basis of the historical process." Thus, the "'discovery' of man in the state of nature provided European reformers" with the means to critically examine the trajectory of their own sociopolitical development; along with "the means to theoretically reconstruct an alternative, universally valid, political community."[8]

This chapter explores the general idea of progress and the work of some of the key contributors to that idea. It outlines the general direction that the path of humankind's universal progress is foreseen to be traveling along and hints at the philosophy of history it foretells. This leads into the following chapter, which presents a more detailed account of where the path of progress is heading, that is, what amounts to a universal theory of civilization. As with the preceding chapter, French, British, and German thinkers provide the majority of the perspectives and material to be discussed. Despite their many differences and variations on a theme, common to virtually all of the contributions discussed herein is an endeavor to situate the newly discovered peoples of the New World, along with other indigenous and native peoples, somewhere on a continuum between the poles of savagery and civilization.[9] At the same time, these thinkers also tended to view the discovery of native peoples in the light of the classical tradition, inserting them, however inappropriate the fit, into a schema handed down through the ages. As Michael Ryan notes, there was a "tendency to compare—if not confuse—ancients with exotics," for the newly discovered "exotics" were thought to "cast their own special light on the noble Greeks and Romans."[10] A good illustration of this is Friedrich Engels's praise of Lewis Henry Morgan's *Ancient Society*, as having found "the key to the most important, hitherto insoluble, riddles of the earliest Greek, Roman and German history."[11]

The degree of interrelation between the concepts of civilization and progress is evident in Nisbet's questioning of "whether civilization in any form and substance comparable to what we have known . . . in the West is possible without the supporting faith in progress that has existed along with this civilization."[12] The object of this chapter is not so much to answer this question but to explore just how the ideal of civilization addressed in the previous chapter relates to the idea of progress. In exploring the nature of this relationship, it becomes evident that these twin ideals have played a significant role in the pursuit of a wide-reaching philosophy of history. The nature and significance of this pursuit is hinted at in Nisbet's claim that "no single idea has been more important than . . . the idea of progress in Western civilization for nearly three thousand years." While ideas such as liberty, justice, equality, and community have their rightful place and should not be discounted, it "must be stressed: throughout most of Western history, the substratum of even these ideas has been a philosophy of history that lends past, present, and future to their importance" (4). Its significance is further revealed when Starobinski's point that "*civilization* is a powerful stimulus to theory" leads to the conclusion: "Despite its ambiguity . . . the temptation to clarify our thinking by elaborating a theory of civilization capable of grounding a far-reaching philosophy of history is thus irresistible."[13] Indeed, in recent centuries it has proved irresistible to a diverse range of thinkers who have endeavored to undertake just such a challenging task.

The Idea of Progress

The distinguished historian J. B. Bury, one of the first to undertake a large-scale investigation of the history of the idea of progress, states that the "idea means that civilisation has moved, is moving, and will move in a desirable direction." In keeping with the irresistibility of promulgating a grand theory from the results of his enquiries, Bury declared, the "idea of human Progress then is a theory which involves a synthesis of the past and a prophecy of the future." This theorizing is grounded in an interpretation of history that regards the human condition as advancing "in a definite and desirable direction." It further "implies that . . . a condition of general happiness will be ultimately enjoyed, which will justify the whole process of civilisation."[14] Nisbet, who has also undertaken one of the more extensive studies on the history of the idea of progress, offers a similar definition. "Simply stated, *the idea of progress holds that mankind has advanced in the past—from some aboriginal condition of primitiveness, barbarism, or even nullity—is now advancing, and will continue to advance, through the foreseeable future.*"[15] In essence, the idea of progress holds that human experience, both individual and collective, is cumulative and future-directed, with the specific objective being the ongoing improvement of the individual, the society in which the individual lives, and the world in which the society must survive. Belief in this idea became so widespread and entrenched in the past two or three centuries, particularly in Europe and North America, that it is described as "a universal religion" (7). As Nannerl Keohane explains, by the nineteenth century the "idea of progress . . . became an article of faith . . . and remained the dominant doctrine" in the West until the mid-twentieth century.[16] This statement hints that, as with the ideal of civilization, so too the idea of progress was tarnished and cast into doubt by the catastrophic events of the early to mid-twentieth century. But as outlined below, in part because of the collapse of communism and the end of the Cold War, the idea of progress and belief in a universal history of humankind has been rehabilitated.

Just as the ideal of civilization encapsulates different aspects—such as the arts and the "hard" and "soft" sciences—so too the idea of progress encompasses a range of elements. The most significant of these are identified by Ruth Macklin in her assertion: "It is wholly uncontroversial to hold that technological progress has taken place; largely uncontroversial to claim that intellectual and theoretical progress has occurred; somewhat controversial to say aesthetic or artistic progress has taken place; and highly controversial to assert that moral progress has occurred." In speaking of moral progress, Macklin is referring to what is "wholly a *social* concept"; one that encapsulates only "events, institutions, and practices in countries, cultures, societies, eras, or periods in history."[17] That is, she is broadly referring to the sociopolitical arena and the organization and conduct of relations within it. As to whether it is highly controversial to assert that there has been progress in the social sphere is open to debate, for this is at odds with the aforementioned point that the idea of progress constituted an "article of faith" for much of the past three centuries. Like Macklin, Goddard and Gibbons note that there is a general historical consensus that "progress has certainly taken place in science, in thought, and in all branches of knowledge." But unlike Macklin, they argue that there has long been a widely held conviction "that progress has taken place in social order and political institutions." They conclude that much of recent history is characterized by a general belief that "all the great branches of human achievement, art, science, religion, politics, society, thought, everything in fact which goes to constitute what we call civilisation, are affected by a discussion of the reality of progress."[18]

As outlined in chapter 2, the aspects of the ideal of civilization most relevant here are those relating to social cooperation or degrees of sociopolitical organization. Analysis herein of the idea of progress, which effectively means the general progress of civilization, is likewise primarily confined to the sociopolitical dimension. The logic underpinning this approach was noted in the preceding chapter and is based on the argument, as seen in Hobbes, that some degree of sociopolitical organization is a basic necessity for the foundation of civilization and, hence, progress. This contention is readily distinguishable in the following well-known passage from Hobbes's *Leviathan*:

> Whatsoever therefore is consequent to a time of Warre, where
> every man is Enemy to every man; the same consequent to the

time, wherein men live without other security, than what their own strength, and their own invention shall furnish them withall. In such condition, there is no place for Industry; because the fruit thereof is uncertain: and consequently no Culture of the Earth; no Navigation, nor use of the commodities that may be imported by Sea; no commodious Building; no Instruments of moving, and removing such things as require much force; no Knowledge of the face of the Earth; no account of Time; no Arts; no Letters; no Society; and which is worst of all, continual feare, and danger of violent death; And the life of man, solitary, poore, nasty, brutish, and short.[19]

What Hobbes is effectively arguing here is that without initial cooperation in (political) society, there is no knowledge of science and technology, no philosophy and fine arts, no personal property, wealth, or well-being and, naturally, "no progress in these things."[20] For Hobbes, at least in the first instance, progress in society and politics comes prior to every other form of progress and, moreover, progress within the other sub-elements of civilization is contingent upon it. Or, as Friedrich von Schiller later put it, "would Greece have borne a Thucydides, a Plato, and an Aristotle, or Rome a Horace, a Cicero, a Virgil, and a Livy, if these two states had not risen to those heights of political achievement which in fact they attained?"[21] Once this initial societal condition is secured, however, there is no reason why progress in other fields should not surpass the rate of progress in the sociopolitical arena. It is for these reasons, first, that civilization primarily concerns social cooperation and organization and, second, that all progress is initially dependent upon advancements in this arena, that this study is primarily concerned with the belief that civilization (or progress) would provide "superior institutions for organising people more rationally."[22]

As suggested above, the idea of progress has a long history, and there are a number of theoretical means by which it came into being. If one follows the categorical distinctions drawn by Charles Van Doren, then those means are identified as either "anthropogenic" or "cosmogenic." The former broadly refers to theories that view humankind as the source of progress, including those based on humankind's collective or accumulative social memory and theories based on humankind's progress through the application of powers of reason. The latter refers to theories of progress in which the source is nonhuman or otherworldly, such as divinely ordained progress or Providence, and progress founded on cosmic processes or principles of nature.[23] In reality it is not so easy to separate and isolate the various theories of progress. Developments within one field can complement arguments in another. These same developments may require only that a particular line of argument requires some reworking, and it need not be to the extent that it is severed from its original moorings. Alternatively, new work on the theorizing of progress may mean that one line of thought either evolves into or gives way to another or splits into divergent strands. And there is also the scenario whereby evidence supporting the idea of progress is interpreted differently by the different traditions, meaning different things to different people, or constitutes different ways of explaining what is ultimately progress directed toward the same ends. With all of this in mind, the following sections give a broad historical outline of the general sources of the idea of progress.

Anthropology and Ethnology

As noted, the idea of progress is in part linked to developments in the sciences, or, as is equally the case, developments in the sciences spring forth from theorizing about the evolutionary progress of the human species. Simply put, just as the fledgling fields of anthropology and ethnology/ethnography were sources of theories of progress of humankind, the identification of distinctly different stages of human progress also provided the foundations of anthropology and ethnography.[24] The arrival of anthropology as a science to be taken seriously is significant. As David Harvey notes, Immanuel Kant "considered that geography (together with anthropology) defined the conditions of possibility of all knowledge and that such knowledge was a necessary preparation—a 'propaedeutic' as he termed it—for everything else."[25] The influence of anthropology on fields of inquiry such as social, political, and legal thought is explored further below.

Christopher Columbus's "discovery" of the New World and the subsequent Spanish encounters with the people of the land they first called *Indias Occidentales* provided further impetus for these new fields of scientific enquiry. Anthony Pagden argues that Bartolomé de Las Casas's *Apologética historia sumaria* (c. 1550), written after years of travel and missionary work among the Amerindians, is effectively the first work of comparative ethnology. Las Casas's work was comparative in that he was comparing Amerindians to Europeans and other known peoples and situating them in what he thought was their rightful place on the savage-civilized continuum. His influence, however, was quite limited, for as with some of Las Casas's other works that sought to ameliorate the treatment and conditions of Amerindians in the Spanish colonies, it remained unpublished in his lifetime. In contrast, following its publication in Spanish in 1590, José de Acosta's *Natural and Moral History of the Indies* was translated into Italian, German, French, English, Dutch, and Latin—the languages of imperial Europe—and thus "for the latter part of the sixteenth and for most of the seventeenth century dominated speculations on the Amerindians and their culture."[26]

Similar to Las Casas, Acosta based his work on his own empirical studies supplemented by "sundry books and reports . . . disclos[ing] the new and strange things that have been discovered in the New World and the West Indies," many of which he was reluctant to place too much faith in.[27] Acosta embarked on his passage to the New World in 1571. Arriving the following year, he spent approximately ten years in the region, one in the Caribbean Islands and the remainder traveling through parts of what is modern-day Peru, Bolivia, Ecuador, Mexico, Guatemala, and Nicaragua. Book 6 of Acosta's *History* is of most interest here, for it is the one in which he addresses the Indian's "customs and polity and government." In it he argues, "It is a proven fact that barbarian peoples show their barbarity most clearly in their government and manner of ruling, for the more closely men approach to reason the more humane and less arrogant is their government." Acosta's investigations of the varying degrees of social organization and systems of government of the various Amerindian groups led him to write: "it must be pointed out that three kinds of government and styles of life have been found among the Indians." Of these, "the chief kind, and the best, has been the realm or monarchy, as was that of the Incas and of Moctezuma." The second system of organization he describes as "free associations or communities, where the people are governed by the advice of many, and are like councils. In time of war these elect a captain who is obeyed by a whole tribe or province. In time of peace each town or group of folk rules itself" under the leadership of prominent men who enjoy the respect of the majority of the group. His description of the third arrangement is reminiscent of Aristotle's reference to the reviled character in Homer, as noted in the preceding chapter. "The third kind of government," declares Acosta, "is absolutely barbarous, and these are Indians who have neither laws nor king nor fixed dwellings but go in herds like wild animals and savages."[28] As Pagden notes, in his study of Amerindian people and society, "Acosta's insistence that barbarism described not one but several different cultural types, [meant] that people could be graded, so to speak, for civility or barbarism by examining their political institutions, religious beliefs and linguistic sophistication."[29]

Acosta was quite well versed in the ways of the different peoples that were known to lie beyond Europe. His grading of the various stages of organizational development among the Amerindians is compared with those of the East Indies, Siam, and Bisnaga. He remarks: "superior to all the others is the greatness and power of the kingdoms of China, whose monarchs have lasted for more than two thousand years according to them, thanks to their splendid form of government."[30] Relying as he did on his own empirical observations, Acosta noticeably makes the point that this is according to the Chinese themselves. As there is no authoritative European verification of their achievements over these millennia, the claim is thus open to suspicion and doubt. The significant point here, though, is Acosta's further indication of a ranking of the organizational qualities of the respective societies.

The Jesuit missionary Father Joseph François Lafitau is the next significant figure to be similarly acclaimed as "the first blaze on the path to scientific anthropology."[31] Like Lewis Henry Morgan who would come after him, Lafitau spent considerable time among the Iroquois and other American Indian peoples. His studies would later be drawn upon by and influence the thinking of people from, among others, the Scottish Enlightenment's Adam Ferguson and his work on civil society to the German romantic Johann Gottfried Herder and his work on language and songs. But I do not want to dwell too long or go into too much detail on Lafitau's extensive studies, other than to note their considerable contribution to the advancement of the topic of human progress being explored herein. A good part of the reason is that Lafitau's studies are in a broadly similar vein to work that preceded it, such as that of Acosta, and work that would follow it.

With further European "discoveries" of aboriginal peoples around the globe in the centuries following Spain's stumbling upon the New World, the theory of stages of progress of the human species became more widely studied and accepted as fact. Based on a broad study of historical societies and aboriginal peoples—including his own extensive observations of Amerindians, particularly the Iroquois Confederation—the American lawyer-cum-anthropologist Lewis Henry Morgan furthered the cause with his elaboration of a yet more detailed hierarchy of human progress. In his influential book of 1877, *Ancient Society*, he wrote, "It can now be asserted upon convincing evidence that savagery preceded barbarism in all tribes of mankind, as barbarism is known to have preceded civilization." He was further convinced "that this sequence has been historically true for the entire human family," because "these three distinct conditions are connected with each other in a natural as well as necessary sequence of progress." Or to put it another way, Morgan was of the opinion that the "history of the human race is one in source, one in experience, and one in progress."[32]

In order to arrive at his stages of humanity theory, Morgan pursued two lines of investigation, one leading through "inventions and discoveries," the other "through primary [social] institutions." In fact, the greater part of his book addresses the "growth of the idea of government" and how it relates to the progression from savagery, through barbarism, to arrival at civilization. Morgan argued that "all forms of government are reducible to two general plans . . . [which] in their bases are fundamentally distinct." The first of these to appear on the scene "is founded upon persons, and upon relations purely personal, and may be distinguished as a society (*societas*)." The "second is founded upon territory and upon property, and may be distinguished as a state (*civitas*)." Whereas the family and loose or fluid coalitions of tribes are the organizational units of the first, the latter is organized through successive stages of integration that range from towns, through to provinces, culminating at the level of the nation. Each of these units is said to be "organized upon territorial areas, and deals with property as well as with persons through territorial relations." And as Morgan states it, "political society is the result," something the former falls short of (4–6).

Morgan's general theory on the progression of the human species and its capacity for sociopolitical organization is succinctly captured in the following passage, which is worth quoting at some length:

> Out of a few germs of thought, conceived in the early ages, have been evolved all the principal institutions of mankind. Beginning their growth in the period of savagery, fermenting through the period of barbarism, they have continued their advancement through the period of civilization. The evolution of these germs of thought has been guided by a natural logic which formed an essential attribute of the brain itself. So unerringly has this principle performed its function in all conditions of experience, and in all periods of time, that its results are uniform, coherent and traceable in their course. These results alone will in time yield convincing proof of the unity of origin of mankind. The mental history of the human race, which is revealed in institutions, inventions and discoveries, is presumptively the history of a single species, perpetuated through individuals, and developed through experience. Among the original germs of thought, which have exercised the most powerful influence upon the hu-

man mind, and upon human destiny, are these which relate to
government, to the family, to language, to religion, and to property. They have a definite beginning far back in savagery, and a
logical progress, but can have no final consummation, because
they are still progressing, and must ever continue to progress.
(59–60)

Regardless of who holds the title as the first anthropologist, according to Sir John Lubbock, writing in 1870, anthropology's particular
significance derives from claims that it constitutes a "natural history of
the human species" encompassing "the complete science of man, body
and soul, in all the modifications of sex, temperament, race, civilization,
etc." On the basis of such claims, anthropology would soon come to inform many other fields of social enquiry too, for it was thought to provide the necessary tools for ascertaining whether there was "a definite
and assured law of progress in human affairs."[33]

In contradistinction to Morgan, the French ethnologist Arthur de
Gobineau—sometimes referred to as the father of ethnographic rac-
ism—insisted that most peoples are incapable of progressing beyond
their present state. Gobineau was convinced "that the racial question
overshadows all other problems in history, that it holds the key to them
all, and that the inequality of the races from whose fusion a people
is formed is enough to explain the whole course of its destiny." He
concludes, "I convinced myself at last that everything great, noble, and
fruitful in the works of man on this earth, in science, art, and civilization, derives from a single starting point; it belongs to one family alone,
the different branches of which have reigned in all the civilized countries
of the universe."[34] Or, in the words of the infamous anatomist Robert
Knox, "Race is everything: literature, science, art—in a word, civilization, depends on it."[35] As Frank Hankins explains, like so many others addressing these broad and beguiling issues, Gobineau could not
resist the temptation to extrapolate from his conclusions a "grand and
sweeping philosophy of history."[36] And as outlined below, there are still
those who are led to not too dissimilar conclusions, albeit it is no longer
overtly stated that race is the discerning factor. Rather, for some, the
West's leading role as an innovator and modernizer in the various fields
of intellectual and technological endeavor is attributed to a cultural or
civilizational superiority. For some of those attuned to Gobineau's line
of thinking, even prior to the appearance of Charles Darwin's *The Descent of Man*, it was thought inevitable that the weaker, less civilized
peoples of the world would be displaced or perish at the hands of the

stronger; that is, Europeans. This was simply thought to be the natural sequence of events.

For instance, Herbert Spencer claimed that nature's "forces at work exterminate" those portions of humankind that stand in the way of progress "with the same sternness that they exterminate beasts of prey and herds of useless ruminants." Just as it is natural that "the savage has taken the place of lower creatures, so must he, if he remained too long a savage, give place to his superior." For Spencer, the "forcible supplantings of the weak by the strong" were not only a natural "phase of civilization" but also prudent and morally right. They aided "civilization by clearing the Earth of its least advanced inhabitants, and by forcibly compelling the rest to acquire industrial habits." As highlighted in following chapters, "the conquest of one people over another has been, in the main, the conquest of the social man over the anti-social man; or, strictly speaking, of the more adapted over the less adapted."[37] The general rule is that the "civilized" do the conquering, and the "uncivilized" are the conquered.

For the purposes here, the significant point is the perceived capacity, or lack of it, of the indigenes of the New World and newly discovered lands elsewhere beyond Europe for social cooperation to the point of political organization. The prevailing thought of the time concerning the peoples of much of the non-European world, particularly those in the Americas, the South Pacific, and Africa, is indicated by the Scottish historian William Robertson's discussion of Amerindians in *History of America*. Robertson reiterates the widely held view that "man existed as an individual before he became the member of a community." As such, the qualities and capacities he possessed as a precommunal being are important considerations when "investigating the manners of rude nations."[38] This statement gives credence to Keohane's point that "throughout history, one favored device for describing human progress has been the analogy between the development of the species and the maturation of a single individual."[39] That is to say that savages and barbarians are often described as childlike or infantile, as such are incapable of caring for themselves, and are hence crying out for protection and tutelage from mature, rational adults, that is, civilized peoples. (Further examples of this are reviewed in chapter 6 below.) In describing these rude nations, Robertson declared: "Their political union is so incomplete, their civil institutions and regulations so few, so simple, and of such slender authority, that men in this state ought to be viewed rather as independent agents, than as members of regular society. The character of a savage results almost entirely from his sentiments or feelings as an individual, and is but little influenced by his imperfect subjection to government and order."[40]

The point being made here is that the character of the savage reflects a general lack of progress or refinement, a consequence of which is the absence of social order and government. The reasons given for this varied. For some it was thought to be racial deficiencies, as seen above, while for others nature or geography was seen to be a significant factor in limiting the degree of progress made through the stages. A prominent and influential proponent of this idea was the French political philosopher Montesquieu. In *The Spirit of the Laws*, he advanced a theory based on environmental considerations to explain the "difference between savage and barbarous nations," and how they are, in turn, distinct from civilized societies. Like other influential accounts discussed here, Montesquieu notes their respective capacities for social cooperation, arguing that "the former are dispersed clans, which for some particular reason cannot be joined in a body; and the latter are commonly small nations, capable of being united. The savages," he adds, "are generally hunters; the barbarians are herdsmen and shepherds."[41] As seen below, Adam Smith draws similar distinctions in his four-stage theory of progress.

From Anthropology to Politics and Philosophy

Having touched on Montesquieu's nature-based contribution to the idea of progress, it is appropriate to discuss further the influence the ideas and theories presented by the human sciences had on the social and political sciences. The significance of anthropology for social theory and political philosophy more generally is perhaps no more evident than in the generous praise Engels heaped upon Morgan's *Ancient Society*. Traversing similar intellectual terrain in his own study, begun with Marx prior to his death, Engels waxes lyrical about the "epoch-making" contribution of Morgan's book in "having discovered and reconstructed" the "prehistoric foundation of our written history." Its specific appeal lies in Engels's claim that "Morgan rediscovered in America . . . the materialist conception of history that had been discovered by Marx forty years ago, and in his comparison of barbarism and civilization was led by this conception to the same conclusions, in the main points, as Marx had arrived at." In fact, Engels states in the preface to *The Origin of Family, Private Property and the State* that it is, "in a sense, the fulfillment of a bequest. It was no less a person than Karl Marx who had planned to present the results of Morgan's researches in connection with the conclusions arrived at by his own . . . materialist investigation of history and thus to make clear their whole significance." As Engels explains the theory, "old society based on sex groups" gives way to "newly-developed social classes; in its place a new society appears, constituted in a state." The state is in turn constituted of units based on territory. It is "a society in which the family system is entirely dominated by the property system," leading to class antagonism and struggles.[42] Engels was so impressed by Morgan's conclusions that he concludes his own book by quoting passages of Morgan's concluding pages, in which Morgan addresses the law of progress, at some length.

The stages of sociopolitical progress theory outlined by anthropologists influenced a wide range of political thinkers who might not usually be grouped together as birds of the same intellectual feather, given their different visions of the ideal political community and the most appropriate or efficient form of governing. As Keohane notes, for Scottish and French Enlightenment figures in particular, the "comparison of Scotland and France with simple hunting tribes in America offered decisive proof of progress in social organization, economic production and commerce, and communication."[43] In France the leading advocates of the idea of progress were Anne Robert Jacques Turgot and Antoine-Nicolas de Condorcet.

French Views on Progress

Turgot advanced what is best described as a cumulative theory of history, arguing that "all the ages are bound up with one another by a succession of causes and effects which link the present state of the world with all those that have preceded it." On this basis he maintained that "the human race, considered over the period since its origin, appears to the eye of a philosopher as one vast whole." Reflecting the analogy noted by Keohane, he continues, "which itself, like each individual, has its infancy and its advancement." In keeping with Hobbes's initial ordering of the realms of progress, Turgot posited that "laws and forms of government succeed one another," following which "the arts and sciences are in turn discovered and perfected, in turn retarded and accelerated in their progress; and they are passed on from country to country."[44] Reaffirming the points made above about sociopolitical cooperation and territorial property being the foundation stones of civilization and towns and villages its building blocks, Turgot writes, the "towns among all civilised peoples constitute by their very nature the centres of trade and the backbone of society" (55).

While Turgot was a firm believer in human progress and viewed the human race as "one vast whole," meaning that the entire species, regardless of race or ethnicity, is progressing along the same path, that is not to say that all members of the species were thought to be progressing at the same rate. Rather, according to Turgot, during his time the known world consisted of peoples who represented all the various stages of progress that humankind had ever passed through or achieved. As he explained it, "the present state of the world, marked as it is by these infinite variations in inequality, spreads out before us at one and the same time all the gradations from barbarism to refinement, thereby revealing to us at a single glance, as it were, the records and remains of all the steps taken by the human mind, a reflection of all the stages through which it has passed, and the history of all the ages" (42). What Turgot proclaimed to be able to see in his survey of the various stages of progress of humankind was a universal history of the species and the path along which it is slowly making its way. The eventual destination he envisioned all humankind heading toward was also clear to Turgot, albeit with some arriving much earlier than others. He described it thus, "Finally, commercial and political ties unite all parts of the globe, and the whole human race, through alternate periods of rest and unrest, of weal and woe, goes on advancing, although at slow pace, towards greater perfection" (41). This is a topic that many theorists of progress and philosophers of history would also take up, and it is one that remains influential and provides the focal point of the following chapter.

J. Salwyn Schapiro notes that, as important as Turgot's contribution was to the idea of progress, he did not manage to develop it into "a system of social philosophy" or a universal history of humankind.[45] Stuart Hampshire makes a similar point about Voltaire,[46] despite him being attributed elsewhere as the first thinker to use the term "philosophy of history."[47] According to Schapiro, that task subsequently fell to Turgot's "friend and disciple," Condorcet.[48] Hampshire acknowledges that the "idea of history" as a narrative of humankind's "progress from superstition and barbarism to an age of reason and enlightenment" was not the brainchild of Condorcet. But he insists that "Condorcet's originality was to extend the doctrine of progress to every department of human activity; he saw history as the story of intellectual, political, economic, social and artistic progress, all necessarily connected."[49] Again, of most interest here is his attention to progress in sociopolitical organization, or what Condorcet referred to as "the social art." He believed that "at a high stage of civilized enlightenment," the social art, or politics, would evolve into "a true theory, founded on general principles that are based on nature, and avowed by reason."[50]

For Condorcet, the study of history had two basic uses. The first was "to establish the facts of progress," and the second was "to discover its laws in order to determine the future development of mankind."[51] What he was hoping to do was equip himself with the tools that would allow him to address the question: "If man can, with almost complete assurance, predict phenomena when he knows their laws . . . why, then, should it be regarded as a fantastic undertaking to sketch, with some pretence to truth, the future destiny of man on the basis of his history?"[52] In short, what Condorcet endeavored to do was observe the passage of history to predict or foresee the future. This emerged from his belief that "the progress of the human mind . . . is subject to the same general laws that can be observed in the development of the faculties of the individual," which is "no more than the sum of that development realized in a large number of individuals joined together in society." Again, we see here the analogy drawn between the maturation of the species and the maturation of an individual. Condorcet goes on to state that history "is a record of change and is based on the observation of human societies throughout the different stages of their development." As such, history "ought to reveal the order of this change and the influence" that each phase has upon the subsequent phase. Ultimately, history ought to reveal all the phases through which humankind has passed, "the path that it has followed, the steps that it has made towards truth or happiness" (4–5). This passage reveals Condorcet's unwavering belief in the direction of human progress and the rosy future he envisions for it.

In articulating his philosophy of the history of humankind, Condorcet reasoned that "if the study of individual beings is useful to the metaphysician and the moralist, why should the study of societies be any less useful to them and to the political philosopher." And that is precisely what he endeavored to do, to study them "side by side" and the "relations between them," and to study them "across the passage of time." What Condorcet found was that "all peoples whose history is recorded fall somewhere between our present degree of civilization and that which we still see amongst savage tribes" (12). Similar to Turgot, he saw an "uninterrupted chain between the beginning of historical time and the [eighteenth] century in which we live, between the first peoples known to us and the present nations of Europe" (8). Between those two extremes—in which Europe could not help but sit at the apex— Condorcet identified ten distinct stages of human progress.[53] The destination that Condorcet envisioned for humanity is explored in the following chapter.

British Views on Progress

Among Scottish Enlightenment thinkers, Adam Ferguson and Adam Smith are most associated with the idea of progress. As Ferguson's work on civil society and the transition of humankind and society from a state of "rudeness" to a "refined" or "polished" state has been discussed in the preceding chapter, the focus here will be a brief account of Smith's schema. Smith can be counted among a group of political economists who Pagden argues "were committed to the view that contemporary commercial society was the highest condition to which man could aspire and that such a society was a possible outcome—possible for all peoples everywhere—of a determinate intelligible, and, to some degree, controllable, historical process."[54] In a discussion of war making and defense in book 5 of *The Wealth of Nations*, Smith outlines four distinct stages to human societal development. The first is "nations of hunters, the lowest and rudest state of society," his prime example being the "native tribes of North America." The second stage is "nations of shepherds, a more advanced state of society," such as that of the Tartars and the Arabs. But such peoples still have "no fixed habitation" for any significant length of term, as they move about on the whim of their livestock and with the seasons in the endless search for feed. The third stage is that of agriculture, which "even in its rudest and lowest state, supposes a settlement [and] some sort of fixed habitation," which in turn presupposes some form of coordination and cooperation for the defense of the village. The fourth and most advanced stage is that of commercial society, which, through its organization and the creation of surplus, has the means to establish a standing army.[55] Edward Harpham suggests that Smith used his four stages theory to "explain why political institutions in a commercial society" had progressed and "were necessarily different from those in earlier stages of society." Smith further set out to explain the appropriate functions of these institutions given the political, social, and economic upheaval that resulted from the transition to a market economy.[56]

Another political economist to address the idea of progress and the development of political society was the Englishman Walter Bagehot. In *Physics and Politics* he argued that "the miscellaneous races of the world be justly described as being upon various edges of industrial civilisation, approaching it by various sides, and falling short of it in various particulars." In speaking of those who fell short, that is, the "condition of primitive man," he claimed that they "neither knew nature, which is the clock-work of material civilisation, nor possessed a polity, which is a kind of clock-work to moral civilisation." Reminiscent of J. S. Mill in some respects, Bagehot reiterates the widely held view that the "progress of *man* requires the co-operation of *men* for its development." In line with the long-held prevailing thinking of the time, he proclaimed: "That which any one man or any one family could invent for themselves is obviously exceedingly limited." The consequences of this are that the "rudest sort of co-operative society, the lowest tribe and the feeblest government, is so much stronger than isolated man, that isolated man . . . might very easily have ceased to exist."[57]

The logical extension of this argument is that the same rings true for societies that occupy the lower end of the scale when they come into contact with those that are more organized and sophisticated. Out of the subject of progress, Bagehot derives two principles. The first "is that man can only make progress in 'co-operative groups,'" which is essentially a restatement of the argument put forward by Hobbes, as discussed above. In accordance with this principle, he insists that "few people would at once see that tribes and nations *are* co-operative groups, and that it is their being so which makes their value." Hence, "unless you can make a strong co-operative bond, your society will be conquered and killed out by some other society which has such a bond." As noted above, this particular view was one that was held by a good many, particularly ethnologists (it is also a topic addressed further in chapter 6). Bagehot's "second principle is that members of such a group should be similar enough to one another to co-operate easily and readily together," for cooperation within a group—particularly a group that has attained the status of political society—requires a "felt union of heart and spirit." Such a union is realizable, he believed, only when there is a genuine and "real likeness in mind and feeling" (213; emphasis in original). Similar sentiments persist to this day among those skeptical of the merits or feasibility of multicultural societies.

German Views on Progress

Distinguishing himself in certain respects from much of the prevailing theorizing on human progress, including his German intellectual sparring partners, was Johann Gottfried Herder, whose thinking is in some ways parallel to that of the Germans outlined in the preceding chapter in regard to distinctions between *civilisation* and *Kultur*. Apart from being regarded as the father of German romanticism, according to Hans Adler and Ernest Menze, Herder is yet another figure described as "the founder of anthropology" and "one of the originators of the modern philosophy of history." But, more than that, Herder's "world history" is interdisciplinary in that he brought to his theorizing a knowledge of "aesthetics, physics, geography, anthropology, theology, mythology, psychology, and many other aspects of human cognition and knowledge," all of which went into his overarching philosophy of history.[58]

Not unlike many other thinkers on these issues, Herder held that the "present [is] pregnant with the past." That is to say, he believed that "the present owes its existence to the past, as the future will be beholden to the present," which is what he termed a "genetical" view of history (5, 8). Like most other thinkers discussed herein, he was of the view that "*on our mother earth all epochs of humankind do yet live and move.*"[59] But that is not to say that Herder conforms to the more widely held view of human progress as a universal march toward perfection or greater civilization. Rather, for Herder, the "universal that makes world history possible" is based on an anthropology that recognizes "the unity of man and humankind in all its diversity."[60] As he simply expressed it, "Is not the good *dispersed* all over earth?" In short, Herder questioned "why should the western extremity of our Northern Hemisphere [Western Europe] alone be the home of civilization? And is that really so?"[61] Essentially, Herder is not convinced by the idea of history as the universal linear march of humankind toward perfection, nor the idea of cyclical history, nor the more skeptical notion that the passage of history is nothing but chaos or chance. As he saw it, progress could not be guaranteed, for he noted that "civilized states may develop where" once deemed virtually impossible, and that "civilized states wither, though we considered them immortal" (46). For Herder, reason is manifold in that human nature or the human spirit does not universally conform to the scientific modeling proposed by many Enlightenment thinkers. His philosophy of history is contingent on the plurality of diverse cultures and societies that make up the species. Speculations on the degree of progress or specific achievements of different peoples should therefore be analyzed in the relevant context, and not abstracted from their all-important cultural grounding. Herder's thoughts on history elicited a response from his one-time teacher, Immanuel Kant, and the two subsequently spent much time disputing or challenging each other's respective philosophical systems.[62] Kant's work in turn sparked much of Georg W. F. Hegel's thinking on the matter, both of whom are discussed below.

In respect to the passage of history and the specific end which he sees it as heading toward, Kant's thinking resembles more that of Condorcet than either of his compatriots, which is not to say that Herder and Hegel have all that much in common on this matter. As Lewis White Beck explains, for Kant, like so many others, the "study of history shows the gradual advance of mankind from barbarism to nationhood," but fewer interpreted it as also giving "the directions needed for its further advance to cosmopolitanism and lasting peace."[63] This aspect of Kant's thought is particularly significant for this book, as it continues to have considerable influence on contemporary liberal thought, particularly that of liberal cosmopolitans, and nowhere more so than in their theorizing on (and, for some, hands-on practice of) international politics, the focus of the following chapter.

Kant's thoughts on history as a narrative of universal human progress are found in his *Idea for a Universal History from a Cosmopolitan Point of View*, in which he argues it is possible "to discern a regular movement in" history. His point is that what might appear to be "complex and chaotic" at the micro level of the individual has a coherence and progressive evolutionary logic when one stands back and looks at the species on a macro level. For Kant, the drivers of progress are reason and what he calls humankind's "unsocial sociability," that is, "their propensity to enter into society, bound together with a mutual opposition which constantly threatens to break up the society." But as with so many other thinkers, for Kant, political society is a crucial apparatus of progress and civilization, for it is only in society that humankind can completely develop all of their inherent capacities, "and more specifically [only] in the society with the greatest freedom."[64] Similar to Condorcet's thought, Kant's philosophy or "Idea of world history" can be described as cumulative. His thoughts on the progress of the state-building process are succinctly captured thus: "If one follows the influence of Greek history on the construction of and misconstruction of the Roman state which swallowed up the Greek, then the Roman influence on the barbarians who in turn destroyed it, and so on down to our own times; if one adds episodes from the national histories of other peoples insofar as they are known from the history of the enlightened nations, one will discover a regular progress in the constitution of states on our continent [Europe] (which will probably give law, eventually, to all others)" (24–25).

And so Europe did to a large extent, as outlined in chapter 5 and elsewhere herein. The fact that Kant is referring to the progress of humankind as a whole and not just select quarters of it is found in his essay *An Old Question Raised Again: Is the Human Race Constantly*

Progressing? Making sure that he is asking the correct questions, he proposes: "If it is asked whether the human race at large is progressing perpetually toward the better, the important thing is not the natural history of man . . . but rather his moral history and, more precisely, his history not as a species according to the generic notion (*singulorum*), but as the totality of men united socially on earth and apportioned into peoples (*universorum*)."[65]

In terms of one of the arguments of this book—that the passage of sociopolitical evolutionary history is shaped by ideas and the enforcement of standards of civilization—Kant's "Idea of world history," as first expounded in *Idea for a Universal History*, raises a significant point. He begins by stating, "Everyone can see that philosophy can have her belief in a millenium, but her millenarianism is not Utopian, since the Idea can help, though only from afar, to bring the millenium to pass." He continues, the "only question is: Does Nature reveal anything of a path to this end? And I say: She reveals something, but very little." He goes on to assert that "human nature is so constituted that we cannot be indifferent to the most remote epoch our race may come to, if only we may expect it with certainty. Such indifference is even less possible for us, since it seems our own intelligent action may hasten this happy time for our posterity."[66] It is here that Kant introduces the idea that humankind may alter or, perhaps more accurately, hasten history's path to its predetermined destination. The idea that the course of history may be shaped is reaffirmed in Kant's *Is the Human Race Constantly Progressing?* during a discussion on "predictive history," in which he suggests: "It was all very well for the Jewish prophets to prophesy that sooner or later not simply decadence but complete dissolution awaited their state, for they themselves were the authors of this fate." To which he adds, "So far as their influence extends, our politicians do precisely the same thing and are just as lucky in their prophecies."[67] This is one of the central arguments of this book: throughout much of recent history, Europeans, and now the (American-led) West more generally, have a particular shape of international society in mind and continue to mould it via the deployment of powerful ideas and concepts such as civilization and progress and through the imposition of standards of civilization. Despite having little else in common with Marx, Kant's proposition is not so different from Marx's famous statement: "Men make their own history."[68] While it may well be that they have little else in common, it does not require too much of a stretch of the imagination to find a common cause running through Enlightenment thought down to the present era.

In reaction to Kant, and not long after Condorcet recorded his thoughts on the prospects and direction of the progress of the human mind, the German philosopher G. W. F. Hegel was convinced that he too knew exactly what "our hopes" were and how they were to be realized. Hegel's philosophy of history is significant here in that it is highly influential and, in particular, provides the foundation for Francis Fukuyama's revival of the idea of progress and history with a purpose following the end of the Cold War (albeit via Alexandre Kojève's idiosyncratic reading of Hegel, and although the end that Fukuyama sees history terminating at is closer to that envisioned by Condorcet and Kant than that outlined by Hegel). Like Condorcet, Hegel embarked on an investigation of the narrative of human history firmly believing in the ideal of human progress. That, however, is pretty much where their similarities end, for his investigation led to a rather different destination. Hegel thought that "the phenomenon we investigate—Universal History—belongs to the realm of the *Spirit*," where "the essence of Spirit is Freedom." Similar to other proponents of the idea of a universal history of human progress and the "impulse of *perfectibility*," Hegel believed that "the History of the world is none other than the progress of the consciousness of Freedom." However, Hegel's "Idea of Freedom" finds expression in a somewhat different form from that of other philosophers, particularly liberal philosophers. For Hegel, "Freedom is nothing but the recognition and adoption of such universal substantial objects as Right and Law, and the production of a reality that is accordant with them—the State."[69] While it is true that many of the figures listed above might agree that cooperative political society is the pinnacle in terms of progress in human social organization, few would sign up to Hegel's particular formulation of the state as the highest unit of organization.

In order to comprehend Hegel's "Idea of Freedom" and its realization in and through the state, it is necessary to have a general understanding of his theory of the state, for they go hand-in-hand. In *The Philosophy of Right*, Hegel makes a clear distinction between the "state as a political entity" and the "state [as] the actuality of the ethical Idea," whereby the "ethical Idea" or "ethical life" is the "Idea of freedom."[70] For Hegel, a person is free only to the extent that she or he is a rational self-determining individual with the ability to think and apply the powers of reason. As mere individuals, however, human beings are incapable of ever being truly free or fulfilling their rationality without the rational state. For it is only in the state that true freedom can be actualized, whereby "right and duty coalesce, and by being in the ethical order a man has rights in so far as he has duties, and duties in so far as he has rights" (109, para. 155). Hegel was of the opinion that in the state individual interests are realized as they become, "of their own accord," one and the same as the collective interests. That is to say, the ends of those individuals that constitute the community are not mutually exclusive, but "consciously aimed at none but the universal end" (160–61, para. 260), that is, an ethical life through the state. But as Hegel explains, a "nation does not begin by being a state"; rather, there is a transition through the stages of family, horde, clan, multitude, and so on, to the point where "political conditions" result in the "realisation of the Idea in the form of that nation." In the absence of this form, that is, a state, a nation "lacks the objectivity of possessing in its own eyes and in the eyes of others, a universal and universally valid embodiment in laws . . . and as a result it fails to secure the recognition of others." Hegel concludes this point by asserting that, so long as a nation lacks the institutions of a state, particularly "objective law" and a "rational constitution, its autonomy is formal only and is not sovereignty" (218, para. 349). As seen in forthcoming chapters, this is a particularly crucial point in terms of the establishment and enforcement of standards of civilization among the society of states. What this means for the hierarchy of nations is that civilized nations are justified in "treating as barbarians those who lag behind them in institutions which are the essential moments of state." Thus, for Hegel, "a pastoral people may treat hunters as barbarians, and both of these are barbarians from the point of view of agriculturalists," and so on, with peoples belonging to a state sitting at the apex (219, para. 351).

Modernization Theory

Georg Iggers makes the point that the "idea of progress in its Enlightenment form represented the first theory of modernization."[71] And this, modernization theory, is the topic I turn to now. As Nisbet notes, the "abundance in the social sciences of foundations and government agencies dedicated to such concepts as 'underdeveloped,' 'modernization,' and 'developed' is tribute to the persisting hold of the idea of progress in the West."[72] Probably the most well-known theory of modernization of the twentieth century is Walt Rostow's five stages of economic growth theory. At the height of the Cold War, and at a time when communism was perceived to pose its greatest threat to capitalist democracy, Rostow proposed what was explicitly a "non-Communist manifesto" for economic development. He identified in his manifesto five distinct stages of societal-economic progress, evolving in the following order: traditional society; the preconditions for take-off; take-off; the drive to maturity; and finally, the age of high mass-consumption. Despite this being labeled an economic theory, sociopolitical organization naturally plays a significant part. For instance, stage one is marked by a "hierarchical social structure" in which "family and clan connexions played a large role in social organization." In the second stage the "decisive feature was often political" transition from "old social structures and values" to "the building of an effective centralized national state." Progression to take-off requires "the emergence to political power of a group prepared to regard the modernization of the economy as serious, high-order political business." The drive to maturity and arrival in the age of consumerism are, in effect, arrival at (Western) modernity, wherein society is rationally organized and efficiently utilizes advances in technology.[73] In elaborating his manifesto, Rostow argued that the stages he identified are "not merely descriptive," nor are they "merely a way of generalizing certain factual observations about the sequence of development in modern societies." Rather, he maintained that they "have an inner logic and continuity. They have an analytic bone-structure, rooted in a dynamic theory of production" (12–13).

More recently, Naeem Inayatullah and David L. Blaney have identified significant "new forms of modernization theory," or what they call "*neomodernization*," emerging in theories of international relations. Included are issues such as the expanding "liberal zone of peace" (as explored further in chapter 4), the workings of globalization, and concomitant discussions of global civil society and global governance. Of particular relevance herein is their discussion of how "modernization theory attempts to eradicate difference" through a "commitment to homogenizing cultural difference." This is pursued, at least in part, through some theorists' attempts to treat the "international system as itself an object of modernization, of the progressive differentiation, integration, and universalization characteristic of liberal modernity."[74] And this is precisely one of the issues central to this study, the shaping of international society and its constituent parts through the ongoing deployment of powerful descriptive-evaluative concepts and concomitant policy techniques.

The relevance of modernization theory for this study is revealed in Gerrit Gong's claim that "one cannot speak of 'modernization,' or the 'process of becoming modern,' in historical perspective without referring to what an earlier age called 'civilization' and the 'process of becoming civilized.'" Gong insists that this conceptualization remains "relevant today," for "there are no value-free models of development or economic and financial interaction."[75] Implied in this statement is an unabashed air of superiority in the claims of Western societies' catalog of achievements in the process of arriving at modernity.[76] To put it another way, modernity is widely regarded as being the world in which Westerners of capitalist liberal democracies live, while the rest of the world—portions of the former communist bloc and the so-called Third World—is thought of as somehow being backward or premodern. From this viewpoint, modernization, or modernity, is achieved via development. World Bank Senior Vice President and Chief Economist Joseph Stiglitz clearly expressed this view in the following account of what it means to be developed.

> Development represents a *transformation* of society, a movement from traditional relations, traditional ways of thinking, traditional ways of dealing with health and education, traditional methods of production, to more "modern" ways. For instance, a characteristic of traditional societies is the acceptance of the world as it is; the modern perspective recognizes change, it recognizes that we, as individuals and societies, can take actions that, for instance, reduce infant morality, extend lifespans, and increase productivity. Key to these changes is the movement to "scientific" ways of thinking, identifying critical variables that affect outcomes, attempting to make inferences based on available data, recognizing what we know and what we do not know.[77]

We see here, as in centuries past, the persistence of the importance placed on "scientific" thinking and methods in distinguishing between evolutionary poles. In Richard Norgaard's more skeptical tone, "Modernity, in short, promised to transform the heretofore slow and precarious course of human progress onto a fast track. . . . At mid-twentieth century, progress somehow still assured peace, equality, and happiness for all." Furthermore, this "confidence in the possibilities of progress was rallied in support of an international economic development that would transform the lives of even the most 'obdurate' landlord and peasant in the most 'backward' reaches of the globe."[78]

As taken up in the following chapter, progress means developing along a particular path toward a particular sociopolitical and economic state of organization—Western modernity. The presumption that all societies are traveling along the same path of progress is further spelled out in Edward Shils's declaration: "There are very few states today which do not aspire to modernity." Furthermore, as has been argued since the foundations of the Enlightenment, "To be modern is to be scientific." What's more, as Hegel pointed out, it is insisted that "modernity requires national sovereignty." This is a point that is elaborated in coming chapters in discussions on standards of civilization. In short, Shils is representative of a significant history and body of thought when he claims: "'Modern' means being Western." Preferably, other peoples would achieve modernity "without the onus of dependence on the West," however, for in the West "it has become part of their nature to be modern and indeed what they are is definitive of modernity."[79] Meanwhile, all other societies remain further back along the path in terms of their progress toward modernity; thus they still fall short of reaching the apex in the hierarchy of civilization.

The "End of History"

As with the general ideal of civilization, two World Wars and the Great Depression dented the confidence of some in the idea of progress. But with the collapse of communism and the end of the Cold War, that faith was significantly revived. In fact, one of the most recent accounts of the idea of the universal progress of civilization has probably won over a whole new generation of believers. This shift came on the back of Francis Fukuyama's declaration that the end of the Cold War marked not just "the passing of a particular period of postwar history, but the end of history as such: that is, the end point of mankind's ideological evolution and the universalization of Western liberal democracy as the final form of human government." When the Berlin Wall came down under the weight of a collective human desire for greater freedom, effectively marking the demise of the world's longest running communist experiment, and with it an alternative path of progress to human perfectibility or utopia, for many in the West it was a moment of triumphalism. For Fukuyama, however, it signified something more again; liberal democracy had outlasted all comers and, as far as forms of governing are concerned, it could not be improved upon. In making such a declaration, Fukuyama was restating the argument that the history of humankind is a story of linear progress in virtually every sense of the word and that there is a point to political, moral, social, cultural, and technological progress. Yet Fukuyama was not just declaring that history has a distinct directionality and is progressing along a given path toward a certain goal, as others have done. He claimed that we have now reached that goal; the triumph of capitalist liberal democracy marks the "end of history as such: that is . . . Western liberal democracy" represents "the final form of human government."[80] In making this claim, Fukuyama is not suggesting that "the occurrence of events, even large and grave events," has come to an end, but History in the Hegelian/Marxist sense; "history understood as a single, coherent, evolutionary process, when taking into account the experience of all peoples in all times." According to Fukuyama's interpretation of Hegel, this evolutionary process culminates in "the liberal state, while for Marx it was a communist society."[81] In essence, Fukuyama argues that at the end of the day, at the end of History actually, Hegel had got it right. But as can be seen in the accounts above, this is an awkward interpretation of Hegel, and as will become clearer in the following chapter, this end resembles more that envisaged by Condorcet and Kant than Hegel.

Robert Wright, an influential American author and scholar, has taken the idea of universal progress to yet another, far broader level in his work on social and cultural evolution, *Nonzero: The Logic of Human Destiny*. Not altogether unlike his many predecessors, he argues that "the more closely we examine the drift of biological evolution and, especially, the drift of human history, the more there seems to be a point to it all." But he goes further in his attempt to explain "the arrow of the history of life, from the primordial soup to the World Wide Web," by claiming that "globalization . . . has been in the cards not just since the invention of the telegraph or the steamship, or even the written word or the wheel, but since the invention of life." He contends that from the Big Bang through to the evolution of the human species, it is inevitable that human societies would grow ever more complex by retaining technologies, political systems, and religious beliefs that foster coordination and cooperation over violent competition. Drawing on game theory, he argues that "both organic and human history involve the playing of ever-more-numerous, ever-larger, and ever-more-elaborate non-zero-sum games."[82] The accumulation of these games over millennia has seen humankind tread what is effectively a predetermined path of progress that would almost inevitably lead to the globalized world in which we live today. The appeal of these ideas is such that, in his final year in office, then US President, Bill Clinton called the book "astonishing" and "fascinating" and instructed all White House staff to read it.[83] As emphasized above, a key point here is that these ideas have an influence on international public policy makers who have the power to shape history via mechanisms that effectively operate as standards of civilization, which in effect makes for self-fulfilling prophesy.

This brings us up to date in terms of the history of the idea of progress and its prominent place in Western thought from the Enlightenment through to the present. While there are obviously some differences of opinion and interpretation among its adherents, Nisbet identifies "at least five major premises" inherent in it. Consistent with much proselytizing about (Western) modernity, they are: "belief in the value of the past; conviction of the nobility, even superiority, of Western civilization; acceptance of the worth of economic and technological growth; faith in reason and in the kind of scientific and scholarly knowledge that can come from reason alone; and, finally, belief in the intrinsic importance, the ineffaceable *worth* of life on this earth."[84] It is not unreasonable to claim that for many, this still rings true; an indicative case in point is the influential American conservative Charles Murray, who in referring to Nisbet's five premises contends "that all these premises are valid—objectively true." He goes on to empirically "prove" each of these premises by cataloging the West's superior inventory of achievements in science and technology, music, literature, the visual arts, and philosophy.[85]

In essence, as Nisbet notes, "From at least the early nineteenth century . . . belief in the idea of progress of mankind, with Western civilization in the vanguard, was virtually a universal religion on both sides of the Atlantic."[86] But there is more to the idea of progress than this, for one of the central elements of most philosophies of progress "is the concept of the unity of man's history," which further necessitates "the conception that civilization is one and universal," that is, there is but "one world history." As Iggers explains it, historically, Europe, "specifically France and the English-speaking world, . . . represents the vanguards of civilization." The history of humankind is therefore thought to be "identical with the history of Western civilization." As such, implicit in the idea of progress from the Enlightenment onward—regardless of whether it is the vision of Condorcet, Hegel, Marx, Auguste Comte, Spencer, Kant, or some other theorist—"is the notion of the civilizing mission of the European nations." For the Enlightenment theorists of progress, from the liberalism of Condorcet to the socialism of Marx, "the history of the West becomes ultimately the history of the non-West, as the West extends it hegemony over the world." Thus, the Nonwestern "world will find the completion of its historical development not in the further development of its own heritage but, because its heritage represents an earlier phase in the progress of mankind, in total Europeanization," or perhaps more accurately today, in total Westernization-cum-Americanization;[87] all at the expense of pluralism and diversity.

It must be asked, though, whether there is sufficient uniformity of thought among Enlightenment thinkers down to the present to make such an assessment. There is, after all, a great range and diversity of thought among the various adherents to the idea of progress, let alone the contributors to the broader Enlightenment. For example, in regard to the idea of progress, one could line up an extensive list of optimists and skeptics on opposing sides. The former would include, among others, Comte, Abbé de Saint-Pierre, Turgot, Condorcet, Hegel, Marx, Mill, and Spencer, while the latter would include, among others, Rousseau, Hume, Aleksandr Herzen, Montaigne, Arthur Schopenhauer, Nietzsche, and Spengler. Despite the diversity of thought, John Gray argues that "it is not too difficult to discern . . . [a core] project in the central Enlightenment thinkers." In essence, the philosophical anthropology of the Enlightenment held that different "cultural identities, along with their constitutive histories, were like streams, whose destiny was to flow irresistibly into the great ocean of universal humanity." And, as Gray argues, it is not unreasonable to assert that "just as the category of *civilization* is a central element in the Enlightenment project, so the idea of *a universal history of the species* is integral to it."[88] And this is the topic addressed in the following chapter: the terminus toward which sociopolitical progress is thought to be heading.

4 The Notion of Universal Civilization: One End for All?

I imagine that the future will bring a series of global civilizations, each evolving out of the previous stage as new economic arrangements, political systems, cultures, and biological conditions emerge. The present global civilization—the one obsessed with globalization itself and still trying to figure out what it means—is only the first, and even it is as yet scarcely born.

Walter Truett Anderson, *All Connected Now: Life in the First Global Civilization*

::::

Introduction: No State, No Civilization, No Entry

The natural question that follows from a discussion of human social and political progress is: Progress to where or to what end? In light of the close relationship between the ideal of civilization and the idea of progress established in preceding chapters, it is apparent that the end is one that approximates the notion of universal civilization. In our increasingly globalized and interconnected world of increasingly uniform states, the envisioned "final universal model of history" is the "One World which the West has brought about and organized as a consequence of technological innovation, and has inescapably laid on all humanity. It is the sequel to the Enlightenment."[1]

For many, the "one world" or "global village" catchphrase has much appeal; it can be seen on T-shirts at music festivals, and it serves a useful purpose for environment and climate change campaigners. At a deeper level, though, there is a problem with this general idea. As Paul Ricoeur recognized some time ago, the "problem is this: mankind as a whole is on the brink of a single world civilization representing at once a gigantic progress for everyone and an overwhelming task of survival and adapting our cultural heritage to this new setting."[2] In assessing this issue and the problem, this chapter examines what is meant by the notion of universal civilization, what it is that is said to be universal across civilizations and within Civilization. It further explores the means by which universal civilization is expected to come about. It delves into competing claims about the most effective way of organizing and governing peoples, particularly those in which the objective is the ordering of the world into a relatively cooperative and peaceful, cosmopolitan international society of states. In doing so, the chapter addresses a series of interrelated and overlapping ideas or concepts, including the international society of states, the ideology of cosmopolitanism, and the "democratic syllogism," particularly its key component, liberal or democratic peace theory. Like the concept civilization, so too these concepts and labels can be used to both describe and evaluate, commend and condemn.

According to Couze Venn, the idea that the multitude of "very different cultures" that constitute our globe "could converge towards a cosmopolitan sameness is inseparable from the twinned birth of European colonialism and modernity." That is, throughout much of their (interrelated) respective histories, both the practice of colonialism and the concept of modernity have inextricable links to the "conceptualization of history as the universal and rational" progression of humankind ever onward and upward toward perfectibility. Put differently, "Enlightenment and post-Enlightenment cosmopolitanism [are] intrinsic to the discourse of modernity." A key element of the universal project of modernity is the proliferation of the modern state and its attendant apparatus, the very foundation of the Westphalian states system. As Venn argues, in Enlightenment thought, "a notion of the nation-state emerges as the central organizing principle for constructing the new progressive community."[3] This is a view that is advanced by a good many Enlightenment thinkers; it is inherent in Kant and receives its strongest statement of endorsement from Hegel.

In regard to the latter's thoughts on the "stateless" peoples of the non-European world, Ranajit Guha notes that, for Hegel, a "people or a nation lacked history . . . not because it knew no writing but because lacking as it did in statehood it had nothing to write about."[4] Recalling

Hegel's thoughts on the philosophy of history and the state from the preceding chapter, added to this is his dismissal of "the New World, and the dreams to which it may give rise . . . [and] pass over to the Old World—the scene of the World's History." Hegel insisted that the only people "capable of history" are those that "comprehend their own existence as independent, i.e., possess self-consciousness." And the means by which this is achieved is the state, or perhaps more accurately, statehood. Taking India as his non-European world example, Hegel asserted that, by and large, "the diffusion of Indian culture is only a dumb deedless expansion; that is, it presents no political action." He continues, the "people of India have achieved no foreign conquests, but have been on every occasion vanquished themselves." Thus, despite India's acknowledged accomplishments in the arts and other arenas of achievement, Hegel concludes, "It is because the Hindoos have no History in the form of annals (historia) that they have no History in the form of transactions (res gestæ); that is, no growth expanding into a veritable political condition."[5] The question for Hegel, and he is not alone here, "is how far a nomadic people . . . or any people on a low level of civilization, can be regarded as a state."[6] Given this, Guha suggests that in the 250 years or so between Hernán Cortés's conquests in the New World and Robert Clive's arrival in India, the "bar was raised" such that inclusion in "World-history"—that is, in the narrative of civilization—shifted from "no writing, no history," to "no state, no history." Moreover, the most efficient and effective means by which "peoples without history . . . got history" was via European colonization.[7] Or, to put it another way, the means by which the uncivilized were to become civilized was through tutelage by European colonial masters.

It was noted in the previous chapter that Hegel's conception of the state is unlikely to be one that many Enlightenment and post-Enlightenment thinkers take comfort in. Nevertheless, it remains the case that an account of the state is inherent to most Enlightenment and post-Enlightenment thought. The best means of organizing society remains central to competing accounts of the good life, as argued by political philosophers, theorists, economists, and policy analysts. The form and role of the state also remains a key issue for international relations scholars and practitioners, regardless of their ideological or theoretical perspectives. As Venn explains, it is widely held that the "nation-state is the artifice which frames the institution of the community as the homogenous community and as the rational and morally ordered form of the good society."[8] Moreover, today more than ever it is the nature of the government of the state that serves as the measuring stick of legitimacy in the international states system. And since the collapse of communism and the appearance of Francis Fukuyama's "end of history" thesis, it is often argued that there is only one kind of ideal state, capitalist liberal democracy, that can lay claim to legitimacy with any wide measure of acceptance.

In a similar line of thinking, albeit "with caution," Ricoeur identifies what he terms "the existence of a rational politics" as an element or stage in the idea of "universal civilization." He further contends that "amid the diversity of familiar political regimes there is the unfolding of a single experience of mankind" in terms of sociopolitical organization, or what he refers to as "unique political technics." More explicitly, he claims that the "modern State, *qua* State, has a recognizable universal structure." Moreover, anticipating Fukuyama, he adds, "Perhaps we must even go further: not only is there the single political experience of mankind, but all regimes also have a certain path in common; as soon as certain levels of comfort, instruction, and culture are attained, we see them all inescapably evolve from a dictatorial form to a democratic form." Ricoeur's caution is prompted by the fact that he made these observations amidst an atmosphere of Cold War tensions, for he was even more wary about noting "the existence of a rational, universal economy."[9] But with the collapse of communism, such claims are now considerably less controversial; the economically globalized post–Cold War world is both more readily identifiable with and receptive to claims of a universal market economy.

That said, there remain many exceptions, many objections, and much opposition to the all-pervasive nature of the capitalist global economy. There is also merit in the argument that the global capitalism that is emerging is not simply universal free-market capitalism but a pluralism of capitalisms, which is to say that "different kinds of capitalism reflect different cultures." For instance, the brand of capitalism that has emerged out of the economies of East Asia is not the product of overtly individualist cultures. Similarly, postcommunist Russian capitalism and the recent reforms undertaken by China have seen the emergence of distinctive indigenous models of capitalism that bear only occasional resemblance to American-style capitalism.[10]

While there might be wide recognition that the state is the most effective and efficient means of organizing and managing a geographically enclosed people—although as with all such issues there are exceptions—whether the proliferation of the state and the expansion of the states system has been an altogether natural process is questionable. Many believe that it is a particularly violent and less-than-organic process, one that more often than not is imposed upon a nation or people by a conqueror-cum-colonizer. As Marx and Engels describe the process in the *Communist Manifesto*:

> The bourgeoisie, by the rapid improvement of all instruments of production, by the immensely facilitated means of communication, draws all, even the most barbarian, nations into civilization. The cheap prices of its commodities are the heavy artillery with which it batters down all Chinese walls, with which it forces the barbarians' intensely obstinate hatred of foreigners to capitulate. It compels all nations, on pain of extinction, to adopt the bourgeois mode of production; it compels them to introduce what it calls civilization into their midst, i.e., to become bourgeois themselves. In one word, it creates a world after its own image.[11]

As outlined in greater detail in following chapters, the standard of civilization in international law and society and concomitant civilizing missions-cum-imperialism have been the weapons of choice for the expansion of the European states system. As David Fidler explains, the function of what is often referred to as the classical "standard of civilization was to provide the common political, economic, and legal foundation for the construction of an international society between diverse cultures." The "function of the new standard of liberal, globalized civilization is the same" (as is addressed further in chapter 7). But more than that, Fidler claims "it also functions to build the foundation for a global society of peoples as well as through the transnationalization of civil society activities." While this might sound reasonably innocuous, a concern is raised here over Fidler's claim that, as a key tool in international law and politics, "the standard of liberal, globalized civilization" aids the "process of civilizational harmonization," a process that "is well under way and has been since the nineteenth century," if not earlier. While Fidler admits that "civilizational harmonization" is not absolutely necessary for the functioning of an international system and its international legal code, he insists that "it is needed in some form to produce international society and global society."[12]

This statement suggests that an international society of states is a more complex and cooperative configuration than an international system. It is not too difficult to discern an outline of the sort of international society that is envisioned as the end toward which human social and political organization is progressing. It is one based on a states system constituted solely of like states that cooperate on the basis of like political, economic, and legal systems, which, in turn, cannot help but influence or affect states' respective social and cultural dimensions. It is a reasonably peaceful international society of economically globalized, interdependent, liberal democratic, cosmopolitan states that are bound together by the "civilizing" ties of commerce.

"Perpetual Peace" in International Society

The war historian Michael Howard states that the "peace invented by the thinkers of the Enlightenment, an international order in which war plays no part, had been a common enough aspiration for visionaries throughout history," but "it has been regarded by political leaders as a practicable or indeed desirable goal only during the past two hundred years." The prize of peace, or "the visualization of a social order from which war had been abolished," shifted from the realm of "millennial divine intervention that would persuade the lion to lie down with the lamb" to "the forethought of rational human beings who had taken matters in to their own hands."[13] According to Norbert Elias though, limited practical progress has been made in this endeavor, for he suggests that at the international "level we are living today just as our so-called primitive ancestors did." He insists that "if the reduction of mutual physical danger or increased pacification is considered a decisive criterion for determining the degree of civilization, then humankind can be said to have reached a higher level of civilization within domestic affairs than on the international plane."[14] While this might well be so, it is not because of lack of thinking and theorizing on the topic, as outlined below.

The essence of the idea of peace and orderly relations between states is expressed by Condorcet in *Vie de Voltaire* (1787) as the "more civilization spreads throughout the earth, the more we shall see war and conquest disappear together with slavery and want."[15] This spread of civilization amounts to the spread of republican government or, for today's theorists, liberal democratic government. The following section illustrates how in recent centuries, as Howard states, the idea has taken such a hold that the pursuit of an elusive peace among the international society of states has become a cornerstone of foreign and domestic policies and international public policy more generally.[16] But first, a brief outline of what constitutes a society of states to put it all in context.

The classical account of international society is that expounded by the English School international relations scholar Hedley Bull. A "*soci-*

ety of states (or international society)," he writes, "exists when a group of states, conscious of certain common interests and common values, form a society in the sense that they conceive themselves to be bound by a common set of rules in their relations with one another, and share in the working of common institutions."[17] Going a little further, international society refers to "a group of states (or, more generally, a group of independent political communities) which not merely form a system, in the sense that the behaviour of each is a necessary factor in the calculations of others, but also have established by dialogue and consent common rules and institutions for the conduct of their relations, and recognize their common interest in maintaining these arrangements."[18] In drawing a distinction between pluralist and solidarist conceptions of international society, Bull identifies no real need for sociocultural recognition or compatibility, instead arguing that pluralist international society merely requires that its member states are sovereign and willing to engage in diplomacy. Contrasted to this is Martin Wight's solidarist conception of international society in which Christian civilization, and Western values more generally, are the bedrock of the international society of states; conformity to these values is a condition of membership.[19] In either account there is a presumption that states precede the society and that preexisting states enter into society with like states under their own volition and in their best interests. But this is not always the case, and it has generally not been the way in which most societies-cum-states have entered into contemporary international society. Most have either sought entry into or been enveloped by international society once it is already established, leaving them with little or no say in the terms of entry or the principles by which it operates.[20] This suggests that inclusion in what was at first effectively European international society was based on a number of qualifiers. First and foremost, a nation or peoples had to constitute an actual political state, as Hegel insisted. Furthermore, it had to be a state that was governed in a particular form.

With the expansion of Europe from the fifteenth century (as explored in chapter 5) and the evolution and export of the European states system as established by the 1648 Peace of Westphalia, the extension of international society was widely seen as the most likely way of expanding the peaceful "family of nations." As Friedrich von Schiller later put it rather optimistically, the "European society of states seems transformed into a great family; its members may have their feuds, but no longer do they tear each other limb from limb."[21] The concern with civilizing relations between states has been around since virtually the foundation of the states system. The express aim of a peaceful and cooperative international society of like states is detectable in the work of influential Enlightenment thinkers discussed in the previous chapter. This is particularly true of Immanuel Kant, whose name is closely associated with the idea of perpetual peace. According to Michael Doyle, it is Kant's "liberal republican . . . theory of internationalism" that "best accounts for what we [Westerners] are."[22] Sentiments similar to Kant's are found earlier in Condorcet, for whom the history of civilization is effectively what Schapiro describes as a liberal history; the *Sketch* is an "expression of the ideals and hopes of that age: its humanitarianism; its cosmopolitanism; its belief in the power of reason and in the innate goodness of human nature; and above all, its faith in progress."[23] Ultimately, what Condorcet envisioned for the future of humankind is an egalitarian and harmonious perpetual peace, both domestically and globally among the "brotherhood of nations." He looked forward to a time when "nations will learn that they cannot conquer other nations without losing their own liberty," a time when "permanent confederations" ensure both independence and security as "mercantile prejudices" evaporate. In short, "When at last the nations come to agree on the principles of politics and morality," then, and only then, "nothing will remain to encourage or even arouse the fury of war."[24]

Martha Nussbaum insists it is "Kant, more influentially than any other Enlightenment thinker, [who] defended a politics based on reason rather than patriotism or group sentiment, a politics that was truly universal rather than communitarian."[25] As to whether this is an accurate characterization is open to question and is discussed further in chapter 6. Nevertheless, it is not unreasonable to assert that Kant—referred to by Howard as the inventor of a peace that was "more than a mere pious aspiration"[26]—remains the intellectual reference point for subsequent and contemporary democratic peace theorists and advocates of cosmopolitanism.

The end that Kant envisaged humanity progressing toward is one that very much resembles the ideal of "Perpetual Peace." In *Idea for a Universal History*, he writes that the "highest purpose of Nature" is realizable only in a "society with the greatest freedom" under a "perfectly just civic constitution,"[27] that is, a republican constitution. This is later reemphasized in *Perpetual Peace*, where Kant states that the "only constitution which derives from the idea of the original compact, and on which all juridical legislation of a people must be based, is the republican." It is based on the "principles of the freedom of the members of a society (as men)," the "principles of dependence of all upon a single common legislation (as subjects)," and "by the law of their equality (as citizens)."[28] The "only question now" for Kant is: Is the republican constitution "also the one which can lead to perpetual peace?" He affirms that the "republican constitution, besides the purity of its origin . . . also gives a favourable prospect for the desired consequence, i.e., perpetual peace." The "reason is this: if the consent of the citizens is required in order to decide that war should be declared (and in this constitution it cannot but be the case), nothing is more natural than that they would be very cautious in commencing such a poor game, decreeing themselves all the calamities of war" (94–95). In essence, Kant held that the spread of the republican form of government, the extension of trading relations between republican states, and the observation of international law among them were the most likely means of securing international peace among such states.[29] The further these conditions spread, the greater the likelihood and reach of an increasingly peaceful and cosmopolitan world order, or what he called "a universal cosmopolitan condition, which Nature has as her ultimate purpose."[30]

The prospect for perpetual peace, or what Lars-Erik Cederman terms Kantian "interdemocratic peace," is based on Kant's claim that republican or democratically elected leaders are required "to take their peoples' pacific preferences into consideration before going to war." But more than that, Cederman argues that for Kant, "the effect of democracy is not limited to this simple cost-benefit mechanism," for Kant "sees no reason why the upward spread of norms has to stop at the democratic state's borders." That is, once "the pathway of normative progress is opened, the rule of law will creep into interstate relations," thus obviating or at least reducing the tendency to resort to threats and or violent confrontation.[31] In this claim, Kant is an important source of the liberal internationalist argument that the nature of politics practiced at the domestic level—for example, liberal democratic as opposed to totalitarian—is a key determinant of the manner in which states conduct politics at the international level.[32] As Kant states it, if there is "more charity and less strife" in the "body politic," then "eventually this will also extend to nations in their external relations toward one another up to the realization of the cosmopolitan society."[33] Bruce Buchan explains that "for Kant, the mutually antagonistic relations between states in the international state of nature would thrust the civilizing process onto the global stage,"[34] just as the "antagonism" among men in society, or their "unsocial sociability," is, for Kant, "in the end, the cause of a lawful order among men."[35]

In respect to the civilizing properties of commerce and economic interdependence, these enterprises have long been seen as essential components of a peaceful, interconnected world. For instance, around the time of Christ, Philo of Alexandria argued that commerce was an expression of the "natural desire to maintain a social relationship," while the first-century historian Lucius Annaeus Florus claimed: "If you destroy commerce, you sunder the alliance which binds together the human race."[36] There is also the testimony of Montesquieu that "commerce is a cure for the most destructive prejudices" and serves to "unite nations."[37] More recently, the political economist David Ricardo stressed that "under a system of perfectly free commerce" between nations, the "pursuit of individual advantage is admirably connected with the universal good of the whole." Thus, "it diffuses general benefit, and binds together by one common tie of interest and intercourse, the universal society of nations throughout the civilized world."[38] The link between commerce and peace is related by Kant in terms of the "spirit of commerce" being "incompatible with war," and "sooner or later" just such a spirit "gains the upper hand in every state." Why? Because despite other uncertainties, "the power of money is perhaps the most dependable of all the powers (means) included under the state power." Therefore, given that trade is said to be beneficial to all contracting parties, in the name of continuing economic prosperity, "states see themselves forced, without any moral urge, to promote honorable peace and by mediation to prevent war wherever it threatens to break out."[39]

The link between commerce, democracy, and peace has more recently been outlined in terms of pacific "democratic values" arising from the "norms of contract that are endemic in developed market economies."[40] But as is highlighted below, democratic polities are not necessarily inherently peaceful. As a counterpoint to the general argument that commerce promotes interdependence and therefore reduces the likelihood of recourse to war, it should be remembered that (as is discussed in the following chapter) the Spanish used infractions of their supposed right to trade as a justification for waging war against the Amerindians of the New World.

International Society as "Realistic Utopia"

Today, the general aim of the architects of the international system remains the development and expansion of an international society of reasonably uniform, liberal democratic states that cooperate and combine to give rise to a globalized liberal cosmopolitan world order. But as Steve Smith asks, if the further expansion of international society is actually possible, is it really any "more than the latest form of imperialism"?[41] This is an important question that is addressed in greater detail below, but it does not present much of an obstacle for those interested in pursuing the Kantian ideal. For instance, John Rawls insists that the "fact of the Holocaust" and the knowledge that humankind is capable of committing such atrocities "should not affect our hopes as expressed by the idea of a realistic utopia and Kant's *foedus pacificum*" or "league of peace."[42] In fact, the "basic idea" for Rawls in *The Law of Peoples* "is to follow Kant's lead as sketched by him in *Perpetual Peace*" in order to come up with a schema that makes possible a pacific federation, or peaceful "realistic utopia." For Rawls, the "Law of Peoples" refers to "a particular political conception of right and justice that applies to the principles and norms of international law and practice."[43] The Law of Peoples is in turn the prescribed governing mechanism of what Rawls describes as a "Society of Peoples." This imagined society approximates the classical definition of international society in that it describes "those peoples who follow the ideals of and principles of the Law of Peoples in their mutual relations" (3). Furthermore, the Law of Peoples that regulates interactions within the Society of Peoples is so right and just that the "Law of Peoples fulfills certain conditions, which justify calling the Society of Peoples a *realistic utopia*" (4; emphasis in original).

The interrelated components of the democratic syllogism are widely thought to be the most appropriate remedy for the inherent volatility and insecurity posed by the anarchic nature of the international states system. The democratic syllogism provides the means to eradicate the "primitive" condition of the international system and replace it with a peaceful, cosmopolitan world order or realistic utopia.[44] Based on Kant's idea of perpetual peace among republics, or the so-called Kantian Tripod, the first and most significant proposition of the syllogism is commonly referred to as liberal or democratic peace theory and is supposedly one of the few nontrivial assertions political scientists can make regarding the realm of international relations. It is worth noting again that Kant was no democrat; rather, he viewed democracy as despotism, but this has not stopped his *Perpetual Peace* from being held up, by international relations scholars in particular, as *the* fundamental statement on democratic peace. Proponents of democratic peace hold that liberal democracies tend not go to war with one another, and, therefore, the further liberal democracy spreads throughout the world, the greater the reaches of the so-called "zone of peace."[45] Based on a survey of wars over the past two centuries, Jack Levy argues that, "marginal deviations" aside, "democratic states have never fought on opposite sides" in wars involving great powers. This leads him to proclaim that "the absence of war between democracies comes as close as anything we have to an empirical law in international relations."[46] Bruce Russett goes so far as to insist that democratic peace theory constitutes "one of the strongest nontrivial and nontautological generalizations that can be made about international relations."[47] Explicitly following Kant and taking into account the rate of the spread of democracy, Michael Doyle has estimated that "global peace should be anticipated, at the earliest, in 2113."[48] Similarly, Rawls thinks that the liberal democratic peace "hypothesis is correct," and as such it "underwrites" his outline of "the Law of Peoples as a realistic utopia."[49] And it is not just liberal international theorists who make such claims. In *An Agenda for Peace*, then United Nations Secretary-General Boutros Boutros-Ghali stated, "Democracy at all levels is essential to attain peace for a new era of prosperity and justice."[50]

None of this necessarily means that liberal democracies are inherently peaceful, although some commentators do claim this to be so. Rather, it is more the case that they are said to be peaceful among themselves. As Doyle acknowledges, despite their claimed pacificity toward their own kind, liberal (or liberal democratic) states "are also prone to make war" on nonliberal states.[51] And when they do, Levy concedes, liberal democracies tend to "adopt a crusading spirit and often fight particularly destructive wars," turning "conflicts of interest into moral crusades."[52] Democratic peace theory remains just that, more theory than cast-iron law. As its critics note, as "scientific" as the search for democratic peace might claim to be, it is not value free. At the same time, it suffers from a degree of ahistoricity in that its many advocates often overlook the fact that values have changed over time. Or as Ido Oren explains it, the claims of democratic peace are not so much about democracies per se as they are "about counties that are 'America-like' or of 'our kind,'" in that the "apparently objective coding rules by which democracy is defined in fact represent current American values."[53]

The second element of the democratic syllogism, and yet another thought-to-be nontrivial generalization, is the correlation between democracy and economic development: democracy is said to be the best form of government for promoting economic development; and the best means of promoting or maintaining a stable democracy is via sustained economic growth. The third and final part of the syllogism—sometimes referred to as the Washington consensus—refers to a set of policy prescriptions that are designed to achieve the commercial and economic interdependence that would encourage peaceful international relations. As noted, the general principles underlying this consensus have been recounted over centuries, including in the work of Montesquieu, Ricardo, and Kant—as described above. The consensus holds that the best way to "open up" a country and promote growth is by completely integrating the country into international trade and investment regimes. This form of economic shock treatment entails measures such as the privatization of state-owned enterprises, floating the currency, and ending subsidies and tariffs.[54] Despite the credibility and coherence of this consensus being undermined by the economic turmoil of the late-1990s, key areas like free trade and unrestrained foreign investment remain at the heart of the democratic syllogism, as is emphasized again chapter 8.

Certain aspects of the democratic syllogism are similar to ideas outlined by Elias in his account of the civilizing of domestic society. In *The Civilizing Process*, Elias writes of "the [expanding] web of human relationships" and "the lengthening of the chains of social action and interdependence," such that "more and more people must attune their conduct to that of others."[55] This is essentially the same argument as that used by democratic peace theorists, who extrapolate the same principles to the global arena. They maintain that states with a complex web of interdependent relations of trade and foreign investment, which are also constrained in the range of actions at their disposal in their international relations by domestic popular public opinion, are more likely to seek peaceful mediation, negotiation, or compromise rather than threatening or using violent force. In short, capitalist democratic states are said to have too much to lose by resorting to violent and expensive conflicts.

The components of the democratic syllogism effectively constitute what is classified as liberal international theory, which is identified by its commitment to "*individual human beings as the primary international actors*" in international affairs. This concern in turn requires that states, the most efficient and effective collective through which these relations take place, act on considerations that are based on both "*self-interest and other regarding.*"[56] According to Francis Fukuyama, the "liberal state must be *universal*" and "it must be *homogenous*," because "it is consciously founded on the basis of open and publicized principles."[57] The key components of liberal international theory are as follows. First, the realm of international relations is being transformed in order to "promote greater human freedom by establishing conditions of peace, prosperity, and justice." Second, imperative to the realization of enhanced overall freedom is the "growth of international cooperation" and interdependence among states. Third, more broadly, the arena of international relations is undergoing a transformation via the "process of modernization that was unleashed by the scientific revolution and reinforced by the intellectual revolution of liberalism." Central to this process are "liberal democracy or republican government; international interdependence; cognitive progress; international sociological integration; and international institutions."[58]

The Dystopia That Is Cosmopolitanism

I noted above that for Kant, the "universal cosmopolitan condition" is the end "which Nature has as her ultimate purpose."[59] Or as a Kantian cosmopolite like Martha Nussbaum states it, "Kant's *Perpetual Peace* is a profound defense of cosmopolitan values." She also suggests that Kant's approach to cosmopolitanism is "saturated with the ideas of ancient Greek and especially Roman Stoicism."[60] The influence of Kant on contemporary cosmopolitan political theory is as evident as his influence on liberal international theory, and, as seen above, in many regards the two spheres of thought overlap. Kantian ethics, particularly his Categorical Imperative—the idea that the human individual constitutes an end in itself and not simply a means to an end—is something of a touchstone for modern cosmopolitan thought. The tone is set by Kant where he writes that the "community of the peoples of the earth" has evolved to the point where the "violation of rights in one place is felt throughout the world." Hence, "the idea of a law of world citizenship is no high-flown or exaggerated notion. It is a supplement to the unwritten code of the civil and international law, indispensable for the maintenance of the public human rights and hence also of perpetual peace."[61]

Kant's direct and widely acknowledged influence is evident in the three central tenets that Thomas Pogge identifies as common to most cosmopolitans: (1) *Individualism*: the primary unit of concern is the individual rather than families; ethnic, cultural, or any other subgroupings; nations; or states. These collectives indirectly derive their concern solely by virtue of the fact that they are made up of individuals who are, first and foremost, rights-bearing beings and, second, by chance happen to be members or citizens of a collective. (2) *Universality*: the primacy of the individual as the central unit of concern is afforded to all human individuals without exception. It is not limited or restricted to people of a certain class, gender, color, creed, religion, or any other subset one wishes to distinguish. (3) *Generality*: the primary concern for the individual extends to all humanity. One's concern for others does not stop at the border. Nor is it the privilege of only those who share one's own race, religion, or other features held in common.[62] While Ulrich Beck's version of cosmopolitanism might vary from that of Pogge, Beck relates what are reasonably widely recognized as the rationales or motivations underpinning much of contemporary cosmopolitanism. They are a raft of pressing issues that "do not fit into national politics" alone; they are global issues that cut across international boundaries, such as terrorism, transnational crime, human migration, and climate change and environmental degradation. Such concerns are "already part of the political agenda—in the localities and regions, in governments and public spheres both national and international," but "only in a transnational framework can they be properly posed, debated and resolved."[63]

For its contemporary advocates, "cosmopolitanism would seem to offer some kind of moral anchorage in a world" of increasing uncertainty. As Anthony Pagden suggests, it is even promoted by some as "a philosophically more interesting, historically grounded version of 'multiculturalism.'"[64] While there might appear to be nothing immediately threatening in these observations, the ground and history on which the cosmopolitan anchor rests is not nearly as morally righteous as its modern adherents would have us believe. Both historically and contemporaneously, cosmopolitanism falls well short of being culturally tolerant, let alone an all-embracing form of multiculturalism. As David Harvey notes, there is a "dreadful cosmopolitan habit of demonizing spaces, places, and whole populations as somehow 'outside the project' (of market freedoms, of the rule of law, of modernity, of a certain vision of democracy, of civilized values, of international socialism, or whatever)."[65]

In order to reveal some of the potential dangers inherent in cosmopolitanism, we need to delve into its Greek and Stoic origins that were so influential on Kant. Stephen Toulmin notes that in ancient Greece the word *cosmos* was used in reference to the "Order of Nature," as embodied in the cycle of the seasons and tidal movements, for example. At the same time, there was also the idea of "Order . . . [in] Society, as evidenced in the organization of irrigation systems, the administration of cities, and other collective enterprises," that was characterized by the term *polis*, wherein a *polis* constitutes a political community. Sooner or later it was inevitable that people would ponder and speculate on the "links between *cosmos* and *polis*," between the Order of Nature, and the Order of Society. Toulmin claims that it was not until the conquests of Alexander the Great that the Greeks broadened their horizon beyond a "preoccupation with single cities, [whereby] we find Stoic philosophers fusing the 'natural' and 'social' orders into a single unit."[66] Whether the role of Alexander was quite so important here is questionable, for it is known that Herodotus had earlier traveled to Egypt, and it is evident from his *Histories* that he was aware of the large political communities of Egypt and also of those in Persia.[67] Irrespective of the precise timing, Toulmin suggests that it came to be held that all things in the world "manifest in varied ways an 'order' which expresses the Reason that binds all together." Thus, the social and natural realms are deemed "aspects of the same overall *cosmos + polis*—i.e. *cosmopolis*." Hence, the "idea that human affairs are influenced by, and proceed in step with heavenly affairs, changes into the philosophical idea, that the structure of Nature reinforces a rational Social Order."[68] Such thinking leads Mike Featherstone to argue that, "while many cultures have assumed there is a direct link between the order of nature and the order of society," come the Enlightenment "the dream of western modernity was that science and technology would eventually discover and exploit the principal forms of order at work in both realms."[69] But this too seems a little off the mark, for a similar scenario has almost always been the case throughout the history of the sciences. Science has always been just one piece of the puzzle short of being able to rationalize and explain all. Today it is superstring theory or a "theory of everything," and tomorrow it will likely be yet another scientific theory that promises to reveal all of the universe's secrets. But that large and unwieldy topic is a digression that is best left alone.

It should be acknowledged that there is a growing body of work that points to a plurality of cosmopolitanisms, including its extension beyond its Western origins.[70] But as Lisa Hill states, "Stoicism is the original source of Enlightenment cosmopolitanism and therefore contemporary internationalism."[71] Hence, the Stoic foundations of and influences on Kant and, in turn, modern cosmopolitanism are the general concern here. Plutarch relays the Stoics' cosmopolitan leanings in *On the Fortunes of Alexander* as follows: "Indeed the *Politeia* of Zeno . . . is directed to this one main point, that our life should not be based on cities or peoples each with its own view of right and wrong, but we should regard all men (*pantas anthrōpous*) as our fellow-countrymen and fellow-citizens, and that there should be one life and one order, like that of a single flock on a common pasture feeding together under a common law."[72] This passage hints at one of the more problematic issues for cosmopolitanism, both past and present: its almost inextricable links to imperialism. But before exploring that charge in greater detail, it is worth noting that what the Stoics were aiming for was the realization of the concept of *oikoumenh*, or a world state. On this point, Featherstone claims that "the cosmopolitan political ideal derives from the

Kantian tradition and entails some notion of a *polis* extended around the globe."[73] But this is something of a misreading or misappropriation of Kant, for Kant clearly advocated a *"foedus pacificum,"* or federation of republican states.[74] While there are contemporary cosmopolitans who do advocate some form of world government, there are many, like Kant, that do not, instead promoting greater global governance. As Charles Beitz notes, "a cosmopolitan conception of international morality is not equivalent to, nor does it necessarily imply . . . world federalism."[75] Rather, many cosmopolitans argue that there is nothing preventing autonomous sovereign states from pursuing cosmopolitan ends. In effect, the Stoics thought of every person as being born into and hence a citizen of two *republicae*: a particular city-state and the greater *cosmopolis*. In the event that this situation should give rise to conflicting loyalties, a citizen's duties to the *cosmopolis* would always prevail.[76]

Not unlike the Stoics, Pogge contends that "persons should be citizens of, and govern themselves through, a number of political units of various sizes, without any one political unit being dominant and thus occupying the traditional role of the state." He adds that "political allegiance and loyalty should be widely dispersed over these units: neighbourhood, town, county, province, state, region, and world at large."[77] In identifying a broader range of political units through which people should organize themselves, Pogge is attempting to move beyond the traditionally dominant role of the modern territorial state. But the alternative units he identifies, like the modern state, could almost all be classified as geographical or territorial units. If one is endeavoring to outline a truly cosmopolitan schema that moves beyond the dominant role traditionally played by geopolitics, then why not include political units that are not geographically based in that schema?[78] Pogge's vision sounds very much like the "concentric circles" analogy that Nussbaum borrows from the Stoic philosopher Hierocles, the first encircling the self, the next the family, and then so on outward until reaching "the largest one, humanity as a whole." This analogy returns us to the problem foreshadowed above, for the nature of the enterprise reveals itself when, citing Hierocles, Nussbaum argues, "Our task as citizens of the world will be to 'draw the circles somehow toward the center,' making all human beings more like our fellow city-dwellers."[79]

The central concern here is highlighted by Pagden who, using Diogenes Laertius's recounting of Zeno, demonstrates how the Stoics fell well short of being all-embracing. To the contrary, Zeno's *cosmopolis* and the Stoics' affection were reserved for "true citizens or friends," wherein "friendship . . . exists only between the wise and the good, by reason of their likeness to one another." As Pagden argues, "In calling upon all men to belong to a common *deme* or polis, Zeno was also, of course, making all men members of the *deme* or polis to which *he* belonged." Moreover, "far from extending a benign cultural relativity to all possible peoples, Stoicism was, in origin, a philosophy particularly well suited to the spread of empire."[80] As Hill explains, the "*cosmopolis* is thus achieved via conquest."[81] Timothy Brennan similarly states that the "ideal of perpetual peace," with its foundations in ancient Greece, constitutes "the search for a constellation into which other nations would be absorbed."[82]

It is not unreasonable to suggest that the intellectual and political origins of cosmopolitanism are not nearly as ethically grounded or above reproach as its advocates would have us believe. Cosmopolitanism is a concept whose origins are distinctively European, and throughout much of its history, its fortunes are intimately tied to Europe's worst universalizing tendencies. As Pagden notes, its history runs a "torturous course" through the "construction of . . . European overseas empires," and "it is hard to see how cosmopolitanism can be entirely separated from some kind of 'civilizing' mission, or from the more humanizing aspects of the various imperial projects with which it has been so long associated."[83] Venn similarly asserts that "Colonialism . . . has been a necessary condition of possibility for the initiation of the project of homogenization and transformation of cultures to produce a cosmopolitan culture." Indeed, colonialism is a "Eurocentric construct, given that Europe was taken for granted as the model and norm which all other cultures should emulate, or indeed would in time resemble once they had 'caught up.'"[84] Despite the charges against cosmopolitanism, and the links and similarities between cosmopolitanism past and cosmopolitanism present, it remains a powerful and influential idea and aspiration.

Giuseppe Mazzini succinctly captures the primary flaw in cosmopolitan thought and practice thus:

> But all these soi disant cosmopolitans, who deny the special mission of the different races, and affect contempt for the idea and the love of nationality, so soon as any question of action and therefore of organisation arises, invariably seek to make the centre of the movement their own country or their own city. They do not destroy nationality, they only confiscate all other nationalities for the benefit of their own. A chosen people, a Napoleon-people, is the last word of all their systems; and all their negations of nationality bear within them the germ of an

> usurping nationalism; usurping—if not by force of arms, which
> is not so easy at the present day—by the assumption of a perma-
> nent, exclusive, moral, and intellectual initiative, which is quite
> as dangerous to those peoples weak enough to admit it, as any
> other form of usurpation.[85]

Given its intellectual heritage, it is difficult see how contemporary
cosmopolitanism is anything other than a reflection of values inherent to
Western liberal democratic societies, "which see themselves as being—
and in some historical sense probably are—the heirs of Kant's representative republics."[86] Featherstone puts the problem succinctly: "The
danger is that cosmopolitan democracy and global governance can be
seen as just an extension of the Enlightenment's Eurocentric humanism, retaining much of its sense of self-importance and universalistic
authority."[87] As Naeem Inayatullah and David L. Blaney recognize, this
"is precisely [the] worry—that claims of universal values are accompanied by a temptation to impose values on the recalcitrant, resulting in
violence and domination." Thus, "Given the tragic consequences of a
society of particularistic states," should we really be "surprised at the
strength of the cosmopolitan impulse to erase or transcend that particularism."[88]

For cosmopolitans there is an inescapable dilemma that by and large
has yet to be addressed. If cosmopolites embrace and advocate only
Western liberal democratic values at the expense of Nonwestern values, then they are not truly multicultural pluralist cosmopolitans at all.
Rather, they are (at best) cultural imperialists, perpetuating the Western Enlightenment's long history of universalism-cum-imperialism. On
the other hand, if, repelled by this prospect, cosmopolitans instead embrace cultural pluralism, that is, if they embrace all (or a broad range
of) values, then it may well be the case that they lack any. This still to be
resolved dilemma confronting cosmopolitans is neatly summarized by
Mazzini in his statement that "the cosmopolitan has but two paths before him. He is compelled to choose between despotism and inertia."[89]
The general fear of the former is highlighted by Michael Walzer, who
notes that a "particularism that excludes wider loyalties invites immoral
conduct, but so does a cosmopolitanism that overrides narrower loyalties. Both are dangerous." Walzer adds that the "crimes of the twentieth century have been committed alternately, as it were, by perverted
patriots and perverted cosmopolitans." If the former is represented by
fascism, then communism is representative of the latter, for is not "repressive communism a child of universalizing enlightenment? Doesn't it

teach an antinationalist ethic" just as contemporary cosmopolitanism does?[90] The charge is difficult to deny.

Contemporary cosmopolitanism can be distinguished between what Pogge calls "legal cosmopolitanism" and "moral cosmopolitanism."[91] The former seeks to move toward a more institutionalized and legally ordered world polity, in which so-called global citizens' rights are guaranteed and protected by something approaching a system of world government. The latter holds that the same goals are achievable within the sovereign states system, providing that the states in that system are liberal democratic and receptive to intergovernmental and transnational institutions devoted to greater global governance. Included here are institutions such as the United Nations and its affiliates, the World Bank, the International Monetary Fund, the Organization for Economic Cooperation and Development, the International Court of Justice, and similar regional bodies. The likelihood that the objectives of legal cosmopolitanism will be realized in the near future, if ever, is highly remote, given that the opposition of most states to ceding any further sovereignty, especially to a world government, is deeply entrenched and unlikely to abate. But it is the case that since the end of World War Two there has been a marked increase in institutional global governance.

In regard to this development, Pagden argues that the world's intergovernmental and financial institutions, "in their quest for a new idiom with which to characterize the new international relations . . . have sought to create a fully cosmopolitan idiom." "It is one," he argues, "which, like Kant's *ius cosmopoliticum*, is suitably flexible about the possible constitutional limits which can be placed upon any particular political system, but it is equally insistent that it can only be achieved within one social and political form of association." He notes that for most of the "earlier European theorists of empire, that had been the European Christian monarchical order; for Kant it was republicanism; for the United Nations and in the rhetoric (if not the policy) of the international monetary agencies it is clearly liberal—or neoliberal—democracy."[92] It might be added that the international financial institutions' policy objectives are also quite clear; one need only browse through the respective institutions' reports and publications to find countless policy prescriptions promoting "good governance" (a topic taken up again in chapter 7).

Pagden suggests that it might be "unduly pessimistic" to speculate that recent enthusiasm for notions of good governance is yet another attempt to impose what are explicitly European or Western social and political values and institutions. But he stresses that it continues to be the case that membership in international society "demands the acceptance of a set of values which those who hold them assume to be, much as Kant did, not the creation of a specific culture, but the expression of a universal human condition" (14). The general sentiment expressed here is a key issue for this book and as such is addressed at length and in detail in the following chapter's account of the development and implementation of the classical standard of civilization in international law or international society. A further concern with cosmopolitan thought is that it "preserves the idea of a single human destiny, a *telos* for all mankind and the conception of the future—and ineluctable—emergence of a single human culture,"[93] as explored in the preceding chapter and as addressed below.

Global Civilization: Uniform not Universal

In reference to the idea of a single human culture or universal civilization, John Gray argues in *Enlightenment's Wake* that there is a readily identifiable project running through the heart of Enlightenment thought. It is a project he sees as still detectable in the "new liberals"—the intellectual descendants of Kantianism. Like their intellectual predecessors, the new liberals "unreflectively subscribe to a version of the Enlightenment philosophy of history in which universal convergence on a cosmopolitan and rationalist civilization . . . was taken for granted as the *telos* of the species." The "core project of the Enlightenment," Gray tells us, "was the displacement of local, customary or traditional moralities, and of all forms of transcendental faith, by a critical or rational morality, which was projected as the basis of a universal civilization. Whether it was conceived in utilitarian or contractarian, rights-based or duty-based terms, this morality would be secular and humanist, and it would set universal standards for the assessment of human institutions." Put differently, he reiterates that the "core project of the Enlightenment was the construction of such a critical morality, rationally binding on all human beings, and, as a corollary, the creation of a universal civilization."[94]

Reaffirming his distaste for this project in *False Dawn*, Gray maintains that Enlightenment thinkers from Thomas Jefferson to Tom Paine, and from John Stuart Mill to Karl Marx, "never doubted that the future for every nation in the world was to accept some version of western institutions and values." As highlighted in the preceding chapter, cultural pluralism was not widely thought of as a lasting or permanent state of human affairs; rather it was merely "a stage on the way to a universal civilization." Despite their ideological differences, these Enlightenment thinkers and their intellectual descendants "advocated the creation of a single worldwide civilization" that would supersede the multitude of cultural traditions with a "universal community founded on reason."[95] For Gray, this is an ongoing project as the contemporary inheritors of the Enlightenment now pursue the "project of a single global market," wherein the aim of a "global free market is the Enlightenment project of a universal civilization." This American-led Western "market utopianism," he asserts, has been successful in appropriating the "faith" that American-style capitalism is "the model for a universal civilization which all societies are fated to emulate" (100–104). But it is not the only version of the universalizing project. As Gray notes, communism and the "former Soviet Union embodied a rival Enlightenment Utopia, that of universal civilization" in which central planning, not markets, would be master (3). He further highlights, in the broader scheme of things, what these rival "utopias have in common is more fundamental than their differences." That is, in "their cult of reason and efficiency, their ignorance of history and their contempt for the ways of life they consign to poverty or extinction, they embody the same rationalist hubris and cultural imperialism that have marked the central traditions of Enlightenment thinking throughout its history" (3).

On a similar note, Ricoeur makes the point that since the idea of "universal civilization has for a long time originated from the European centre," Europeans have "maintained the illusion that European culture was, in fact and by right, a universal culture." At the same time, Europeans perceived that their "superiority over other civilizations seemed to provide the experimental verification of this postulate." But as demonstrated in the preceding chapters' discussion of civilizational hierarchy, just as significantly, "the encounter with other cultural traditions was itself the fruit of that advance and more generally the fruit of Occidental science itself."[96] The nature of the broader concern for Nonwestern societies as outlined above and in the preceding chapter is captured in Ricoeur's question: "In order to get onto the road toward modernization, is it necessary to jettison the old cultural past which has been the *raison d'être* of a nation?" The problem is one of "unearth[ing] a country's profound personality," a personality that has been suppressed and denied under the yoke of colonialism by the imposition of a foreign personality. For Nonwestern peoples or Nonwestern states, this unearthing process gives rise to a dilemma Ricoeur explains thus:

On the one hand, [a Nonwestern state] has to root itself in the
soil of its past, forge a national spirit, and unfurl this spiritual
and cultural revendication before the colonialist's personality.
But in order to take part in modern civilization, it is necessary at
the same time to take part in scientific, technical, and political
rationality, something which very often requires the pure and
simple abandon of a whole cultural past. It is a fact: every culture cannot sustain and absorb the shock of modern civilization.
There is the paradox: how to become modern and to return to
sources; how to revive an old, dormant civilization and take part
in universal civilization.[97]

But are Nonwestern states permitted to pursue an alternative development path even if they wish to? The limitations on their options (and
the nature of the threat) are explicit in David Fidler's assertion that the
"Western standard of civilization prevailed in the clash of civilizations
because the Western countries were the builders of the new international
society and exercised their superior power to ensure that the society was
built in their image."[98] While his conclusions are sometimes contentious,
on this issue at least, Samuel Huntington makes a fair point in his esti-
mation that the notion of world community or international society is
little more than a "moniker" that has superseded the "free world" as the
"euphemistic collective noun" used to give "global legitimacy to actions
reflecting the interests of the United States and other Western powers."
While this might overstate the point, Huntington is not far off the mark
when he adds, "Decisions made at the UN Security Council or in the International Monetary Fund that reflect the interests of the West are presented
to the world as reflecting the desires of the world community."[99]
    The point to be emphasized here is that an element of danger is in-
herent in the very idea of a cosmopolitan, globalized, peaceful international society. While this end might sound desirable and the general
intent admirable, the pursuit of a "realistic utopia" has very real implications for those peoples and societies that do not measure up or conform to the norm. Gertrude Himmelfarb identifies this inherent danger
when she states that the "ideal of a utopia not only belittles any kind of
progress that can be achieved short of utopia, making anything short of
perfection seem radically evil, but the pursuit of that idea—whether absolute reason, absolute liberty, absolute virtue, or any combination of
these—makes it all too easy to justify the use of absolute power."[100] The
violence committed against so-called uncivilized peoples in the name

of "civilization" and "civilizing missions" in the past five hundred plus years is evidence enough of this danger.

The final point to be made here is that claims such as Fukuyama's "End of History" thesis and his insistence on the universality of a consumption-oriented human nature, or assertions that we are converging on a single global civilization, or that a universal international society is beginning to emerge, are unfounded, seriously flawed, and require far more scrutiny on a range of levels. If there is anything at all in these claims, it is not so much that the late twentieth and early twenty-first centuries have witnessed the emergence of a slow and steady but ultimately inevitable coming together of a *universal* civilization or international society—as has long been envisioned in Enlightenment and cosmopolitan thought. Rather, it is that after centuries of civilizing-cum-imperial missionary zeal that has sought to expunge from the earth "uncivilized" peoples and their "backward" cultures and ways of life, we just might (regrettably) be being coerced toward a homogenized *uniform* civilization—a uniform civilization, or empire of uniformity, brought about by an international society of largely uniform liberal democratic states and intergovernmental institutions, all based on Western norms, values, and social and political institutions. One of the driving forces behind the homogenization of the states in international society is the international legal apparatus known as the "standard of civilization." The emergence of this tool of civilization and empire is explored in the following chapter.

Part Two: The Art and Science of Empire

The conquest of the earth, which mostly means the taking it away from those who have a different complexion or slightly flatter noses than ourselves, is not a pretty thing when you look into it too much. What redeems it is the idea only. An idea at the back of it; not a sentimental pretence but an idea; and an unselfish belief in the idea—something you can set up, and bow down before, and offer a sacrifice to.   **Joseph Conrad, "Heart of Darkness," 1899**

5

The Expansion of Europe and the Classical Standard of Civilization

"I love the University of Salamancha; for when the Spaniards were in doubt as to the lawfulness of their conquering America, the University of Salamancha gave it as their opinion that it was not lawful." He spoke this with great emotion, and with that generous warmth which dictated the lines in his "London," against Spanish encroachment. **James Boswell, *Boswell's Life of Dr. Johnson*, 1791**

The vocabulary of international law, far from being neutral, or abstract, is mired in this history of subordinating and extinguishing alien cultures.
Antony Anghie, "Francisco de Vitoria and the Colonial Origins of International Law"

: : :

Introduction

The means by which peoples or nations have historically been admitted into or barred from the international society of states is the legal mechanism known as a standard of civilization. Standards of civilization are a direct consequence of the twin concepts of civilization and progress and the associated idea of a civilizational hierarchy ranging from savages to the civilized, as outlined in chapters 2 and 3. As introduced in the preceding chapter, standards of civilization in effect serve to produce an international society of reasonably uniform states based on shared values, norms, and institutions. What follows is an account of the origins and character-istics of what is often referred to as the classical standard of civilization in international law or international society, that is, the original European standard as was prompted by the foundation of the Westphalian states system and ongoing encounters between European nations and peoples beyond the (fuzzy and shifting) borders of Europe. The significance of the classical standard of civilization cannot be understated in terms of the vi-olent European civilizing missions that it helped give rise to, as is outlined in the following chapter. But first, I want to describe in some detail the origin and evolution of the standard and precisely what it entails.

Gerrit W. Gong, who has undertaken one of the few comprehensive studies of the classical standard, describes it as a set of "tacit and explicit" "assumptions" that form the criteria for any given civilization to identify "those that belong to [their] particular society from those that do not." Out of this distinction arises a situation whereby "those [nations] who fulfil the requirements of a particular society's standard of civilization are brought inside its circle of 'civilized' members," while those nations that do not measure up are excluded "as 'not civilized' or possibly 'un-civilized.'"[1] Gong's book received something of a mixed reception at the time of its publication; it was a bit of an oddity in the field of international relations in that it dealt explicitly with the exclusivist nature of European-cum-Western international society. More recently it has experienced a sort of second coming as a small but significant minority of international relations scholars become increasingly concerned about the historical and contemporary plight of the "Other," as is the case herein.

Gong's study begins by asserting that the "confrontation which oc-curred as Europe expanded into the non-European world during the nineteenth and early twentieth centuries was not merely political or economic," nor was it solely military. Rather, it was "fundamentally a confrontation of civilizations and their respective cultures." He ar-gues that at "the heart of this clash were the standards of civilization by which these different civilizations identified themselves and regulated their international relations." As such, other standards inevitably ex-isted among societies beyond Europe. But "because the standard of 'civi-lization' which originated in Europe during the nineteenth century was applied throughout the world," Gong contends that by that century's end, "confrontation" gave rise to a situation whereby "the international society of European states was evolving into an international society of self-proclaimed 'civilized' states" (3–5). So while European civilization might have met or confronted other collectives of peoples, their level of political society was deemed not to meet the requirements of Civilization. Thus, any nation that did not meet the prerequisites for membership in European international society—which was much, if not all, of the non-European world—was, by definition, "uncivilized."

There are two important points to be made in regard to these remarks by Gong, in which he outlines the temporal and spatial setting of the entire book. First, to refer to European expansion and interaction with the rest of the world as simply being some form of cultural or civilizational "confrontation" is a little misleading. On practically every front, expansion by European nations was by and large an aggressive act involving what was usually the violent conquest and suppression of indigenous peoples. Second, in implying that European expansion and the "civilizational clashes" that followed were limited to the nineteenth and early twentieth centuries, Gong takes something of a short-sighted view of the history of imperial expansion by the European powers, ignoring much earlier forays into the world beyond. Furthermore, by omission, Gong overlooks the possibility that similar civilizational or cultural meetings-cum-clashes were also taking place among and between the many different non-European civilizations of the world.

Going by Gong's account, it is apparent that the expanding Europe at the heart of these civilizational confrontations was a Europe bearing many of the hallmarks of the evolving Westphalian states system. Around the same time, as outlined in chapter 3, the very concept of civilization was arising out of Enlightenment Europe and, with it, the growing recognition of the existence of an array of unique and differing, albeit inferior, peoples and civilizations. Despite the absence of a recognized system of sovereign states and the concept of civilization prior to this era, that is not to say that something similar to Gong's "confrontation of civilizations" had not long been taking place between various peoples, faiths, and or cultures of the world. For instance, in contradistinction to Gong, but still using the concept of civilization, Robert A. Williams predates Western expansion and the consequent confrontations to the thirteenth century and the time of "Pope Innocent's letters to the Great Khan of the Mongols." He states, "The 'West' has sought to impose its version of truth on non-Western peoples since the Middle Ages. In seeking the conquest of the earth, the Western colonizing nations of Europe and the derivative settler-colonized states produced by their colonial expansion have been sustained by a central idea: the West's religion, civilization, and knowledge are superior to the religions, civilization, and knowledge of non-Western peoples. This superiority, in turn, is the redemptive source of the West's presumed mandate to impose its vision of truth on non-Western peoples."[2] Williams goes on to argue "that law, regarded by the West as its most respected and cherished instrument of civilization, was also the West's most vital and effective instrument of empire during its genocidal conquest and colonization of the non-Western peoples of the New World" (6).

Given the significance of imperial expansion by the nations of Europe and the nature of their encounters with the non-European world in the development of the law of nations, or what we today know as international law, this chapter takes a longer term view of the confrontation between civilizations and its impact on the evolution of that law, particularly in reference to the international legal standard of civilization. To that end, it traces the origins and evolution of what was to become the legally entrenched standard of civilization that Gong sees as emerging in its most concrete manifestations in the nineteenth century. In doing so, this chapter highlights how modern international law has its origins in the centuries-old European Law of Nations. It further demonstrates how international law in general, and the standard of civilization in particular, helped to serve the cause of European imperialism.

Before that, I want to return momentarily to Williams's claims and his dating of Western imperial expansion and oppressive exploitation. Like so many large-scale histories, including this one to some extent, Williams's conception of the West is a retrospective construction. This poses some problems in that it oversimplifies and relies on a high level of abstraction to link the past with the present by using a descriptive term like "the West" in relation to "Europe" of the Middle Ages; even the use of *Europe* is somewhat problematic. It implies a degree of social, cultural, and even religious homogeneity and cohesion among the various peoples of the European continent and associated islands, which was anything but the case. It also suggests that the peoples of Europe exercised a monopoly on the use of violence against and exploitation of non-European peoples and that this violence and exploitation was directed against only outsiders. History shows us that this was not the case. The various civilizations and empires which at different times dominated the checkerboard of geographical space that is now Europe all resorted to violent conquest to further their cause and expand their dominion. And for centuries this violence and exploitation was directed inward toward conquering immediate neighboring peoples just as much as it was directed against distant peoples. It was not until the seventeenth and eighteenth centuries that cleavages began to ameliorate, slowly being replaced by a modicum of cohesion and solidarity, at least among (Western) European nations. On the whole, the use of "the West" to describe "Europe" of the Middle Ages is something of an ideological construct that belies the political realities of the time. If there is an identity trait that links medieval and modern Europe, it is probably Christianity, but the Reformation and the Religious Wars make even this link tenuous and obscure when trying to identify a direct descendant in the modern West to hold accountable for more than half a millennium of oppression. That said, it is undeniable that colonial expansion by European nations and the European Law of Nations are the foundation for much subsequent international law. Hence, they will be used as both a starting point and a point of reference throughout much of the account of the classical standard of civilization that follows.

Popes and Infidels in the Medieval Era

According to James Muldoon, expansion by powers based in Europe actually began a couple of centuries prior to Williams's thirteenth-century designated starting point. He contends that it effectively began in "1095, the year in which Pope Urban II (1088–1099) proclaimed the first crusade." Muldoon acknowledges that even during the medieval era, "religious motivation" was never the "sole hallmark" of expansion. From the very "first [crusade], economic and social motives were inextricably associated in a religious culture." And Urban II was only too aware of "the profits to be made in winning land and treasure from the infidel."[3]

As legal developments are primarily key to the immediate investigation, the chosen point of entry for the "confrontation of civilizations" (for want of a better term) between the powers of Europe and the non-European world is 1245. This is the year in which Pope Innocent IV (1243–1254) began to articulate the nature of papal-infidel—or civilized-uncivilized—relations in his commentary on Pope Innocent III's (1198–1216) decretal *Quod super his*. Innocent IV, who has been described by Frederic Maitland as "the greatest lawyer that ever sat upon the chair of St. Peter,"[4] is particularly significant because of the influence he would have on jurisprudential successors like Franciscus de Vitoria and Hugo Grotius, both widely regarded as the founding fathers of international law. The former in particular is a central figure in this and the following chapter. Prompted by issues of dominion raised by the Crusades, Innocent IV sought to address the question: "Is it licit to invade a land that infidels possess or which belongs to them?" This is one of the questions that goes to the very heart of colonial expansion and conquest for the best part of seven centuries to come; hence Innocent's opinion is a most significant and influential one. In response to the problem, Innocent offered the following legal opinion: "Men can select rulers for themselves. . . . Sovereignty, possessions, and jurisdiction can exist licitly, without sin, among infidels, as well as the faithful." However, he was adamant that as the "vicar of Jesus Christ," the pope "has power not only over Christians but also over infidels." And "the pope can grant indulgences to those who invade the Holy Land for the purpose of recapturing it although the Saracens possess it . . . [for] they possess it illegally." Furthermore, "if infidels prohibit preachers from preaching, they sin and so they ought to be punished." And "if the infidels do not obey" the pope's licit commands, "they ought to be compelled by the secular arm and war may be declared upon them by the pope and not by anyone else."[5] In his commentary, Innocent was effectively claiming that as the Saracens had illegally seized control of the Holy Land in an unjust war, the pope had the right to authorize an invasion to secure its return to its rightful Christian inhabitants. If this was not justification enough, he further insisted that "the Holy Land was rightfully Christian because Christ's life and death there had consecrated the land. His followers, not those of Mohammed, should therefore dwell there."[6] While it is difficult to draw direct lines of cause and effect across so many centuries, claims about rights—and wrongs—of possession and occupation continue to trouble the region to this day and will likely do so for a long time to come.

Innocent's commentary on *Quod super his* was issued from Lyons on the eve of the First Council of Lyons. The summer prior he had been forced to relocate the papal seat from Rome in order to evade the invading excommunicated Hohenstaufen Emperor Frederick II. His thinking on papal-infidel, or what would come to be classified as civilized-uncivilized, relations was both influenced by and is nicely demonstrated in the following account of an early "civilizational confrontation." It is an account that clearly establishes Europe's claims on the role of keeper of the keys to the kingdom of civilization and its role as civilizer-in-chief. Fearful of Western Christendom's state of vulnerability, in March 1245 Innocent IV sent forth from Lyons two diplomatic missions—one Dominican, the other Franciscan—to meet with the Great Khan of the imposing Mongol Empire to the east.[7] Traveling by way of the Near East, the Dominican mission headed by Friars Ascelinus and Andrew of Longjumeau met with limited success, in 1247 reaching only as far as the camp of Baiju, a Mongol commander out-posted in Armenia and Mesopotamia. Even then, within a few weeks the missionaries managed to overstay their welcome and estrange their hosts by insisting that Baiju and his followers immediately receive baptism. The arrogant tone of Friar Ascelinus's baptismal demands is reputed to have almost led to his execution, but Baiju relented and instead sent the overzealous diplomat and his entourage back to Lyons under escort.[8]

The second diplomatic mission was led by Friar John of Plano Carpini, a disciple of St. Francis of Assisi, and his companion Friar Laurence of Portugal, who would later fall ill and be left behind at a Mongol outpost part way into the arduous journey.[9] The Franciscans' predetermined route took them north though Russia, along the way passing through Poland, where Brother Benedict joined the diplomatic caravan to act as Friar John's "interpreter and the companion of his labour and cares."[10] After fifteen months and more than 3,000 miles, the diplomatic convoy arrived in the heartland "of the Tartars on the Feast of Mary Magdalene [July 22nd] . . . at a great encampment which is called Syra Orda," where they stayed for four months. During this time, they were privileged to be present for the election and coronation of the Great Khan of the Mongols, Guyuk (also recorded as Cuiuckan or Guyak), a grandson of Genghis Khan. Brother Benedict related that "they had both seen about 5,000 princes and great men . . . assembled for the election of the king . . . [and] that there were about [another] 3,000 ambassador envoys from different parts of the world present, bringing letters, answers, and every kind of tribute and gift to the court" (81). It was on the third day of ceremonies that Innocent's emissaries were accorded an audience with Guyuk Khan, at which time Friar John presented the Emperor with the two letters from Pope Innocent IV, which had been entrusted to his care.

In the first of these letters, Innocent sought to introduce the Great Khan to the mores and manners of Christian doctrine. He wrote:

> He [Jesus] handed to him [St. Peter] the keys of the kingdom of heaven by which he and, through him, his successors, were to possess the power of opening and of closing the gate of that kingdom to all. Wherefore we, though unworthy, having become, by the Lord's disposition, the successor of this vicar, do turn our attention, before all else incumbent on us in virtue of our office, to your salvation and that of other men, and on this matter especially do we fix our mind, sedulously keeping watch over it with diligent zeal and zealous diligence, so that we may be able, with the help of God's grace, to lead those in error into the way of truth and gain all men for Him.[11]

Innocent went on to introduce his envoys as "men remarkable for their religious spirit, comely in their virtue and gifted with a knowledge of Holy Scripture," before urging the Mongol Emperor to follow "their salutary instructions [such that] you may acknowledge Jesus Christ the very Son of God and worship His glorious name by practising the Christian religion."

In the second letter, Innocent sought to admonish the Emperor Khan for having "invaded many countries belonging both to Christians and to others and . . . laying them waste in a horrible desolation." He further protested that "with a fury still unabated you do not cease from stretching out your destroying hand to more distant lands." The pope maintained that, in taking such ruinous actions, the Mongol Empire was "breaking the bonds of natural ties," the divine natural law, "the very elements which go to make up the world machine," which united "not only men but even irrational animals." This is a point that would be reiterated and reaffirmed by many of his successors in Western legal and political thought, from Vitoria to Immanuel Kant, among others. Having made known his displeasure at past Mongol advances, Innocent went on to forewarn the Emperor:

> Desist entirely from [further] assaults of this kind and especially from the persecution of Christians, and that after so many and such grievous offences you conciliate by a fitting penance the wrath of Divine Majesty, which without doubt you have seriously aroused by such provocation; nor should you be emboldened to commit further savagery by the fact that when the sword of your might has raged against other men Almighty God has up to the present allowed various nations to fall before your face; for sometimes He refrains from chastising the proud in this world for the moment, for this reason, that if they neglect to humble themselves of their own accord He may not only no longer put off punishment of their wickedness in this life but may take greater vengeance in the world to come.

Pope Innocent then concluded the second letter by demanding that the Emperor Khan "make fully known to us through these same Friars what moved you to destroy other nations and what your intentions are for the future."

Upon the conclusion of their business with the Mongol Emperor, "the Friars were sent back by the Emperor to carry letters to the Lord

Pope signed under his own seal."[12] For the first fifteen days of their return journey, the Friars were escorted by envoys of the Soldan of Babylon to ensure their safe passage back to the west. Once safely back in Lyons, Brother John promptly passed on Guyuk Khan's letter of reply, a reply that Innocent had now been waiting on for close to two years. It is difficult to know exactly what kind of response Pope Innocent IV might have been expecting, but it is almost certain that it was not the reply he received. Guyuk Khan's letter was anything but conciliatory and should have left the pope in no doubt that he was dealing with a man of formidable intellect. The Great Khan replied:

> You have . . . said that supplication and prayer have been offered by you, that I might find a good entry into baptism. This prayer of thine I have not understood. Other words which thou hast sent me: "I am surprised that thou hast seized all the lands of the Magyar and the Christians. Tell us what their fault is." These words of thine I have also not understood. The eternal God has slain and annihilated these lands and peoples, because they have neither adhered to Chingis [Ghengis] Khan, nor to the Khagan, both of whom have been sent to make known God's command, nor to the command of God. Like thy words, they also were impudent, they were proud and they slew our messenger-emissaries. How could anybody seize or kill by his own power contrary to the command of God?
>
> Though thou likewise sayest that I should become a trembling Nestorian Christian, worship God and be an ascetic, how knowest thou whom God absolves, in truth to whom He shows mercy? How dost thou know that such words as thou speakest are with God's sanction? From the rising of the sun to its setting, all the lands have been made subject to me. Who should do this contrary to the command of God?
>
> Now you should say with a sincere heart: "I will submit and serve you." Thou thyself, at the head of all the Princes, come at once to serve and wait upon us! At that time I shall recognize your submission.[13]

In effect, Guyuk Khan directly contested Innocent's assertion that he as pope was God's spokesperson on earth. Although Guyuk seems less than absolutely certain as to his own claim on the title, Innocent must have been infuriated by the logical presentation of his claims to the post.

How could the expansion of the Mongol Empire via successive military conquests have been permitted to succeed if it was "contrary to the command of God?" This was a well-made point indeed.

Innocent's growing impatience with the Mongol Emperor was most clearly demonstrated in a follow-up letter he sent back to Guyuk Khan in 1248 with the returning representatives of Baiju, who had accompanied the Dominican mission on its return journey to Lyons. In the letter, Innocent stressed that his interest in the Mongols was purely in regard to the salvation of their souls. For this he now held even graver fears because, "having heard of the truths of Christianity from the friars who had visited them, the Tartars could no longer plead ignorance of the true faith when God called them for judgement."[14] This was an argument that would be closely followed by Vitoria in his legal reasoning over Spain's divine right of conquest of the Amerindians of the New World. History shows us that Pope Innocent IV and the Mongol Emperor Guyuk Khan were never presented with the opportunity to test their competing claims to being God's messenger on Earth. Within two years of his coronation, and only shortly after receiving Innocent's final letter, Guyuk Khan died and was succeeded by Oghul Ghaymish, who would divert his attention from Europe in the west to the Moslem east and Mesopotamia.[15] So too, Innocent's reign would last for only another six years before he was succeeded by Alexander IV (1254–61). While this rather engaging encounter between Pope Innocent IV and the Mongol Emperor might come across as a meeting of near equal egos and empires, according to Martin Wight, the "papal claims" represent "the earliest version of the European assertion of superiority." For the "Papacy trumped the imperial ace by playing the universality promised to the Christian religion," and when the "tide of Mongol conquest ebbed, their empire became a mission field" for Christian Europe.[16] As we shall see, this is a theme that persisted through the colonial era, just as claims about Western universality persist to this day.

The Old World Meets the New

Muldoon insists that Innocent IV is significant not only for the active role he played in formulating law and policy for dealing with infidels while he was alive, but also because of the precedents he set that would influence the thinking of others—rulers and jurists among them—long after his death. His "discussion of the natural right of infidels to govern themselves was an important step in the development of international law. It was often quoted in the sixteenth-century debate over the rights of the inhabitants of the New World in the face of the Spanish conquest of the Americas."[17] Accordingly, we now skip forward to the sixteenth century and consider the work and influence of Innocent's jurisprudential descendant, the Spanish theologian Franciscus de Vitoria and his *De Indis et de Iure Belli Relectiones*, which was dedicated to this very topic.[18]

According to James Brown Scott, Vitoria and his *Relectiones* are of great significance because they "set forth his law of nations, which was to become the international law not merely of Christendom but of the world at large." By Scott's admiring eye, Vitoria's work "attributes to the discovery of America the expansion of international law until it has become a universal rule of conduct," proclaiming "an international community composed of all nations."[19] According to Anthony Pagden's less glowing reading, Vitoria's is "one of the earliest and probably the most consistently influential text on the question of the legitimacy of European imperialism."[20] Vitoria's significance in respect to the consequences of European encounters with the New World is born out in the claim that "international law, such as it existed in Vitoria's time, did not *precede* and thereby effortlessly resolve the problem of Spanish-Indian relations; rather, international law was created out of the unique issues generated by the encounter between the Spanish and the Indians."[21] This encounter might be described as yet another forerunner to Gong's nineteenth-century "confrontation of civilizations and their respective cultural systems,"[22] and had a major impact in shaping the soon-to-be legally entrenched European standard of civilization.

The task Vitoria set for himself in the *Relectiones* was to establish ground rules for addressing the "controversy and discussion . . . started on account of the aborigines of the New World, commonly called Indians, who came forty years ago into the power of the Spaniards, not having been previously known to our world."[23] These peoples were widely thought of as living in a state of sociopolitical organization that "is absolutely barbarous, and these are Indians who have neither laws nor King nor fixed dwellings but go in herds like wild animals and savages."[24] In the first instance, Vitoria endeavored to establish an argument that would discredit the long-held opinion that under the highest of laws, divine law, the pope was granted universal jurisdiction and thus authorized to sanction the military conquest of the New World. In lieu of this conventional or divine basis of Spanish claims to title over the Indians, Vitoria set about constructing a new secular international law governing relations with the Indians founded on a Thomistic or humanist natural law. He began by asking himself "whether the aborigines in

question were true owners in both private and public law before the arrival of the Spaniards; that is whether they were true owners of private
property and possessions and also whether there were among them any
who were the true princes and overlords of others."[25]

In considering this question, Vitoria ponders an extensive set of arguments for and against. Recalling that Aristotle "neatly and correctly
says" that " 'some are by nature slaves . . . who are better fitted to serve
than to rule,' " he posits that "these [Indians] are they who have not sufficient reason to govern even themselves, but only to do what is bidden."
Therefore "the aborigines in question are slaves," and, as Aristotle has
proven, " 'a slave can have nothing of his own.' " He adds that "they
[Indians] really seem little different from brute animals and are utterly
incapable of governing, and it is unquestionably better for them to be
ruled by others than to rule themselves. Aristotle says it is just and natural for such to be slaves." Another of the propositions considered by
Vitoria is drawn from the Bible. After quoting Genesis chapter 1, " 'Let
us make man in our own image and likeness that he may have dominion
over the fish of the sea,' etc.," Vitoria argues, it "appears therefore that
dominion is founded on the image of God," and as "the sinner [Indians]
displays no such image . . . he has no dominion."[26]

Having considered all of the arguments that came to him, Vitoria
somewhat equivocally comes to the conclusion that the "Indian aborigines are not barred on this ground [the use of reason] from the exercise
of true dominion. This is proved from the fact that the true state of the
case is that they are not of unsound mind, but have, according to their
kind, the use of reason." So too "the barbarians in question can not
be barred from being true owners, alike in public and private law, by
reason of the sin of unbelief or any other mortal sin, nor does such sin
entitle Christians to seize their goods and lands." Vitoria further suggests that "it is through no fault of theirs that these aborigines have for
many centuries been outside the pale of salvation, in that they have been
born in sin and void of baptism and the use of reason whereby to seek
out the things needful of salvation. Accordingly I for the most attribute
their seeming so unintelligent and stupid to a bad and barbarous up-
bringing." Despite coming to these conclusions, upon returning to the
issue of slavery and dominion, Vitoria concludes that "the Philosopher
[Aristotle]" does not "mean that, if any by nature are weak of mind, it
is permissible to seize their patrimony and enslave them and put them
up for sale." Rather, "what he means is that by defect of their nature
they [Indians/aborigines] need to be ruled and governed by others and
that it is good for them to be subject to others, just as sons need to be

subject to their parents until of full age, and a wife to her husband."[27] In this statement we have one of the earliest expressions of the idea of the "burden of civilization"—that it is the job of the civilized to take charge of the uncivilized.

Following these first two propositions, Vitoria continues to articulate a further five claims by which the Spanish are justified in intervening in the affairs of and gaining dominion over the Indians of the New World. But I will set these aside for the moment and take them up again in the following chapter on European "civilizing missions" in the New World and elsewhere. For it is Vitoria's speculations on the unsuitability or inability of the Amerindians to govern themselves that is of most significance here in terms of the rise of standards of civilization as a tool of empire.

Extending the vein of thought running through the first claim, Vitoria concludes the first *Relectio* by raising an eighth and "doubtful" claim, one which he "dare not affirm . . . nor . . . entirely condemn." "It is this: Although the aborigines in question are (as has been said above) not wholly unintelligent, yet they are little short of that condition, and so are unfit to found or administer a lawful State up to the standard required by human and civil claims."[28] In this passage we find Vitoria's most explicit reference to something akin to a standard of civilization, a standard based on the capacity for sociopolitical organization and self-government—"a lawful State"—whereby the Spaniard's system of governing is the natural benchmark.

Following this proposition, Vitoria proceeds to make a statement that is clearly inaccurate and was quite likely known by him to be so. He continues:

> Accordingly they have no proper laws nor magistrates, and are not even capable of controlling their family affairs; they are without any literature or arts, not only the liberal arts, but the mechanical arts also; they have no careful agriculture and no artisans; and they lack many other conveniences, yea necessaries, of human life. It might, therefore, be maintained that in their own interests the sovereigns of Spain might undertake the administration of their country, providing them with prefects and governors for their own towns, and might even give them new lords. (161)

And then, further prefiguring the language of the "white man's burden" or "burden of civilization," Vitoria adds:

I say there would be some force in this contention; for if they are all wanting in intelligence, there is no doubt that this would not only be permissible, but also a highly proper, course to take; nay, our sovereigns would be bound to take it, just as if the natives were infants. The same principle seems to apply here to them as to people of defective intelligence; and indeed they are no whit or little better than such so far as self-government is concerned, or even the wild beasts, for their food is not more pleasant and hardly better than that of beasts. Therefore their governance should in the same way be entrusted to people of intelligence. (161)

At the end of this passage, Vitoria returns to his starting point of Aristotle's musings on slaves, professing that "herein some help might be gotten from the consideration . . . that some are by nature slaves, for all the barbarians in question are of that type and so they may in part be governed as slaves are" (161). It is evident that although Vitoria recognized that "according to their kind" the Indians might have some primitive or rudimentary form of government, it was not one that was thought to be anywhere near sophisticated enough to deal with the well-organized and well-governed sovereign Spanish state on an equal footing.[29]

As Antony Anghie points out, the Indian personality according to Vitoria has two distinct features. First, like the Spaniard and the rest of humankind, the Indian belongs to the universal realm, for, as Vitoria reluctantly acknowledges, they "have, according to their own kind," a limited facility of reason and thus a means of comprehending the universally binding *ius gentium*. Second, the Indian and the Spaniard differ significantly in that the Indian's "social and cultural practices are at variance with the practices required by the universal norms." That is, it is the "particular cultural practices of the Spanish [that] assume the guise of universality as a result of appearing to derive from the sphere of natural law." (As discussed in the preceding chapter, cosmopolitanism's claims about the universal applicability of Western mores and values share a similar secular logic.) Thus, according to Anghie, in the mind of Vitoria, the Indian of North America is "schizophrenic, both alike and unlike the Spaniard." While the Indians may possess the potential to be accepted into the universal, that is, the Spanish fold, this "potential can only be realized . . . by the adoption or the imposition of the universally applicable practices of the Spanish"—effectively meaning they are not truly "universal" values and practices at all. It follows that "the universal norms Vitoria enunciates regulate behaviour" not only between the Indians of the New World and the Spanish, but also between the various collectives of Indian nations, granting the Spanish "an extraordinarily powerful right of intervention."[30]

In terms of giving rise to the European standard of civilization, "we see in Vitoria's work the enactment of a formidable series of maneuvers by which European practices are posited as universally applicable norms with which the colonial peoples must conform if they are to avoid sanctions and achieve full membership."[31] This is the very essence of the function of a standard of civilization. If in the eyes of the Spanish the Amerindians are unable to measure up to European social and cultural practices and, more importantly, systems of sociopolitical organization and government that are assumed to be the universal norm, then the Indians are deemed barbarous, uncivilized, or infantile—in any event, inferior.

The chance discovery (and more coordinated conquest) of the New World—and in no small part, Vitoria's findings on its legal implications—would serve to lay the international legal groundwork for how other indigenous peoples would be treated by Europeans in future encounters or "confrontations of civilizations." The classification of the Amerindians as somehow being substandard or uncivilized, based in large part on their sociocultural practices and their capacity for self-government, and the subsequent entrenchment of a European standard of civilization would have serious ramifications for the rest of the non-European world long into the future. As Anghie has argued, "Non-European peoples have been continuously characterized as the barbarians compelling the further extension of international law's ambit."[32]

The following section traces this extension of international law as it navigates through what is often referred to as the era of the classical standard of civilization and the work of the publicists over whom Vitoria would cast such a long jurisprudential shadow.[33] In speaking of this influence on his own generation of publicists, one of international law's leading nineteenth-century exponents, John Westlake, claimed that "men like Vitoria . . . were the worthy predecessors of those who now make among us the honourable claim to be 'friends of the aborigines.'"[34] Just how good a friend they turned out to be we shall see.

The Classical Standard of Civilization

The importance of international law to the expansion of European empires and the role of those that did so much to develop it can be found in the words of another of its best-known practitioners and scribes, Henry Wheaton. Referring to the publicists who came after Vitoria such as Hugo Grotius, Samuel von Puffendorf, Christian Wolff, Emerich de Vattel, and Cornelius van Bynkershoek, Wheaton enthusiastically asserts that "it would be difficult to name any class of writers which has contributed more to promote the progress of civilization than 'these illustrious authors— these friends of human nature—these kind instructors of human errors and frailties—these benevolent spirits who held up the torch of science to a benighted world.' "[35] Note again here the prominence of science or "modern" scientific methods in advancing civilization.

The further Europeans explored and the more indigenous peoples they encountered, the more it came to be held that the hallmark of "primitive societies" was an "absence of any definite machinery for the enactment, enforcement and administration of Law." This perception led observers to conclude "that the savage knows nothing of Law in any true sense, but is enslaved in a vast mesh of custom which dictates every act, every thought, every word he utters."[36] Sidney Hartland was in no doubt that this was the case. "The savage," he tells us, "is hemmed in on every side by the customs of his people, he is bound in the chains of immemorial tradition, not merely in his social relations, but in his religion, his medicine, his industry, his art, and every aspect of his life."[37] An example of the extremes this line of thought was taken to is found in Carleton Kemp Allen's *Law in the Making*, in which he declared: "There is not a very vast difference between the automatism of an ant and the tribal habits of an Australian aboriginal; the ant, indeed, in many respects has the better of the comparison."[38] It may come as a surprise to only a few that this favorable comparison of ants with Aborigines retained its place in the subsequent third edition of 1939, only being expunged in the fourth edition of 1946.

In a similar line of thought, following an argument first proposed by Vitoria, the German philosopher-jurist Christian Wolff wrote in *Jus Gentium*, "We call a nation barbarous . . . which cares but little for intellectual virtues, consequently neglects the perfecting of the intellect. Therefore, since barbarian nations do not develop their minds by training, in determining their actions they follow the leadership of their natural inclinations and aversions." In contrast, Wolff identifies a "cultured and civilized nation" as one which "cultivates intellectual virtues" and "desires to perfect the intellect" and develop "the mind by training. And that is called a civilized nation which has civilized usages or usages which conform to the standard of reason and politeness." This line of argument bears some resemblance to the thinking of Hobbes, and others, about the order and prerequisites for civilization and progress as outlined in chapters 2 and 3 above. Having drawn a distinction between the two, Wolff positions barbarous and civilized nations as absolute opposites, adding that "since barbarous nations have uncivilized usages, therefore to a barbarous nation is opposed a nation cultured and civilized." Of the two, civilized nations are the superior, and "a nation ought to be cultured . . . and therefore ought to develop the mind by training" and, hence, "ought not to follow the leadership of its natural inclinations and aversions, but rather that of reason." Wolff concluded that "because nations ought to be civilized," and "since the perfection of a nation consists in its fitness for attaining the purpose of the state, and since the form of government of a nation is perfect, if nothing is lacking in it, which it needs for attaining that purpose; nations in perfecting the intellect ought always to consider the purpose of the state and those things which they need for attaining this purpose, consequently they ought to direct all their efforts to this end."[39] The importance attributed here to achieving sovereign statehood, the pinnacle of civilization, has parallels with the esteemed standing that Hegel would later attribute to the state, as discussed in chapter 3. From this assessment, it was just a short leap to the assumption that the governed and enlightened nations of "civilized" Europe, taking the form of states, were the norm to which the "barbarous" might aspire. It was an equally short leap to the assumption that it was the task of the civilized to assist with the training of the uncivilized in their aspiring to the realms of the civilized world, should their minds be sufficiently pliable and adept to accept such conditioning. Thus, we come to the era in which the "perfected" states of Europe precipitate Gong's "confrontation of civilizations and their respective cultural systems"[40] as they continue to stretch their imperial wings across the globe.

The challenges and complexities that European encroachment into the non-European world posed for a still incipient body of international law was not lost on all of those practitioners who were in the midst of it at the time. In contradistinction to opinions cited above, the jurist Robert Ward—who would later serve in the British House of Commons and in executive posts—observed: "When the New World was opened to the spirit and adventure of the Old, it was reasonable to expect what was found; new laws and customs, as well as a new people and language." That is, new civilizations. In his jurisprudence, Ward was of the belief that natural law, and hence the law of nations, was not a universal system. Rather, he held it to be dependent upon interpretations grounded in the cultural context of each nation. This led him to recognize that "each

Class of Peoples may be said to have a different Law of Nations. . . .
The North American Indians have one; The Indians of the South Sea
another; The Negroes a third; The Gentoos a fourth; The Tartar Nations a fifth; The Mahometans a sixth; The Christians a seventh, and so
on." That is not to suggest, however, that the respective laws of nations
of these civilizations were afforded equal respect when they confronted
one another. That was certainly not the case, for Ward hastened to add
that "it was not reasonable to expect, that the intercourse between the
Spaniards and the Mexicans should be governed by the same customs as
the intercourse of Nations in Europe."[41] In this regard, Ward and most
of his predecessors, contemporaries, and successors were in agreement,
for as Wolff insisted, despite acknowledging that "by nature all nations
are equal the one to the other . . . it is plain . . . [and] has to be admitted,
that what has been approved by the more civilized nations is *the* law of
nations."[42] The precedence of the law of nations observed by the exploring civilized states of Christian Europe is reaffirmed again and again by
publicists such as William Hall, who maintained that "international law
is a product of the special civilisation of modern Europe, and is intended
to reflect the essential facts of that civilisation so far as they are fit subjects for international rules."[43]

The idea that international law is founded on the principles of Christian morality, as reciprocally practiced between the Christian states of
Europe, finds explicit expression in the legal opinion of Wheaton. Ap-
provingly quoting Friedrich Carl von Savigny, he asserts that the "progress of civilization, founded on Christianity, has gradually conducted
us to observe a law analogous to this in our intercourse with all the
nations of the globe, whatever may be their religious faith, and without reciprocity on their part." Wheaton's legal opinion lends his juridical authority to reinforce Ward's opinion on the limited extension and
protection afforded by the Law of Nations of civilized Europe. Asking
himself: "Is there a uniform law of nations?" Wheaton assuredly declares, "There certainly is not the same one for all the nations and states
of the world." In Wheaton's opinion, "public [international] law, with
slight exceptions, has always been, and still is, limited to the civilized
and Christian people of Europe or to those of European origin."[44] Full
recognition before international law and membership in what Westlake
referred to as civilized "international society" is therefore limited to
that "society of states, having European civilisation." Wherein civilized
Christian international society "comprises—*First*, all European states.
These, as explained in speaking of the Peace of Westphalia, form a sys-

tem intimately bound together by the interests of its members. . . . *Secondly*, all American states. These, on becoming independent, inherited the international law of Europe. . . . *Thirdly*, a few Christian states in other parts of the world, as the Hawaiian Islands, Liberia and the Orange Free State."[45]

Beyond Europe's borders and those of its fledgling settler colonies, much of the non-European world was widely thought to consist of what Ward referred to as uncivilized "nations that are still approaching to a state of nature." Expressing sentiments that were held by the majority of his predecessors and successors, Ward explicitly states, "If we look to the *Mahometan* and *Turkish* nations . . . their ignorance and barbarity repels all examination, and if they have received any improvement since the days when they first set foot in Europe, it is probably from their connection with people professing the very religion which they most hate and despise." He adds that the "same inferiority in this sort of conduct, is to be found even among the Chinese, so famed for eminence in every other branch of knowledge, and in the science of morals itself. Their wars have always been carried on with *Eastern* barbarity, and their known laws against strangers would alone demonstrate the point."[46] This point about distinctly savage or barbarian forms of war making is an issue that is taken up again in chapters 6 and 7.

An explicit distinction between civilized and uncivilized peoples in the eyes of international law gained such currency in the work of so many publicists that it was virtually beyond contention. For example, Wheaton makes just such a distinction in outlining the legal status of the "barbarians of Africa" and the "savage tribes" of North America.[47] This further distinction between these two groups of "uncivilized" peoples had been proposed and established many years prior. As noted in earlier chapters, no lesser authority than Montesquieu stated, "There is this difference between savage and barbarous nations: the former are dispersed clans, which for some particular reason cannot be joined in a body; and the latter are commonly small nations, capable of being united. The savages are generally hunters; the barbarians are herdsmen and shepherds."[48] Wheaton, in drawing his distinction between the civilized and uncivilized worlds, echoes the sentiments of Ward in claiming that "Turks are not a civilizing people." Rather, they "are a nation of soldiers, who care little for the peaceful pursuits of trade, literature, and science; while many of their [Christian] subjects are capable of attaining to the highest forms of civilization." This leads Wheaton to observe that "the governing race in Turkey has remained nearly stationary, while many of its subjects, and all the neighbouring States, have been rapidly progressing."[49] This is clearly a misrepresentation of the true state of affairs, yet it is a view that was widely held.[50]

The clearest distinctions or legal hierarchy of peoples is that outlined by the publicist James Lorimer. Following Montesquieu to a certain extent, Lorimer's legal opinion is also influenced by the work of anthropologists and ethnologists, such as the aforementioned Lewis Henry Morgan and Arthur de Gobineau (see chapter 3). Lorimer stridently proclaims, "No modern contribution to science seems destined to influence international politics and jurisprudence to so great an extent as that which is known as ethnology, or the science of races." The influence of ethnology led him to conclude that "as a political phenomenon, humanity, in its present condition, divides itself into three concentric zones or spheres—that of civilised humanity, that of barbarous humanity, and that of savage humanity."[51] Of these three classifications, Lorimer firmly believed that "savages are incapable of municipal organisation beyond its most rudimentary stages; and yet it is by means of municipal organisation that men cease to be savages" (2:191). This is the essence of the argument about the nature of civilization as detailed in chapter 2 above. This line of reasoning led him to argue, "Grotius lays it down that a band of robbers is not a State. On this ground the Barbary States were never recognised by European nations; and the conquest of Algeria by France was not regarded as a violation of international law." He concedes that had "Algeria come to respect the rights of life and property, its history would not have permanently deprived it of the right to recognition" (1:160–61). But when speaking of the Muslim world in general, he goes so far as to declare, "To talk of the recognition of Mahometan States as a question of time, is to talk nonsense" (1:123). Why? Because "in order to be entitled to recognition, a State must . . . possess" both "the will . . . [and] the power to reciprocate the recognition which it demands" (1:109). This was clearly, and mistakenly, seen as something that was altogether alien to Muslim peoples. As I have noted earlier, this was also a criterion that Hegel strenuously argued is a prerequisite for civilization.

Effectively then, the degree of sociopolitical organization and the form of government established within the nations of the non-European world became one of the key features in determining whether or not they were sufficiently equipped to be admitted to the civilized family of nations. Westlake explicitly expressed the capacity for self-government in accordance with European standards as a prerequisite for civilized status under the heading, "*Government the International Test of Ci-*

vilisation."[52] In a similar fashion, according to Hall, "Theoretically a politically organised community enters of right . . . into the family of states and must be treated in accordance with the law, so soon as it is able to show that it possesses the marks of a state."[53] But as we all know, things do not always work in practice as they do in theory. The significance of a non-European nation's degree of functioning government lay in its capacity to reciprocate the legal guarantees on offer by the states of Europe under their Law of Nations. Wheaton captured this imperative thus: "The rules of international morality . . . are founded on the supposition, that the conduct which is observed by one nation towards another, in conformity with these rules, will be reciprocally observed by other nations towards it. The duties which are imposed by these rules are enforced by moral sanctions, by apprehension on the part of sovereigns and nations incurring the hostility of other States, in case they should violate maxims generally received and respected by the civilized world."[54]

And so it came to be that the European law of "civilized" Christian nations was established as the guiding principle as to whether a nation was civilized, barbarous, or savage, thus determining its admissibility or exclusion from European international society. In order to meet the requisite standard of civilization and be admitted to the family of international law-abiding nations, non-European societies were required to organize themselves in a manner that would be immediately recognizable by European states as reflecting their own, supposedly universal standards of sociopolitical organization. Commenting on the classical standard of civilization decades after its entrenchment in international law, the jurist Georg Schwarzenberger neatly summarized it thus: "The test whether a State was civilised and, thus, entitled to full recognition as an international personality was, as a rule, merely whether its government was sufficiently stable to undertake binding commitments under international law and whether it was able and willing to protect adequately the *life, liberty and property of foreigners.*"[55] Almost inevitably, the foreigners in question were understood to be citizens of civilized states—that is, Europeans.

In essence and in practice, this meant that any nation or people that did not share the laws and customs of Europe was automatically excluded from international society. Such arbitrary exclusions are seen in the Italian publicist Pasquale Fiore's definition of "uncivilized tribes." He asserted that an "uncivilized tribe is composed of a group of persons, formed by the union of families. It lacks a definite political organization and has neither the laws nor the customs of civilized peoples." He added, "Barbaric people, even when they settle in a territory where they live as they please and recognize the authority of their chief, cannot be considered as persons of the *Magna civitas*."[56] A similar exclusion by definition (where to describe and label is to evaluate and pass judgment) is found in Wheaton, who proclaimed, "A State is also distinguishable from an unsettled horde of wandering savages not yet formed into a civil society."[57] Again, we see here the importance of sovereign statehood. Furthermore, it is readily apparent that the leading international lawmakers of the time thought it likely that few "uncivilized" nations would ascend to the ranks of the "civilized" international society of states any time soon. As Hall comments, "Apart from the rare instances in which a state is artificially formed, as was Liberia, upon territory not previously belonging to a civilised power, or in which a state is brought by increasing civilisation within the realm of law, new states generally come into existence by breaking off from an actually existing state."[58]

International Law: "A Friend of the Aborigines"?

The clear-cut legal distinction between the civilized and uncivilized worlds and the unavoidable interactions between the two led to what became known as the unequal treaty system, or the system of capitulations and the right of extraterritoriality. As Fiore makes clear, the "object of the Capitulations is to determine and to regulate the relations between civilized and uncivilized states, as regards the exercise of their respective sovereign rights with respect to the citizens of civilized states who reside in the countries where Capitulations are in force." He adds, "In principle, Capitulations are derogatory to the local 'common' law; they are based on the inferior state of civilization of certain states of Africa, Asia and other barbarous regions, which makes it impracticable to exercise sovereign rights mutually and reciprocally with perfect equality of legal condition."[59] This did not automatically mean that nations deemed uncivilized and outside the bounds of international society and thus lacking equal recognition under international law were afforded no place within the ambit of international law. Their precise status in international law is outlined by Fiore, who asked, "Can barbarous tribes, whatever their degree of culture, be denied the capacity of being considered subject to international law?" To which he replied, "acknowledging the authority of a chief, they cannot be placed on the same footing as the other members of the *Magna civitas*." He adds, "One could not, however, refuse to apply international law to them as a means of regulating *de facto* relations which may be established between them and civilized states" (34). Despite having quasi-legal status, like Vitoria's

Indians who occupied an ambiguous position in international law—partially subjected to it, but afforded minimal protection under it—Fiore is adamant that "uncivilized tribes are not indeed in the same condition as civilized peoples; the 'common' law cannot be applied in the same way, whatever the degree of culture may be" (45). So while non-European peoples might have been regarded as having some measure of "culture," they were not regarded as having "civilization," something which was still uniquely European.

The authority of the publicists of the late eighteenth to early twentieth century was such that by the end of the First World War, the classical standard of civilization was well and truly entrenched in the annals of international law. In speaking of the esteemed place held by publicists in international affairs, Wheaton postured: "Without wishing to exaggerate the importance of these writers, or to substitute, in any case, their authority for the principles of reason, it may be affirmed that they are generally impartial in their judgement. They are witnesses of the sentiments and usages of civilized nations, and the weight of their testimony increases every time that their authority is invoked by statesman."[60] As outlined in the opening pages of this book, this self-congratulatory sentiment is a powerful testament to the power of ideas, the power of language, and the power of thinkers to influence holders of important public offices and decision making and policy making more generally.

In 1921 the American Alpheus Henry Snow, partially quoting the French publicist Antoine Rougier, gave the following account, which notes the origins of the standard of civilization in international society: "Those States which recognize themselves as obligated to fulfill the functions which are necessary to the existence of all organized society, by maintaining order and justice under a regular government and securing the human rights of their inhabitants 'form a community or society, anciently called the Community of Christian States, now the community of civilized States.'"[61] Those that failed to measure up to the European standard of civilization—the inferior non-Christian world, the ungoverned or ungovernable, the uneducated, essentially the majority of the Nonwestern world—were relegated to the second- or third-class uncivilized world of savages and barbarians. The members of these nations or states were thought to require further training at the hands of the civilized empires of Europe in the ways of civilization before they could hope to graduate to the ranks of the civilized.

Schwarzenberger succinctly captures a good measure of the rationale underpinning the origins and enforcement of the classical standard of civilization thus: "Once civilisation is related to the basic types of human association, it is no longer necessary to be content with the mere enumeration and description of a bewildering number of civilisations," as suggested by Lucien Febvre's supposedly purely "ethnographic" definition of civilization. But as has been argued, the concept of civilization is both descriptive and evaluative, and, given its normative demands, it is "then possible to evaluate and to measure individual civilisations in the light of a universally applicable test of the degree of civilisation which any such particular endeavour has attained."[62] Lingering on well into the twentieth century, far longer than many of the colonial states and some of the jurists of the time thought appropriate, the classical standard of civilization was eventually made redundant, at least in terms of its formal place in international law, upon the settlement of the Second World War. The total abrogation of the laws of war as witnessed by the nature of the totalitarian aggression perpetrated by members of the thought-to-be civilized world effectively put paid to the notion of maintaining a world legally divided between the "civilized" and the "uncivilized." The evolution and deployment of nuclear weapons and the subsequent concept of mutually assured destruction served to further undermine the principle (229–34). No less significantly, in the wake of the Second World War, numerous anticolonial nationalist movements rapidly emerged in many of Europe's colonial possessions, all seeking the newly recognized right to national self-determination, unexempted state sovereignty, unqualified inclusion in international society, and full recognition under international law.

Even prior to the war, a number of leading jurists recognized that adhering to a standard of civilization was "considered anachronistic and insulting by the growing number of non-European countries which were becoming for both political and legal reasons full International Persons and members of the Family of Nations."[63] Hersh Lauterpacht, for instance, was highly critical of Lorimer's explicit legal distinction between civilized, barbarous, and savage societies. The latter two excluded from recognition "because they are unable to fulfil the fundamental condition of what Lorimer calls a 'reciprocating will,'" or what Lauterpacht referred to as Lorimer's "picturesque descriptions of varying degrees of civilization with reference to recognition." Indignant at the perpetuation of the dichotomy, Lauterpacht declared: "Modern international law knows of no distinction, for the purposes of recognition, between civilized and uncivilized States or between States within and outside the international community of civilized States."[64] The philosopher R. G. Collingwood expressed similar sentiments, for he thought that the standard was not only inappropriate and redundant, but had long been so.

Referring to the "dichotomy of civilized and barbarous societies" in a lecture of 1940, he exclaimed, "There are still people who accept it; but to accept it in the middle of the twentieth century is a sure sign of retarded development: of being a century and a half behind the times in your habits of thought."[65] Commenting on this juncture in the debate, there is more than a little irony in Schwarzenberger's statement: "At this point doctrine reaches the other extreme. The standard of civilisation has vanished, and States are supposed to be under a legal duty to recognise even non-civilised States and their governments."[66] It is all too evident that while the classical standard of civilization might have been on the way out in terms of postwar international law, the notion that some peoples of the world remained uncivilized persisted in certain quarters. And as outlined in chapters 7 and 8, Collingwood's death knell was brief at best, for the idea continues to persist in world politics in various guises.

It is appropriate to bear this in mind when assessing the legacy of international law, and the classical standard of civilization in particular, that emerged, expanded, and took root on account of European encounters with the non-European world. According to Anghie, the significance of Vitoria and the international law to which he gave rise lies in the development of a "set of concepts" and the construction of a "set of arguments" that ever since have been deployed "by western powers in their suppression of the non-western world and which are still regularly employed in contemporary international relations in the supposedly post-imperial world." They are a set of concepts that are simultaneously used to describe and evaluate, compare and contrast, commend and condemn. Furthermore, Vitoria's work is indicative of the European tendency to posit one's own practices as "universally applicable norms with which the colonial peoples must conform if they are to avoid sanctions and achieve full membership" in civilized international society. A further consequence of the jurisprudence that followed is the construction of the "uncivilized" "other," who is subject to the law's sanction but deprived of any real measure of protection afforded by it. Thus, it "creates an object against which sovereignty may express its fullest powers by engaging in an unmediated and unqualified violence which is justified as leading to conversion, salvation, civilization."[67] As outlined and argued throughout, irrespective of their age and origins, descriptive-evaluative concepts such as civilization and progress not only persist but remain influential drivers of policy and policy justification.

The so-called civilizational confrontations and the consequences that flowed from them were not meetings between equal sovereigns; rather, they were between the sovereign states of Europe and the nonsovereign or quasi-sovereign Amerindians and other indigenous peoples of the world. Once it was determined that the colonial world lacked civilization and thus lacked sovereignty, it was almost inevitable that international law would create for itself "the grand redeeming project of bringing the marginalized into the realm of sovereignty, civilizing the uncivilized and developing the juridical techniques and institutions necessary for this great mission." Thus, it is not unreasonable to assert that the principle of a legal standard of civilization is implicated in a long-running, universalizing Western imperial project. As an instrument of international law and a tool for extending international law's ambit, the standard of civilization "is mired in this history of subordinating and extinguishing alien cultures."[68] How it did so, by way of violent "civilizing missions" that were intended to "civilize" the "uncivilized," as carried out for the past five hundred plus years, is examined in the following chapter.

6

The Burden of Civilization and the "Art and Science of Colonization"

I am as free as nature first made man,
E're the base laws of servitude began,
When wild in woods the noble savage ran.
John Dryden, *Conquest of Granada,* **1670**

The history of the world is the triumph of the heartless over the mindless.
Sir Humphrey Appleby, *Yes, Prime Minister*

: : :

Introduction

I have described in preceding chapters how the coming together of Europeans and different civilizations or peoples
led to the identification of a hierarchy of civilizations, or,
more accurately, civilization, savagery, and barbarism. This
taxonomy in turn led to the establishment of the classical
standard of civilization in international society. I have argued that, as a legal and political tool imposed exclusively
by the self-proclaimed "civilized" against the "uncivilized,"
the classical standard is implicated in the subordination and
extinguishing of peoples and cultures deemed inferior. The
justification for these offenses, or the high moral ground

claimed by the civilized states of Europe that conferred upon them the right and, to some extent, the duty to "civilize" the "uncivilized," goes by the name of the "white man's burden" or the "burden of civilization." The means by which civilized Europe undertook this process were the often violent and overly zealous civilizing missions or *mission civilisatrice*, missions that were generally designed to ameliorate—where and when thought possible—the conditions of the world's savages and barbarians, usually through tutelage, training, and conversion to Christianity. What follows is an account of these missions down though the ages, from the discovery of the New World through to the late twentieth century. What becomes evident is that there is a certain consistency and continuity (particularly in concepts, language, and practice) across time and space, irrespective of which particular European nation (or European settler colony) is acting in the name of civilization and administering the civilizing.

When in 1492 Christopher Columbus stumbled upon the bountiful islands of the New World, he took "possession of them all for their Highness" the King, "and no opposition was offered." As for the Amerindians already living in these "islands which I have found," he observed that they "all go naked, men and women, as their mothers bore them. . . . They have no iron or steel or weapons, nor are they fitted to use them." This was not because of any physical shortcomings, for Columbus records they are of "handsome stature." Rather, it was because they are "incurably timid." In fact, he thought them to be "the most timorous people in the world," some even "cowardly to an excessive degree." But they were generous to a fault, "refusing nothing that they possess, if it be asked of them; on the contrary, they invite any one to share it and display as much love as if they would give their hearts." Through such generosity they accepted "even the pieces of the broken hoops of the wine barrels and, like savages, gave what they had." One of Columbus's sailors even exchanged a thong for "gold to the weight of two and a half castellanos, and others received much more for other things which were worth less." But Columbus insists the trade was generally fair, for he "gave them a thousand handsome good things . . . in order that they might conceive affection for us and, more than that, might become Christians and be inclined to the love and service of Your Highness and of the whole Castilian nation." These were sentiments and actions he was convinced they were ready and willing to do. He also believed they had the desire to "strive to collect and give us of the things which they have in abundance and which are necessary to us."[1]

Despite Columbus's apparently generous and affectionate appraisal of the natives and the gracious welcome he received from them—believing him, by his own account, to be literally Heaven-sent—he had no reservations about taking "some of the natives by force, in order that they might learn and might give me information of whatever there is in these parts." He also did not hesitate to relieve the land of some of its "incalculable gold," nor did he see anything wrong in bringing home to Spain "with me Indians as evidence" of his discoveries. On the whole he thought that the Amerindians, apparently lacking any form of structured government or civilized mores, would not only do well to embrace Christianity and the ways of the Spaniards, but would welcome the imposition of such measures, regardless of the means (196, 200). With this assessment, Columbus effectively outlined the basic guiding images and principles that would determine the nature of future European encounters and relations with the non-European world for close to the next five hundred years.

Within fifty years of Columbus's discovery of the Americas and its inhabitants, for many, "the great question of the Indies" was "beyond all doubt the most important in the world." As Bartolomé de la Vega exclaimed at the time, "what is at stake is nothing less than the salvation or loss of both the bodies and souls of all the inhabitants of that recently discovered world."[2] While this might sound like something of an overstatement, the significance of the events taking place in the Americas— particularly the Spanish treatment of the Amerindians—for the future of relations between diverse peoples was far greater than Vega's immediate concerns allowed him to imagine. The precedents and laws established following contact by Europeans with the peoples of the New World would thereafter inform the nature of subsequent European encounters with indigenous peoples around the globe. As Columbus observed, in the Americas and elsewhere, indigenous peoples who came into regular contact with European explorers and settlers either adopted European ways and assimilated, or risked perishing.

Precisely which of these outcomes it would be depended in large part on the assessment of colonial conquerors as to how far from and how amenable to civilization the natives in question were. For a significant but incalculable number of native peoples, it was thought best that they "simply be cleared away." That is, it was deemed quite reasonable and legitimate to drive them from their land, enslave and work them to death, sometimes hunt them for "sport," or, perhaps somewhat more humanely, allow them to die-out on reservations. The remaining native peoples, that is, "the more advanced [or less stubborn] among them are absorbed into the lower reaches" of civilization by varying measures of "compulsion," "periods of discipline," and training and tutelage in the ways of civilized Europeans.[3] Regardless of their "progress," however, at all times they fell short of perfect (European) civilization and thus occupied the bottom rung in the social hierarchy and were limited to living on the fringes of the society into which they were being absorbed and assimilated. In respect to the immediate postdiscovery phase of the New World Amerindians, Tzvetan Todorov gives a good indication of their plight and the "intensity" of the encounter in his assessment that "the sixteenth century perpetrated the greatest genocide in human history."[4]

As discussed in the previous chapter, the conquest of uncivilized peoples was not invented with Europeans' adventures in the New World, although they did precipitate its legal legitimization and formalization. The English, for instance, honed the techniques they employed in the Americas and elsewhere in the centuries prior, through conquest and expansion into the Celtic lands of Wales and Ireland, where "administrators were acutely aware that settler minorities faced a war of cultural attrition in which the first victim would be their English civility."[5] To counter this threat, the English resorted to legal declarations, such as the Statute of Rhuddlan of 1284, also known as the Statute of Wales, and the Statute of Kilkenny of 1366. The latter, renewed in 1498 and supplemented in 1536, reads: English settlers "forsaking the English language, dress, style of riding, laws and usages, live and govern themselves according to the manners, dress and language of the Irish enemies, and had also contracted marriages and alliances with them whereby . . . the allegiance to the lord king and the English laws there are put into subjection and decayed."[6] As John Darwin notes, the "intolerance and savagery" with which such regulations were routinely enforced appears to be at "odds with the pretensions to cultural superiority that underlay English expansion then and later."[7] Both the violence and its rationale are revealed in an account by Sir John Davies, King James's attorney general of Ireland, regarding the English Crown's difficulties in subduing the Irish. Davies wrote that "the Husbandman must first break the land, before it be made capable of good feed: and when it is thoroughly broken and manured, if he do not forthwith cast good seed into it, it will grow wilde again, and bear nothing but weeds. So a barbarous Country must first be broken by a war, before it will be capable of good Government; and when it is fully subdued and conquered, if it be not well planted and governed after the Conquest, it will eft-soons return to the former Barbarism."[8] With these earlier experiences closer to home, it did not require too much of an adjustment in thinking for European conquerors to extend similar ideas, labels, and practices to "breaking" and "supplanting" Amerindian and other indigenous "weeds" in preparing colonial soil for good government or civilization.[9]

As established in the preceding chapter, "positivist international law distinguished between civilized states and non-civilized states and asserted further that international law applied only to the sovereign states that composed the civilized 'Family of Nations.'" Having identified the gap "between the civilized European and uncivilized non-European world," European conquerors proceeded to devise a range of means of eradicating or "bridging this gap—of civilizing the uncivilized."[10] Thus, the European world took upon itself the burden of civilization, the challenge of bringing enlightenment and salvation to the uncivilized hordes of the world, either that or eliminate them in the endeavor.

With their respective ways of life threatened, some non-European peoples met European occupiers with concerted resistance—a good example outside of the "Indian Wars" in the Americas being the opposition met in Afghanistan. The extent of what was at stake for native peoples is all too evident when one recalls Herbert Spencer's prescription for dealing with the problem of savages, as outlined in chapter 3. Extending that line of thought, he was adamant that "wild races deficient in the allegiance-producing sentiment, cannot enter into a civilized state at all, but have to be supplanted by others which can." If left to their own devices and "uncontrolled, the impulses of the aboriginal man produce anarchy." Therefore, "Either his individuality must be curbed or society must dissolve."[11] Similar prescriptions were proposed by the German philosopher Eduard von Hartmann in his speculations on progress and "the improvement of the race." Translated and readily accessible in English shortly after its publication in German, Hartmann's philosophy was an attempt to bring together and reconcile the views of Schopenhauer, Hegel, Friedrich von Schelling, and Gottfried Leibniz. In attempting to do so, he was insistent that one of the ways human evolution takes place is through "the competition of races and nations in the struggle for existence, which is waged among mankind under natural laws just as pitilessly as among animals and plants." From this position he argued:

> No power on earth is able to arrest the eradication of the inferior races of mankind, which, as relics of earlier stages of development once also passed through by ourselves, have gone on vegetating down to the present day. As little a favour is done the

dog whose tail is to be cut off, when one cuts it off gradually, inch by inch, so little is there humanity in artificially prolonging the death-struggle of savages who are on the verge of extinction. The true philanthropist, if he has comprehended the natural law of anthropological evolution, cannot avoid desiring an acceleration of the last convulsions, and labouring for that end.[12]

There are some serious problems of logic with Hartmann's general argument, for he recognizes that the "inferior races" are actually part and parcel of humankind. As such, he also acknowledges that they are in a state of development that the white race also passed though. Therefore, despite their supposed arrested state of development, his reasoning suggests there is no good reason why other races will not in time experience similar progress. But the point Hartmann is making here is that, by their very presence here on earth, the inferior races are holding all races back. As seen in chapter 3, this kind of thinking was not uncommon among eighteenth and nineteenth century theorists of progress, race, and evolution. A good many of these theorists believed it inevitable that the weaker, less civilized peoples of the world would either be absorbed by or perish at the hands of stronger and more resilient peoples.

Despite the persistence of such views, just over four hundred years after Columbus's arrival in the Americas, on the eve of the United States's entry into the colonial enterprise in the Philippines, Puerto Rico, Guam, and soon Cuba, Alpheus Henry Snow stated in *The Question of Aborigines*:

> It is acknowledged . . . that the year 1898 marks the beginning of a new epoch in the art and science of colonization, in which civilized States have recognized more and more definitely that guardianship of aboriginal tribes implies not merely protection, not merely a benevolence toward private missionary, charitable, and educational effort, but a positive duty of direct legislative, executive, and judicial domination of aborigines as minor wards of the nation and of equally direct legislative, executive, and judicial tutorship of them for civilization, so that they may become in the shortest possible time civil and political adults participating on an equality in their own government under democratic and republican institutions.[13]

It is apparent that the principle of the "sacred trust of civilization" became widely accepted among the conquering and colonizing states of Europe. And even well into the mid-twentieth century, it still found explicit expression in international law, being referred to in the judgment handed down by the International Court of Justice in the South West Africa Cases of 1966. In the second phase of the cases, decided by the court president's casting vote, the court held that the applicant states (Ethiopia and Liberia), despite being member states of the League of Nations, did not have an established legal right or legitimate interest in alleging that the Republic of South Africa had contravened its League of Nations Mandate for South West Africa (Namibia).[14] In issuing the judgment, one of the seven dissenting justices, Judge Tanaka, stated that the "idea that it belongs to the noble obligation of conquering powers to treat indigenous peoples of conquered territories and to promote their well-being has existed for many hundreds of years, at least since the era of Vitoria."[15]

As argued in the preceding chapter, Vitoria's influence on international law and colonial policy is both significant and lasting, as seen in Judge Tanaka's judgment. Hence, it is the era of the Spanish "discovery" and conquest of the New World, and the justifications for it presented by Franciscus de Vitoria and others, to which I now turn.

Saving the Souls of the Uncivilized

In 1542 King Charles of Spain was informed that Spanish *conquistadores* in the New World were committing unspeakable atrocities against the Amerindians, including a form of slavery known as "*repartimiento* or *encomienda* (a satanic invention, never before heard of)." Under the advisement of "men from every expert and learned council," Charles issued a ban on slavery and directed that all such enslaved natives be freed. Believing they had been robbed of what was rightfully theirs, some *conquistadores* rebelled against the king's orders and continued their profitable slaughter and plunder. Other dissenters sought out men of "learning who could attack the imperial laws with solid legal arguments" in the hope that Charles might be convinced to reverse his decision. The man they found for the job was the Spanish royal historian, Juan Ginés de Sepúlveda, who, in *On the Just Causes of War*, sought to attack the validity of the new laws without actually making explicit reference to them as he launched a four-point defense of Spanish conquest of the Amerindians.[16]

In presenting his case, Sepúlveda's primary argument was that Amerindians "are barbaric, uninstructed in letters and the art of government, and completely ignorant, unreasoning, and totally incapable of learning anything but the mechanical arts." Furthermore, "they are sunk in vice, are cruel, and are of such character that, as nature teaches, they are to be governed by the will of others." Calling on the authority of Saint Augustine, he insisted that, "for their own welfare," natural law demands that the Indians "obey those who are outstanding in virtue and character"—the Spaniards. It followed that, once warned, if the Amerindians "refuse to obey this legitimate sovereignty, they can be forced to do so for their own welfare by recourse to the terrors of war." Sepúlveda then cited the authority of Aristotle (chapters 2, 3, and 5 of the *Politics*), scripture ("the fool *shall be* servant to the wise of heart," Proverbs 11:29), and Saint Thomas Aquinas (who held "first place among scholarly theologians"), to assert that such a war is "just both by civil and natural law." And if that was not sufficient proof, "all political philosophers, basing themselves on this reason alone, teach that in cities, kingdoms, and states those who excel in prudence and virtue should preside with sovereignty over the government so that government may be just according to natural law." This is why Augustine saw it as just to force someone to do something against their will if it is in their best interest. And it is the reason why Aquinas approved of the Romans' subjugation of other nations as just and proper. Irrespective of these points, Sepúlveda added that, even if the Amerindian "barbarians . . . do not lack capacity, with still more reason they must obey and heed the commands of those who can teach them to live like human beings."[17]

Sepúlveda's second key point of argument was that the Amerindians "must accept the Spanish yoke so that they may be corrected and punished for the sins and crimes against the divine and natural laws," especially the sins of idolatry and human sacrifice. The third point was closely related to the second, while Sepúlveda's final argument concerned the "spread and growth of the Christian religion" among the Indians. He argued that this end "will be accomplished if" the New World is tamed and controlled, such that "the gospel of Christ can be preached by consecrated men safely and without any danger." A similar point was made centuries earlier by Pope Innocent IV, as outlined in chapter 5. Sepúlveda concluded his defense of Spanish conquest by asserting that "it is totally just, as well as most beneficial to these barbarians, that they be conquered and brought under the control of the Spaniards, who are the worshippers of Christ," for Pope Alexander VI's "decree to the College of Cardinals declared armed expeditions against the Indians to be just." Thus, seeing as it was undeniable that "wars undertaken by God's command are just, no one will deny that a war is just that God's Vicar . . . declares to be justified" (13–16).

One of the first to take up the task of fighting for the rights of Amerindians was Bartolomé de Las Casas. Las Casas responded by stating that he "detected in" Sepúlveda's pleadings for the repeal of the laws, "poisons disguised with honey." Furthermore, the arguments presented by Sepúlveda "are partly foolish, partly false, [and] partly of the kind that have the least force."[18] That is, he charged Sepúlveda with making "certain counterfeit arguments that favour the greediest cravings of tyrants by twisting texts from the sacred books and the doctrines of the holiest and wisest fathers and philosophers."[19] Las Casas then set about proving to an assembly of noted theologians, jurists, and the King's Council of the Indies—and prove it he did in large part—that God did not despise the Amerindians such "that he willed them to lack reason and made them like brute animals, so that they should be called barbarians, savages, wild men, and brutes." "On the contrary," he argued, "they are of such gentleness and decency that they are . . . supremely fitted and prepared to abandon the worship of idols and to accept . . . the word of God and the preaching of the truth."[20] This in itself is a significant point, for it still provided the grounds for justifying intervention in Indian affairs and daily life for the sake of their souls and their civilization. Las Casas adds that, despite "the fact that the Indians are barbarians it does not necessarily follow that they are incapable of government and have to be ruled by others, except to be taught about the Catholic faith and to be admitted to the holy sacraments." Although they might well be barbarians, he was convinced that they were neither ignorant, nor inhuman, because "long before they heard the word Spaniard they had properly organized states, wisely ordered by excellent laws, religion, and custom." Thus, was it not proved that "Reverend Doctor Sepúlveda has spoken wrongly and viciously" against the peoples of the Americas (42)?

While Las Casas might have proved much of his case to the commission, which judged in his favor on some points and left others open and unresolved, this did not halt Spanish enterprises in the Americas. As outlined in chapter 5, it was Franciscus de Vitoria who had the greater impact on the establishment of laws regulating the conduct between "civilized" conquerors and the "uncivilized" conquered. A good indicator of this is the fact that it was Vitoria's intellectual home, the Salamanca School, that Samuel Johnson heaped praise upon for supposedly offering the opinion that the conquering of the Americas "was not lawful."[21] Others likewise saw Vitoria as something of a champion of Indians' rights. For instance, in the 1949 edition of *The Law of Nations*, the jurist J. L. Brierly proclaims that Vitoria's "examination of the title of the Spaniards to exercise domination over the inhabitants of the New World . . . is remarkable for its courageous defence of the rights of the Indians."[22] In contrast, there are others, such as Robert Williams, who protest in much harsher terms that Vitoria "initiated the process by which the European state system's legal discourse was ultimately liberated from its stultifying, expressly theocentric, medievalized moorings and was adapted to the rationalizing demands of Renaissance Europe's secularized will to empire."[23]

The contested nature of Vitoria's rightful place in the history of international law becomes more fathomable the further one delves into the *Relectiones*, particularly section 3 of *On the Indians*. Here he outlines the "lawful and adequate titles whereby the Indians might have come under the sway of the Spaniards." Influenced by Innocent IV's argument regarding "the bond of natural ties" that constitutes "the world machine,"[24] Vitoria begins his case for just Spanish title over the Amerindians by arguing for what he calls a title of "natural society and fellowship." According to this title, the "Spaniards have a right to travel into the lands in question and to sojourn there, provided they do no harm to the natives, and the natives may not prevent them." Following similar logic to that employed by Innocent IV in his letter to Guyuk Khan, his proof is "derived from the law of nations (*jus gentium*), which either is natural law or is derived from natural law." According to Vitoria, people have enjoyed the title of "natural society and fellowship" since "the beginning of the world (when everything was in common)," and it "was never the intention of peoples to destroy" this reciprocal right "by the division of property." A further proof of this title was that "to keep certain people out of a city or province as being enemies, or to expel them when already there, are acts of war." Implying that "the Spaniards are doing no harm," Vitoria claimed that "the Indians are not making a just war"; hence, "it is not lawful for them to keep the Spaniards away from their territory."[25]

Among the other proofs presented by Vitoria is the idea that "the Spaniards may lawfully carry on trade among the native Indians" without hindrance from "native princes." The proof of this title rests in a "rule of *jus gentium* that foreigners may carry on trade." And if this was not enough, by Vitoria's reckoning "similar proof lies in the fact that this is permitted by divine law." Furthermore, "the sovereign of the Indians is bound by the law of nature to love the Spaniards. Therefore the Indians may not causelessly prevent the Spaniards from making their profit." Two further proofs proposed by Vitoria are, "If there are among the Indians any things which are treated as common both to citizens and to strangers, the Indians may not prevent the Spaniards from a communication and participation in them." And, despite the absence of a corresponding concept of citizenship among the Amerindians, "If children of any Spaniard be born there and they wish to acquire citizenship, it seems they can not be barred either from citizenship or from the advantages enjoyed by other citizens" (152–54).

Having outlined the first of the titles by which Spain may legally hold power over the Indians, Vitoria then asserted that should the "natives wish to prevent the Spaniards from enjoying any of their above-named rights under the law of nations . . . the Spaniards ought in the first place to use reason and persuasion to remove scandal." However, "if after this recourse to reason, the barbarians decline to agree and propose to use force," Vitoria insists that "the Spaniards can defend themselves and do all that consists with their own safety," including the declaration of war. If after having taken all reasonable measures and used "all diligence" to secure their safety, the Indians continue to pose a threat, Vitoria compels his fellow Spaniards to "make war on the Indians, no longer as on innocent folk, but as against forsworn enemies." As such they are authorized to employ "all the rights of war, despoiling them of their goods, reducing them to captivity, [and] deposing their former lords and setting up new ones." He is also careful to point out that "it is a universal rule of the law of nations that whatever is captured in war becomes the property of the conqueror." Vitoria concludes that this "then is the first title which the Spaniards might have for seizing the provinces and sovereignty of the natives" (154–56). One cannot help but suspect that had there been any suggestions that Amerindians had a corresponding set of entitlements should they land on the shores of Spain, it would have been greeted with outright indignation.

A second proposed title by which Spain might legally gain dominion over the Indians was by way of what Vitoria called the "propagation of Christianity"; and as "the Indians are not only in sin, but beyond the pale of salvation . . . it seems that they are bound to do so." Moreover, it is a task "entrust[ed] to the Spaniards" by none other than the pope, "to the exclusion of all others." For "if there was to be an indiscriminate inrush of Christians from other parts to the part in question, they might easily hinder one another and develop quarrels, to the banishment of tranquillity and the disturbance of the concerns of the faith and of the conversion of the natives." More is the point, as it was the Spaniards who "had the good fortune to discover the New World, it is just that this travel should be forbidden to others and that the Spaniards should enjoy alone the fruits of their discovery" (156–57). In making this point, Vitoria conveniently overlooks that the logic underpinning his argument clearly contradicts his own arguments concerning the title of "natural society and fellowship" and its accompanying rights of freedom of travel, trade, and association.

It followed from this second title that "if the Indians . . . prevent the Spaniards from freely preaching the Gospel, the Spaniards, after first reasoning with them in order to remove scandal . . . may then accept or even make war, until they succeed in obtaining facilities and safety for preaching the Gospel." Waging war was also deemed a legitimate response if Indians sought to "hinder conversion" or deter their fellows from seeking the same. In essence, the propagation of Christianity title "demonstrates that, if there is no other way to carry on the work of religion, this furnishes the Spaniards with another justification for seizing the lands and territory of the natives and for setting up new lords there and putting down the old lords and doing in right of war everything which it is permitted in other just wars" (157). Vitoria articulates five further titles by which the Spaniards might legally take possession of the New World, including a title "found in the cause of allies as friends." His rationale is the precedent of the expansion of the Roman Empire, which was "approved by St. Augustine and by St. Thomas [Aquinas] as a lawful one" (160). On the whole though, these further titles are little more than variations on a theme, and thus warrant no further examination here.

Vitoria's lasting influence on the foundation and evolution of international law, and the esteem with which he is still held by many, no more so than by jurists, is beyond question. According to Ernest Nys's introductory words to the Carnegie edition of *Relectiones*; "Because of the vigor of his reasoning, the nobility of his sentiments, and his profound love of mankind, Franciscus de Vitoria is still in our day [1913] an imposing personality." Furthermore, "He was modest, simple, good; a sturdy defender of truth and justice."[26] In a similar fashion, James Brown Scott concludes his commentary on Vitoria and his law of nations by declaring that "Vitoria was a liberal. He could not help being a liberal. He was an internationalist by inheritance. And because he was both, his international law is a liberal law of nations."[27] That might be so, but if it is so, it does not necessarily say a lot for the foundations of liberal international law. The question that remains unresolved is: When all is said and done, is Vitoria's influence primarily positive or negative when it comes to assessing the overall impact on native peoples? It may well be that he sought to find compassionate and humane grounds on which Spain might legitimately undertake its conquest of the New

World. Many still believe that this was the case. However, in the end, Vitoria undermines his own apparent convictions and betrays the inevitably violent nature of the conquest by his admission, "I personally have no doubt that the Spaniards were bound to employ force and arms in order to continue their work there." He at least concedes, "I fear measures were adopted in excess of what is allowed by human and divine law" in the undertaking of that conquest.[28]

The true extent of Vitoria's compassion for the Amerindians is difficult to gauge, for, under the heading "*On the Law of War*," he claims that "sometimes it is lawful and expedient to kill all the guilty." Such "is especially the case against unbelievers, from whom it is useless ever to hope for a just peace on any terms" (183). Furthermore, in a possible indication of his true feelings and motivations, Vitoria concludes his discussion "on the Indians lately discovered" by stating that "even if there be no force in any of the titles which have been put forward"—although he clearly believes there is—"There would be no obligation to stop trade" with the Amerindians. Such a "grave hurt of the royal treasury (a thing intolerable)," is not conceivable, for "there are many commodities of which the natives have a superfluity and which the Spaniards could acquire by barter" (161–62). In sum, it is not too unfair to say that in the *Relectiones* Vitoria essentially sets out to establish a series of titles and arguments for the inevitably violent Spanish conquest of the Indians (and their land and possessions) of the New World. Furthermore, it was not only inevitable, but apart from being of great material benefit to the Spanish, it was also thought to be of great overall benefit to the Amerindians. They were to be the beneficiaries of a generous and superior benefactor, Spain, who would take them under its imperial wing and bring salvation while governing them on their behalf. In short, Vitoria's categorization of the Amerindians as being uncivilized and less than human, based on their social mores and cultural practices, and their perceived lack of capacity for self-government, set the wheels of imperialism and colonialism in motion.

In the seventeenth century, Juan de Solórzano Pereira cited both Sepúlveda and Vitoria in *De Indiarum Jure* to further legitimize Spanish occupation and possession of land in the New World. In essence, the Spanish relied on papal authority to justify their role in the Americas. As early as 1493, Alexander VI's papal bull *Inter caetera* relied on Columbus's observations of natives "going unclothed" to take responsibility for their salvation. Despite their nakedness, he deemed them "sufficiently disposed to embrace the Catholic faith and be trained in good morals." Thus, the "process of Christianizing" the Amerindians under

Spanish control and care was thought to "precede the process of civilizing them."[29] In effect, civilization was not attainable without Christianity, and for the Spanish, Catholicism in particular.

By this time the English were making their own claims on parcels of the New World, but in their case they appealed to an even higher authority. In 1620, King James I authorized a patent for the Council of New England which stated that "within these late Yeares there hath by God's Visitation raigned a wonderfull Plague, together with many horrible Slaughters, and Murthers, committed amoungst the Savages and bruitish People . . . to the utter Destruction, Devastacion, and Depopulacion of that whole Territorye." This "wonderful plague" of violence was all part of God's master plan, favoring the English as He did with "his Mercie and Favour, and by his Powerful Arme," such that the land in question, "deserted as it were by their naturall Inhabaitants, should be possessed and enjoyed by such our Subjects and People."[30] Whereas Spanish claims on the New World rested on the authority of God's vicar in Rome, English claims to occupation and possession cut out the middleman, so to speak, and called directly on the authority of God.

Exporting Civilization through Colonization

God's will aside, the degree of indigenous occupation and usage of land became a significant factor in the European usurpation of newly discovered territories. One of the most influential figures on this issue was John Locke. Locke was more than just a political philosopher and man of ideas, taking an active role in colonial policy as coauthor, with the Earl of Shaftesbury, of the Fundamental Constitutions of Carolina. He also served as secretary of the Council of Trade and Plantations from 1673 to 1675. While Locke was opposed to Spanish-style conquest, he was of the opinion that "where there being more *Land*, than the inhabitants possess, and make use of any one has liberty to make use of the waste."[31] And as far as he could see, this was widely the case in the New World. He wondered "whether in the wild woods and uncultivated wast[e] of America left to Nature, without any improvement, tillage or husbandry, a thousand acres will yield the needy and wretched inhabitants as many conveniences of life as ten acres of equally fertile land doe in Devonshire where they are well cultivated?"[32] Therefore, if the natives were not going to till, sow, and reap the land European-style, then the English were perfectly entitled to do so, and having mixed their labor with the land, they were then also entitled to take possession of it. Locke, like the English utilitarian and liberal thinkers who would come after him, such as

James Mill and John Stuart Mill, is a good example of the power of ideas, the relationship between political ideas and political practice, and the far-reaching influence they can have on policy making and practice.

The influence of such thinking is evident in the philosopher-jurist Emerich de Vattel's musings on "the discovery of the New World" and "whether a Nation may lawfully occupy any part of a vast territory in which are to be found only wandering tribes whose small numbers can not populate the whole country." For Vattel, "cultivation of the soil [is] . . . an obligation imposed upon man by nature." Therefore, it was against the laws of nature that there are peoples "who, in order to avoid labor, seek to live upon their flocks and the fruits of the chase." Peoples "who still pursue this idle mode of life occupy more land than they would have need of under a system of honest labor, and they may not complain if other more industrious Nations, too confined at home, should come and occupy part of their lands." In Vattel's mind then, it was very much the case that the lazy Amerindians were not properly utilizing the vast lands they merely "roamed over," rather than "inhabited." As such, their "uncertain occupancy" was not "a real and lawful taking of possession," thus making way for Europeans to "lawfully take possession of them and establish colonies in them."[33]

In a similar manner, Pasquale Fiore later argued that "as a matter of principle, colonization and colonial expansion cannot be questioned." For it is entirely appropriate "that civilized countries, in order to find new outlets for their ever increasing activity, need to extend their present possessions and to occupy those parts of the earth which are not of any use to uncivilized peoples."[34] This is a classic argument for imperial expansion based on the expansionist demands of capitalism and its need for new sources of input and new markets.[35] Furthermore, on Lockean principles, Fiore adds "that the earth is in general designed to serve the needs of everyone and that it is not permissible that savages who are unable to derive any profit from natural products should be allowed to leave sources of wealth unproductive, leaving the ground uncultivated."[36]

In time, it was not only the cultivation of land that Europeans thought themselves obliged to undertake, for arguments like the following from the publicist James Lorimer increasingly became the norm. He insisted that "colonisation, and the reclamation of barbarians and savages, if possible in point of fact, are duties morally and jurally inevitable; and where circumstances demand the application of physical force, they fall within necessary objects of war." The responsibility for upholding this obligation did not necessarily fall upon "individual States," rather, Lorimer thought it best undertaken "by a central authority, emanating from the whole body of recognised and recognising States, and that the process of civilisation should thus become the common task of civilised mankind."[37] At the time, this effectively meant the international society of civilized states based on Western Europe, and perhaps, begrudgingly, North America.

In speaking of intervention more generally, in quite prophetic language in terms of contemporary calls for humanitarian intervention, the French publicist Antoine Rougier argued that a "government which fails in its function by ignoring the human interests of the governed commits what may be called a perversion of its sovereignty." In the absence of sovereignty, that is, "when the violations of the law of human solidarity occur in the case of a barbarous or half-civilized State, in which the disorders have a durable and permanent character, the civilized powers must of necessity have recourse to a more energetic method of control— a control adapted to prevent the wrong-doing rather than to repress it or cause reparation to be made." This more energetic method meant that "instead of the right of ordinary intervention there then arises the right of permanent intervention."[38]

The general rationale behind this line of argument and the driving force behind colonial policy are highlighted by another prominent and influential jurist, John Westlake. He argued that "wherever the native inhabitants can furnish no government"—which he claimed was essentially the case wherever Europeans made contact with native peoples— "the first necessity is that a government should be furnished." It was taken for granted that the "inflow of the white race cannot be stopped where there is land to cultivate, ore to be mined, commerce to be developed, sport to enjoy, curiosity to be satisfied." Moreover, if any "fanatical admirer of savage life argued that the whites ought to be kept out, he would only be driven to the same conclusion by another route, for a government on the spot would be necessary to keep them out."[39] This is another example of circular reasoning, wherein the conquest of uncivilized indigenous peoples and the usurpation of their land was inevitable no matter what the rationale.

The idea that organized, well-governed, civilized peoples—such as those of Europe—generally have an advantage over less organized, ungoverned, uncivilized peoples—as most newly discovered natives were characterized—has a long history when it comes to matters of conquest. Continuing the ideas outlined in chapter 3, Hegel further comments that "it arises above all in the *Iliad* where the Greeks take the field against the Asiatics and thereby fight the first epic battles in the tremendous opposition that led to the wars which constitute in Greek history a turning-

point in world-history." He continues, "In a similar way the Cid fights
against the Moors; in Tasso and Ariosto the Christians fight against
the Saracens, in Camoens the Portuguese against the Indians. And so in
almost all the great epics we see peoples different in Morals, religion,
speech, in short in mind and surroundings, arrayed against one another;
and we are made completely at peace by the world-historically justified
victory of the higher principle over the lower which succumbs to a brav-
ery that leaves nothing over the defeated." The conclusion Hegel draws
from this is that "in this sense, the epics of the past describe the triumph
of the West over the East, [the triumph] of European moderation, and
the individual beauty of a reason that sets limits to itself."[40] Furthermore,
as he writes elsewhere, the "inner dialectic" of a civilized society drives
it "to push beyond its own limits and seek markets" in territories that
are "generally backward in industry," in turn generating the "colonizing
activity . . . to which the mature civil society is driven."[41] The conquest
of native peoples, therefore, whether the Amerindians in the Americas,
the Aborigines of Australia, or the various peoples of Africa, is seen as
a largely natural and inevitable series of events that conform to recent
patterns in world-history.

It was not always the case, however, that the supposedly more
civilized triumphed over the less civilized. Adam Smith argues that in
"ancient times, the opulent and civilised found it difficult to defend
themselves against the poor and barbarous nations. In modern times,
the poor and barbarous nations find it difficult to defend themselves
against the opulent and civilized." The reason for this change is that in
"modern war the great expense of firearms gives an evident advantage
to the nation which can best afford the expense; and, consequently, to
an opulent and civilized, over a poor and barbarous nation." Smith's
observations here highlight the almost inevitably violent nature of the
European exportation of civilization to the uncivilized corners of the
world. He adds that the "invention of firearms, an invention which at
first sight appears to be so pernicious, is certainly favourable, both to the
permanency and to the extension of civilization."[42]

Presenting another side to the argument were Enlightenment era
anti-imperialists, such as Johann Gottfried Herder, Denis Diderot,
and Immanuel Kant.[43] As discussed earlier, the last of these thinkers
in particular is often cited as a champion of cosmopolitanism and an
avowed anti-imperialist who believed "colonial conquest is morally un-
acceptable."[44] Kant wrote in *Perpetual Peace* that a state "is a society of
men whom no one else has any right to command or to dispose except
the state itself." Furthermore, "to incorporate it into another state, like

a graft, is to destroy its existence as a moral person, reducing it to a thing." He went on to highlight the dangers that Europe had brought upon itself by engaging in such folly.[45] But the political entities Kant is talking about here are sovereign states exclusively, which brings us to the other side of Kant's thought.

Despite his stance against Europe taking colonial possessions, and claims like Martha Nussbaum's that he promoted "a politics that was truly universal,"[46] Kant's toleration fell well short of a benevolent "live and let live." This is most evident in his rarely discussed *Geography*. David Harvey makes the legitimate point that "the fact that Kant's *Geography* is such an embarrassment is no justification for ignoring it."[47] Today it is difficult to get one's hands on the work, which is somewhat surprising given the cottage industry that Kant's other more recognized works have given rise to. The following passage is drawn from a recent French translation and translated into English by Harvey: "In hot countries men mature more quickly in every respect but they do not attain the perfection of the temperate zones. Humanity achieves its greatest perfection with the white race. The yellow Indians have somewhat less talent. The negroes are much inferior and some of the peoples of the Americas are well below them."[48] George Tatham summarizes his translation of passages from the German thus: "All inhabitants of hot lands are exceptionally lazy; they are also timid and the same two traits characterize also folk living in the far north. Timidity engenders superstition and in lands ruled by Kings leads to slavery. Ostoyaks, Samoyeds, Lapps, Greenlanders, etc. resemble people of hot lands in their timidity, laziness, superstition and desire for strong drink, but lack the jealousy characteristic of the latter since their climate does not stimulate their passion greatly."[49] Elsewhere, Kant argues that ordinarily we "assume that no one may act inimically toward another except when he has been actively injured by the other." And this assumption is "correct if both are under civil law, for, by entering into such a state, they afford each other the requisite security through the sovereign which has power over both." There are, however, exceptions, as Kant's thoughts on the less civilized races led him to claim that "Man (or the people) in the state of nature deprives me of this security and injures me, if he is near me, by this mere status of his, even though he does not injure me actively (*facto*); he does so by the lawlessness of his condition (*statu iniusto*) which constantly threatens me. Therefore, I can compel him either to enter with me into a state of civil law or to remove himself from my neighborhood."[50]

Kant is not so different from the many other advocates of European civilizing missions that are designed to elevate the natives from a state of nature into the realms of law-governed political organization, or civilization. Should this fail, or not go according to plan, the same missions become the more violent missions of conquest that compel the threatening savages to "remove" themselves to a neighborhood where they pose less of a threat to the civilized. Or as Harvey explains it, "What happens when [Kant's] normative ideals get inserted as a principle of political action into a world in which some people are considered inferior and others are thought indolent, smelly, or just plain ugly?" In effect, "it boils down to this: either the smelly Hottentots and the lazy Samoyards have to reform themselves to qualify for consideration under" Kant's supposedly universal ethical code, or in reality it is that his "universal principles operate as an intensely discriminatory code masquerading as universal good."[51]

Robert van Krieken accurately notes that the civilizing process "is accompanied by aggression and violence towards those who remain uncivilized, largely because of the threat they pose to the fragility of the achievements of civilization." Equally, "it is this aggression which then underlies the associated civilizing offensives." In effect, civilization and the "state monopolization of violence in fact involved the *exercise* of that violence on groups seen to lie outside the prevailing standards of civilization."[52] Just as this is evident in Kant, it is also found in J. S. Mill, who makes the point that a "civilized government cannot help having barbarous neighbours." As a consequence, like Kant, he argues that when it does, "it cannot always content itself with a defensive position, one of mere resistance to aggression." After an indeterminate but intolerably wary time, almost inevitably "it either finds itself obliged to conquer them, or to assert so much authority over them" that the uncivilized neighbor gradually falls into a state of dependence on the civilized nation. This, Mill insists, accounts for the history and nature of the relations between the British government and the "native States of India." As he explains it, Britain was never "secure in its own possessions until it had reduced the military power" of neighboring Indian "states to a nullity."[53]

In referring to relations between civilized and uncivilized societies more generally, Mill argues that it is a "grave error" to "suppose that the same international customs, and . . . rules of international morality, can obtain . . . between civilized nations and barbarians." Why? Because the "rules of ordinary international morality imply reciprocity," something that savages and barbarians are deemed incapable of. He contends that the "minds" of the uncivilized "are not capable of so great an effort," and they "cannot be depended on for observing any rules." Furthermore,

Mill adds that barbarous nations have not progressed "beyond the period during which it is likely to be for their benefit that they should be conquered and held in subjection by foreigners." The rationale here is that the "independence and nationality" essential to the development of more civilized peoples is thought a general "impediment" to the uncivilized. Therefore, the "sacred duties which civilized nations owe to the independence and nationality of each other" under the law of nations are not extended to uncivilized societies, for Mill exclaims that "barbarians have no rights as a *nation*." As a result of this legal principle, he insists that the "criticisms, therefore, which are so often made upon the conduct of the French in Algeria, or the English in India," are more often than not based "on a wrong principle."[54]

Edward Said relates a good example of these ideas at work in *Orientalism*, in which he cites Arthur Balfour's speech to the British House of Commons of June 13, 1910, as a spirited yet one-sided and inadequate defense of the British role in Egypt. As noted, it was often the case that European conquerors believed that they knew "exotic" civilizations better than those people themselves and were therefore best equipped to act as their overseer. Balfour similarly insisted, "We know the civilization of Egypt better than we know the civilization of any other country. We know it farther back; we know it more intimately; we know more about it." According to Balfour, the well-being of Egypt and its people was best entrusted to the hands of the British. He continued, "Western nations as soon as they emerge into history show the beginnings of those capacities for self-government." But beyond Europe, "one may look through the whole history of the Orientals . . . and you never find traces of self-government. . . . Conqueror has succeeded conqueror; one domination has followed another; but never in all the revolutions of fate and fortune have you seen one of those nations of its own motion establish what we, from a Western point of view, call self-government. That is the fact." And with that "fact," Balfour believed that he had more than found a good and just cause for British colonial occupation of not just Egypt, but the Empire at large. He further justified Britain's moral case for taking up this responsibility by insisting, "I think that experience shows that they have got under it far better government than in the whole history of the world they ever had before, and which not only is a benefit to them, but is undoubtedly a benefit to the whole of the civilised West. . . . We are in Egypt not merely for the sake of the Egyptians, though we are there for their sake; we are there also for the sake of Europe at large."[55] Thus, as Snow states, by the end of the nineteenth century, it was "established as a fundamental principle of the law of nations that aboriginal tribes are the wards of civilized States."[56] Colonization and the sacred trust of civilization were not only for the sake of Europe, but for the sake of the entire uncivilized world.

The Scramble for Africa

By the late-nineteenth century, the vast majority of the world that was suitable for occupation by Europeans had been laid claim to. All the while, as Cecil Rhodes insisted, "Africa is still lying ready for us [and] it is our duty to take it." The so-called dark continent to the south had been known, traded with, and repeatedly partially conquered and partially occupied for centuries, particularly following Vasco da Gama's discovery of a sea route to India in 1498. But until the late nineteenth century, most of these exploits had been limited to trading ports and settlements along Africa's coasts and in the more arid north. Attention was now turned to the largely unexplored interior, for people such as Rhodes saw it as a "duty to seize every opportunity of acquiring more territory." He insisted, "we should keep this one idea steadily before our eyes that more territory simply means more of the Anglo-Saxon race more of the best the most human, most honourable race the world possesses"; as opposed to the "most despicable specimens of human beings" that presently inhabited much of the continent.[57] Other European colonial powers had similar designs on Africa and had begun to establish footholds there. And so, in 1884–85 the Berlin Conference on Africa was convened by the European powers, initially with the primary intent of easing tensions over issues of sovereignty and trading rights in the Congo basin. As history shows, though, the conference also resulted in the European powers carving up and allotting Africa among themselves. The process behind the divided Africa that emerged from Berlin is described by Michael Doyle as a series of "brilliant exercises in obscure African genealogy and even more fanciful geography." As the European powers staked their claims and counterclaims and argued over borders, all along "explorers, officials, traders, and missionaries went about the slow business of making effective the paper annexations accredited in Berlin."[58]

As with European adventures elsewhere, the idea of the "sacred trust of civilization" was a significant influence on much of European thinking as the imperial powers embarked on the "scramble for Africa."[59] Accordingly, under article 6 of the Berlin Conference's General Act, in "exercising sovereign rights," signatories were mandated "to watch over the preservation of the native tribes, and to care for the improvement of the conditions of their moral and material well-being." To this end, they were required, "without distinction of creed or nation, [to] protect and favour all religious, scientific, or charitable institutions and undertakings created and organised for the above ends, or which aim at instructing the natives and bringing home to them the blessings of civilization." And so it was that, rather generously, "Christian missionaries, scientists, and explorers, with their followers, property, and collections, shall likewise be the objects of especial protection."[60]

Other significant provisions of the Berlin Act include article 34, which required that European nations newly establishing or taking possession of a stretch of African coastline, or assuming "protectorate" status thereof, must notify the other signatory powers of this action for the claim to be recognized. Following it, article 35 held that in order to legitimately possess a stretch of coastal Africa, the occupying nation also had to establish sufficient authority there and in the hinterland to which they were also entitled, "to protect existing rights" and "freedom of trade and transit." In combination, these two articles introduced—or perhaps adapted from the balance of power theory—a "spheres of influence" doctrine and a doctrine of "effective occupation." Together they were supposed to render the conquest and occupation of Africa a less violent and bloody process.

It should not be deduced from this that just because the idea of the sacred trust of civilization had found its way into legally binding documents, that by the late nineteenth and early twentieth century the colonizing process had become a peaceful and nurturing experience. On the contrary, in Africa as elsewhere, it continued to be a violent and bloody one.[61] Hartmann gleefully pointed out in advocating the "eradication" of inferior races and peoples that "one of the best means is the support of missions, which . . . has done more to further this purpose of Nature than all the direct attempts of the white race at the annihilation of savages."[62] And as Charles Henry Alexandrowicz states, by the nineteenth century, "International law shrank into a Euro-centric system which imposed on extra-European countries its own ideas including the admissibility of war and non-military pressure as a prerogative of sovereignty." At the same time, it "also discriminated against non-European civilisations and thus ran on parallel lines with colonialism as a political trend."[63] The African experience of colonialism, particularly in sub-Saharan Africa, was total and brutal. For many colonies-cum-countries, this brutality lasted well into the second half of the twentieth century. Slavery, the legacies of colonialism, and the ongoing struggles for true independence continue to have a lasting impact on the continent and its peoples.

From Colony to Colonizer: The Rise of American Imperialism

The end of the Spanish-American war in late 1898 brought the victor, the United States, to the verge of formally entering the colonial enterprise.[64] Following the war, formal peace arrangements were outlined in the Treaty of Paris and signed by Spain and the United States on December 10, 1898, with Spain ceding its former colonies Puerto Rico, Guam, and the Philippines to the United States, and Cuba gaining its short-lived independence. With the signing of the treaty, opinions in the United States and debate in the Senate were sharply divided over whether it should be ratified, thus thrusting the United States into the company of the imperial nations of Europe as an occupier and enforcer of civility. For many, such as Henry Cabot Lodge, it was a matter of the indignity of being "branded as a people incapable of taking rank as one of the greatest world powers" if the treaty were to be rejected. Among the anti-imperialists was Senator George Frisbie Hoar, who argued that the "Treaty will make us a vulgar, commonplace empire, controlling subject races and vassal states, in which one class must forever rule and other classes must forever obey." On the other side of the argument, Senator Knute Nelson insisted that "Providence has given the United States the duty of extending Christian civilization. We come as ministering angels, not despots." Best of intentions aside, this was the same argument that so many European civilizers, thinking themselves enlightened and benevolent, had put forward as their justification for subjecting native peoples, as they instead went quickly on to become oppressive despots. It is also an early example of one of the more persistent but less admirable tendencies of too many administrations and wielders of US power, the inability or unwillingness to learn from the lessons of the past. Despite the objections, the US Congress ratified the Treaty of Paris on February 6, 1899, fifty-seven votes in favor and twenty-seven opposed. The following day President McKinley signed the treaty and the United States formally became a colonial power, taking possession of the Philippines, Guam, and Puerto Rico, and in the not too distant future, Cuba.[65]

According to Snow, "the entry of the United States into the civilized world as a colonizing power" was marked by the recognition "that domination of distant communities by a Republic was permissible when needful." A further qualifier was that it was only thought permissible when the colonizer "recognized and fulfilled the positive and imperative duty of helping these dominated communities to help themselves by teaching and training them for civilization, as the wards and pupils of the nation and of the society of nations." One of the cornerstones of US policy was purported to be the promotion of "democracy and republicanism," but it was not to be promulgated by destroying the ignorant or the unbelievers. Rather, it was to be achieved "by the positive, helpful, propagandist work of republics in converting to these principles the nondemocratic and nonrepublican part of the world."[66] One cannot help but observe from the vantage point of the early twenty-first century that recent US foreign policy objectives have a familiar ring to them, as will be discussed in following chapters.

Anders Stephanson suggests in *Manifest Destiny* that these general sentiments have their roots as far back as George Washington's first inaugural address, which "typified the mixture of biblical and classical language with its call for the preservation of 'the sacred fire of liberty and the destiny of the republican model of government.' Nothing illustrates the moment better . . . than the many poetic odes to the 'rising glory' of America." As a genre, these odes "combined science and commerce, empire and millennium, into a final vision of 'endless peace' under universal US benevolence."[67] A century and a half later, Woodrow Wilson also saw the United States as having a "special calling or mission." To Wilson, America had been "allowed to see the light and was bound to show the way for the historically retrograde." In fact, it had a "duty to develop and spread to full potential under the blessings of the most perfect principles imaginable." Stephanson suggests that this "vision has been constant throughout American history," but that it has been expressed in two quite distinct manifestations toward the rest of the world. At different times America has held itself up as an exemplar detached from the "corrupt and fallen world," urging others to follow their lead as best as possible. At other times, reflecting Wilson's own position, it has undertaken "regenerative *intervention*" to hurry others along (xii; emphasis in original). But it is the former that has tended to dominate much US domestic and foreign policy, with the occasional outbreak of what is usually misguided adventurism.

Despite the high-minded claims and aspirations, like so many other colonizers, the United States's track record through the twentieth century as a colonial power falls well short of its stated aims and objectives. Nevertheless, by Snow's judgment, the "United States has, in the Philippines particularly, fulfilled this duty of tutorship with a conscientiousness and zeal entitling it to take the lead in any future development of the law of nations in this respect."[68] If one asks the Filipinos for their opinion of the occupying force, however, a far different assessment and account of events is provided.[69]

As history shows, with a newfound confidence in itself as an emerging and substantial power, and a colonial one at that, the United States began to take on the responsibility of developing principles of foreign intervention. In his annual address to the Congress on December 6, 1904, President Theodore Roosevelt outlined what became known as the Roosevelt Corollary to the Monroe Doctrine. Intended to warn-off European powers from intervening too strongly in Latin America, Roosevelt stated that as yet, there is "no judicial way of enforcing a right in international law." Hence, if "one nation wrongs another or wrongs many others, there is no tribunal before which the wrongdoer can be brought." Therefore,

> Until some method is devised by which there shall be a degree of international control over offending nations [that do wrong by international law], it would be a wicked thing for the most civilized powers, for those with most sense of international obligations and with keenest and most generous appreciation of the difference between right and wrong, to disarm. If the great civilized nations of the present day should completely disarm, the result would mean an immediate recrudescence of barbarism in one form or another.

In a perhaps somewhat prophetic statement, given President George W. Bush's recent declarations on the threat posed by "evil" regimes, Roosevelt added, "A great free people owes it to itself and to all mankind not to sink into helplessness before the powers of evil." He continued:

> Chronic wrongdoing, or an impotence which results in a general loosening of the ties of civilized society, may . . . ultimately require intervention by some civilized nation, and in the Western Hemisphere the adherence of the United States to the Monroe Doctrine may force the United States, however reluctantly, in flagrant cases of such wrongdoing or impotence, to the exercise of an international police power.

Not so prophetically, Roosevelt further declared:

> If every country washed by the Caribbean Sea would show the progress in stable and just civilization which with the aid of the Platt Amendment Cuba has shown since our troops left the

island, and which so many of the republics in both Americas are
constantly and brilliantly showing, all question of interference
by this Nation with their affairs would be at an end. Our interests and those of our southern neighbors are in reality identical.
They have great natural riches, and if within their borders the
reign of law and justice obtains, prosperity is sure to come to
them. While they thus obey the primary laws of civilized society
they may rest assured that they will be treated by us in a spirit of
cordial and helpful sympathy.

In regard to these matters, neither did Cuba continue to proceed
along the path the United States had planned for it, nor did the United
States abstain from intervening in the affairs of its southern neighbors.
Somewhat ironically, while the Monroe Doctrine was intended to prevent European intervention and meddling in the Western Hemisphere,
in effect, Roosevelt's corollary served as a justification for American
intervention throughout the same hemisphere and, in the future, beyond. The potential extreme ends the doctrine might be extended to
are plain to see in a statement of 1912 made by Roosevelt's successor,
President William Howard Taft. A one-time governor-general of the
Philippines (1901–1904), Taft, as president, contended that the "day is
not far distant when three Stars and Stripes at three equidistant points
will mark our territory: one at the North Pole, another at the Panama
Canal and the third half the South Pole." The rationale on which Taft
based such claims is reminiscent of Spencer and other racial suprema-
cists, for he added that the "whole hemisphere will be ours in fact as, by
virtue of our superiority of race, it already is ours morally." Taft's math-
ematical shortcomings aside—three halves make more than one whole
hemisphere—the United States's intermittent interventionist and expansionist tendencies are on the record for all to see. Fortunately for the
United States's northern and southern neighbors, Taft lost the support
of Roosevelt, and in turn lost the presidency after one term to the Democratic nominee and committed internationalist Woodrow Wilson—a
man with his own set of ideas about intervention and making the world
"safe for democracy."

Despite Snow's glowing appraisal of the United States's qualities as
a colonial power, John A. Hobson's assessment of the situation comes
closer to the mark. He asserts:

> Here is a country which suddenly breaks through a conserva-
> tive policy, strongly held by both political parties, bound up

with every popular instinct and tradition, and flings itself into a rapid imperial career for which it possesses neither the material nor the moral equipment, risking the principles and practices of liberty and equality by the establishment of militarism and the forcible subjugation of peoples which it cannot safely admit to the condition of American citizenship.

Was this a mere wild freak of spread-eaglism, a burst of political ambition on the part of a nation coming to a sudden realisation of its destiny? Not at all. The spirit of adventure, the American "mission of civilization," were as forces making for Imperialism, clearly subordinate to the driving force of the economic factor.[70]

While this suggests that the United States's primary motivation for venturing into the affairs of empire were economic benefit, this does not necessarily mean that the "mission of civilization" aspect is unimportant in justifying and "selling" such adventurism to domestic constituencies, to the colonized, and even in the minds of policy makers themselves. As has been emphasized, certain ideas, concepts, and language are powerful tools that can at once describe, evaluate, and justify. Indeed, Vitoria undertook a similar exercise and arrived at similar conclusions. And as can be found in Locke, Mill, and others, the two objectives are not necessarily mutually exclusive. Rightly or wrongly, these are charges that continue to be leveled against the United States more than one hundred years on in an era that is marked by both the age of globalization and the "Washington consensus," and the US-led global war on terror(ism).

The "Sacred Trust of Civilization" after Colonialism

As noted in the preceding chapter, the end of the Second World War gave rise and a voice to numerous anticolonial nationalist movements in many of Europe's colonial possessions. The Philippines had already fought for and won its independence, and by the mid-1960s much of sub-Saharan Africa had either done likewise or was on the verge of doing so, with some cases more bloody than others. While there were some colonial powers hanging on to the remnants of empire with a ruthless and bloody tenacity—such as Portugal in southern Africa, perhaps because it represented the last vestiges of a long-dissipated pretence to significant global power—on the whole, colonialism's time was largely thought of as having come and gone.

But that is not to be taken as meaning that the idea of the sacred trust of civilization had also passed its use-by date. On the contrary, in what were settler colonies such as Australia—where there were significant numbers of indigenous peoples to be "administered"—the issue of their "civilizing" continued to be a salient one. For instance, as the Commonwealth Minister for Territories and the chairperson of a Native Welfare Conference, Paul Hasluck, "without apology to either the cynics or the scientists," made the following statement to the Commonwealth Parliament of Australia on October 18, 1951.

> The blessings of civilisation are worth having. For many years past, people have been rather nervous of using phrases about carrying the blessings of civilisation to the savage for fear that they may be accused of cant and humbug. The world today, however, is coming around again to the idea that inevitable change can be made a change for the better. We recognise now that the noble savage can benefit from measures taken to improve his health and his nutrition, to teach him better cultivation, and to lead him into civilised ways of life. We know that culture is not static but that it either changes or dies. We know that the idea of progress, once so easily derided, has the germ of truth in it. Assimilation does not mean the suppression of the aboriginal culture but rather that, for generation after generation, cultural adjustment will take place. The native people will grow into the society in which, by force of history they are bound to live.[71]

Hasluck's statement is not so far removed from one issued almost fifty years later by then World Bank Senior Vice President and Chief Economist Joseph Stiglitz. Outlining what it means to be developed, as recounted at length in chapter 3, he argued that modernization requires a transformation of society away from traditional ways of thinking and dealing with health, education, and manufacturing, to more modern means that increase life chances and productivity.[72] But as is only too evident in the stated intentional outcomes of Hasluck's assimilation policy, Western-style modernization programs raise new issues of imperialism. For instance, Dean Tipps argues that, while not "all modernization theorists are necessarily apologists of American expansionism," nevertheless, it is a theory that tends to necessitate a "form of 'cultural imperialism.'" This is "an imperialism of values which superimpose American or, more broadly, Western cultural choices upon other societies, as in the tendency to subordinate all other considerations (save political stability perhaps) to the technical requirements of economic development."[73] This begs the question: In a supposedly postcolonial or postimperial age, has all that much really changed; have not formal empires and imperialism merely been superseded by some sort of informal imperialism? This question will be explored further in part 3.

In 1910 a French advocate of colonialism by the name of Jules Harmand argued that it was necessary "to accept as a principle and point of departure the fact that there is a hierarchy of races and civilizations, and that we [Europeans/Westerners] belong to the superior race and civilization, still recognizing that, while superiority confers rights, it imposes strict obligations in return." He further contended that the "legitimation of conquest over native peoples is the conviction of our superiority, not merely our mechanical, economic, and military superiority, but our moral superiority." He thought that our dignity and the dignity of the enterprise "rests on that quality, and it underlies our right to direct the rest of humanity."[74]

To this day, much of the general issue of imperialism continues to revolve around claims to superiority and the notion of a hierarchy of civilizations, races, states, or whatever the particular collective might be. Just as important is the persistence of the related idea that humanity universally progresses along an evolutionary path from savagery to civilization. Throughout much of history, Europeans thought of themselves as representing the highest stage of that process, and it was a condition that other peoples at various stages of arrested development were encouraged to aspire to. In more recent times, it is the United States that holds itself up as the shining light of progress and civilization, the epitome of a fully developed, individualist, and commercial and consumer society. And to this day it is still argued by many that "traditional" or "underdeveloped" societies still require a good measure of tutelage to help them achieve a similar state of "development." While much time has passed between the first discoveries of savages which ushered in far-reaching civilizing missions and the more recent identification of traditional societies in need of intervention, much of the accompanying language and the ideas that underpin that intervention remain remarkably familiar.

As with J. S. Mill's "one very simple principle" in *On Liberty*, there are exceptions regarding to whom liberty and full self-government are extended. Then, as now, like children, "backward states of society in which the race itself may be considered at its nonage" are excluded. Although it is unlikely today to be explicitly stated in terms of race, culture often being the preferred label, it remains the case that societies at this stunted stage of development are still thought to "require being taken care of by" civilized developed states and "must be protected against their own actions." And, as Mill insisted, for such "traditional" or "underdeveloped" societies, paternalistic "despotism is a legitimate mode of government . . . provided the end be their improvement, and the means justified by actually effecting that end."[75] The point to reemphasize here is that such thinking was, and still is, driven by powerful descriptive-evaluative concepts such as civilization and associated ideas about universal progress. While the language used by today's institutions, theorists, policy makers, and practitioners has changed slightly from that used by Mill, though not so much as to be unrecognizable, the intent and the implications remain constant. It was suggested in the preceding chapter that standards of civilization are supposed to be a relic of the past, and thus the civilizing missions that accompany them are also thought of as consigned to history. However, as suggested above, and as the following chapters demonstrate, so long as certain hierarchical distinctions continue to be drawn between the different societies that make up our world, and so long as powerful concepts such as civilization continue to be employed for certain means and ends, neither is quite the case.

Part Three: New Barbarism, Old Civilization, Revived Imperialism

Roman, remember by your strength to rule
Earth's peoples—for your arts are to be these:
To pacify, to impose the rule of law,
To spare the conquered, battle down the proud.
Virgil, *Aeneid*

All former empires rose, the work of guilt,
On conquest, blood or usurpation built:
But we, taught wisdom by their woes and crimes,
Fraught with their lore, and born to better times;
Our constitutions form'd on freedom's base,
Which all the blessings of all lands embrace;
Embrace humanity's extended cause,
A world our empire, for a world our laws.
David Humphreys, "A Poem on the Happiness of America"[1]

7

New Barbarism and the Test of Modernity

I do know, that there is no greater necessity for men who live in communities than that they be governed, self-governed if possible, well-governed if they are fortunate, but in any event, governed.

Walter Lippman; quoted in Samuel P. Huntington,
Political Order in Changing Societies

: : :

New Barbarism and the Coming Anarchy

This final section is intended to demonstrate how the influential ideas, concepts, and associated policy tools explored in the preceding sections continue to have a significant impact on contemporary thinking and policy making. The influence of descriptive-evaluative concepts such as civilization and associated ideas like progress, modernization, and development remain far-reaching despite claims that public discourse is overrun by political correctness, rendering such ideas largely unfashionable.

It was noted in the preceding section that R. G. Collingwood was quite adamant that the "dichotomy of civilized and barbarous societies" is outdated.[2] Georg Schwarzenberger made a similar, albeit more ambiguous, statement that the standard of civilization is likewise a relic of the past.[3] Nevertheless, I want to suggest here that news of their demise is premature. It is largely true that anthropological and legal distinctions between civilized and uncivilized societies no longer abound. This in turn has seen the legally codified classical standard of civilization expunged form the annals of international law. That said, given that certain descriptive and normative ideas associated with civilization persist and are regularly applied—labels such as developed, modern, and underdeveloped—so too certain standards or benchmarks continue to include, exclude, and distinguish between the varied members of the states system. This has been the case in the realm of international politics since the post–Second World War anticolonial drive for independence, when the classical standard was thought redundant. As Martin Wight noted, during the subsequent Cold War, the states system remained "divided still concentrically between the world city and the world rural district." Out of this two-tiered states system came "one of the unwritten understandings of the Cold War," that "the peace of Europe shall be warily preserved while the struggle is pursued for influence and position throughout the Third World."[4] In the time since Wight made these observations, the collapse of the longest running communist experiment and the subsequent break-up of the Soviet Union brought the Cold War era to an end. Nevertheless, the notion that there exists a "hierarchy of states" is one that has outlived colonialism and the Cold War and continues to gather adherents.[5] While it is a notion that is interpreted and described in a range of ways, its "key theme is that disparities in capability are reflected, more or less formally, in the [membership and] decision making of the society of states."[6] That is, just as in the past, distinctions continue to be made through the articulation of certain standards or requirements that set the benchmark for inclusion and exclusion from international society.

In exploring the maintenance of a hierarchy within the international states system, this chapter examines some of the claims made about those societies that constitute the different tiers of the system. Many of the arguments concerning the persistence of clear-cut distinctions between the types and quality of societies that constitute the international system are presented, more or less tactfully, in terms of legitimacy. No doubt influenced by earlier discourses of civilization and savagery, some accounts bemoan a return to some form of "essential barbarism" of one description or another, particularly in the postcolonial Third World, where there is a perceived proliferation of tribal or ethnically motivated violence. These arguments have considerable influence in important decision-making quarters. They underpin increasingly strident calls for the en-

forcement of an explicit standard of civilization for the twenty-first century. What follows is a catalog of the more influential of these accounts
and the calls for a reinvigorated standard of civilization to which they
have given rise.

Commentators of various intellectual leanings and allegiances lament
what they variously term the "retreat of civilization," a "return to barbarism," a "descent into barbarism," or the rise of "new barbarism."
Some consider this barbarism to be sporadic or geographically (or culturally) isolated, but nevertheless, they generally feel that it has wider
ramifications in that it threatens to spill over into neighboring regions
and among diasporas. This barbarism justifies the perpetuation of states
or geographical zones being classified as more or less civilized, more or
less barbaric. In large part, many observers attribute this ongoing division of the world to the nationalist, ethnic, or religious dimensions of
the many conflicts that have erupted in various regions of the world following the end of the Cold War.[7] For instance, Eric Hobsbawm claims
that "barbarism has been on the increase . . . and there is no sign that
this increase is at an end." It is a barbarism to which he sees two sides.
First, it is marked by "the disruption and breakdown of the systems
of rules and moral behaviour by which *all* societies regulate the relations among their members and, to a lesser extent, between their members and those of other societies." Second, there is a distinct stalling or
reversal of the Enlightenment project, "namely the establishment of a
universal system of such rules and standards of moral behaviour, embodied in the institutions of states dedicated to the rational progress of
humanity."[8] In a similar fashion, Clifford Poirot harks back to an earlier
period of European division, suggesting that in the Balkans in particular the collapse of communism "produced a return to the sort of barbarism that . . . was latent in late nineteenth century Germany."[9] In the
immediate aftermath of the Cold War's end, Nathan Gardels described
the divergence of two worlds within one: one disintegrating under the
forces of "nationalist resentment" and wounded by the "humiliation of
subjugation, disrespect, and disregard." It is a world that is "also largely
unwired and technologically slow—sunk in the hopeless realm of past
hurts, not future possibilities." The other world, the privileged Western
hemisphere, is said to be affluent, integrated, connected, and interdependent. The depth of the chasm between these two worlds leads him to
pose the question: "Can two civilizations so historically out of sync, the
civilizations of the soil and of the satellite, coexist?"[10]

Some of the most graphic and influential arguments along these
lines have come from journalists describing what they perceive to be

the largely irrational "tribal" violence that stems from some kind of essential savagery, a remnant of incomplete "civilizing missions" of the colonial era. The most prominent of these is Robert Kaplan's widely read *Atlantic Monthly* article "The Coming Anarchy," an apocalyptic Malthusian premonition of the future of our planet and its population, as modeled on the state of affairs in troubled western Africa. He insists that strife-torn Sierra Leone is indicative of "West Africa and much of the underdeveloped world: the withering away of central governments, the rise of tribal and regional domains, the unchecked spread of disease, and the growing pervasiveness of war."[11] In short, the drugs, disease, crime, and violence that Kaplan sees as pervading much of the Nonwestern world renders much of it virtually ungovernable.

To paint a graphic picture of a world sharply divided between the ungovernable and the well-governed, Kaplan draws on the work of environmental security specialist Thomas Homer-Dixon. He asks us to "think of a stretch limo in the potholed streets of New York City, where homeless beggars live. Inside the limo are the air-conditioned post-industrial regions of North America, Europe, the emerging Pacific Rim, and a few other isolated places, with their trade summitry and computer-information highways. Outside is the rest of mankind, going in a completely different direction."[12] Kaplan goes on to add further graphic images to the analogy: "Outside the stretch limo would be a rundown, crowded planet of skinhead Cossacks and *juju* warriors, influenced by the worst refuse of Western pop culture and ancient tribal hatreds."[13] Curiously, the root of Kaplan's pessimism is not too dissimilar to Francis Fukuyama's thinking on the specificities of human rights and human nature; violence is an inherent aspect of human nature, and it is only once "people attain a certain economic, educational, and cultural standard" that this trait abates.[14] Furthermore, the modern state is said to be "a purely western notion," and Kaplan sees no evidence "that the state, as a governing ideal, can be successfully transported to areas outside the industrialized world." All of this leads him to conclude, "We are entering a bifurcated world." More particularly, "Part of the globe is inhabited by Hegel's and Fukuyama's Last Man, healthy, well fed, and pampered by technology. The other, larger, part is inhabited by Hobbes's First Man, condemned to a life that is 'poor, nasty, brutish, and short.'"[15] Such thinking is inevitably influenced by the long history of ideas about civilization, savagery, and barbarism and its relationship to sovereignty and statehood, as outlined in part 1 above. Equally, the powerful imagery of Africa as the "dark continent," with its inherent savagery and virtual ungovernability, not only draws on but perpetuates centuries of European characterizations of the continent and its peoples as largely being beyond the pale of civilization. It would seem that postcolonial optimism was fleeting at best.

In order to distinguish the new wave of post–Cold War "Malthus-with-guns" apocalypticism from earlier Malthusian dystopianism, Paul Richards suggests the moniker "New Barbarism" to accommodate the latest doomsayers. In taking on the "new barbarism thesis," and in particular Kaplan's account of the supposedly "meaningless" nature of the atrocities committed in western Africa and the nihilistic future he envisions for it, Richards presents a thorough rebuttal of new barbarism's general premise. He demonstrates how Kaplan is wrong in attributing a lack of logic to events in West Africa. On the contrary, there is a rationale behind the brutal methods employed there, just as there is elsewhere. Like so many Westerners before him (think Dr. Livingstone, Sir Henry Morton Stanley, or Lord Lugard), Kaplan seems unable to grasp or appreciate the history behind such tactics, given his rather distorted Western lens of what constitutes acceptable methods of warfare.[16] The important point here is that, while Kaplan's view of the world is not a terribly sophisticated or rigorously argued account of events, such views are taken seriously in significant quarters. One of the reasons for this is that Kaplan's view draws on ideas, labels, and characterizations that have been long engrained in the collective psyche. For instance, shortly after its publication, Tim Wirth, a former US Senator and at the time a Clinton Administration Under Secretary of State for Global Affairs, is known to have had copies of Kaplan's article faxed to every American embassy around the globe. The same article is also said to have "so rattled top officials at the United Nations that they called a confidential meeting in New York to discuss its implications."[17]

It seems undeniable that a good many commentators, theorists, policy makers, and politicians adhere to the notion that zones of "barbarism" are reasonably well entrenched in certain corners of the globe. The identification of such disparate states of order and disorder in the international system effectively constitutes a de facto division of the world into "civilized" and "uncivilized" spheres. Wherever there are different standards, or even cultural diversity within an international system, and wherever there is contact between and across the divide(s), we are likely to find standards of civilization or functional equivalents. Given the historical association with strident European expressions of racial and civilizational superiority that led to the violent civilizing missions that became colonialism, the term "standard of civilization" was eschewed in the immediate postcolonial era. However, with the collapse of communism and the absence of a major ideological competitor to capitalist liberal democracy, when combined with emotive accounts of civil strife like that of Kaplan, not to overlook the more recent operating atmosphere since September 11, 2001, much has changed in the international political arena. The short-lived stigma of past injustices has lifted and ushered in ever more calls (implicit and explicit) for renewed standards of civilization. Hand-in-hand with this is the similarly short-lived demise of the old formal hierarchy of human collectives, the explicit distinction once drawn between "savage," "barbarian," and "civilized" peoples. In its stead is an expanded vocabulary of terms that perpetuate the hierarchy of civilization.

Reviving Standards of Civilization

In his account of the classical standard of civilization, written in the last decade of the Cold War, Gerrit Gong suggests that "at least two possible successors may have arisen as new standards in contemporary international society." The first of these is a "standard of non-discrimination or standard of human rights," and the second a "standard of modernity."[18] In noting the first, Gong was building on the work of the Oxford jurist Ian Brownlie, who earlier argued that "by 1965, at the latest, it was possible to conclude that the principle of respect for and protection of human rights had become recognized as a legal standard."[19] As with the origins of its predecessor, the classical standard, Gong notes that the "willingness and ability to protect human rights has become a new standard for Europe." Citing Greece's full admission to the European Economic Community on January 1, 1981, he further notes that the European Human Rights Convention is the only convention of its kind empowered to enforce compulsory jurisdiction over its constituents. With its "ability to guarantee human rights," he contends it "retains something of its old role as shibboleth for those seeking to enter Europe." A case in point is the protracted negotiation process behind Turkey's bid to enter Europe, with one of the stated justifications for the exhaustive process being its poor human rights record.[20] Furthermore, Gong argues that with its "supranational conventions and court systems, Europe appears to be setting a standard of transnationalism in an age" characterized by the strident assertion of national sovereignty. In this respect, despite their protestations that they are not mere imitations, Gong insists that "groups like the Association of South East Asian Nations" effectively remain "quasi-European Communities, just as their nineteenth-century predecessors were labelled quasi-sovereign or semi-sovereign states" during the era of the classical standard of civilization.[21]

The second proposed successor, the "standard of modernity," takes two possible forms: one "vindicates the nineteenth-century assumption that the laws of science, being universal, undergirded a rational cosmology which would bring the 'blessings of civilization' to all." Its primary significance is related in terms of the "standard of living" and "quality of life" that can be achieved universally via the application of science and technology to issues of health, nutrition, and the like, as identified in Joseph Stiglitz's claims of what it is to be "modern." The other shape a standard of modernity might take comes in the guise of a "contemporary cosmopolitan culture," reflecting the "shared values, moral norms, and experiences" given popular expression in terms like the "global village" and "global city." Elsewhere, he refers to this standard as a globalizing or globalized cosmopolitan standard of civilization.[22] In essence, it is the acclaimed universal cosmopolitan civilization outlined and dissected in chapter 4.

Like Wight, Gong was making his observations in the midst of a world that was sharply and bitterly divided between East and West by the tensions of the Cold War. At this juncture in history, there was no agreement on universally shared values and norms, let alone experiences. On the contrary, the Cold War divide served to engender an environment that inhibited the formation or, more accurately, the potential for what some describe as an all-encompassing international society based on shared ideological values and norms.[23] Rather, given the opposing camps' desperation to win over allies at virtually any cost, and their willingness to bring them into the fold regardless of the nature of the regime, the Cold War made for some seemingly odd alliances of convenience. This situation is not unique. One need only look to history to find examples of alliances or mini "international societies" that were made to suit the order of the day; the outwardly incongruous alliances struck up during the Napoleonic Wars are but one example. The end of the Cold War, however, ushered in an era that was acclaimed as the coming of a "new world order" in which capitalist liberal democracy as a system of government had defeated all comers. International politics entered an environment in which the concepts of individual rights, participation in government via some modicum of democracy, and unhindered access to the goods and services available via the marketplace are widely thought of as the aspirational norm.

The "triumph of the West" or, perhaps as significant, the triumphalism of the now dominant and largely unchallenged West (the issue of extremist terrorism aside) allows it to set the agenda in terms of shaping and redefining standards of civilization for the twenty-first century. In Ulrich Beck's terms, "Today, for the first time, the West has *carte blanche* to define and promote universal values."[24] This claim raises two issues, the first of which is less relevant here and relates to issues addressed in preceding chapters: Is it really the first time that the West, or its forerunner, Europe, has claimed the moral high ground? The evidence suggests otherwise. The more immediately significant point is, if the West has to first define and then promote these values among the multitude of societies in the Nonwestern world, are they really universal values at all? Again, the evidence would suggest not. Mehdi Mozaffari notes that the "role of formulating" and setting the principles that constitute a standard of civilization "is incumbent upon the predominant civilization." When the Roman Empire dominated Europe, Rome set the standard; when the balance shifted toward Islamic civilization, Islamic principles dominated; and "when Christianity was predominant, the dominant values were Christian." And so it is today, for Mozaffari asserts, the "global standard of civilization is therefore defined—primarily—by the dominant Western civilization, which happens to be democratic," liberal, and economically globalized.[25] But these are not necessarily values and practices that are shared by all. In essence, a variation of the "might equals right" logic prevails (and it is widely argued to be rightly so): as it is the West that dominates, it is the West that sets the standard.

Standards of Human Rights and Democracy

Given the sustained prominence and ongoing influence of concepts such as civilization, progress, and modernity in the theorizing and practice of world politics, what follows is an account of the twists and turns through the post–Cold War era of the not-quite-defunct standard of civilization in international society. It quickly becomes evident that Gong was not far wide of the mark in proposing two possible successors to the classical standard of civilization, albeit not necessarily as the distinct alternatives he postulates. It is increasingly clear that Gong's two alternatives, the standard of human rights and the standard of modernity, have tended to converge or have largely been conflated.

Perhaps facilitated by the more hospitable post–Cold War environment, John Rawls, one of the twentieth century's most eminent political philosophers, presents a case whereby some measure of human rights norms are the benchmark of the international system. While he makes no explicit reference to standards of civilization as such, it is very much implied in his outline of a legal scheme of interaction between what he calls "liberal" and "hierarchical" societies. Rawls sets out what he sees as the minimum requirements that states must fulfill in order to gain full membership in international society, or in his words, membership in a just and fair "Society of Peoples." He argues that human rights "are a special class of rights of universal application and hardly controversial in their general intention. They are part of a reasonable law of peoples and specify limits on the domestic institutions required of all peoples by that law. In this sense they specify the outer boundary of admissible domestic law of societies in good standing in a just society of peoples."[26]

Following the groundwork prepared by Gong, Rawls, and others, Jack Donnelly is more explicit in his claim that, despite "still common scepticism towards international human rights . . . internationally recognized human rights have become very much like a new international 'standard of civilization.'" Using Kaplanesque language, he pleads that "a standard of civilization is needed to save us from the barbarism of a pristine sovereignty that would consign countless millions of individuals and entire peoples to international neglect." At this "present historical juncture," so far as Donnelly can see, only the ideals and principles contained in "the *Universal Declaration of Human Rights* and the international human rights covenants, [seem] capable of playing such a role." His intent is most clearly expressed in the statement that "human rights represent a progressive late twentieth-century expression of the important idea that international legitimacy and full membership in international society must rest in part on standards of just, humane or civilized behaviour." This is despite Donnelly's acknowledgment that the "language of 'civilization'" carries the "fatal tainting" of "abuses carried out under (and by the exponents of) the classic standard of civilization" and his admission that "internationally recognized human rights share a similar legitimating logic."[27] Like Gong, Donnelly emphasizes the leading role played by Europe—based on the authority of its Commission on Human Rights and the power of its Court of Human Rights—as he takes up the argument that this "fatal tainting" has been overcome by giving "greater emphasis" to the "positive demands of 'civilization.'" In spite of the centuries of oppression and conquest carried out in the name of civilization, as outlined herein, the term is now said to be imbued with a new and enlightened postcolonial meaning by "shifting attention from the exclusive or particularist, intercultural dimensions of 'civilization' to the inclusive and universal." Precisely what the inclusive and universal dimensions of civilization are is not clearly defined. As explained in part 1, claims about universality and universal history have almost always been part and parcel of the discourse of civilization, and therein lays the link to imperial overtones. Nevertheless, with this supposed shift, according to Donnelly, "European human rights initiatives have been missionary in the best sense of that term, seeking to spread the benefits of (universal) values enjoyed at home" (15). One might interpret this as implying that it will inevitably require yet more Western intervention in the "uncivilized" world to save the wretched of the earth from home-grown "barbarism." Setting aside the content of the catalog of human rights, if the (very) broad set of values that Donnelly is referring to here require propagation abroad, then are they truly universal? Might it not be that some are culturally contingent? This is a debate that also surrounds the idea of democracy,[28] which Donnelly tentatively suggests might one day constitute an appropriate standard of civilization. While he laments that "the emerging norm of electoral legitimacy is unlikely to displace power, interest and sovereign equality," he notes that "states today face political costs for [undemocratic] practices that just two decades ago were standard." For instance, "the dramatic upsurge in international election monitoring indicates growing acceptance of an active international interest in national electoral democracy."[29]

Donnelly is not alone in his thinking on the democratic entitlement. A similar line of argument is more explicitly and forcefully pursued by the jurist Thomas Franck, who places democratic governance at the core of his argument that state legitimacy is essential in order to secure full membership in international society. Moreover, it is in Franck's account that we find an explicit link between the role of standards of civilization and democratic peace theory, or the democratic syllogism. Explicitly following Kant, who is claimed to have "discerned a three-way link between democracy, peace, and human rights," Franck maintains "that compliance with the norms prohibiting war-making is inextricably linked to observance of human rights and the democratic entitlement." He insists that the "democratic entitlement is welcomed from Malagache to Mongolia, in the streets, the universities, and the legislatures, not only for its promise of a new global political culture . . . but also because it opens up the stagnant politics, economies, and culture of states to development." He adds that the "problems of underdevelopment can only be addressed successfully in a world of stable, peaceable nations, which in turn presupposes a world of open democracies."[30] Franck follows this by outlining what amounts to a democratic standard of civilization in international society and its accompanying regimes. He insists that "the right of each state to be represented in international organs, and to share in the benefits of international fiscal, trade, development, and security programs should be dependent upon its government satisfying the system's standard for democratic validation." He is even prepared to consider "limit[ing] collective security measures to cases of attack against democratic states." Asking, "Would it help Kuwait to establish democratic internal order if its future protection by UN-authorized collective measures depended upon such a transformation?" he acknowledges that it "is a change in the system's rules which is unlikely to come about in the near future." But he believes "it is worth contemplating."[31]

Franck is clearly of the opinion that some form of democratic governance should be a prerequisite for full admission into the international society of states. He even claims that the human rights-cum-democracy-cum-peace entitlement already "appears with increasing clarity in both normative texts and practice" (137). Whether this has been established as formally or as forcefully as Franck would like us to believe is open to question. Nevertheless, some notable figures have added their intellectual weight to the case for the affirmative. For instance, Amartya Sen contends that in the twentieth century "the idea of democracy became established as the 'normal' form of government to which any nation is entitled—whether in Europe, America, Asia, or Africa."[32] As seen in chapter 4, such "normality" is advocated by United Nations secretaries general, among a host of other world leaders and prominent international figures. Significantly, the promotion of democracy has been a stated principle of successive US administrations. In 1982 President Ronald Reagan announced before the British Parliament "a global campaign for democratic development." This policy carried over into the administration of George H. W. Bush and was restated by Bill Clinton in 1992 while campaigning and again once elected. And the administration of George W. Bush promoted democracy (unevenly) in Afghanistan, Iraq, and the wider Middle East—in much of its rhetoric, anyway.[33]

Conflating Human Rights, Democracy, and Modernity

It was noted above that in his account of the classical standard of civilization, Gong pointed to two possible successors to that standard; a "standard of human rights," and a "standard of modernity."[34] In this sense modernity is widely regarded as being the world in which Westerners of capitalist liberal democracies live, while the rest of the world—parts of the former communist bloc and the Third World or underdeveloped world—is thought of as somehow being backward or premodern. As Firoze Manji and Carl O'Coill describe it, in what they see as a commonplace attitude toward Africa, no longer are Africans regarded as "uncivilized," rather they are now "underdeveloped." But irrespective of what descriptive-evaluative label is applied, it is the "civilized" or "developed" West that "has a role to play in 'civilizing' or 'developing' Africa."[35]

Recalling Stiglitz's account of what it means to be developed, as outlined at length in chapter 3, from this viewpoint modernization, or modernity, is achieved via Western-style development. That is, the transition from underdeveloped to developed entails a shift away from traditional means of subsistence to the application of scientific methods to virtually all aspects of life. Bearing this definition in mind, there is evidence to suggest that the emerging standard of civilization—a measure of human rights and democracy, for argument's sake—conflates Gong's possible alternative standards. At the very least, in the tradition of universal history and modernization theory, there is a belief in some quarters that in the march of human progress, human rights, democracy, and Western-style modernity (or development) are so interdependent that they cannot be separated. For instance, the economic historian David Landes claims that not all cultures "are equally suited to successful high productivity in a material sense." Those not suited he describes as "toxic cultures which handicap the people who cling to them." He contends that, while these people may draw "all the consolation they want" from their culture, in the end "it handicaps them in their ability to compete in a modern world."[36] Such a belief is also found in Franck's "three-way link between democracy, peace, and human rights," from which basis he argues that "the democratic entitlement . . . opens up the stagnant politics, economies, and culture of states to development." He adds that "the problems of underdevelopment can only be addressed successfully in a world of stable, peaceable nations, which in turn presupposes a world of open democracies."[37] In essence, this line of argument contends that the observation of human rights and arrival at modernity via economic development—which means full membership in international society—are all achieved via the medium of democratic government. An integral part of this process is the third component of the aforementioned democratic syllogism, full integration into liberal international financial and trading regimes. All of these, as described in chapter 4, are widely thought to enhance the likelihood of world peace via the expansion of the pacific federation of free-market oriented liberal democracies.

The conflation of human rights, democracy, and scientific modernity is explicitly expressed by Francis Fukuyama and links directly to the idea of progress and his vision of how a universal history of humankind should look. He argues, "Human rights as understood in contemporary liberal democracies . . . comes as part of a larger package." He continues:

> These rights express the moral aspirations and priorities of modern societies, that is, of societies based on the systematic employment of science and technology for the satisfaction of human needs. To seek to export only the human rights part of that package to societies that are either traditional, non-democratic or otherwise based on contrary political principles can often be counterproductive and, if the country in question is powerful, dangerous as well. Human rights can be said to be universal only in a developmental sense: they become explicit aspirations primarily of societies that are both economically and politically developed.[38]

While Fukuyama's recognition or acknowledgement of cultural diversity and contingency is to be welcomed, the conclusions he extrapolates from the existence (if not the value) of difference are not. The assertion that one can only expect to have basic human rights—like the right to life, liberty, and freedom from torture or degrading punishment—observed once a society reaches the point of economic and political modernity is a highly contentious one. Its advocates have yet to provide a convincing case as to why the observation of the general principles of human rights is incompatible with societies that do not resemble or conform to the Western "ideal" model. Equally, a society that chooses not to opt for the peculiarities associated with science and technology and the material world need not be labeled "backward," as something to be looked down upon and in need of saving. Individuals freely opt out of such societies all the time to pursue alternative lifestyles. Being "traditional" may simply be being different. But more to the point, modernization or economic development in the Nonwestern world need not also demand cultural Westernization at the expense of cultural pluralism.

Global Standards of Market Civilization

The issue of economic development brings us to David Fidler's identification and promotion of an economically liberal standard of civilization, which also conflates human rights, democracy, and economically globalized liberal modernity. The direction that Fidler sees the standard as heading toward—if not already at—is what he terms a "standard of liberal, globalized civilization." This standard comes about by what he identifies as parallel or concurrent "standards of civilization and globalization." While the "historical contexts" of the classical standard of civilization and the new standard of globalization are said to be "dramatically different, the substance of the two standards is not." Just as the classical "standard of civilization required the creation and maintenance of certain conditions that would allow Westerners to conduct commerce and trade safely and effectively in non-Western countries," so does the standard of globalization, because the "standards of civilization and globalization share the central objective of improving the conditions of economic interaction between the West and the rest." This effectively suggests that the rationale behind such standards has not changed all that much from the Spanish discovery of the Americas and Vitoria's justifications for Spanish domination. Much like Gong and Donnelly, Fidler sees the classical standard and the standard of globalization as sharing the same origins: the former reflecting the norms of European civilization of an earlier era, the latter reflecting "the norms of the same civilization now expanded beyond the confines of Europe and North America."[39]

In a nutshell, Fidler contends that the "confluence of the standards of civilization and globalization at the end of the twentieth century produces the composite *standard of liberal, globalized civilization*." Reflecting many of the ideas and conflations outlined above, while adding a trade and economic component, the defining characteristics of the new standard of civilization are "(1) respect for basic civil and political human rights; (2) respect for the importance of civil society in domestic and international politics; (3) commitment to democratic governance; (4) commitment to the 'rule of law' domestically and internationally; (5) commitment to free market economics domestically and free trade and investment internationally; and (6) commitment to developing and applying science and technology to political, legal, economic, and social challenges" (409; emphasis in original).

The commitment to economic liberalism and the application of science and technology to virtually all facets of social policy have become cornerstones of international public policy. In this respect, Ronnie Lipschutz has argued that "liberalism—with the individual at its core" effectively represents the "dominant 'operating system' in global politics." Adopting language and terminology reminiscent of the colonial era, he contends that the "principles of economic and political liberalism thus come to represent something like the *jus civile* of the civilized community."[40] To this end they are promoted in various intergovernmental forums and by key international financial and trade institutions, such as the World Bank, the International Monetary Fund, the Bank for International Settlements, and the World Trade Organization (WTO). Not only do these institutions and regimes promote these policy principles, but membership or participation in most of them actually requires the adoption of and commitment to such policy measures. In this regard these organizations all play key roles in setting and enforcing international standards of civilization as they relate to areas such as government transparency and corruption, fiscal and monetary policy, and arbitration and dispute settlement, just to name a few.[41] Particularly since the financial crises that hit Asia, Latin America, and Russia in the mid-to-late 1990s, and lingered on into the following century, a "standard of financial modernity" of sorts now regulates actors and transactions in the international financial system. The primary objective of the standard is to guarantee offshore investments and property, including against nationalization or expropriation, through quarantining domestic operations against corruption and arbitrary interference by promoting transparency and the free exchange of information. As with other standards, the standard of financial modernity distinguishes between what are routinely referred to as "developed economies," "emerging economies," and "nonmarket economies" in the contemporary international financial system. Gong describes the function of the "standard of financial modernity" thus: if states wish to attract trade and foreign investment or maintain credit, in order to be full members of the modern financial and trading system, they "must adapt and adhere to a new standard increasingly ensconced in the international system."[42]

China's recent accession to the WTO provides an example of the workings of the system. Before being granted membership, China had to make concessions on a raft of what were once largely sovereign domestic economic policy issues. These included antidumping and countervailing measures; industrial policy, including subsidies; judicial review, uniform administration, and transparency; product-specific safeguards; quantitative import restrictions, including prohibitions and quotas; sanitary and phytosanitary measures; trade-related aspects of intellectual property rights; and transitional review mechanisms.[43] It is not a straightforward process; there are many hoops to jump through before a country can be said to measure up to the requisite standards of economic and market civilization. In a similar manner, international credit rating agencies, such as Standard and Poor's and Moody's, play a significant role in setting internationally accepted standards of economic governance. Some ratings agencies issue country sovereignty ratings; a poor rating or a rating downgrade can have a significant impact on a country's capacity to attract foreign investment or source commercial loans.[44] It is worth remembering that matters of economics and trade cannot be divorced from other arenas of sociocultural activity. As Anthony Pagden notes, "the world economy, which has come to constitute a new kind of human environment," is also a creation of Western cosmopolitan culture. Therefore, "belonging to that environment demands signing up to its political and social values as well." Furthermore, as outlined in chapter 4, it is difficult to separate Western cosmopolitan culture from its imperial moorings when one considers that "the entire development project," as carried out by the West in the "underdeveloped" Nonwestern world, continues to be motivated by the notions of "humanity" and "benevolence" that justified civilizing missions of old.[45] Not to be overlooked here is the ongoing influence of the concept of civilization and associated ideas such as progress and modernity that are all tied up in this development project.

Similar to Fidler, Mehdi Mozaffari contends that "the rise of a 'global standard of civilization' reflects the transformation of the world" that is currently taking place under the "ongoing process of globalization." In essence, he claims that "globalization has considerably reduced the differences between various [competing] world visions."[46] Much like the standards set forth in other accounts, the "global standard of civilization refers to a set of laws, norms, values, and customs" regulating interactions between "international actors." And like many of those accounts, Mozaffari's account duly recognizes the significance of the earlier classical standard or "European code of conduct," noting that the "global standard of civilization is a product of the European standard of civilization that has been formulated through the centuries in a cumulative fashion" (252). This is to say that influential ideas such as hierarchies of civilization have not really dissipated but have merely evolved and persist in various forms. Reviewing the historical process of globalization and its impact on international law, Mozaffari concludes that "since the beginning of the *Renaissance*, and particularly after the Peace of Westphalia in 1648, only European civilization has succeeded in producing a set of norms and creating various institutions and organizations with a global/universal scope and dimension." By contrast, he contends that the "old civilizations"—which presumably means archaic or premodern civilizations, for they continue to survive—"be they Chinese, Islamic, Indian and so on" have failed to make "any successful attempts at elaborating an alternative 'international law.'" In explaining his conclusions,

Mozaffari attributes the Nonwestern world's "weak contribution to the improvement and correction of dominant norms" to the overall "lack of democracy and the weakness of civil society" (257–58). This criticism seems to be little more than Western triumphalism of the worst kind and a rehashing of the might-equals-right logic when it comes to setting norms and standards. It does not explain the implication that Western-style democracy and civil society are supposed to have been contributing factors to the establishment of international law. This is particularly so given the demonstration in chapter 5 that the foundations of modern international law are rooted in a Europe in which democracy was still largely unknown and civil society nascent at best.[47]

A World Divided after September 11

The most recent and dramatic event to set off further appeals to civilization in defending against barbarism are the terrorist attacks on New York and Washington, DC, of September 11, 2001. Four days after the attacks, a headline on the front page of the *New York Times* implored: "US Demands Arab Countries Choose Sides." In a speech to the Congress on September 20, 2001, US President George W. Bush reiterated, "Every nation, in every region, now has a decision to make. Either you are with us, or you are with the terrorists." He further declared that the terrorists responsible for the attacks on New York and Washington were "the heirs of all murderous ideologies of the twentieth century . . . they follow in the path of fascism, and Nazism, and totalitarianism." Then, being careful to avoid language that characterized the "war on terrorism" as a "clash of civilizations," or a war between the Judeo-Christian Western world and the Islamic East, Bush cast the war as a "fight *for* civilization." Leaving no observer in any doubt as to which side of the battle line the United States occupied, the president confidently added that "the civilized world is rallying to America's side."[48] The casting of the attacks of September 11 as an assault by a "barbarous" terrorist organization and its sponsors on the entire "civilized" world was echoed widely. For instance, pledging his country's "full solidarity" with the United States, then German Chancellor, Gerhard Schroeder, denounced the attacks as not just an attack on America "but also against the entire civilized world." Similarly, on the day after the attacks, *The Independent* of London editorialized that "the terrorists can only truly be said to have won if civilized nations abandon civilized values."[49] This unremitting stance both confirms and reflects the trend that the world is once more explicitly divided into opposing camps. The nations of the world are called upon to identify with and stand by one or the other. Failure to expressly support the civilized United States and its civilized allies means risking being classified by default as an uncivilized sympathizer that gives comfort to barbarous terrorists. In the prosecution of the global war on terror(ism), opting for some form of neutral middle ground or abstaining from taking sides is not an option. For the Bush Administration and its allies, it is as simple as that. There is black and there is white; there are no shades of gray.

Four months after the September 11 attacks, in his State of the Union address, President Bush reiterated that "the civilized world faces unprecedented dangers." Then, claiming to "know their true nature," he declared that regimes like those in power in North Korea, Iran, and Iraq have "something to hide from the civilized world. States like these and their terrorist allies," he continued, "constitute an axis of evil."[50] With these declarations, the die was cast. For the Bush Administration, the world was effectively divided into two spheres: a self-declared "civilized" world fighting for the cause of "good" was at war against an "uncivilized" or "barbarous" sphere of fundamentalist terrorists and their sympathizers said to be acting in the name of "evil." In a similar vein, Ayman al-Zawhiri, al-Qa'ida's second in command, has similarly outlined a "dichotomous struggle for God's sovereignty on earth [which] eliminates the middle ground and sets the stage for a millennial, eschatological battle between good and evil."[51] One cannot help but detect in the choice of language and the ensuing claims an uncanny resemblance and certain parallels with the thirteenth-century standoff between Pope Innocent IV and the Mongol Emperor Guyuk Khan, as outlined in chapter 5.

The characterization of the attacks of September 11 as an "attack on civilization" by "barbarians," and the subsequent casting of the war on terrorism as a war fought on behalf of or for Civilization against some less-than-civilized Other—terrorists and their cohorts—is a significant point. The deliberate choice of language and the image being generated and marketed here is one of a war between the civilized defenders of everything that *Civilization* represents and the barbarous terrorists who oppose it and want to tear it down. (A similar argument, ironically enough, is posited by Osama bin Laden and others on the other side of this Manichean divide.) Right or wrong, this image is not exactly new, and thus the war on terror is not exactly a war like no other—contrary to what we are regularly told by its prosecutors. Rather, as preceding chapters have recounted, history and precedents in which powerful descriptive-evaluative concepts such as civilization and barbarism have been employed have a lot to tell us about the present and how this war on terror is being conducted.

Recall that J. S. Mill claimed that in barbarous and "savage communities each person shifts for himself; except in war (and even then very imperfectly) we seldom see any joint operations carried on by the union of many." And nowhere is the capacity for cooperation more important than in the theatre of war. Mill continues: "Look even at war, the most serious business of a barbarous people; see what a figure rude nations, or semi-civilized and enslaved nations, have made against civilized ones, from Marathon downwards. Why? Because discipline is more powerful than numbers, and discipline, that is, perfect co-operation, is an attribute of civilization."[52] As noted in chapter 6, the idea that organized, well-governed, civilized peoples generally have an advantage over less organized, ungovernable, uncivilized peoples has a long history when it comes to matters of conquest. Key to my purposes here, as indicated by Mill, is that an important aspect of the organizational capability of civilized societies is a capacity for self-defense and an understanding of and willingness to adhere to the "civilized" laws of war making. As noted by the American anthropologist Harry Holbert Turney-High, in his study *Primitive War*, the "war complex fits with the rest of the pattern of social organization, which in turn seems to have a close correlation with victory in technological and economic configurations."[53] The same point was made earlier by Adam Smith in the *Wealth of Nations*.

It has been demonstrated herein and elsewhere that arising out of centuries of encounters with savage and barbarian Others, Europe and the West more generally have proclaimed a strategic and technological capability that remains unrivaled on the battlefield. At the same time, Europeans-cum-Westerners have long laid claim to a monopoly on the moral high ground when it comes to questions of *ius ad bellum* (just causes of war) and *ius in bello* (laws governing the conduct of war).[54] As noted, one of the key criteria in determining a people's or society's approximation to civilization is their conduct in war, a topic worth recalling in light of the claims outlined above in relation to the war on terrorism.

The "military horizon" was a figurative line drawn in the sand to distinguish "civilized" European warfare, which was supposedly organized, constrained, and chivalrous, from the chaotic nature of the undisciplined and opportunistic "primitive" warfare practiced by savages and barbarians. As Turney-High put it, the "military horizon depends . . . not upon the adequacy of weapons but the adequacy of team work, organization, and command." Because of a perceived lack of organization and cooperation, that is, of civilization, and "despite their face-painting and sporadic butchery," uncivilized peoples are thought to fall short of the military horizon. Thus they are "not soldiers" and nor do they "contain the rudiments of the arts of war."[55] Characterizations such as these draw on work like that of José de Acosta's *Natural and Moral History of the Indies*, as discussed at length in parts 1 and 2. The various and varied first-hand accounts emanating from the frontiers of the Americas to Europe carried great influence and are discernible in such celebrated texts as William Robertson's *History of America*, in which he wrote:

> When polished nations have obtained the glory of victory, or have acquired an addition of territory, they may terminate a war with honor. But savages are not satisfied until they extirpate the community which is the object of their hatred. They fight not to conquer, but to destroy. . . . If they engage in hostilities, it is with a resolution to never to see the face of the enemy in peace, but to prosecute the quarrel with immortal enmity. . . . With respect to their enemies, the rage of vengeance knows no bounds. When under the dominion of this passion, man becomes the most cruel of all animals. He neither pities, nor forgives, nor spares. . . . They place not their glory in attacking their enemies with open force. To surprise and destroy is the greatest merit of a commander, and the highest pride of his followers.[56]

The casting of the warfare of Amerindians as savage when compared to that of Europeans or settlers—however inappropriate, misguided, or downright inaccurate the comparison—even made its way into such monumental documents as the United States of America's Declaration of Independence, July 4, 1776. In the Declaration, Thomas Jefferson charges that the British king "has excited domestic insurrections among us, and has endeavored to bring on the inhabitants of our frontiers, the merciless Indian savages, whose known rule of warfare is an undistinguished destruction of all ages, sexes, and conditions." The Declaration is revered to this day, despite such tasteless characterizations and aspersions. Robert Ward claimed of non-Europeans closer to home, "Their wars have always been carried on with *Eastern* barbarity."[57] So it was not just newly discovered natives who were thought to employ uncivilized means of warfare.

One of the critical questions arising out of the "barbarous" or "savage war" thesis was posed by the American jurist Quincy Wright in the wake of the French bombardment of Damascus in October 1925 (Syria being a French mandate at the time). Wright asked: "Does international law require the application of laws of war to people of a different civilization?" To which he immediately replied:

> The ancient Israelites are said to have denied the usual war restrictions to certain tribes against which they were sworn enemies, the ancient Greeks considered the rules of war recognized among Hellenes inapplicable to barbarians, and medieval Christian civilization took a similar attitude toward war with the infidel. An English writer in 1906 draws attention to "the peculiarly barbarous type of warfare which civilized Powers wage against tribes of inferior civilization. When I contemplate," he adds, "such modern heroes as Gordon, and Kitchener, and Roberts, I find them in affiance with slave dealers or Mandarins, or cutting down fruit trees, burning farms, concentrating women and children, protecting military trains with prisoners, bribing other prisoners to fight against their fellow countrymen. These are performances which seem to take us back to the bad old times. What a terrible tale will the recording angel have to note against England and Germany in South Africa, against France in Madagascar and Tonquin, against the United States in the Philippines, against Spain in Cuba, against the Dutch in the East Indies, against the Belgians in the Congo State." Possibly the emphasis, in most accounts of the recent bombardment of Damascus, upon the fact that relatively slight damage was done to Europeans and Americans indicates the existence of this distinction in the moral sense of western communities.[58]

Wright's rueful lament of French heavy-handedness in Syria—which he equates to "a policy of terrorism" (273)—is an exception to the rule when it comes to self-assessments of the West's conduct in its dealing with other civilizations. In response to Wright's assessment of the legality of the French bombing of Damascus—and the broader moral turpitude of which it was symptomatic—Eldridge Colby, a captain in the United States Army, replies, "however Professor Wright may deplore the fact—[there is] one matter which must be faced. The distinction is existent." Colby continues:

> It is based on a difference in methods of waging war and on different doctrines of decency in war. When combatants and non-combatants are practically identical among a people, and

savage or semi-savage peoples take advantage of this identity to effect ruses, surprises, and massacres on the "regular" enemies, commanders must attack their problems in entirely different ways from those in which they proceed against Western peoples. When a war is between "regular" troops and what are termed "irregular" troops the mind must approach differently all matters of strategy and tactics, and, necessarily also, matters of rules of war.[59]

In support of his argument, Colby draws on a range of juridical and military authorities to demonstrate that things could not be any other way. In *The Reformation of War*, Colonel J. F. C. Fuller of the British Army writes: "In small wars against uncivilized nations, the form of warfare to be adopted must tone with the shade of culture existing in the land, by which I mean that, against peoples possessing a low civilization, war must be more brutal in type."[60] The British *Manual of Military Law* states that "the rules of International Law apply only to warfare between civilized nations, where both parties understand them and are prepared to carry them out. They do not apply in wars with uncivilized States and tribes."[61] Colby further argues that the "long list of Indian wars in which the troopers of the United States have defended and pushed westwards the frontiers of America bear eloquent testimony to the unified tribal action in war [with men, women, and children as combatants], and to the almost universal brutality of the red-skinned fighter."[62] While he acknowledges that it is "good to be decent," it is "good to use proper discretion," and it is "good to observe the decencies of international law," he insists that "it is a fact that against uncivilized people who do not know international law and do not observe it, and would take advantage of one who did, there must be something else" (287). Setting aside the dubious point being made here, just two of the obvious problems with this line of argument are: How can one knowingly take advantage of something they do not know exists? And does this give the other party the right to turn their back on a set of laws they claim to abide by and which are held up as a marker of their civilization? Colby concludes that the "real essence of the matter is that devastation and annihilation is the principal method of warfare that savage tribes know" (285). As such, "civilized" Westerners are somehow supposed to be justified in adopting "more brutal" methods as they go about devastating and annihilating the "uncivilized" hordes.

Even prior to September 11, 2001, terrorism was regarded as some form of "new barbarism" or contemporary "savage war." The military historian and theorist Everett Wheeler contends that the "shock of modern terrorism resembles the outrage of seventeenth- or eighteenth-century European regulars in North America when ambushed by Indians who ignored the European rules of the game."[63] (Wheeler is another who is unwilling to acknowledge or fails to recognize that it is impossible to ignore rules that one does not know exist.) Terrorism is denounced for "the shock value of unexpected savagery toward innocent victims [which] creates the impression of civilization teetering on the brink of anarchy" (6). And in the tradition of the "savage war" thesis, Wheeler contends that "conventional warfare requires, above all, open battle and observance of rules, although many remain unwritten," while "terrorism like primitive warfare is unconventional in its most literal sense: the parties in conflict lack a shared set of values." Like the warfare attributed to the savages and barbarians who once roamed the Americas, Australasia, Africa, Asia, the Middle East, and even Eurasia, "above all, terrorists avoid pitched battle and confrontation with regular armed forces, relying on the tactics of primitive warfare—surprise, ambush, deception, and hit-and-run maneuvers" (14–15).

In the immediate aftermath of the September 11 terrorist attacks, the distinguished British military historian Sir John Keegan wrote an opinion piece for *The Telegraph* of London (reprinted in newspapers around the world) in which he proclaims that "Westerners fight face to face, in stand-up battle, and go on until one side or the other gives in. They choose the crudest of weapons available, but observe what to non-Westerners may well seem curious rules of honor. Orientals, by contrast, shrink from pitched battle, which they often deride as a sort of game, preferring ambush, surprise, treachery and deceit as the best way to overcome an enemy." Keegan further claims, "Relentless as opposed to surprise and sensation is the Western way of warfare." He says it is a style of war making that is "deeply injurious to the Oriental style and rhetoric of war making." Keegan goes on to outline what he believes to be the obvious link between the savages of the past and the savages of the present; declaring that "Oriental war-makers, today terrorists, expect ambushes and raids to destabilize their opponents, allowing them to win further victories by horrifying outrages at a later stage."[64] Speaking elsewhere of the al-Qa'ida terrorist network, Keegan suggests that it is "very Islamic, but particularly very Arab—and you can see that it has its roots in Islamic but particularly Arab Islamic style of war-making that goes back to the seventh century AD. The surprise attack . . . victory . . . killing for its own sake."[65] Despite the benefit of greater knowledge and understanding of other traditions and civilizations, these sentiments are not too dissimilar from those put forward by chroniclers of the New World and other "savage lands" based on mere speculation, invention, and the unreliable accounts of travelers.

In contrast, most leaders of the Western world allied against al-Qa'ida and its hosts have been at pains to emphasize that the war on terrorism is not a war against the Islamic or Arab worlds; it is not, they stress, a "clash of civilizations." Likewise, most have gone to lengths—then Italian Prime Minister Silvio Berlusconi being a notable exception[66]—to ensure that they do not portray Islamic or Arabic civilization as inferior to Western civilization. This, however, does not mean that commentators in the West have felt obliged to follow suit. For instance, Keegan concluded his observations on the war on terrorism with the following ill-considered diatribe that recalls ignorant observations of centuries past.

> This war belongs within the much larger spectrum of a far older conflict between settled, creative, productive Westerners and predatory, destructive Orientals. It is no good pretending that the peoples of the desert and the empty spaces exist on the same level of civilization as those who farm and manufacture. They do not. Their attitude to the West has always been that it is a world ripe for the picking. When the West turned nasty, and fought back, with better weapons and superior tactics and strategy, the East did not seek to emulate it but to express its anger in new forms of the raid and surprise attack.[67]

In an "Address to the Nation" from Fort Bragg in North Carolina on June 28, 2005, George W. Bush further underlined the notion that tactics employed by parties to a conflict reflect their degree of civility: the civilized supposedly chivalrous and noble; the uncivilized barbarous and cowardly. Bush declared, "We see the nature of the enemy in terrorists who exploded car bombs along a busy shopping street in Baghdad, including one outside a mosque. We see the nature of the enemy in terrorists who sent a suicide bomber to a teaching hospital in Mosul. We see the nature of the enemy in terrorists who behead civilian hostages and broadcast their atrocities for the world to see. These are savage acts of violence." He went on to state, "We're fighting against men with blind hatred—and armed with lethal weapons—who are capable of any atrocity." These modern savages, like the Amerindians and the Viet Cong before them, "wear no uniform; they respect no laws of warfare or morality."[68] When combined with the mantra that the war on terror

is a "war like no other" against an enemy that is "pure evil" and refuses
to "fight by the rules," the inference is that this war demands tactics and
means of warfare that are necessarily more brutal than might otherwise
be employed.[69]

Terrorists have indeed committed atrocious and criminal acts—as
have those fighting the war on terrorism. For the former, atrocities and
acts of callousness are prescribed policy.[70] Those fighting the war on
terror try to justify or explain away atrocities as isolated incidents committed by a handful of rogue troops, such as the shameful events at Abu
Ghraib prison in Iraq. There have been many other unsavory incidents
and instances, such as widespread "collateral damage," enough to suggest that there is something more going on than isolated incidents of
brutality. It seems that what is really going on is that, in response to
atrocities or acts of savagery by an uncivilized foe, the West, in the
name of civilization and the battle of good over evil, is seeking to justify a turn to any means necessary, including "more brutal" means of
warfare. A war against such an evil and unscrupulous barbarous enemy
cannot be won by conventional means; rather, fire must be fought with
fire—so the argument goes. But perhaps it is more the case that those
more base instincts and "uncivilized" means have been at their disposal
and employed by the West all along. The history of "civilizational confrontations" outlined herein, particularly from the discovery of the
Amerindians on, suggests as much. Powerful descriptive-evaluative
concepts like civilization and its opposites, barbarism and savagery, and
associated dichotomies between the civilized, uniformed, chivalrous
combatant and the opportunistic, treacherous savage have consistently
proven to have violent consequences. In this regard, it is worth recalling
Walter Benjamin's poignantly made point: "There is no document of
civilization which is not at the same time a document of barbarism."[71]

Implications of Standards of Civilization

The conduct of war is only one arena in which serious implications arise
out of the articulation of hierarchical distinctions and the employment
of emotive language that at once describes and in doing so commends or
condemns. More generally, the rationale behind hierarchies of peoples
or societies and concomitant calls for new standards of civilization are
not so different from the logic and language underpinning the classical standard outlined in chapter 5. As Schwarzenberger noted in 1955,
"Once civilisation is related to the basic types of human association,
it is no longer necessary to be content with the mere enumeration and

description of a bewildering number of civilisations. It is then possible to evaluate and to measure individual civilisations in the light of a universally applicable test of the degree of civilisation which any such particular endeavour has attained. This criterion gives the key to understanding whether, and to what extent, democratic States may claim to be more civilised than totalitarian or authoritarian systems."[72]

Although more than fifty years on from Schwarzenberger, contemporary advocates of enforceable standards of civilization go beyond a modicum of democracy in governance as the measure of civilization. In the context set out above, today the term "modern liberal democracy" has much more riding on it than just electoral democracy; it entails issues of human rights, globalized free markets and free trade, and economic and cultural globalization. At the beginning of the twenty-first century, it is increasingly the case that in order to measure up to the revised standard of civilization, a growing set of criteria must be met. While it is an evolving standard, at present for a state to be considered a full member of the international society of civilized states, it must commit itself, at minimum, to the following principles: human rights and the rule of law, representative democracy in governance, economic liberalism and free markets open to international trade and foreign investment, religious and cultural pluralism, and the efficacy of science and technology. If, in the process of becoming globalized and liberalized, a state can claim to promote and adhere to these principles, then it is deemed to have arrived at that exalted condition known as modernity, or more accurately, Western modernity. In contrast, states like Iraq, Afghanistan, Sudan, Somalia, and much of sub-Saharan Africa, among others, are said to have "failed the modernity test." These failed or rogue states are characterized as uncivilized by comparison to the civilized liberal democratic states of the West. Furthermore, for some, the only hope they have of reaching modernity is "with a proper teacher—the west."[73]

It is difficult to deny that there are distinct similarities and parallels between the present and the past in terms of the division of the world into civilized and uncivilized spheres. Not only are there parallels, but the ideas, concepts, and labels that are used to justify and describe the divide, concepts such as civilization (and its opposites) and associated ideas like progress and modernization, remain central to the existing divisions. At the beginning of the twenty-first century, it is readily apparent that many Western theorists and commentators, not to mention political practitioners, continue to hold to a world order characterized by divisions according to what might be called different shades of civilization. Whether this division is characterized as a dichotomy between the "well-ordered" and the "not well-ordered," the "civic" and the "predatory," the "good" and the "evil," or the "civilized" and the "savage" is a matter of semantics. Like the classical standard, the current measure of civilization revolves around the capacity of Nonwestern states to govern and conduct themselves in such a manner that they can engage with the West on its terms, whether that be through trade or at war. At the very least we have reached a point at which "emerging liberal thinking about the international legal order argues increasingly that it is possible to divide the world into zones." As Benedict Kingsbury notes, there exists in practice "a liberal zone of law, constituted by liberal states practising a higher degree of legal civilization, to which other states will be admitted only when they meet the requisite standard." This amounts to the "continuation of recurrent patterns in the history of Western legal thought, traceable, for example, in the sixteenth century European divisions between Christians and infidels, or in James Lorimer's late-nineteenth-century division of the world into a hierarchy of civilized nations, barbarous humanity, and savage humanity." For some, the identification of different zones or levels of civilization is defended as nothing more than a description of existing or emerging political realities. But as argued throughout this book, on another level there is a normative side to the story that promotes the West as the gatekeeper of liberal international order. As Kingsbury suggests, "its many normative advocates see the liberal West as the vanguard of a transformed global legal order."[74]

The theory of different zones or grades of civilization, however they may be drawn, necessitates "differential treatment where the boundaries of the liberal zone are crossed, conferring privileges based on membership in the liberal [or civilized] zone, and setting high barriers to entry." As Kingsbury correctly notes, the "new standard of civilization is defended normatively as the means to promote the advancement of the backward." This is not new. As seen in preceding chapters, it was called on by Vitoria and it served as the justification for the civilizing missions that were undertaken during the colonial era. Moreover, Kingsbury is right to question "why human flourishing is better promoted by the construction of an identifiable 'other,' and 'us' and 'them' from amongst the myriad ways of understanding and classifying the world." The consequence of such constructions "seems likely to be the maintenance of a classificatory system which is itself both an explanation and a justification for those at the margins remaining there for generations"

(90–91). Such a conclusion is evidenced by the fact that the classification of which particular societies or types of societies are deemed "civilized" has barely changed since Lorimer's declaration of over a century ago.

Beyond this there are further consequences that proponents of a division of the world into different spheres or grades of civilization and the enforcement of corresponding standards of civilization either overlook or refuse to acknowledge. As outlined in the following chapter, just as the division of the world into spheres of barbarous, savage, and civilized humanity in the era of the classical standard of civilization led to the violent civilizing missions that became colonialism, so too there are serious implications for how the contemporary "civilized" world intervenes in the supposedly "uncivilized" world—be it in the form of humanitarian intervention, preemptive/preventative war, or under the guise of development assistance—as it is coaxed toward modernity.

8

The "New Realities" of Imperialism

We're an empire now, and when we act, we create our own reality. And while you're studying that reality—judiciously, as you will—we'll act again, creating other new realities, which you can study too, and that's how things will sort out. We're history's actors . . . and you, all of you, will be left to just study what we do.   **Senior adviser to US President George W. Bush, 2002[1]**

: : :

Introduction

This chapter represents a contemporary or updated version of the story outlined in chapter 6, as Europe sought to export civilization to the non-European world through colonial civilizing missions. To that end, it demonstrates how policy making continues to be influenced by a set of ideas and associated labels addressing how domestic and international society should be organized. As demonstrated in the previous chapter, there is a widely held view that a significant number of Nonwestern states fall well short of meeting the ideals of civilization, or what has been termed the test of modernity. Much like the cycle of events described in part 2, the articulation of civilizational hierarchies and enforcement of contemporary standards of civilization similarly lead to imperial-like civilizing missions or policies that are intended to close the gap between the civilized and the uncivilized. These missions come in different shapes and sizes—depending in part on those doing the civilizing and those being civilized—and take various names, from preemptive war to development assistance, yet in essence they are increasingly referred to and recognized as exercises in imperialism. This is an interesting development given that, not so long ago, Michael Doyle suggested that imperialism is "not in the mainstream" of scholarship on world politics.[2] But much has changed in the past two decades or so, and empire and imperialism have returned with gusto to the forefront of thinking about and explaining world politics, particularly since September 11, 2001.[3]

The previous chapter outlined how influential actors in Western political thought and practice continue to divide our world between a sphere of civilized international society made up of fully sovereign states, and a less than civilized sphere of barely legitimate quasi-states. Between the extremes of civility and chaotic savagery or the barbarism of terrorists are a range of states that occupy intermediate positions on the scale, some developing ever more characteristics and institutions that are the hallmark of fully civilized states, others sliding further away from the Western ideal. Those toward the uncivilized end of the scale are said to have failed the test of modernity in that they are collapsed states, rogue states, or something in between or approaching one of these conditions. Either way, they fall short of meeting the requirements for being granted absolute sovereignty by the full and sovereign members of the international society of states. For some commentators on international affairs, drawing a line between these worlds is an exercise in normative theory, but this is also how international politics effectively works in practice. Given that such divisions persist, aspects of contemporary world politics inevitably continue to be regulated by contemporary standards of civilization; employing much of the same language to bar membership, deny sovereignty, and justify intervention. In the colonial era the classical standard was associated with a tendency to intervene in the uncivilized world: to conquer and colonize it, to coax and train it toward civilization. More recently the existence of uncivilized states has not always been a pressing concern for the broader international society (or "international community" as it is often termed in popular public discourse). So long as they posed no immediate threat, they could be isolated, or at least kept at arm's length, and presented a problem only for themselves. But this was a short-lived exception to the long-standing general rule, for the terrorist attacks of September 11, 2001, and the ongoing threat of terrorism have had dramatic ramifications. Once again a similar interventionist tendency has taken hold, and once again, as outlined in the previous chapter, the language of civilization and barbarism is a prominent force behind the justifying rationale of such foreign policies. The fleeting deference to political correctness has been passed over as troubled states are again seen as posing a threat to civilized states, in part because of what they are, but more so because of what they might harbor, the primary concern being terrorists and other rogue elements.

The intervention by the West in the name of security currently being advocated, contemplated, and in some cases undertaken in dysfunctional states and societies is more than just petty interference. There are increasingly loud arguments from both the left and right of politics for a return of some form of imperialism as the best means of dealing with failed and failing states, states deemed incapable of effective self-government, or civilization, by contemporary standards. To suggest, however, that the West is speaking with one voice on this matter would be seriously misleading, for there is considerable debate and disagreement among the Western powers over the where, when, why, who, and how aspects of intervention. Furthermore, all manner of imperialisms have been proposed as the ideal remedy for the affliction of instability and disorder: economic, cultural, liberal, humanitarian, democratic, Western, and American being the more frequently mentioned. The multitude of voices and perspectives swirling around the debate about "new imperialism" has served more to cloud than clarify the issue. As Doyle noted, "in a field in which Hobson warned about the use of 'masked words' to rally bemused intellectual support for brutal policies, in which Lenin feared the impact of jingoistic ideas on a labor aristocracy bought by imperialistic gold, and in which Schumpeter discussed the use of imperialism itself as a 'catchword,' one has to be especially careful not to contribute to obfuscation."[4] Thus, it is worth making at least a modest attempt to define imperialism in the most general of terms in order to corral the discussion herein.

Doyle warns that "empires, like international politics," do exhibit certain traits and regularities across time and space, but we must bear "in mind that broad analogies can yield illusory similarities as readily as illusory differences." That said, "Empires have conventionally been defined in narrow terms as the formal annexations of conquered territory," as is largely described in part 2 above. However, they are also defined more "broadly as any form of international economic inequality, as international power, as international exploitation, and as international order—even as the extension of civilization (presumably that of the conquerors)." This final characteristic is precisely the form of imperial civilizing missions explored in this book. And it is the form of imperialism that is largely the focus of this chapter: the extension of civilization to societies that are deemed less than civilized by modern standards of economic civilization, legal civilization, cultural civilization, and or sociopolitical civilization. Ultimately, Doyle defines empire as "a relationship, formal or informal, in which one state controls the effective political sovereignty of another political society. It can be achieved by force, by political collaboration, by economic, social, or cultural dependence." And "Imperialism is simply the process or policy of establishing or maintaining an empire."[5] Particularly in respect to informal relationships, this definition explains in part why the label imperialism is attached to so many of the unequal power relationships that constitute the vast web of connections in an increasingly globalized world. It is worth reiterating, as argued throughout, that a close connection persists here between ideas and outcomes, or thought and practice: "the imperial *decision-making elite* relies in the short term on the *interpretive elite*—intellectuals, writers, scholars, journalists, and so on—to give it support in the form of perspectives and visions that justify and reinforce its exercise of power."[6]

The first question that must be asked in relation to new imperialism is: Why imperialism at all? The argument generally offered in defense is: "Empires are in the business of producing world order."[7] And at the present juncture in world politics, the United States and its closest allies are convinced that the world is in need of a dose of order—imposed by themselves, of course. Or as Michael Ignatieff has put it, "imperialism doesn't stop being necessary just because it becomes politically incorrect. Nations sometimes fail, and when they do, only outside help—imperial power—can get them back on their feet."[8] Ignatieff claims elsewhere that the "case for empire is that it has become, in a place like Iraq, the last hope for democracy and stability alike."[9] This begs the question: Why is Western intervention (and nothing less than annexation, at that) the last hope for countries like Iraq and Afghanistan? Does this not imply a certain skepticism or doubt in the aptitude or capacity of Iraqis and other Nonwestern peoples to govern themselves? Why is imperialism the only alternative? Why, for instance, cannot internally instigated changes of regime—such as the "velvet," "rose," "orange," and "tulip" revolutions that swept governments from power in the former Eastern Bloc—be legitimate options for failing nations? This question becomes even more relevant when one considers recent declarations by the world's most powerful leader, US President George W. Bush, the man fulfilling the role of the new emperor in overseeing this imperial adventurism.[10] In the recent *National Security Strategy of the United States of America*, the president insisted that there is "a single sustainable model for national success: freedom, democracy, and free enterprise."[11] Such statements cannot help but remind one of the arguments outlined in chapter 4, that a key goal of international public policy is the construction of an international society of states modeled on Western liberal democratic market capitalism and the values and institutions inherent to it.

While it might seem all well and good to seek to impose some kind of order on the international states system, as Charles Maier highlights, "not all orders are alike: some enhance freedom and development; others oppress it." Furthermore, one of the more general issues for separating order and disorder—and that is a good part of what empires are about, policing the frontier—is the problem that "for every greater inclusive effort, there must still be those left outside the expanded walls clamoring to enter, or those not willing to participate vicariously in the lifestyles of the rich and famous—and those, indeed, embittered by the values of secular consumerism (which contemporary empires rely on to generate public loyalties) and imbued with far more zealous and violent visions of fulfillment." As was the case in the colonial era, the "issues of inclusion and exclusion, belonging and estrangement, the peace of empire and the violence it generates despite its efforts, [are] what twenty-first-century politics, certainly since September 11, is increasingly about."[12]

In respect to fundamentalist terrorism directed at the West, Naeem Inayatullah and David Blaney make the point that "the attacks of September 11, 2001," might "not have come as much of a surprise" had more in the West anticipated "that others, at home and elsewhere, have alternative narratives of what we call 'modernization' or 'civilization.'" Moreover "we might have predicted the humiliation, anger, and violent response to what are seen as colonizing projects."[13] This is a good pointer to the ongoing narrative of civilization and associated terms such as *progress* and *modernization* and their consequences more generally. For there is more to the story of new imperialism than that which was ushered in by the post–September 11 wave of enthusiasm for intervention in rogue states. To the contrary, for some time now there have been pundits advocating the imposition of some form of imperialism-cum-colonialism in failed or collapsing states, or what some describe as humanitarian imperialism.

Humanitarian Imperialism

It was noted above that the existence of states on the verge of collapse has not always prompted the international community into action, particularly when there was nothing much at stake in terms of self-interest. But Richard Shweder also makes a fair point in arguing that "with the end of the Cold War, the temptation in the 'West' to engage in 'Enlightened' interventions into other peoples' ways of life has become irresistible, once again."[14] The rationale behind this humanitarian style of interventionism is not so much geo-strategic, as in the manner of Cold War interventions. Rather, it seems to have more in common with the logic of good old fashioned "civilizing missions" that seek to bring the blessings of governance as dictated by the rationale of progress and the moral imperative of civilization. The language used to justify such interventions appears to indicate as much. It is worth noting here that while this temptation might sometimes prove irresistible, this is not to suggest that the West has just stepped in anywhere and everywhere the opportunity presents itself. On the contrary, for one reason or another—determinations of national interest high among them—the Western penchant for intervention is applied rather selectively: too little, too late in Rwanda; belatedly near all-out in the former Yugoslavia; and not at all in Sudan.

An early advocate of such interventionism was Paul Johnson in a 1993 feature article in the *New York Times Magazine*, bluntly titled "Colonialism's Back—and Not a Moment Too Soon." He began by arguing that in much of the Third World, and in Africa in particular, the "the most basic conditions for civilized life have disappeared," primarily because these countries are unable to govern themselves. His claim here is remarkably similar to those made five hundred years earlier about the plight of other savage peoples who were incapable of self-government; his solution similarly reflects an earlier era. The problems and "horrors" of Africa and elsewhere, he insists, are neither a hangover from nor the vestiges of colonialism, and nor are they caused by "demographics or natural disasters or shortage of credit." Rather, they come about because of "bad, incompetent and corrupt government, usually all three together, or by no government at all." This incapacity for self-government, he claims, has made way for the "revival of colonialism, albeit in new form," a trend that "should be encouraged . . . on practical as well as moral grounds." Colonialism, he argues, has a long and proud history; it was "invented" by the Greeks who "founded city-colonies to spread their civilization." The Romans then followed suit, and so on down to the "European powers and then Russia and the United States."[15] While colonialism does have a long history, and colonialists have indeed been proud of their exploits, this is very much a rose-tinted view of colonialism.

Johnson insists that the option of giving these countries more time to right the ship is not prudent; in fact, he thinks it counterproductive. In support of such a claim, he points to Haiti and Liberia—countries that have been self-governing for 200 and 150 years respectively—as "two of the world's most chronically unstable and poorest black states." With "no security for property or even life," he maintains that the "ordinary citizens" of both these countries have "clamored for Western intervention" (43). More than a decade on from this assertion, US intervention in Haiti has proved to be less than effective, which does not auger well for the much larger and more complicated US-led reconstruction missions presently being undertaken in Afghanistan and Iraq. Intervention in Liberia has primarily been left to its West African neighbors under Nigerian leadership (under both dictatorship and democratic governments), one of the very countries Johnson highlights as a basket case and prime candidate for further Western tutelage. Johnson's questionable reading of history and the lasting impact of colonialism aside, even when highlighting recent European interventions in Africa, such as the so-called "rescue missions" of France and Belgium in central Africa, he only sees part of the story. Much of the chaos in the former Belgian Congo can be attributed (either directly or indirectly) to Belgian colonial policy there. In the year following Johnson's article, "Operation Turquoise," France's intervention in Rwanda during the genocide of Tutsis and moderate Hutus, if anything, served to prolong, not bring an end to, the killing.[16] But that is a matter for somewhere other than here. Johnson claims that for more than thirty years now, the "international community has been treating symptoms not causes." Because of the trend toward political correctness, with echoes of J. S. Mill and others, he maintains that there is an unwillingness to admit that "some states are not yet fit to govern themselves." He continues, "there is a moral issue here: the civilized world has a mission to go out to these desperate places and govern."[17] The continuity with the West's history of similar thinking and intervening, as outlined in earlier chapters, particularly chapter 6, is plain enough to see. So is the ongoing use of the language of civilization and its opposites to describe, justify, and judge.

In *The Wrath of Nations*, William Pfaff likewise calls on the language and demands of civilization to draw distinctions similar to those discussed in the preceding chapter between the "modern" Western world and "backward" postcolonial Africa. He argues that the "new elites of the new African nations governed unsophisticated and illiterate populations, agricultural or pastoral peoples living at levels of social and economic development that had characterized Northern Europe centuries earlier." At best, this represents "backwardness by the criteria of social, economic, and political development imposed by contemporary civilization."[18] As a result of their social, economic, and political backwardness, or lack of social, economic, and political civilization, Pfaff concludes that the "immediate future of Africa, including that of majority-ruled South Africa, is bleak, and it would be better if the international community would reimpose some form of paternalist neo-colonialism in most of Africa, unpalatable as that may seem" (158). Unpalatable indeed, but soon thereafter, Ali Mazrui, acclaimed as one of Africa's leading intellectuals, wrote that the "successive collapse of the state in one African country after another during the 1990s suggests a once unthinkable solution: recolonization." As a result of widespread "War, famine and ruin," he thinks that "external colonization under the banner of humanitarianism is entirely conceivable."[19] While recolonization might be one option, one wonders why it will necessarily provide the solution to Africa's problems, unless you are of the opinion that colonialism was successful the first time around in creating the conditions for stable independent indigenous government. But the evidence suggests that its legacy is not so constructive and that it has done far more harm than good. At least in Mazrui's advocacy of recolonization, he concedes that "it is time for Africans to exert more pressure on each other, including through benevolent intervention, to achieve a kind of Pax Africana." Best of all in Mazrui's mind would "be self-conquest. But that," he adds, "implies an African capacity for self-control and self-discipline rarely seen since before colonialism" (18–19). This last statement implies that these attributes—the absence of which was often cited as the justification for colonialism, through which they would be instilled—have in actual fact been suppressed or extinguished by the yoke of colonialism.

Both Michael Walzer and Ignatieff suggested a decade or so ago that a return to old-style trusteeships or protectorates, lasting years if necessary, where the institutions of state and civil society can be nurtured, might be a workable option for failing states. Walzer proposed that two styles of "long-lasting intervention," trusteeship and protectorate, both of which he acknowledges have past associations with "imperial politics, now warrant considering." Under trusteeship, the "intervening power actually rules the country it has 'rescued,' acting in trust for the inhabitants." Under a protectorate system, intervening forces bring "some local group or coalition of groups to power," which is then sustained only defensively to guard against the return of a "defeated regime or the old lawlessness." Despite the best of intentions, as has almost always been proclaimed in matters colonial, it is not too hard to imagine how a powerful intervening force could abuse either of these proposals. In any case, Walzer thought at the time that they might not get the chance to be implemented given the opposition to the return of such practices, both within likely target states and within states best equipped to undertake such occupations.[20] Ignatieff also thought that such options were likely to be untenable in a supposedly postimperial age.[21] But how quickly times have changed, particularly for Ignatieff. Further to his endorsement of imperialism noted above, more recently he has stated that twenty-first century imperialism "is a new invention in the annals of political science." It is what he calls "an empire lite, a global hegemony whose grace notes are free markets, human rights and democracy, enforced by the most awesome military power the world has ever known," the United States.[22] Fitting neatly with the arguments outlined in the preceding chapter, this is a mantra that has been around in post–Cold War development discourse well before the events of September 11, 2001, the trigger which prompts Ignatieff's more recent musings on empire.

It is not an insignificant point that, particularly "since the end of the cold war, nation-building has become a multi-billion dollar business." And as Ignatieff and countless others assert (including the various multilateral government and nongovernmental agencies and the international financial institutions), the "new mantra of this industry is governance." A further argument is made that "economic development is impossible and humanitarian aid is a waste of time," unless the particular country being intervened in "has effective governance: rule of law, fire walls against corruption, democracy and a free press."[23] The central tenets of this general argument are not particularly new; "governance" or "good governance" might be the catch-phrase of the times, but as is argued throughout much of this book, a capacity for competent self-government has long been the measuring stick of civilized society, or civilization. And if a society is deemed incapable of self-government, at present as in the past, there are ready and willing tutors and governance professionals waiting to show the ill-governed how it is done.

Despite his advocacy of such interventionist programs, Ignatieff recognizes that there is a downside, noting, "Nation-building isn't supposed to be an exercise in colonialism, but the relationship between the locals and the internationals is inherently colonial." The United Nations (UN) nation-builders in Afghanistan, for example, "all repeat the mantra that they are here to 'build capacity' and to 'empower the local people.'" This, Ignatieff argues, is supposed to be the "authentic vocabulary of the new imperialism," but as he rightly points out, this vocabulary is also not "as new as it sounds. The British called it 'indirect rule.'" And this is what best describes what is taking place in "Afghanistan: the illusion of self-government joined to the reality of imperial tutelage" (31). If the UN presence engenders a mix of awkwardness, unease, and begrudging necessity among Afghans, then those sentiments are sharpened and multiplied by the US military presence. As Ignatieff states, "the Special Forces aren't social workers. They are an imperial detachment, advancing American power and interests in Central Asia. Call it peacekeeping or nation-building, call it what you like—imperial policing is what" they are doing in Afghanistan (28). While none of this is altogether new, particularly in the case of Afghanistan, the times have changed. Colonial empires of old were in part sustained by the promise to restless subjects—and perhaps just as important, the promise to nervous constituents at home—that independence would one day come, albeit not before a long and exhaustive period of preparation for that day. For today's occupiers under the repackaged "new imperialism, the promise of self-rule cannot be kept so distant."[24] Both the occupied and the citizen's at home want to know what the "exit strategy" is and when it will be implemented. The invasion and ongoing intervention in Iraq is a classic case in point.

Not all left-leaning thinkers support such interventionism. For those opposed, it is still the case that there are no excuses for imperialism, even if it is dressed up as humanitarian intervention on behalf of an oppressed or endangered minority. For instance, following the NATO intervention in Kosovo on what were widely regarded by most observers as humanitarian grounds, Ellen Meiksins Wood pleaded: "Where . . . are the tens, even hundreds, of thousands who used to come out to protest US imperialism, in Vietnam or Central America? Where, in particular is the left? Have people stopped caring, or is it possible that people don't recognize imperialism when they see it?"[25] Perhaps one of these explanations provides the answer, but as explored further below, perhaps it is more the case that many Americans no longer object quite so much to US interventionism abroad, especially in the wake of September 11. Or at least that may have been the case until the intervention in Iraq started to become particularly unpalatable. At the time, Wood's protestations had more to do with the left's long-standing objections to economic imperialism. Her ire had been sparked by one of then US President Bill Clinton's statements on Kosovo to the effect that NATO intervention there had as much to do with advancing US economic interests as it did with saving Kosovars. He is reported to have said, "If we're going to have a strong economic relationship that includes our ability to sell around the world, Europe has got to be key. . . . That's what this Kosovo thing is all about."[26] Maybe it is what the "Kosovo thing" was all about, and maybe it was not; maybe there was more to it. In all likelihood there was a humanitarian side to the story as well; rarely are such issues black and white. If it means that the United States benefits economically while leading the charge in coming to the aid of Kosovars, then shades of gray it is. Whatever the circumstances of this particular case—which few of us will ever know for sure—this leads us to the general issue of economic globalization and its association with Western/Northern/American economic imperialism—depending upon who is laying the charges. It would be misleading, however, to suggest that the United States is the sole developed world beneficiary of expanding economic globalization.

Economic Imperialism

Much has been written about economic imperialism, particularly by those on the left of politics in relation to neoliberal economic orthodoxy and economic globalization, including on the continuities between globalization and earlier manifestations of economic imperialism.[27] While there is little point in repeating or rehashing these arguments, there are a couple of issues relating to standards of economic civilization that are worth highlighting. The first relates to an interesting perspective on World Bank and IMF structural adjustment programs (SAPs), particularly the argument that they represent the modern equivalent of the colonial era's system of capitulations, as discussed in chapter 5. Standards of economic civilization are also at play in the second point, which has to do with how, particularly since September 11, 2001, the spread of free markets has become an imperative of the Bush administration's endeavors to shore up national security. But first, the literature on the successes and failures of structural adjustment programs is vast,[28] and there is no need to rework that ground here. However, in line with points made in chapter 5 concerning the system of capitulations and the right of extraterritoriality, David Fidler's claim that "SAPs represent the capitulations of the era of globalization" is worthy of closer examination.[29]

Before that, it is worth giving a brief outline of what SAPs entail, which is basically the implementation of the "Washington consensus" set of policies outlined in chapter 4. In a nutshell, structural adjustment programs are economic and monetary policies that (usually poorer or indebted) countries must follow in order to qualify for ongoing World Bank and IMF lending, whether it be for particular development projects or simply to service debt. Although SAPs are usually tailored to individual country needs, they are marked by a set of general guiding policy principles or prescriptions. Included in these are the privatization and liberalization of monopoly state enterprises and utilities, the promotion of export-led growth, and the "opening up" of the economy to unfettered foreign investment and "free" market enterprise. SAPs also usually demand that a country devalue its currency (to enhance exports); abolish tariffs, quotas, and any other impediments to imports and exports, including the removal of subsidies and price controls; and deliver a balanced budget, usually through tax increases and lower spending on social services.

Fidler argues that, in effect, "Capitulations and SAPs are kindred in their fundamental message," that those on the receiving end do not measure up to certain standards of economic civilization, or civilization more generally. Furthermore, "SAPs are also kin of extensive 'rule of law' [legal civilization] and 'good governance' [sociopolitical civilization] efforts" presently being pursued apace around the globe. He asserts that "to engage fully in international relations, your behavior has to conform to expectations, policies, and rules established by the prevailing powers" (389). The more specific point is that "SAPs aim to establish some fundamental conditions for economic interaction between the developed and developing worlds;" as was the aim in the colonial era. The primary objective is the reduction of "political, economic, and legal uncertainty and risk for private enterprise" when it comes to "trade and investment between developed and developing countries." Fidler suggests that "because much of what is required under a SAP involves legal changes, SAPs can be seen as a sophisticated form of legal harmonization to facilitate the conduct of global trade and investment." And, as was the case with the colonial era's system of "capitulations, this harmonization is imposed on the developing world country by country, slowly building up a systemic harmonization in international relations," or what was described in chapter 4 as an empire of uniformity. The crux of the issue is that, instead of "a harmonization based on mutual negotiation and compromise, Western forms of economic policy and law have been selected as the basis of harmonization and imposed on the developing countries through SAPs" (399). As Fidler pertinently highlights, this means that to "be considered a globalized state, a developing country subject to a SAP has to admit the inadequacy of its government and society and permit massive interference with its internal affairs." Ultimately, in line with the general argument made in chapter 4, "Just as capitulations laid the groundwork for the universal extension of the

Western system of states and conception of international law, SAPs help lay the groundwork for the universal extension of the processes of globalization."[30]

The second significant development in the realm of economic imperialism, the determination to expand free trade, is something of an oddity. It is not so much an oddity in and of itself, for, as demonstrated in chapter 4 and as has been argued elsewhere, liberals have long seen trading relations and the mutual benefits of commerce as a means of pacifying and civilizing unruly states and their leaders. Rather, what makes it a bit of an oddity are the circumstances and the name under which this single-minded endeavor is pursued: national security. Shortly after the terrorist attacks of September 11, 2001, US President George Bush declared that the "terrorists attacked the World Trade Center, and we will defeat them by expanding and encouraging world trade."[31] The point to be made here is that the relentless pursuit and expansion of trade equals national security would seem to be a rather unusual observation to make in the immediate wake of such a tragically momentous occasion. Or perhaps it is not so odd, for the depth of faith much of the American leadership has in markets is epitomized by then US Federal Reserve Bank Chairman Alan Greenspan's statement: "Markets are an expression of the deepest truths about human nature and . . . as a result, they will ultimately be correct."[32]

The Bush administration's commitment to free trade as a weapon to combat barbarous terrorists and their uncivilized hosts and sponsors is reaffirmed in the US National Security Strategy (NSS), issued a full year after the attacks of the previous September. This suggests that key administration personnel had plenty of time to think the strategy over and that Bush's initial remarks were more than just a spur of the moment sound bite. The document sounds more like a trade policy than a security strategy. In the preface, the president declares: "We will actively work to bring the hope of democracy, development, free markets, and free trade to every corner of the world."[33] Section 6 of the NSS, titled "Ignite a New Era of Global Economic Growth through Free Markets and Free Trade," contains even more specific policy prescriptions to fight terrorism and shore up national security, recommending measures such as "lower marginal tax rates—that improve incentives for work."[34] The same section lays the Bush administration's master plan out in greater detail again. It reads, the "concept of 'free trade' arose as a moral principle even before it became a pillar of economics. If you can make something that others value, you should be able to sell it to them. If others make something that you value, you should be able to buy it.

This is real freedom, the freedom for a person—or a nation—to make a living" (18). Interestingly, this argument borrows from and relies on reasoning similar to that used by Vitoria to justify Spain's presence in the Americas nearly five hundred years earlier.

In speaking of the "exertion of such indirect imperial control," Anatol Lieven argues that "it is possible to draw a rather straight line from the Monroe Doctrine to the Bush Doctrine." Others have made similar imperial arguments about earlier White House administrations, and it would be wrong to suggest that American hegemony or imperialism is simply a child of the war on terrorism. On a related note, Lieven suggests that the difference between the imperialism of the Clinton administration and that of the current Bush administration is that "Clinton packaged American imperialism as globalism." And Clinton, he argues, "was also genuinely motivated by a vision of global order in which America would lead rather than merely dictate." The imperialism of the Bush administration, on the other hand, is an imperialism driven by "the domestic political fuel" of a "wounded and vengeful nationalism." And like any other nationalist sentiment or movement, the administration is "absolutely contemptuous of any global order involving any formal check whatsoever on American action" and expressions of power.[35] Precisely what President Clinton's vision was is difficult to determine, but the assessment of the Bush administration as driven by a brand of neoconservative nationalism married to *laissez-faire* market liberalism seems close to the mark. Commenting on the distinction between the respective administrations' imperial pursuits, Lieven makes the point that, "to put it at its crudest, imperialism, like any other program, can be conducted intelligently or stupidly" (29). How one assesses the respective administrations' imperial pursuits probably depends in large part on one's ideological leanings, but, for many, it remains the case that any imperial enterprise, economic or otherwise, is an objectionable one. Again, it would be misleading to imply that the United States is alone in promoting such neoliberal economic orthodoxy. Like the United States, Europe (European Union member states in particular) and Japan have also profited considerably from the expansion of world trade and unhindered access to developing world markets. As now are China and India in particular.

American Imperialism

I want to turn now to a discussion of US imperialism more generally, or what some refer to as "the empire that dared not speak its name."[36]

In chapter 6 I noted that ideas about American exceptionalism have abounded for centuries, ebbing and flowing with the stridency with which they are projected onto the wider world. As Anders Stephanson notes, there has long existed the idea "that civilization was always carried forward by a single dominant power or people." Moreover, the "historical succession" of the vanguard of civilization "was a matter of westward movement." Hence, it is readily recognizable "why this was an attractive idea. To the American eye, it gave historical sanction to becoming the next great embodiment of civilization."[37] Thus, the baton of standard bearer and forger of civilization was believed to have passed from Europe to America. And at the dawn of the twenty-first century, American power and influence is thought to be greater than ever before. Paul Kennedy has suggested that nothing past or present "has ever existed like this [present] disparity of power" between the United States and its allies and rivals. Influential conservative columnist Charles Krauthammer is even more strident in insisting, "The fact is no country has been as dominant culturally, economically, technologically and militarily in the history of the world since the Roman Empire."[38] Thus, it is the United States which is inclined to take the lead and seeks to set the tone across all manner of spheres: political, economic, legal, military, technological, cultural, and more.

Despite the shift of power and influence across the Atlantic, around a century ago Theodore Roosevelt shunned the idea that there was any comparison between America's recent expansionism and earlier European colonial expansion. He insisted that the "simple truth is there is nothing remotely resembling 'imperialism' . . . involved in the development of that policy of expansion which has been part of the history of America from the day she became a nation." He bluntly declared that there "is not an imperialist in the country that I have met yet."[39] Today, US leaders still protest that there is no American empire. For instance, President Bush stated in a speech to graduating cadets at West Point on June 1, 2002, that "America has no empire to extend or utopia to establish." This statement seems to be at least partially at variance with his promotion of the ideal state as outlined in the NSS. Similarly, when then US Secretary of Defense Donald Rumsfeld was asked by a reporter on April 28, 2003, about empire building, he responded: "We don't seek empires. We're not imperialistic. We never have been. I can't imagine why you'd even ask the question."

Despite the protestations and declarations to the contrary, if Theodore Roosevelt was alive today he would not have such a hard time finding advocates and enthusiasts of American empire. As early as 1989,

Craig Snyder, a former program director of the World Affairs Council of Philadelphia, claimed that, beyond exporting democracy, the United States's "efforts to see a better world in the new century must involve all three components of our [American] social system . . . political, economic, and social."[40] Such policy thinking allows Krauthammer to assert, "People are now coming out of the closet on the word 'empire.'" In a similar vein, Kennedy—who not so long ago was forecasting the decline of US power because of overreach—now claims that the United States is "an empire in formation," not on the slide. Unlike Rumsfeld, he recognizes that "From the time the first settlers arrived in Virginia from England and started moving westward, this was an imperial nation, a conquering nation."[41] On this matter Kennedy would likely argue that Henry Cabot Lodge was closer to the mark than Theodore Roosevelt, when in 1895 he stated, "We [Americans] have a record of conquest, colonization and expansion unequalled by any people in the nineteenth century."[42]

In a *Foreign Policy* article provocatively titled "In Praise of Cultural Imperialism?" David Rothkopf suggests that "the decline of cultural distinctions may be a measure of the progress of civilization." While this might be putting a particularly kind "spin" on the diminution of cultural pluralism, it is harder to argue with Rothkopf's claim that "the United States . . . is the 'indispensable nation' in the management of global affairs."[43] For the time being, this is probably undeniable; the United States is the most significant nation when it comes to maintaining, or upsetting, some semblance of world order. This includes global economic and financial order, which the United States might have limited control over but is nonetheless central to, as evidenced by the so-called subprime mortgage crisis and associated credit squeeze from 2007 to 2008 on. One can even understand the assertion that "it is in the economic and political interests of the United States to ensure that if the world is moving toward a common language, it be English; that if the world is moving toward common telecommunications, safety, and quality standards, they be American; that if the world is becoming linked by television, radio, and music, the programming be American; and that if common values are being developed, they be values with which Americans are comfortable" (45). All of these developments are in the interests of the United States; there is no denying that, just as they would be in the interests of Russia, France, or the Maldives if they were in a similar predominant position. What is arguable is the oft-implied assumption that if something is in the interest of the United States, then it is in the interest of or for the good of the rest of the world. All too often this is not so. Such an assumption is evident in Rothkopf's insistence that "Americans should not shy away from doing that which is so clearly in their economic, political, and security interests—and so clearly in the interests of the world at large." Even more disconcerting is the claim that the "United States should not hesitate to promote its values. In an effort to be polite or politic, Americans should not deny the fact that of all the nations in the history of the world, theirs is the most just, the most tolerant, the most willing to constantly reassess and improve itself, and the best model for the future" (48–49). Here is a direct statement that neatly conforms to arguments outlined in chapter 4 about ideal states and mistaken claims to universality. Beyond the lack of understanding and appreciation of the world beyond the American shore, there are serious problems and dangers inherent in such a statement, whether coming from an American or a citizen of any other nation. Too many conflicts of the past have their roots in similar thinking about civilizational moral superiority and concomitant expansionist aspirations and missionary zeal.

In respect to the Bush Administration and the general idea that empires are about establishing or maintaining order, Sebastian Mallaby argues in *Foreign Affairs* that the "logic of neoimperialism is too compelling for the Bush administration to resist." Why? Because the "chaos in the world is too threatening to ignore, and existing methods for dealing with that chaos have been tried and found wanting." He is presumably referring here to multilateral bodies such as the United Nations. By Mallaby's reckoning, "a new imperial moment has arrived, and by virtue of its power America is bound to play the leading role." Therefore, the "question is not whether the United States will seek to fill the void created by the demise of European empires but whether it will acknowledge that this is what it is doing."[44] Stephen Rosen, Director of the Olin Institute for Strategic Studies at Harvard University, similarly asserts that a "political unit that has overwhelming superiority in military power, and uses that power to influence the internal behavior of other states, is called an empire." But he insists that the United States is not like earlier empires. Because it "does not seek to control territory or govern the overseas citizens of the empire, we are an indirect empire, to be sure, but an empire nonetheless." Rosen adds that if this is the most appropriate description of the United States, then "our goal is not combating a rival, but maintaining our imperial position, and maintaining imperial order."[45]

Despite the absence of terms such as *empire* or *imperialism*, this is essentially the goal that is outlined in the Bush Administration's National

Security Strategy, warding off the "enemies of civilization" to maintain the United States's position at the vanguard of progress. As canvassed in the preceding chapter in relation to the war on terror, Rosen notes that when it comes to waging war in the name of empire, "Imperial wars to restore order are not so constrained" as conventional wars. In imperial wars the "maximum amount of force can and should be used as quickly as possible for psychological impact—to demonstrate that the empire cannot be challenged with impunity" (as seen perhaps in recent US military demonstrations of "shock and awe"). Rosen further argues that during the Cold War, the United States "did not try very hard to bring down communist governments." But he suggests that "now we are in the business of bringing down hostile governments and creating governments favorable to us" (31). Afghanistan and Iraq are examples that might fall into this category, while supporting the less than legitimate and largely unpopular government of Pakistan might be considered the other side of this policy coin.

Rosen's assertion that the United States is an indirect empire is one that some take issue with, arguing that it is behaving ever more like territorial empires of old. Chalmers Johnson, for instance, suggests that, given the number of United States military personnel and bases spread across so many continents, it is time to acknowledge that American democracy has given rise to a "global empire."[46] Such a contention is discernible even in Rosen's insistence that, unlike when conventional wars end and the troops return home, when "Imperial wars end . . . imperial garrisons must be left in place for decades to ensure order and stability. This is, in fact, what we are beginning to see, first in the Balkans and now in Central Asia,"[47] and also the Middle East. This might not equate to usurping full sovereignty, as colonial empires such as Great Britain once did, but installing friendly governments and maintaining an ongoing military presence comes very close to asserting extraterritorial rights or capitulations.

Precisely what the future holds for the American hegemonic exercise-cum-imperial enterprise is difficult to determine.[48] There are those who predicted its downfall even before it was acknowledged as resembling an empire.[49] And there are those who argue that it has yet to peak. Some have looked to history for clues, including the work of Arnold Toynbee, who made a point to the effect that empires do not die by murder, but by suicide. While this does not apply to all of history's empires, it is a point worth remembering nonetheless. Another thought for the Bush administration—and its successors—to keep in mind as it single-mindedly pursues foreign policy goals at the head of the thinnest of "coalitions of the willing" is Finnegan's reminder that "even empires need allies."[50] Bearing these points in mind, Lieven makes a further pertinent assessment: "Given its immense wealth, the United States can afford a military capable of dominating the earth; or it can afford a stable, secure system of social and medical entitlements for a majority of its population; or it can afford massive tax cuts for its wealthiest citizens and no tax rises for the rest. But it cannot afford all three."[51] At the very least, it is highly unlikely that the United States would be able to sustain all three for any significant length of time. And if it decides to forgo social services at home in order to maintain its military domination, then, as Toynbee forewarned, the empire might just crumble from within.

Imperial Urgency since September 11

As noted in the preceding chapter, the threat of fundamentalist terrorism has had a significant impact on the landscape of world politics. The rise of the international terrorist threat has ongoing implications for world order and security in two respects. First, the September 11, 2001, attacks on New York and Washington, DC, and subsequent attacks on Madrid trains on March 11, 2004, and on the London transit system on July 7, 2005, eroded the general sense of security and undermined the notion that the world had settled into a reasonably peaceful post–Cold War "new world order," an order that was overseen and maintained by the worldwide reach of the United States as the sole remaining superpower. Second, those attacks and the general unpredictability of the terrorist threat directly challenged the United States's standing and, as a consequence, have added a new impetus and sense of urgency to the hegemon's traditional task of imposing and maintaining a semblance of world order. The imposition and maintenance of world (or regional) order is regarded as the true mark of any great world power or empire, as is outlined above.

The magnitude of the damage done to the American and other Western nations' psyche by the terrorist attacks of September 11 and the fear of more to come are captured in an address by the late Daniel Patrick Moynihan on the occasion of the 2002 Harvard University commencement. Moynihan was a former four-term United States Senator from New York, ambassador to India and to the United Nations, adviser to four US presidents, and a one-time Harvard professor. He was a man of considerable experience who was widely respected by people of virtually all political persuasions, not the least because he was usually level-headed and chose his words carefully. That is to say, he was unlikely to be mistaken for an ultra-conservative reactionary or a left-wing radical. Nevertheless, he ended his speech by noting that fifty-five years prior, on the same occasion, "General George C. Marshall summoned our nation to restore the countries whose mad regimes had brought the world such horror." Moynihan went on to declare, "History summons us once more in different ways, but with even greater urgency. Civilization need not die. But at this moment, only the United States can save it."[52] This is a statement of considerable gravity. It gives a good indication of how the United States perceives its all-important place in the world—in essence, as the linchpin and guardian of civilization. Moynihan was effectively suggesting that the shadow of terrorism poses a potential threat to civilization equal to or even greater than the specter of Nazism and fascism that loomed large and threatened to envelop all of Europe.[53] Given that Moynihan was aware of what the Nazis had in mind for those that did not fit into their master plan for the world, whereas General Marshall might have been still to discover the true extent of Nazi horrors, this makes Moynihan's declaration a very big call. But for him, and so many other Americans, this time it was the United States under threat and under attack; the much-cherished American and Western way of life more broadly, and all that it represents, was and is being directly challenged.

This brings us to the global war on terror(ism). In the previous chapter I outlined in more detail how the events of September 11 and the all-out war on terrorism that it set in motion have further sharply divided the world between a self-designated "civilized" sphere and an opposing realm occupied by "barbarous" terrorists and their "uncivilized" supporters. For the most part, the states and nonstate actors that make up this uncivilized world are reasonably clear in the eyes of the judges. But there are, or were, societies teetering on the brink that quickly had to decide which side of the line they were on, Pakistan being a good example. As suggested by Moynihan's speech and as clearly spelled out in a number of statements issued by the Bush administration and other Western governments, the terrorist attacks of September 11 and thereafter are characterized as an "attack on civilization" by "barbarians." So too, the subsequent war on terrorism is widely cast and prosecuted as a war between the "civilized" world and an "uncivilized" mix of despots, rogue states, terror networks, and assorted sympathizers. The war on terrorism could just as readily be cast as a war on behalf of the empire of civilization, a war against the enemies of enlightenment, progress, modernity, and civilization. Or to put it differently again, it is a modern-day civilizing war, as strange as that might sound. And as Rosen suggests and as was foreshadowed in chapter 7, such imperial wars are generally fought with unrelenting aggression and minimal restraint to send the message loud and clear "that the empire cannot be challenged with impunity."[54] In a rather forthright manner, Ignatieff contends that, in actual "fact, America's entire war on terror is an exercise in imperialism."[55]

For some, this is not the unwanted or denigrating assessment it once was. A rather disconcerting case in point is that, based on the United States's unchallenged status as the lone superpower, prominent American foreign policy identities are casting the war on terrorism as something like "the new Rome meets the new barbarians."[56] Taking such an analogy further, Krauthammer insists that the United States does not need to dress up its reawakened interventionist penchant in the sky blue berets of the United Nations. He thinks that the "liberal internationalist view of the world, [in which] the US is merely one among many—a stronger country, yes, but one that has to adapt itself to the will and needs of 'the international community'" is absolute "folly." Rather, "America is no mere international citizen. It is the dominant power in the world, more dominant than any since Rome." On this basis, "America is in a position to reshape norms, alter expectations and create new realities. How? By unapologetic and implacable demonstrations of will."[57] But as Lieven presciently points out, at the best of times "imperialism isn't pretty. Add a sense of righteousness and victimhood and it's downright dangerous."[58] Significant here is that once again the ideas of civilization and barbarism are called upon to explain and justify the extension of power to the point of domination or even conquest.

Calls for the United States to be more aggressive in asserting its will come from a range of sources across the political spectrum. Another commentator who does not bother to diplomatically dress up calls for greater US-led Western intervention in states that are thought to be the well-spring of terrorists is Max Boot of *The Wall Street Journal*, who proposes that a "dose of US imperialism may be the best response to terrorism." He contends that "the September 11 attack was a result of insufficient [American] involvement and ambition. The solution is to be more expansive in the US's goals and more assertive in their implementation." According to Boot, "US imperialism—a liberal and humanitarian imperialism, to be sure, but imperialism all the same—appears to have paid off in the Balkans." Therefore, it should work elsewhere too. He believes "Afghanistan and other troubled lands today cry out for the sort of enlightened foreign administration once provided by self-confident Englishmen in jodhpurs and pith helmets." Unlike Krauthammer, Boot at least pays deference to the UN and the broader international community, adding that "the US can lead an international occupation force under UN auspices, with the co-operation of some Muslim nations"—presumably client nations such as Kuwait, or maybe even Indonesia, or Malaysia—which would represent a "huge improvement in any number of lands that support or shelter terrorists."[59] Again, it appears that Boot has a rather rose-colored perspective of the "enlightened foreign administration" once undertaken by the British Empire in far-flung corners of the globe in the name of civilization. And just as the British were once bogged down in Afghanistan, before eventually retreating, as did the Soviet Union later, the US-led intervention there is not proving to be as straightforward or as successful as such language presupposes.

Robert Cooper, a senior British diplomat and shaper of former British Prime Minister Tony Blair's doctrine of internationalist interventionism, is one of the more influential foreign policy gurus to openly advocate the resurrection of some form of imperialism. He insists that the threat posed by terrorism to world order requires "a new kind of imperialism," a "defensive" or "neighbourly" imperialism that is supposedly "acceptable to a world of human rights and cosmopolitan values." The interventions in Afghanistan and Iraq fit this definition. But the neighborhood is virtually boundless, for, in Cooper's words, "Usama bin Laden has now demonstrated for those who had not already realised, that today all the world is, potentially at least, our neighbour."[60] The impact of Cooper's thinking is plain to see in Blair's speech to the British Labour Party three weeks after the terrorist attacks of September 11. The prime minister made it clear that a Blair-led Britain was ready and willing to lead the charge in taking on the "burden" of "reorder[ing] the world around us." With faint echoes of Britain's imperial past ringing in the background, Blair stated his intention of making the "war on terrorism" a "fight for justice" that brings the "values of democracy and freedom to people around the world."[61]

The intent here is not to deny that the terrorist attacks of September 11 and others thereafter are horrendous crimes for which those responsible must be held to account. But waging war or threatening to occupy the numerous countries that the West believes may be host to possible or even potential threats is not the appropriate response. The division in the world intensified by the threat of terrorism and the antiterror war it has spawned is reminiscent of the one so graphically sketched by Robert Kaplan, as outlined in the previous chapter. But whereas Kaplan advocated putting up barriers and isolating the affluent Western world from the spiraling chaos of the uncivilized premodern world, the West is instead being led by a wounded superpower determined to exact what it believes to be a commensurate measure of justice in its "new Cold War on terrorism."[62] And this is effectively what President Bush launched in an address to a joint session of Congress on September 20, 2001, when he declared a "war on terror [that] begins with al Qaeda, but . . . does not end there. It will not end until every terrorist group of global reach has been found, stopped and defeated."[63] To that end, the United States and its closest allies seem determined to intervene, militarily if need be, in the uncivilized world where and whenever they can to eliminate future threats, real or imagined. On that count, Cooper's warning is all too clear, for the majority of states that constitute our world fall outside of the Western articulated boundaries of the liberal democratic "civilized world." Hence, all are at least potential candidates for Western "neighborly imperialism." It seems, however, that reviving some form of imperial rule in the name of national security will only serve to alienate a large percentage of the world's population.

Almost exactly one hundred years prior to Bush's declaration of the global war on terror, when an anarchist named Leon Czolgosz assassinated President William McKinley on September 14, 1901, his successor, Theodore Roosevelt, similarly called for a crusade to exterminate terrorism everywhere. Theodore Roosevelt did not mange to eradicate terrorism and neither will George W. Bush. Terrorism has rarely, if ever, been defeated by waging war on it. It is not solely a military matter; it requires a more holistic approach and a combination of tactics on various fronts: politics, diplomacy, economics, law enforcement, religion, civil society, and more. At best, the war on terror–cum–imperial project that was kicked into gear by September 11 will ensure that the world remains divided and the war on terrorism is an endless one.

Why Imperialism?

Having outlined how our world remains divided, both in theory and practice, between a civilized international society and what is regarded as a more chaotic realm of collapsing quasi-states, this chapter has highlighted some of the consequences of this divide. It has noted that today, as in the past, the descriptive-evaluative language of civilization and barbarism is used to describe, rationalize, and justify these divisive processes and outcomes. As in the past, when a clearly demarcated and closely guarded qualifier led to the civilized conquering and colonizing the uncivilized, so too contemporary standards of civilization have led to similarly motivated interventions. What the classical standard of civilization and its latter day reincarnations have in common is that they render those societies that fall outside of civilized international society less than fully sovereign. Such "rogue," "predatory," or "uncivilized" societies are perceived as a threat to the security, stability, and general well-being of the broader international society of states, particularly immediate neighbors. Hence, as has often been the case throughout much of history, but even more so in an era of globalization when the entire globe is seen as one's own interconnected neighborhood, the civilized world is wont to intervene in the affairs of its less civilized neighbors. The aim in doing so is generally to civilize them and bring them into the empire of civilization. This is not just an altruistic gesture by the self-proclaimed civilized. Rather, they see it as an act of mutual beneficence, bringing security to themselves and civility and all that it entails to the conquered. Whatever one's view of it, ultimately it is an exercise in creating the new realities of imperialism. Whether it is termed humanitarian imperialism, liberal imperialism, or imperialism dressed up as national security is of little consequence.

Michael Ignatieff makes the point that the "moral evaluation of empire gets complicated when one of its benefits might be freedom of the oppressed."[64] There is some truth to this; it does get complicated. But empires have often claimed to be acting in the best interests of those taken under their wing, allegedly freeing them from one burden, oppressor, or another, only to overstay their welcome and take up a similar overbearing role. There is also the consideration that, just as the European civilizing missions of old had the effect of barbarizing the civilizers—or, perhaps more accurately, legitimizing the ruthless and barbaric impulses of the civilized—modern-day civilizing missions or imperial wars have a similar effect. Preemptive or preventative wars against "rogue" states that are largely carried out through aerial bombing and the use of "smart" bombs serve to desensitize, if not dehumanize, those pulling the strings and giving the orders from afar.[65] It also gives rise to sanitized terms such as "collateral damage" in a rather perverse attempt to skirt around the seriousness of what is actually going on. Unconscionable acts such those committed by US troops at Abu Ghraib prison in Iraq only confirm the worst suspicions and fears among these broader concerns.

Karl Marx once wrote, "Hegel remarks somewhere that all facts and personages of great importance in world history occur, as it were, twice. He forgot to add: the first time as tragedy, the second time as farce."[66] Perhaps imperial civilizing missions would be farcical the second time around if there was not so much at stake. The language of new barbarism and old civilization, the return of contemporary standards of civilization, and the concomitant push for a revival of imperialism are yet another case of refusing to learn lessons from history, some of it all too recent history. In the wake of the "discovery" of the New World and for centuries thereafter, either directly or indirectly, civilizing missions led to the virtual extermination of countless thousands of peoples. Whole cultures and ways of life were expunged, and for those that survived it was a largely a life of oppression. A good measure of this was done in the name of expanding civilization's empire. It is not too much of an exaggeration to say that the devastation caused to so many Nonwestern peoples by colonial civilizing missions has become something of a forgotten holocaust. But as Seumas Milne notes, "the battle over history" is rarely exclusively "about the past—it's about the future." And many of "those who write colonial barbarity out of twentieth century history want to legitimise the new liberal imperialism."[67]

It is something of a mystery why so soon after it was relegated by many writers to the pages of history as a retrograde and largely racist concept, imperialism is once again being dusted off and coated in a new sheen of respectability. While it might no longer be portrayed simply as "the white man's burden," it is not too far removed from it, for as John Lloyd argues, contemporary imperialism is largely about "reconstituting a kind of neo-colonial directory of states willing to bear the rich man's burden."[68] Equally difficult to comprehend is the advocacy of economic imperialism, for it is recognized by many to be of more benefit to wealthy than poor nations.

Despite the claims from advocates on the Left, Right, and Center of contemporary Western politics, imperialism need not be the only answer or last hope for that portion of the world experiencing problems of state legitimacy or shortcomings in the capacity to carry out the regular functions of a sovereign nation. There is no reason to suppose that largely nonviolent revolutions, which have overthrown corrupt and tired governments in Eastern Europe and the former Soviet Bloc, could not be enacted elsewhere. The current political climate in Zimbabwe, for example, would appear to make it a prime candidate for a change of regime instigated by its own people: there exists an organized opposition, the country's economy is in virtual free-fall thanks largely to government mismanagement, and there is a widespread perception among the population that recent elections have been anything but free or fair. Given the allegiance of the military and police to the governing ZANU-PF (Zimbabwe African National Union Patriotic Front), a popular uprising might not be absolutely bloodless like many of those in Eastern Europe. But in those too, a previously loyal military correctly gauged the mood of the nation and realized that the time for change had come, opting to stand aside with a watchful eye and let events take their course instead of intervening on behalf of the government.

Mozambique provides another example. It is now pulling itself out of the mire and taking tentative steps along the road to recovery after years of civil war, largely because of the death of one warlord. In Nigeria, it took a fatal heart attack to end the reign of one of its most despicable dictators; soon thereafter the country was holding elections to choose its first nonmilitary leader in years. Admittedly, Nigeria is a less-than-perfect democracy with its share of problems (it is not alone here), but it is endeavoring to make changes for the better and is looking to encourage similar stability among its smaller West African neighbors.

These are just a few examples of what is possible; there is no telling what combination of circumstances can make for sudden and drastic change in the fortunes of what was once a collapsing or pariah quasi-state. And they are all examples of political change that is taking place under domestic momentum for changes for the better, not as a result of direct Western intervention such as imperial occupation in the name of nation building. In most countries there is a widespread desire and willingness among the people, diverse as they might be, to effectively govern themselves in an orderly and just manner, and, equally as importantly, there is no good reason to suppose that there is not also the capacity. Imperialism denies and suppresses both of these virtues. Admittedly, in many countries there are formidable obstacles that will have to be overcome before such transitions can even hope to get underway, not the least of which are serious ethnic and social divisions, many of which are legacies of imperial rule. The concern for some in the West, particularly the advocates of the new imperialism, is that domestically generated political change might not lead to the type of liberal democratic, market capitalist, consumerist states and societies that are held up as the ideal type and the model for all societies.

9

Conclusion: The Future of Intercivilizational Relations

The exemplary history of the conquest of America teaches us that Western civilization has conquered, among other reasons, because of its superiority in human communication; but also that this superiority has been asserted at the cost of communication with the world. Having emerged from the colonialist period, we vaguely experience the need to evaluate such communication with the world; here again, the parody seems to precede the serious version.

Tzvetan Todorov, *The Conquest of America*

. . :

Back to Civilization

In an article written in 1994 after the collapse of communism and with it the Soviet Union, Jay Tolson suggested, "We have come to a peculiar pass." The "we" he is referring to here is not spelled out. It is possible that he means all humanity, but more likely that he is referring to Westerners. The peculiar pass Westerners have supposedly come to concerns the "the ideal of civilization," whereby civilization is claimed to be, "of course, Western civilization." The traits of Western civilization, and hence the ideal of civilization more broadly, are described as a "perhaps unholy" blend of diverse legacies, such as Judeo-Christian religion, "Roman and Germanic law, Hellenic rationalism, Renaissance individualism, Enlightenment progressivism, assorted democratic and parliamentary traditions, and, not least, scientific, technological, and industrial know-how"—many of the same ideas and issues that are discussed and problematized throughout this book. The peculiar pass is said to come about thus:

> Civilization, thought to be on its last legs, staggers through the last round of a long and bloody fight and unexpectedly—*mirabile dictu*—KO's its biggest challenger. Stunned, punch-drunk, and lurching back to its corner, victorious civilization stares into the crowd of its screaming fans and recognizes . . . almost no one. Shaking its head in disbelief, it is not even sure what it is anymore, much less what the stakes of the fight were or what the prize is. The fans don't seem to care, either. They're having fun, though it looks like a violent, savage sort of fun. This, then, is where we stand: in the parking lot outside the arena where civilization scored its last-round stunner, uncertain where to go next.[1]

While this passage sounds rather poetic, particularly to those on the sidelines cheering market capitalist liberal democracy's victory over central planning authoritarian communism, there is much to take issue with. First, many of the characteristics attributed to Western civilization, save perhaps strident individualism, democratic traditions, and the open expression of religious faith, are equally identifiable with communism. At the same time, some of these traits are not exactly unknown to Nonwestern civilizations, as is explained below. As outlined in the beginning of this book and again in chapter 4, the ideological battle between East and West that manifested itself in the Cold War was not a struggle between Western Enlightenment and a tradition of thought with an altogether different intellectual heritage. On the contrary, capitalist liberal democracy and state socialism more accurately represent competing visions of Enlightenment utopianism that both originate from within the same Enlightenment tradition. They are two divergent or rival paths to the utopian end that is universal civilization.

Second, the suggestion that civilization no longer knows what it is or what it represents is a long way off the mark. Since its self-identification or self-realization, civilization has always been quite certain of what it is and equally certain about who or what is not civilization: the conditions of savagery and barbarism that are presented as its opposite, or at times its antithesis. As this book has demonstrated, virtually since its inception as a concept, the ideal of civilization has entailed a capacity for social cooperation, sociopolitical organization, and the requirement that the resulting society be capable of self-government if it is to be regarded as civilized, and hence sovereign. Similarly, the claim that civilization no longer knows what it is fighting for or what spoils go to the victor is equally wide of the mark. This book has shown that some of civilization's greatest fans are triumphalist Western liberals who know exactly what the prize is. The prize is an expanding liberal democratic empire of civilization in which world order is based on the Kantian ideal of "perpetual peace" among an international society of uniform, cosmopolitan states based on the Western model.

The third point to take issue with is Tolson's assertion that civilization has scored a last-round knockout victory over the last of its challengers and is unsure where to turn next. This statement would be erroneous even without the subsequent rise of the international terrorist threat to Western interests and individual well-being. But that threat does serve to highlight just how serious a collective misjudgment has transpired here. As outlined in part 3 herein in particular, the language of civilization and barbarism continues to be deployed to explain and justify a range of actions in world politics in much the same manner that they have been used for centuries, despite the unsavory baggage that comes with it. This particular miscalculation by Tolson, and some Western triumphalists more generally, is the result of a general lack of long-range historical perspective—limited to roughly the period from the late nineteenth century through the end of the Cold War—which in turn causes short-sightedness when looking to the future. As chapters 7 and 8 highlight, the self-appointed guardians of civilization are well aware that the fight goes on; there remains much to do before the goal of universal civilization is achieved and the prize of lasting peace among the uniformly liberal cosmopolitan states of international society is claimed.

The final point to be made about this passage is that the violent, savage fun that Tolson sees the fans of civilization—the civilized, or the representatives of civilization itself—engaging in is not new. It is the same violent savagery that is described above in chapter 6 as the supposedly civilized world attempted to export civilization to what it saw as the uncivilized hordes that populated the world beyond Europe. And it is the same violent savagery that is part and parcel of the global war on terror. Like the character Kurtz in Joseph Conrad's novel *The Heart of Darkness*, the violence that is the imperial civilizing mission cannot help but affect the psyche of the civilized. Or, to put it more accurately, this book has further demonstrated that violent savagery is as much a part of civilization as it is of any other condition; the distinction is that it is deemed legitimate, even necessary, when the violence is committed by the civilized against the uncivilized.[2] To add insult to injury, this violently repressive tutelage is all too often claimed to be for the good of the uncivilized in the name of advancing universal civilization.

It was noted at the beginning of this book that the concept of civilization has been resurrected in the lexicon of the social and behavioral sciences and in the practice of world politics, a point fleshed out in part I and reaffirmed from discussions of contemporary international affairs in part 3. The point was also made that with its revival as a tool of social scientific analysis and policy making, the concept of civilization has all too often been misappropriated, manipulated, or is poorly understood; the passage quoted above is a good indication of this. In an attempt to rectify some of these misunderstandings, this book has demonstrated that from its inception through to the twenty-first century, the ideal of civilization has consistently referred to a peoples' capacity for sociopolitical cooperation and self-government. This is when the concept of civilization is at its most powerful: when it is a value-laden measuring stick as opposed to a descriptive means of distinguishing one collective of peoples from another. (As noted throughout, however, the two uses are not readily separable.) This power, often violent and oppressive, is most clearly expressed in terms of the consequences that follow from the establishment and enforcement of standards of civilization. Throughout much of the last millennium, the thinking common to most civilized societies has held that if a foreign people are incapable of advanced social organization and lack the capacity for self-government, and perhaps thus pose a threat, then they are best governed by a state or institution that does have the capacity to govern and exploit the resources at hand. Or to put it slightly differently, if a society is deemed to be less than fully civilized, then it is also less than fully sovereign, thus making interventions in its affairs by the civilized world legitimate. An earlier version of this particular logic is a factor behind the English oppression of the Irish from the twelfth century on. It extends to the Spanish conquest of the Amerindians following their discovery of the New World in the late fifteenth century. And it is a factor that still dictates the actions of the United States and its allies in Afghanistan and Iraq in the early twenty-first century. This book has demonstrated that the application of this principle has caused much harm to countless peoples and entire cultures or ways of life, much of it in the names of civilization, progress, and, ironically but tragically, peace.

Civilization and Its Others

It is argued that one of the reasons why a growing number of people identify new barbarians among us and thus advocate reinvigorated explicit standards of civilization is because they tend to either overlook or are unaware of the consequences that followed such actions in the past. I would like to believe that it is based on an ignorance of history or an unwillingness to fully learn from the lessons available in it. In this regard, Tzvetan Todorov makes a nice point in noting, "If we are ignorant of history, says another adage, we risk repeating it; but it is not because we know history that we know what to do. We are like the conquistadors and we differ from them; their example is instructive but we shall never be sure that by *not* behaving like them we are not in fact on the way to imitating them, as we adapt ourselves to our new circumstance. But their history can be exemplary for us because it permits us to reflect upon ourselves, to discover resemblances as well as differences: once again self-knowledge develops through knowledge of the Other."[3]

But it may well be that these influential intellectual advocates and powerful policy makers are aware of the oppression and violence that such civilizational hierarchies and standards beget. On those occasions when commentators or policy makers do try to draw some lessons from history in order to address similar issues in a contemporary context, it would seem that too many are picking up the wrong lessons. For instance, in an article titled "Democratic Imperialism," Stanley Kurtz argues that "the problem of a postwar occupation of Iraq is rather more similar to the challenges faced by [J. S.] Mill than to any experience with which Americans are familiar." Kurtz suggests, therefore, that the United States "would do well to learn from" what he sees as "Mill's cautious, thoughtful, and in many ways successful program of democratization" in India. According to Kurtz, "Mill's belief in democratic gradualism was not only realist; it was also liberal."[4] If this is the case, then given the record of the British in India and the role of Mill and his father James in formulating and implementing British imperial policy there, it reflects rather poorly on the idea of realist, liberal democratic gradualism. At the very least, it makes for a less than ideal model to follow in Afghanistan, Iraq, or the wider Middle East. It also conveniently overlooks India's own extensive democratic history prior to British occupation.[5] But more importantly, while the very idea of an appropriate model is problematic, the more fundamental question is that of intervention and imposition in general.

Another of the underlying reasons behind the division of our world into different shades of civilization, or what is described in chapter 7 as the new barbarism thesis, is captured rather neatly by Jean Starobinski. He writes that today the West feels "anxious about the emergence of savage subcultures, about the revival of superstition, about phenomena of intellectual and moral regression that put the tools (and weapons) of civilization into the hands of individuals incapable of controlling them."[6] Robert Nisbet expresses just such an anxiety in his work on the idea of progress when he insists that the West's problem now is that the "official philosophies or religions of those nations which are the most formidable threats to Western culture and its historical, moral, and spiritual values" are daring to modernize and borrow ideas and technologies too efficiently. For Nisbet and others in the West, this represents "one more instance of the capacity for Western skills and values to be exported, corrupted, and then turned against the very West that gave them birth."[7] A classic case in point is the present hysteria over weapons of mass destruction falling into the hands of terrorists and then being turned on their creators, a cruel irony that the manufacturers and stockpilers of these weapons should be thinking about more deeply. Complaints like Nisbet's seem a bit rich when one considers, for instance, how Europeans adopted and adapted Chinese inventions, like gunpowder and the compass, and then put them to extremely damaging and profitable use as they plundered and pillaged the globe.[8] In effect, the general message that this sort of thinking sends to the Nonwestern world is that while it is okay to develop and modernize to a certain extent, do not get too far ahead of yourself—always remember your place in the civilizational hierarchy.

More generally, this line of thinking is highly indicative of the West's propensity for "continental chauvinism," as outlined by Martin Bernal in *Black Athena*.[9] On this general point, Eric Wolf notes:

> We have been taught, inside the classroom and outside of it, that there exists an entity called the West, and that one can think of this West as a society and civilization independent of and in opposition to other societies and civilizations. Many of us even grew up believing that this West has a genealogy, according to which ancient Greece begat Rome, Rome begat Christian Europe, Christian Europe begat the Renaissance, the Renaissance the Enlightenment, the Enlightenment political democracy and the industrial revolution. Industry, crossed with democracy, in

turn yielded the United States, embodying the rights to life, liberty, and the pursuit of happiness.[10]

As Wolf aptly notes and is outlined herein, such a narrow understanding of the genealogy of the Western tradition—and by default other histories and traditions of thought—is misleading, possibly even dangerous. This commonly adopted and often warmly embraced evolutionary schema renders history as some sort of hierarchical "moral success story," a tale of civilization and progress, a race through time in which successive runners pass on the torch of progress and liberty. "History is thus converted into a tale about the furtherance of virtue, about how the virtuous win out over the bad guys" (4–5). In essence, the story runs along lines to the effect that the West has led this particular race from the get go, no other peoples, race, culture, civilization, or whatever has come close to the West in the hierarchy of world civilizations.[11]

The pointlessness of such civilizational chauvinism and scorekeeping is highlighted by simply noting some of the East's influences in the realm of ideas and innovations that were introduced to the West. To take just a few examples, Arabic/Islamic breakthroughs in the field of mathematics, particularly in algebra and trigonometry, were critical early developments in the field and crucial to its development. The term *algebra* actually derives from the title of an important work written in 830 CE by al-Khwārizmī (c. 780–850 CE), *Hisab al-jabr w'al-muqabala*, the *al-jabr* in the title was translated around three centuries later as *algebra*. By the ninth century many Muslim mathematicians and astronomers agreed that the Earth was spherical, not flat, calculating its circumference to a less than 200-kilometer margin of error. The Arabic/Islamic world also made significant advancements in health, hygiene, and medicine. Zakariyya al-Razi's (c. 865–925 CE) medical writings, for instance, were translated, reprinted, and widely available across Europe, representing required reading for would-be Islamic and European physicians alike for centuries. Similarly, Ibn Sīnā (also known as Avicenna, 980–1037 CE), a Persian philosopher and physician—and important interpreter of Aristotle in the Islamic world—wrote a one million word *Canon of Medicine* which was a key medical and physiology text for centuries in both the Middle East and Europe through twelfth-century Latin translations. And it was a tenth-century Muslim surgeon named al-Zahrawi (930–1013 CE) who introduced to the world many of the surgical instruments that have become commonplace, including the scalpel and forceps. In 1206 a Muslim engineer named al-Jazari authored the *Book of Knowledge of Ingenious Mechanical Devices*, in which he introduced a number of inventions, from combination locks to water clocks, including none more important than the crankshaft. The modern check also comes to us from the East; it is thought that in the ninth century a businessman from what we now call the Middle East could cash a check in China, drawing on his bank in Baghdad. These are just some of the ideas and inventions that have their origins in the East. Added to these are things such as quilting and carpets, gunpowder and the compass, and others from chess to the three-course meal.[12]

When it comes to the much cherished Western values that are supposedly being misappropriated and turned against the West, the story is also not necessarily as cut-and-dried as we have been led to believe. For instance, let us take a concept that is thought of as central to the Western tradition of political thought and sociopolitical progress: democracy. At present, as conflict rages in Afghanistan and Iraq, and as tensions simmer elsewhere, no concept is more topical and contentious than democracy and democratization, particularly exporting democracy and imposing it in places and cultures that are thought to be totally alien to the basic principles of democracy. Perhaps more than any other idea or concept, democracy is regarded by many to be a uniquely and exclusively Western idea. But is this really the case?

The Western conception of democracy tends to emphasize the importance of democratic institutions and processes largely associated with Western liberal democracies, such as those in Europe, North America, and Australasia. But democratic-like processes and practices are also to be found in the histories of many Nonwestern peoples and places. Let us begin with a little background to illustrate that democracy and the principles underlying the concept are not necessarily exclusively a Western invention. The idea and practice of democracy is widely thought to have its roots in ancient Greece around two-and-half millennia ago (c. sixth century BCE). The oldest and best known of the Greek democracies is ancient Athens, a city-state something like modern Singapore but considerably smaller. Recent discoveries, however, suggest that some rudimentary form of democracy or predemocracy might have first emerged centuries earlier in the Late Bronze Age (c. 1600–1100 BCE) around Mycenae in the northeast Peloponnese. Furthermore, relatively recent archaeological explorations suggest that the ancient Greeks might not have been the first to make use of self-governing assemblies. That honor, rather, might actually belong to the peoples of the East who once occupied the land that is modern-day Iran and Iraq. From there these early or predemocratic ideas of decision making by discussion spread toward the east and the Indian subcontinent, and westward to Phoenician port cities such as Byblos and Sidon before arriving in ancient Athens.[13] The point to be made here is that the ideas and ideals behind democracy are not the sole preserve of the Western world. On the contrary, they have a long and prominent history in the East, the West, and beyond; with undoubtedly more than a little borrowing taking place between one and all. A renewed understanding of the history and origins of democracy further undermines the persistent contention in the history of Western thought that Nonwestern peoples are sociopolitically retarded and incapable of self-government or civilization.

One of the inhibiting factors in giving the Nonwestern tradition of predemocracy the attention it warrants is that scholarship tends to focus on the state as the foremost evolutionary political institution, as Hegel in particular, among others (contemporary scholars included), painfully makes clear. There is a saying, however, that all politics is local, and this is certainly the case for much of human history. Steven Muhlberger and Phil Paine make the point that the vast majority of "human government has been a matter of councils and assemblies," often incorporating a reasonably significant proportion of the community, which adopts a "surprising degree of democratic procedure." To put it another way, "humanity possesses a long history of government by discussion, in which groups of people sharing common interests make decisions that affect their lives through debate and consultation, and often enough by voting." Of all the human beings who have ever walked the Earth, a large majority of them have lived in small agricultural villages. And of these untold millions of agricultural communities, both past and present, most "have employed some democratic techniques of government" in their decision making and in choosing leaders. No matter what period or place in history one looks at, virtually all villages across time and space have made use of some form of village council system.[14]

The supposedly exclusively Western idea of democracy is just one key example of how ideas or values that are thought to originate in or "belong" to one particular civilization or people are in fact shared across civilizations. Another is the ethic of reciprocity, or the so-called Golden Rule, which is a fundamental moral principle common to virtually all of our world's major religious, cultural, or civilizational groups. While it is expressed in a range of ways, the essence of the ethic of reciprocity is captured in the phrase, "treat others as you would like to be treated."[15] A similar point can be made about the importance of human dignity and its prominent place in a plurality of cultural groupings. The same can be said of the supposedly exclusively Western or Judeo-Christian principle of toleration.[16] In essence,

John Donne's phrase, "No man is an island, entire of itself,"[17] applies equally as much to any civilization—Western civilization and civilizations of the East included. Rather, for millennia there have been back and forth movement of peoples and exchanges of ideas, inventions, and innovations between East and West and beyond. Who invented what is not or should not really be the key issue of debate; as with any idea or invention, people borrow and redesign and rethink and improve on the original. That is how progress is made that spreads far and wide to the benefit of all: through the exchange and sharing of ideas and inventions, not through keeping knowledge and know-how in-house to the exclusion of others. That, however, does not mean that all societies need eventually come to resemble one another or follow a particular developmental path. It simply means that certain core values are shared across various divides and expressed via manifold ways and means. The most important lesson to take from this is in terms of opportunities for enhanced mutual understanding.

Guizot's Question Reconsidered

I want to return now to the question posed by Guizot with which this book started: Is there a cumulative universal history of human civilization and its destiny to be written?[18] Guizot and other serious thinkers and chroniclers before and since him have thought so, with the musings of some of the more prominent believers explored herein. I have argued here that the reading of history that sees it as heading toward an end that resembles universal civilization is far from a natural or inevitable passage of history. Rather, it represents what is closer to a crafted passage of history that is motivated by the pursuit of a Kantian-style peace among a civilized international society of cosmopolitan liberal democratic states based on their common culture and interests. I have termed this the expansion of an "empire of civilization" that is not so much based on values and a way of life that are universal, but a set of Western values, ideals, and institutions that are being inculcated across the globe to slowly but surely realize a degree of political, social, legal, economic, and cultural homogeneity—an empire of civilization that is more uniform than universal. I have characterized it as a process of conscientiously or proactively making History, and I have also described the often damaging influence this exercise has had on peoples powerless to stem the tide of civilization/progress/history. For many in the West, this course of action is thought to be a natural and rational one: Western civilization and its values are said to be the most advanced; therefore, it makes sense that the rest of the world wants and aspires to what the West has. Why would they not? How could they not? As noted in chapter 4 in particular, throughout much of history, dominant cultures or civilizations have tended to see their social and political institutions and the values and way of life that they hold dear and by which they live not as the child of their specific culture, but as a universal condition aspired to by all.

This general line of thinking is essentially what underpins Daniel Lerner's claim that "the Western model of modernization exhibits certain components and sequences whose relevance is global." Lerner is representative of many in believing that "the same basic model reappears in virtually all modernizing societies on all continents of the world, regardless of variations in race, colour, creed."[19] US President George W. Bush makes essentially the same claim, insisting that there is "a single sustainable model for national success: freedom, democracy, and free enterprise."[20] Or, to interpret this general view another way, wherever someone of this inclination sees Westernization taking place, they see modernization; in the absence of Westernization, they see "tradition," or "backwardness"; at the very least, something short of the achievements of Western civilization. Underlying this general view is the notion that Western society is an expression of the Western rationality which more traditional and hence irrational Nonwestern societies supposedly aspire to. This general line of thought lies behind George W. Bush's comments on the first anniversary of September 11, 2001, which are undoubtedly directed toward the same Middle East region that Lerner's study is based on. Bush declared:

> America's greatest opportunity is to create a balance of world power that favors human freedom. We will use our position of unparalleled strength and influence to build an atmosphere of international order and openness in which progress and liberty can flourish in many nations. A peaceful world of growing freedom serves American long-term interests, reflects enduring American ideals and unites America's allies. We defend this peace by opposing and preventing violence by terrorists and outlaw regimes. We preserve this peace by building good relations among the world's great powers and we extend this peace by encouraging free and open societies on every continent. . . . As we preserve the peace, America also has an opportunity to extend the benefits of freedom and progress to nations that lack them. We seek a just peace where repression, resentment and

poverty are replaced with the hope of democracy, development, free markets and free trade.[21]

The pursuit of such misguided and poorly informed foreign policy goals relate directly to David Fidler's claim that Western standards of civilization and globalization are prevailing in the so-called clash of civilizations because Western globalized countries are exercising their superior power as the builders of international society to ensure that it is crafted in their image.[22] This kind of thinking and policy making and practice relates directly to the contention made in the book's introductory chapter that Francis Fukuyama's "end of history" thesis and Samuel Huntington's "clash of civilizations" thesis are complimentary, or at least they are both potentially implicated in the pursuit of this end—two sides of the same coin, so to speak. To restate the point, using the coercive language of civilization, savagery, and barbarism to justify imperial-like civilizing missions, for many centuries now—following the discovery of the New World to the global war on terror—much international public policy has been designed and directed toward pursuing a peaceful civilized international society of uniformly cosmopolitan, liberal democratic states organized around Western institutions, values, and ways of life.

One of the aims of this book is to highlight the steps through which this vision of universal civilization or manufactured narrative of history unfolds. If one was to read, say, chapter 3 of this book on the idea of progress, and then proceed to chapter 8 on new imperialism, they might not see many immediate or obvious connections between the respective topics. In and of themselves, the ideas, concepts, and policies explored in the separate chapters are potentially deployed for specific or more immediate objectives. But they can also be seen as a set of interconnected ideas and policy justifications in the service of greater ends—an expansive empire of civilization—such that when taken together the chapters have a sequential coherence, telling a "big picture" story about how a number of smaller stories (both ideas and actions) are intimately linked. As stated at the beginning of this book, the linking of the ideas, events, trends, and arguments offered herein is unlikely to satisfy all in terms of explaining the best part of the last millennium of politics among peoples, nations, states, and or civilizations. While skeptics and critics might write it off as another overcooked conspiracy theory against Europe and it successor, the West, the connections and continuities are laid out to be evaluated on their merits. Central to the story is the ideal of civilization and the way in which it has been deployed over a long period of time and across much space to describe, explain, rationalize, and justify all manner of interventions and sociopolitical engineering.

Ultimately, the endeavor to expand the empire of civilization based largely on uniquely Western values and institutions via the extension of some form of imperial-like civilizing missions to the unenlightened reaches of our world is doomed to fail, in no small part because of the violence generated by the civilized center in the name of civilization. Particularly so soon after the at times violent and bloody end of the colonial era, the suggestion that some form of new and enlightened imperialism is the remedy to the challenges of international order and disorder brought about the world's trouble spots and newly emerged threats is short-sighted to say the least. Few stable and lasting transitions to the way societies are organized and governed have come about through external imposition. While they might sometimes be bloody and drawn-out contests, internally generated upheavals and transitions are generally perceived to be more legitimate and thus have enjoyed greater long-term success. Naturally, each and every case is contingent, and there are exceptions to every guiding rule, but the key point here is (to reiterate the argument outlined in chapter 8) that Western imperialism is not the last and only hope for those societies experiencing problems of state legitimacy or capacity. For instance, there is no reason to suppose that the largely nonviolent revolutions which have seen corrupt, incompetent, and even dictatorial governments removed from office in the former Eastern Bloc will not catch on elsewhere. As has been the case in so many places around the world across various points in history, there is no telling what combination of circumstances can usher in unexpected or even longed-for changes in the management of states and societies on the brink. As outlined above, most parts of the world have histories involving reasonably well-organized and stable governments of some form at least at the micro level, if not necessarily as postcolonial states. Just as importantly, in most countries, despite challenges such as those posed by diversity and a lack of material resources, there is a general desire and willingness to self-govern in an orderly and just manner. Moreover, there is no good reason to suppose that there is not also the capacity. As Johann Gottfried Herder remarked so long ago, "Is not the good *dispersed* all over earth?" Surely "it could not be encompassed by one face of humankind, by one region of the compass."[23] Imperialism denies that this is the case, suppressing capacity and will in the process.

As much of the past five hundred plus years of history have demonstrated, the division of our world into varying hierarchies or shades of civilization and the concomitant enforcement of standards of civilization accompanied by imperial civilizing missions have potentially dire consequences for those branded uncivilized. While there is a need to distinguish between different states and societies on the basis of legitimacy, the value-laden measuring stick of civilization is overburdened by a particularly violent and heavy-handed moral crusade which attributes different moral worth to different peoples. As Naeem Inayatullah and David Blaney propose, surely "a world of live-and-let-live—a negative utopia of tolerance—is preferable to the bloodletting associated with moral crusading across political and cultural borders."[24] Precisely what constitutes the ideal means of drawing the appropriate distinctions remains to be found; and as it is a large and complex issue, it cannot be done justice within the bounds of this book. But it is an issue that requires further serious thought by anyone interested in a future that seeks to avoid repeating mistakes of the past. What can be emphasized here, though, and which is a general concern herein, is that the categorization of certain states and societies as uncivilized, premodern, backward, or something other than civilization is not the ideal answer. The reification or deification of the ideal of civilization is loaded with risks. For centuries the drawing of hierarchical distinctions has had devastating consequences for those societies that fall short of meeting the requirements of civilization. Contemporary commentators who draw lines in the sand based on a society's proximity to the ideal of civilization or those who advocate the ruthless enforcement of standards of civilization either conveniently overlook or are blind to this point. Imperial-style interventions, even when they are classified as humanitarian and in the name of saving the uncivilized from themselves, have serious and often unwelcome consequences that must be taken into account and weighed up. There is nothing to be gained by arbitrary distinctions between "civilized" and "uncivilized" societies, the former looking down upon the latter with an unjustifiable sense of superiority closely accompanied by a missionary zeal.

Almost inevitably there will be those who say, "So what?" to the entire case presented here. Quite likely they are the same people who see nothing wrong with the way the European-cum-Western world has violently intervened in the affairs of other peoples down through the past five hundred plus years. Those that hold such a view will likely never be convinced that the nature of relations between the "West and the rest" needs to change. At the same time, they will dismiss perspectives like those outlined above as naive "romanticism" about native or "traditional" societies. But there are also a lot of people who recognize

the errors and injustices of the past and would not want to see them re-
peated, even if they are unknowingly accomplices to or implicated in the
perpetuation of similar injustices, as Todorov notes is possible. The reasons why the issues raised herein cannot be dismissed with a "so what"
is that they are important issues that have serious implications for how
the Western world interacts with the Nonwestern worlds in the present and into the future. There are many lessons to be learned by international actors—from states to the international financial institutions,
from the United Nations and its various entities to nongovernmental aid
organizations—from the history of European/Western intervention in
the Nonwestern world. The question is: Will it be a case of perpetuating
the pattern of injustices of the past, in part because they are not recognized, or will there be a serious rethink?

While the project of universal civilization is unlikely to reach the
destination it seeks, serious damage can be done by continuing to pursue this goal at any cost, as we are now seeing, for instance, with the
rise of fundamentalist terrorism. The extent of what is at stake cannot
be understated or underemphasized; it is nothing less than the continued suppression of ways of life that are thought of as belonging to another time, which ultimately results in the further diminution of social,
political, legal, economic, and, most importantly, cultural pluralism. It
need not be this way. There is no one-and-only way of being; basic human rights, a decent standard of living, and a just system of government
are achievable in societies that are something other than replicas of the
Western archetype.

According to Paul Ricoeur in *History and Truth*, human truth lies in
the "process in which civilizations confront each other more and more
with what is most living and creative in them." He goes on to suggest
that human "history will progressively become a vast explanation in
which each civilization will work out its perception of the world by confronting all others." But he writes that "this process has hardly begun"
and that it is likely to be a task thrust upon "generations to come" to
make better sense of. Looking back on the West's history of relations
with Nonwestern peoples and cultures, he was unsure of what will become of Western civilization "when it has really met different civilizations by means other than the shock of conquest and domination." In
this regard, he was compelled to "admit that this encounter has not yet
taken place at the level of an authentic dialogue." Ricoeur thought at
the time that "we are in a tunnel, at the twilight of dogmatism and the
dawn of real dialogues." Since he wrote these words, momentous events
such as September 11 and the subsequent war on terrorism, and even

the riots that spread across his homeland, France, not long after his death have cast a shadow on this optimism. At the level of diplomatic and international relations, today I fear we are probably closer to midnight than to the dawn of an authentic dialogue between civilizations wherein a dialogue or exchange of ideas takes place in the true two-way (or multidirectional) sense of the word, not a one-way dictation from a "superior" to "inferior" civilizations. The need for authentic intercivilizational dialogue and understanding has rarely been more urgent. Ricoeur went on to make the point that "every philosophy of history is inside one of these cycles of civilizations. That is why we have not the wherewithal to imagine the coexistence of these manifold styles; we do not possess a philosophy of history which is able to resolve the problems of coexistence."[25]

Ricoeur is on the money on this last point. He captures the essence of the obstacles that must be negotiated before there is tolerance, understanding, and reconciliation between the West and much of the rest of the world (including within the rest of the world). The bloody and contested nature of the relations that have historically transpired between Europe and its colonies, and settler colonies and indigenous peoples, continues to cast a long shadow over contemporary domestic and international relations between peoples of diverse cultural heritage. Until the West resolves to seek out a philosophy of history that is more accommodating of Nonwestern peoples and cultures, and treats them with greater respect as different yet of equal moral value, then there is a danger that we are destined to continue along the same misguided path.

That said, as with many momentous turning points in history, along with great challenges come great opportunities which must be seized upon by people operating at all levels. And in this regard there is cause for hope. While some world leaders have missed the opportunity and chosen a more treacherous course, at another level, gatherings such as the World Social Forum and similar events are doing their bit to facilitate and advance intercivilizational dialogue. Another cause for hope is the coming together of diverse states and communities to find a united approach to address urgent global issues such as environmental degradation and climate change. Similarly, ranging from the level of individuals to larger collectives and communities of faith, each and every day multiple dialogues and exchanges of ideas are taking place, some of them face to face, many of them over the Internet; all of them adding to and aiding the cause of shared understandings. As we engage in these dialogues and debates, we would do well to keep in mind a point reiterated by Edward Said in the preface to the twenty-fifth anniversary edition of *Orientalism*: "Rather than the manufactured clash of civilizations, we need to concentrate on the slow working together of cultures that overlap, borrow from each other, and live together in far more interesting ways than any abridged or inauthentic mode of understanding can allow."[26]

For one reason or another, conflict and what sets different peoples apart always seems to attract more attention than cooperation and what we have in common, and that is the case for much of this book too. To many observers, the various comings together of the "West and the rest" are defined by a recurring or ongoing series of confrontations and clashes, from the eleventh-century Crusades (1095–1291) through to the modern-day Huntingtonian "clash of civilisations" being played out in the Middle East, Afghanistan, and beyond. But this preoccupation with clashes and confrontations obscures what many civilizations or sociocultural groups share in common and sidelines centuries of migration and mingling, peaceful cooperation, cultural borrowing, and exchanges of ideas. There is much to be gained by directing greater attention toward what the "West and the rest" have in common and have shared and shaped together. As briefly outlined above, Western civilization and the myriad of other Nonwestern civilizations or cultural groupings have overlapped and freely borrowed from one another and share more in common than is generally acknowledged.

In highlighting the need for more attention to cooperation over conflict as we seek out opportunities for genuine intercivilizational dialogue and greater shared understanding, I would like to conclude by borrowing from Will Durant's idea that civilization is a stream with banks, and that at times the stream is filled with blood from people killing, stealing, shouting, and doing the things that tend to attract our attention; while on the banks, unnoticed, people build homes, make love, raise children, sing songs, write poetry, and even whittle statues.[27] Much like Durant's interpretation of the story of civilization, the tale of where intercivilizational relations go from here can and should be more about what happens on the banks rather than the perpetuation of oppression and bloodshed that has fouled the stream throughout too much of human history. The choice should be an easy one.

Notes

1. INTRODUCTION

1. François Guizot, *The History of Civilization in Europe*, trans. William Hazlitt (*1828*; Harmondsworth: Penguin, 1997), 12.

2. Robert Wright, *Nonzero: The Logic of Human Destiny* (New York: Vintage, 2001), 3, 7.

3. Some relevant notable exceptions include David Armitage, *The Ideological Origins of the British Empire* (Cambridge: Cambridge University Press, 2000); William Bain, *Between Anarchy and Society* (Oxford: Oxford University Press, 2003); Duncan Bell, *The Idea of Greater Britain: Empire and the Future of World Order, 1860–1900* (Princeton, NJ: Princeton University Press, 2007); Edward Keene, *Beyond the Anarchical Society: Grotius, Colonialism and Order in World Politics* (Cambridge: Cambridge University Press, 2002); Bruce Mazlish, *Civilization and Its Contents* (Stanford, CA: Stanford University Press, 2004); Nicholas Greenwood Onuf, *The Republican Legacy in International Thought* (Cambridge: Cambridge University Press, 1998); Jennifer Pitts, *A Turn to Empire: The Rise of Imperial Liberalism in Britain and France* (Princeton, NJ: Princeton University Press, 2006); Mark B. Salter, *Barbarians and Civilization in International Relations* (London: Pluto, 2002); Brian Schmidt, *The Political Discourse of Anarchy* (Albany: State University of New York Press, 1998); Richard Tuck, *The Rights of War and Peace: Political Thought and the International Order from Grotius to Kant* (Oxford: Oxford University Press, 2001); and R. B. J. Walker, *Inside/Outside: International Relations as Political Theory* (Cambridge: Cambridge University Press, 1993).

4. Samuel P. Huntington, *The Soldier and the State: The Theory and Politics of Civil-Military Relations* (Cambridge, MA: Harvard University Press, Belknap Press, 1957), vii.

5. Francis Fukuyama, *The End of History and the Last Man* (London: Penguin, 1992); and Samuel P. Huntington, *The Clash of Civilizations and the Remaking of World Order* (London: Simon & Schuster, 1997).

6. See for instance, Roger Scruton, *The West and the Rest: Globalization and the Terrorist Threat* (London: Continuum, 2002). Similar terminology was used much earlier by the anthropologist Marshall Sahlins and the historian Arnold J. Toynbee; see especially Toynbee's 1952 BBC Reith Lectures, *The World and the West* (London: Oxford University Press, 1953).

7. Samuel P. Huntington, "The West Unique, Not Universal," *Foreign Affairs* 75, no. 6 (1996): 28–46; and *Clash of Civilizations*.

8. Richard A. Shweder, "On the Return of the 'Civilizing Project,'" *Dædalus* 131, no. 3 (2002): 118.

9. On the idea of an "empire of uniformity," see James Tully, *Strange Multiplicity: Constitutionalism in an Age of Diversity* (Cambridge: Cambridge University Press, 1995), esp. chap. 5.

10. See, for instance, Robert Wright et al., "The World's Most Dangerous Ideas," *Foreign Policy* 144 (2004): 32–49.

11. John Maynard Keynes, *The General Theory of Employment, Interest and Money* (London: MacMillan, 1936), 383–84.

12. Naeem Inayatullah and David L. Blaney, *International Relations and the Problem of Difference* (New York: Routledge, 2004), 7.

13. Important early works include, J. G. A. Pocock, "The History of Political Thought: A Methodological Enquiry," in *Philosophy, Politics, and Society*, 2nd ser., ed. Peter Laslett and W. C. Runicman (Oxford: Blackwell, 1962), 183–202; John Dunn, "The Identity of the History of Ideas," *Philosophy* 43 (1968): 85–104; and Quentin Skinner, "Meaning and Understanding in the History of Ideas," *History and Theory* 8, no. 1 (1969): 3–53.

14. Duncan S. A. Bell, "Language, Legitimacy, and the Project of Critique," *Alternatives: Global, Local, Political* 27, no. 3 (2002): 332.

15. Ken Booth, "Discussion: A Reply to Wallace," *Review of International Studies* 23, no. 3 (1997): 374.

16. Quentin Skinner, "Rhetoric and Conceptual Change," *Finnish Yearbook of Political Thought* 3 (1999): 61; and Skinner, "Language and Social Change," in *Meaning and Context: Quentin Skinner and His Critics*, ed. James Tully (Cambridge: Polity, 1988), 122.

17. Skinner, "Rhetoric and Conceptual Change," 61.

18. Skinner, "Meaning and Understanding," 42n176; emphasis in original.

19. Pocock, "History of Political Thought," 183, 195.

20. Dunn, "Identity of the History of Ideas," 86.

21. Bell, "Language, Legitimacy, and the Project of Critique," 336.

22. Keith Tribe, translator's introduction to *Futures Past: On the Semantics of Historical Time*, by Reinhart Koselleck, trans. Keith Tribe (Cambridge, MA: MIT Press, 1985), xiii.

23. Terence Ball, James Farr, and Russell L. Hanson, introduction to *Political Innovation and Conceptual Change*, ed. Terence Ball, James Farr, and Russell L. Hanson (Cambridge: Cambridge University Press, 1989), 4.

24. Melvin Richter, *The History of Political and Social Concepts: A Critical Introduction* (Cambridge: Cambridge University Press, 1995), 124; and chap. 6, "Pocock, Skinner, and *Begriffsgeschichte*," more generally. See also Kari Palonen, "Rhetorical and Temporal Perspectives on Conceptual Change," *Finnish Yearbook of Political Thought* 3 (1999): 41–59.

25. See, for instance, Reinhart Koselleck, *Futures Past: On the Semantics of Historical Time*, trans. Keith Tribe (Cambridge, MA: MIT Press, 1985).

26. Skinner, "Rhetoric and Conceptual Change," 62–63.

27. Ball, Farr, and Hanson, introduction, 4.

28. Martin Wight, "Why Is There No International Theory?" in *Diplomatic Investigations: Essays in the Theory of International Politics*, ed. Herbert Butterfield and Martin Wight (London: Allen & Unwin, 1966), 26.

29. Skinner, "Meaning and Understanding," 53.

30. Ball, Farr, and Hanson, introduction, 4–5.

31. Wolf Schäfer, "Global Civilization and Local Cultures: A Crude Look at the Whole," *International Sociology* 16, no. 3 (2001): 302.

32. Raymond Williams, *Keywords: A Vocabulary of Culture and Society*, rev. ed. (New York: Oxford University Press, 1985), 87.

33. Jean Starobinski, "The Word Civilization," in *Blessings in Disguise; or, The Morality of Evil*, trans. Arthur Goldhammer (Cambridge, MA: Harvard University Press, 1993), 20.

34. Friedrich von Schiller, "The Nature and Value of Universal History: An Inaugural Lecture [1789]," *History and Theory* 11, no. 3 (1972): 325–27.

35. James Lorimer, *The Institutes of the Law of Nations* (Edinburgh· William Blackwood & Sons, 1883), 1:12.

36. "Statute of the International Court of Justice," in *Basic Documents in International Law*, ed. Ian Brownlie, 3rd ed. (Oxford: Clarendon, 1994), 397; emphasis added.

37. Norbert Elias, *The Civilizing Process*, trans. Edmund Jephcott, rev. ed. (1939; Oxford: Blackwell, 2000), 431.

38. Samuel P. Huntington, *Political Order in Changing Societies* (New Haven, CT: Yale University Press, 1968), 1.

39. John Gray, *Enlightenment's Wake: Politics and Culture at the Close of the Modern Age* (London: Routledge, 1995), 123.

2. THE IDEAL OF CIVILIZATION

1. For related exercises, see Patrick Thaddeus Jackson, *Civilizing the Enemy: German Reconstruction and the Invention of the West* (Ann Arbor: University of Michigan Press, 2006); Martin Hall and Patrick Thaddeus Jackson, eds., *The Production and Reproduction of "Civilizations" in International Relations* (New York: Palgrave, 2007); Mazlish, *Civilization and Its Contents*; Iver B. Neumann, *Uses of the Other: "The East" in European Identity Formation*

(Minneapolis: University of Minnesota Press, 1998); Jacinta O'Hagan, *Conceptualizing the West in International Relations: From Spengler to Said* (Basingstoke: Palgrave, 2002). See also the special issue on civilization(s), *International Sociology* 16, no. 3 (2001).

2. Anthony Pagden, *Lords of All the World: Ideologies of Empire in Spain, Britain and France c.1500–c.1800* (New Haven, CT: Yale University Press, 1995), 1–2.

3. Fernand Braudel, *A History of Civilizations*, trans. Richard Mayne (New York: Allen Lane / Penguin, 1987), 4.

4. Émile Benveniste, "Civilization: A Contribution to the History of the Word," in *Problems in General Linguistics*, trans. Mary Elizabeth Meek (Coral Gables, FL: University of Miami Press, 1971), 289.

5. Gerrit W. Gong, *The Standard of "Civilization" in International Society* (Oxford: Clarendon, 1984). This study and the classical "standard of civilization" are discussed in further detail in chapter 5.

6. Samuel P. Huntington, *Clash of Civilizations*; and Huntington, "The Clash of Civilizations?" *Foreign Affairs* 72, no. 3 (1993): 22–49.

7. Huntington, *Clash of Civilizations*, 40–41.

8. Skinner, "Rhetoric and Conceptual Change," 61; and Skinner, "Language and Social Change," 122.

9. Fernand Braudel, *On History*, trans. Sarah Matthews (London: Weidenfeld & Nicolson, 1980), 213.

10. Guizot, *History of Civilization in Europe*, 11–12.

11. Benveniste, "Civilization," 292.

12. Quoted in Starobinski, "The Word Civilization,", 1; emphasis in original.

13. Lucien Febvre, "*Civilization*: Evolution of a Word and a Group of Ideas," in *A New Kind of History: From the Writings of Febvre*, ed. P. Burke, trans. K. Folca (London: Routledge & Kegan Paul, 1973), 220–21.

14. M. Boulanger, *Antiquité dévoilée par ses usages* (Amsterdam, 1766), vol. 3, book 6, chap. 2, 404–5; quoted in Febvre, "*Civilization*," 222; emphasis in original.

15. Benveniste, "Civilization," 290; and Starobinski, "The Word Civilization," 3.

16. Braudel, *History of Civilizations*, 4.

17. Quoted in Starobinski, "The Word Civilization," 2; emphasis in original.

18. Starobinski, "The Word Civilization," 3.

19. Benveniste, "Civilization," 289, 292.

20. Starobinski, "The Word Civilization," 3.

21. Quoted in Starobinski, "The Word Civilization," 2.

22. Starobinski, "The Word Civilization," 2–5, quote at 5.

23. Starobinski, "The Word Civilization," 7–8. As Skinner argues, however, in employing such concepts or "speech-acts," there can be no neutral reading, they both describe and evaluate, commend and condemn. Skinner, "Rhetoric and Conceptual Change," 61.

24. Febvre, "*Civilization*," 220.

25. Volney, *Éclaircissements sur les États-Unis*, in *Oeuvres complètes* (Paris: F. Didot, 1868), 718; quoted in Febvre, "Civilization," 252n51.

26. James Boswell, *Boswell's Life of Johnson* (1791; Oxford: Clarendon, 1934), 2:155; emphasis in original.

27. Adam Ferguson, *An Essay on the History of Civil Society 1767*, ed. Duncan Forbes (Edinburgh: Edinburgh University Press, 1966).

28. The letter is quoted in Benveniste, "Civilization," 295.

29. The context of Hume's letter suggests that Ferguson had been working on the manuscript for some time and that Hume had read an earlier draft still.

30. Duncan Forbes, introduction to *An Essay on the History of Civil Society 1767*, by Adam Ferguson (Edinburgh: Edinburgh University Press, 1966), xix.

31. A. Ferguson, *Essay*, 1.

32. Forbes, introduction, xx.

33. Adam Ferguson, *Principles of Moral and Political Science* (1792; Hildesheim, Germany: Georg Olms Verlag, 1975), 1:252.

34. John Stuart Mill, "Civilization" [1836], in *Essays on Politics and Culture*, ed. Gertrude Himmelfarb (Garden City, NY: Doubleday, 1962), 51; emphasis in original.

35. See, for instance, Edmund Burke, "India," in *Selections: With Essays by Hazlitt, Arnold and Others*, ed. A. M. D. Hughes (Oxford: Clarendon, 1921), 111–27. See also Jennifer M. Welsh, *Edmund Burke and International Relations: The Commonwealth of Europe and the Crusade against the French Revolution* (New York: St. Martin's, 1995), in which Welsh identifies similar issues in Burke's thinking surrounding his "presumption of homogeneity."

36. Mill, "Civilization," 53, 57.

37. Adam Smith, *An Inquiry into the Nature and Causes of the Wealth of Nations* (1776; London: T. Nelson & Sons, 1869), 295–96.

38. Herbert Spencer, *Social Statistics*, rev. ed. (London: Williams & Norgate, 1892), 249.

39. Elias, *Civilizing Process*, rev. ed., 5–6; and Schäfer, "Global Civilization and Local Cultures," 304–10.

40. Elias, *Civilizing Process*, rev. ed., 10; emphasis in original.

41. The term *Bildung* is used instead of *Zivilisation* throughout the work of Johann Gottfried Herder, one of the early German Romantic thinkers. However, there is no real English language equivalent, and it is translated into English as *civilization*. See Herder, *Philosophical Writings*, ed. Michel N. Forster (Cambridge: Cambridge University Press, 2002).

42. Elias, *Civilizing Process*, rev. ed., 24.

43. This is nowhere more evident than in the French Declaration of the Rights of Man of 1789 and in Napoleon Bonaparte's blunt declaration: "*Ce qui est bon pour les français est bon pour tout le monde*" (What is good for the French is good for everybody). See Anthony Pagden, *Peoples and Empires* (London: Weidenfeld & Nicholson, 2001), 138.

44. See also Darrin M. McMahon, *Enemies of the Enlightenment: The French Counter-Enlightenment and the Making of Modernity* (New York: Oxford University Press, 2001).

45. Oswald Spengler, *The Decline of the West*, ed. Helmut Werner, trans. Charles Francis Atkinson (New York: Knopf, 1962), 23–24.

46. Jeffrey Herf, *Reactionary Modernism: Technology, Culture, and Politics in Weimar and the Third Reich* (Cambridge: Cambridge University Press, 1984), 49.

47. Adam Kuper, *Culture: The Anthropologists' Account* (Cambridge, MA: Harvard University Press, 1999), 6–7.

48. See Alexander von Humboldt, *Cosmos: A Sketch of a Physical Description of the Universe*, trans. E. C. Otté (London: Henry G. Bohn, 1864–65).

49. See Braudel, *History of Civilizations*, 5. These lectures later became the basis for Hegel's, *The Philosophy of History*, trans. J. Sibree (New York: Dover, 1956).

50. Sigmund Freud, *The Future of an Illusion*, trans. W. D. Robson-Scott (1928; London: Hogarth Press and the Institute of Psycho-analysis, 1949), 8–9.

51. Karl Marx and Frederick Engels, "Manifesto of the Communist Party," in *Selected Works* (Moscow: Foreign Languages, 1958), 1:39.

52. Thomas Mann; quoted in Braudel, *On History*, 182.

53. Braudel, *History of Civilizations*, 5; and Robert K. Merton, "Civilization and Culture," *Sociology and Social Research* 21, no. 2 (1936): 110.

54. Wilhelm Mommsen; quoted in Braudel, *On History*, 182.

55. Elias, *Civilizing Process*, rev. ed., 7.

56. Starobinski, "The Word Civilization," 28.

57. Friedrich Nietzsche, "Aus dem Nachlass der Achtzigerjahre," in *Werke* (Munich: Carl Hanser Verlag, 1966), 3:837.

58. Kuper, *Culture*, 8.

59. G. Kuhn (1958); quoted in Braudel, *On History*, 182.

60. Address by Victor Hugo to the French National Assembly meeting in Bordeaux on March 1, 1871; quoted in Starobinski, "The Word Civilization," 20–21.

61. Braudel, *On History*, 183.

62. Huntington, *Clash of Civilizations*, 41.

63. E. Durkheim and M. Mauss, "Note on the Notion of Civilization," *Social Research* 38, no. 4 (1971): 811. Originally published in *L'année sociologique* 12 (1913): 46–50.

64. Arnold J. Toynbee, *Civilization on Trial* (New York: Oxford University Press, 1948), 24.

65. Arnold Toynbee, *A Study of History*, rev. and abr. ed. (London: Thames & Hudson and Oxford University Press, 1972), 44–45.

66. Robert P. Kraynak, "Hobbes on Barbarism and Civilization," *Journal of Politics* 45, no. 1 (1983), 90; emphasis in original.

67. Thomas Hobbes, *Leviathan*, ed. C. B. MacPherson (1651; Harmondsworth: Penguin, 1985), chap. 46, p. 683.

68. Kraynak, "Hobbes," 90–91.

69. Aristotle, *The Politics* (London: Dent & Sons, 1912), 3, para. 1252b.

70. Kraynak, "Hobbes," 93.

71. Aristotle, *Politics*, 4–5, para. 1253a.

72. Anthony Pagden, "The 'Defence of Civilization' in Eighteenth-Century Social Theory," *History of the Human Sciences* 1, no. 1 (1988): 39.

73. R. G. Collingwood, "What 'Civilization' Means," appendix 2 in *The New Leviathan*, ed. David Boucher (Oxford: Clarendon, 1992), 502–8.

74. Zygmunt Bauman, *Legislators and Interpreters: On Modernity, Post-Modernity and Intellectuals* (Ithaca, NY: Cornell University Press, 1987), 93; emphasis in original. See also, John Keane, *Reflections on Violence* (London: Verso, 1996), 19.

75. Starobinski, "The Word Civilization," 31.

76. Pagden, "Defence of Civilization," 33.

77. Starobinski, "The Word Civilization," 32; emphasis in original.

78. Elias, *Civilizing Process*, rev. ed., 5; emphasis in original.

79. For commentary on these works as critiques of colonialism, see Sven Lindqvist, *"Exterminate All the Brutes,"* trans. Joan Tate (London: Granta, 1998), 77–79.

80. On this see Brett Bowden, "The River of Inter-civilisational Relations: The Ebb and Flow of Peoples, Ideas and Innovations," *Third World Quarterly* 28, no. 7 (2007): 1359–74.

81. F. C. S. Schiller, introduction to *Civilisation or Civilisations: An Essay in the Spenglerian Philosophy of History*, by E. H. Goddard and P. A. Gibbons (London: Constable, 1926), vii.

82. Guizot, *History of Civilization in Europe*, 16; emphasis in original.

83. Febvre, *"Civilization,"* 229–30; emphasis in original.

84. Quoted in Febvre, *"Civilization,"* 230.

85. Starobinski, "The Word Civilization," 17; emphasis in original.

3. CIVILIZATION AND THE IDEA OF PROGRESS

1. Joel Colton, foreword to *Progress and Its Discontents*, ed. Gabriel A. Almond, Marvin Chodorow, and Roy Harvey Pearce (Berkeley: University of California Press, 1982), ix. See also Ludwig Edelstein, *The Idea of Progress in Classical Antiquity* (Baltimore: Johns Hopkins University Press, 1967).

2. See Robert Nisbet, *History of the Idea of Progress* (London: Heinemann, 1980), 9; and J. B. Bury, *The Idea of Progress: An Inquiry into Its Origin and Growth* (New York: Dover, 1960), 19.

3. Ronald L. Meek, *Social Science and the Ignoble Savage* (Cambridge: Cambridge University Press, 1976), 1; compare J. H. Elliot, *The Old World and the New, 1492–1650* (Cambridge: Cambridge University Press, 1970).

4. Beate Jahn, *The Cultural Construction of International Relations: The Invention of the State of Nature* (Basingstoke: Palgrave, 2000), 95.

5. Tzvetan Todorov, *The Conquest of America: The Question of the Other*, trans. Richard Howard (New York: HarperPerennial, 1984), 4.

6. John Locke, *Two Treatises of Government* (1690; New York: New American Library, 1965), book 2, p. 343, para. 49; emphasis in original.

7. A. Ferguson, *Essay*, 80.

8. Jahn, *Cultural Construction of International Relations*, 95.

9. See William Brandon, *New Worlds for Old: Reports from the New World and Their Effect on the Development of Social Thought in Europe, 1500–1800* (Athens: Ohio University Press, 1986); and Wolfgang Haase and Meyer Reinhold, eds., *The Classical Tradition and the Americas* (Berlin: W. de Gruyter, 1994).

10. Michael T. Ryan, "Assimilating New Worlds in the Sixteenth and Seventeenth Centuries," *Comparative Studies in Society and History* 23, no. 4 (1981): 529–31.

11. Frederick Engels, *The Origin of Family, Private Property and the State* (Moscow: Progress, 1948), 6.

12. Nisbet, *History of the Idea of Progress*, 9.

13. Starobinski, "The Word Civilization," 33–34; emphasis in original.

14. Bury, *Idea of Progress*, 2, 5.

15. Nisbet, *History of the Idea of Progress*, 4–5; emphasis in original.

16. Nannerl O. Keohane, "The Enlightenment Idea of Progress Revisited," in *Progress and Its Discontents*, ed. Gabriel A. Almond, Marvin Chodorow, and Roy Harvey Pearce (Berkeley: University of California Press, 1982), 21.

17. Ruth Macklin, "Moral Progress," *Ethics* 87, no. 4 (1977): 370; emphasis in original.

18. E. H. Goddard and P. A. Gibbons, *Civilisation or Civilisations: An Essay in the Spenglerian Philosophy of History* (London: Constable, 1926), 1–2.

19. Hobbes, *Leviathan*, chap. 13, p. 186.

20. Charles Van Doren, *The Idea of Progress* (New York: Praeger, 1967), 376.

21. Friedrich von Schiller, "Nature and Value of Universal History," 329.

22. Richard B. Norgaard, *Development Betrayed: The End of Progress and a Coevolutionary Revisioning of the Future* (London: Routledge, 1994), 51.

23. Van Doren, *Idea of Progress*, 26–30.

24. Certain race-related aspects of these fields of study, such as phrenology, have since been termed quasi-science or straight-out bad science, or not science at all.

25. David Harvey, "Cosmopolitanism and the Banality of Geographic Evils," *Public Culture* 12, no. 2 (2000): 534.

26. Anthony Pagden, *The Fall of Natural Man: The American Indian and the Origins of Comparative Ethnology* (Cambridge: Cambridge University Press, 1982), 122, 146, 198; and Walter D. Mignolo, introduction to *Natural and Moral History of the Indies*, by José de Acosta, ed. Jane E. Mangan, trans. Frances M. López-Morillas (1590; Durham, NC: Duke University Press, 2002), xviii.

27. José de Acosta, *Natural and Moral History of the Indies*, ed. Jane E. Mangan, trans. Frances M. López-Morillas (1590; Durham, NC: Duke University Press, 2002), 8.

28. Acosta, *Natural and Moral History of the Indies* (2002), 329, 345–46, 359.

29. Pagden, *Fall of Natural Man*, 198.

30. Acosta, *Natural and Moral History of the Indies* (2002), 346.

31. William N. Fenton and Elizabeth L. Moore, introduction to *Customs of the American Indians Compared with the Customs of Primitive Times*, by

Joseph François Lafitau, ed. and trans. William N. Fenton and Elizabeth L. Moore (1724; Toronto: Chaplain Society, 1974), xxix.

32. Lewis H. Morgan, *Ancient Society; or, Researches in the Lines of Human Progress from Savagery through Barbarism to Civilization* (Chicago: Kerr, 1907), v–vi, 3, vi.

33. Sir John Lubbock, preface to the American edition of *The Origin of Civilisation and the Primitive Condition of Man: Mental and Social Condition of Savages* (New York: Appleton, 1870), iii–iv.

34. Count Joseph Arthur de Gobineau, *Essai sur l'inégalitié des races humaines*, 4 vols. (1853–55); quoted in Frank H. Hankins, *The Racial Basis of Civilization* (New York: Knopf, 1926), 34.

35. Robert Knox, preface to *The Races of Men: A Philosophical Inquiry into the Influence of Race over the Destinies of Nations*, 2nd ed. (London: Henry Renshaw, 1862). Outside of his work on race, Knox's infamy derives from his "business" association with William Burke and William Hare, the notorious body snatchers-cum-serial killers of Edinburgh who sold the cadavers of their victims to Edinburgh medical schools on an "ask no questions basis." This episode subsequently provided the inspiration for Robert Louis Stevenson's novels *The Strange Case of Dr Jekyll and Mr Hyde* and *The Body Snatchers*.

36. Hankins, *Racial Basis of Civilization*, 34.

37. Spencer, *Social Statistics*, 234–36. See also, Frederick Farrar, "Aptitude of the Races," *Transactions of the Ethnographical Society of London* (1867); and J. C. Prichard, "On the Extinction of Human Races," *Edinburgh New Philosophical Journal* 28 (1839): 166–70.

38. William Robertson, *The History of America*, 12th ed. (London: Cadell & Davies, 1812), 2:59–60. Contrast this with the views of Adam Ferguson.

39. Keohane, "Enlightenment Idea of Progress Revisited," 40

40. Robertson, *History of America*, 2:60.

41. Montesquieu, *The Spirit of the Laws*, trans. Thomas Nugent (1748; New York: Hafner, 1949), book 18, chap. 11, p. 276. In prominent contemporary analysis, environment and geography are still seen as important developmental factors; see, for example, Jared Diamond, *Guns, Germs, and Steel: The Fates of Human Societies* (New York: Norton, 1997).

42. Engels, *Origin of Family, Private Property and the State*, 5–6.

43. Keohane, "Enlightenment Idea of Progress Revisited," 34.

44. Anne Robert Jacques Turgot, "A Philosophical Review of the Successive Advances of the Human Mind," in *Turgot on Progress, Sociology and Economics*, ed. and trans. Ronald L. Meek (Cambridge: Cambridge University Press, 1973), 41.

45. J. Salwyn Schapiro, *Condorcet and the Rise of Liberalism* (New York: Octagon, 1963), 240.

46. Stuart Hampshire, introduction to *Sketch for a Historical Picture of the Progress of the Human Mind*, by Antoine-Nicolas de Condorcet, trans. June Barraclough (London: Weidenfeld & Nicolson, 1955), x.

47. See Lewis White Beck, editor's introduction to *Kant: On History* (Indianapolis: Bobbs-Merrill, 1963), xii; and Hans Adler and Ernest A. Menze, "Introduction: On the Way to World History: Johann Gottfried Herder," in *On*

World History: An Anthology, by Johann Gottfried Herder, ed. Hans Adler and Ernest A. Menze, trans. Ernest A. Menze and Michael Palma (Armonk, NY: Sharpe, 1997), 9. See also Voltaire, *The Philosophy of History* (Reprint of the original 1766 ed.; London: Vision, 1965).

48. Schapiro, *Condorcet and the Rise of Liberalism,* 240.

49. Hampshire, introduction, x.

50. Hampshire, introduction, xi; partially quoting Condorcet.

51. Schapiro, *Condorcet and the Rise of Liberalism,* 241.

52. Antoine-Nicolas de Condorcet, *Sketch for a Historical Picture of the Progress of the Human Mind,* trans. June Barraclough (1795; London: Weidenfeld & Nicolson, 1955), 173.

53. The stages are: (1) Men are united in tribes. (2) Pastoral peoples through to the transition to agricultural peoples. (3) The progress of agricultural peoples up to the invention of the alphabet. (4) The progress of the human mind in Greece up to the division of the sciences around the time of Alexander the Great. (5) The progress of the sciences from their division to their decline. (6) The decadence of knowledge to its restoration around the time of the crusades. (7) The early progress of science from its revival in the West to the invention of printing. (8) From printing to the era when philosophy and the sciences shook of the yoke of authority. (9) From Descartes to the foundation of the French Republic. (10) The future progress of the human mind.

54. Pagden, "Defence of Civilization," 34.

55. A. Smith, *Wealth of Nations,* 289–96, and book 5 in general.

56. Edward J. Lapham, "Liberalism, Civic Humanism, and the Case of Adam Smith," *American Political Science Review* 78, no. 3 (1984): 769.

57. Walter Bagehot, *Physics and Politics* (London: Kegan Paul, Trench, Trubner, [1875]), 16, 19, 212–13; emphasis in original.

58. Adler and Menze, introduction, 3–4, 8.

59. Johann Gottfried Herder, *On World History: An Anthology,* ed. Hans Adler and Ernest A. Menze, trans. Ernest A. Menze and Michael Palma (Armonk, NY: Sharpe, 1997), 45; emphasis in original.

60. Adler and Menze, introduction, 13.

61. Herder, *On World History,* 41, 47; emphasis in original.

62. Immanuel Kant, "Reviews of Herder's *Ideas for a Philosophy of the History of Mankind*" [1785], in *Kant: On History,* ed. Lewis White Beck (Indianapolis: Bobbs-Merrill, 1963), 27–39. See Beck, editor's introduction," viii–ix, for a discussion of their intellectual divergence.

63. Beck, editor's introduction, xi. In "Perpetual Peace," Kant writes of a "deep contempt" for "the attachment of savages to their lawless freedom," regarding it as "barbarity, rudeness, and a brutish degradation of humanity." See "Perpetual Peace," in *Kant: On History,* 98.

64. Immanuel Kant, "Idea for a Universal History from a Cosmopolitan Point of View" [1784], in *Kant: On History,* 11, 15–16.

65. Immanuel Kant, "An Old Question Raised Again: Is the Human Race Constantly Progressing?" [1798], in *Kant: On History,* 137.

66. Kant, "Idea for a Universal History," 22.

67. Kant, "Old Question," 137–38.

68. Karl Marx, "The Eighteenth Brumaire of Louis Bonaparte" [3rd ed., 1885], in *Selected Works*, by Karl Marx and Frederick Engels (Moscow: Foreign Languages, 1958), 1:247.

69. Hegel, *Philosophy of History*, 16–17, 54, 19, 59; emphasis in original.

70. G. W. F. Hegel, *Philosophy of Right*, trans. T. M. Knox (Oxford: Clarendon, 1958), 105, para. 142.

71. Georg G. Iggers, "The Idea of Progress in Historiography and Social Thought since the Enlightenment," in *Progress and Its Discontents*, ed. Gabriel A. Almond, Marvin Chodorow, and Roy Harvey Pearce (Berkeley: University of California Press, 1982), 65.

72. Nisbet, *History of the Idea of Progress*, 308.

73. W. W. Rostow, *The Stages of Economic Growth: A Non-Communist Manifesto* (New York: Cambridge University Press, 1961), 4–11.

74. Inayatullah and Blaney, *International Relations and the Problem of Difference*, 93–95.

75. Gerrit W. Gong, "Asian Financial Crisis: Culture and Strategy," paper presented at the ICAS Fall Symposium, University of Pennsylvania, September 29, 1998; and Gong, "Standards of Civilization Today," in *Globalization and Civilizations*, ed. Mehdi Mozaffari (London: Routledge, 2002), 80.

76. For more of such claims, see Charles Murray, *Human Accomplishment: The Pursuit of Excellence in the Arts and Sciences, 800 B.C. to 1950* (New York: Harper Collins, 2003).

77. Joseph E. Stiglitz, "Towards a New Paradigm for Development: Strategies, Policies, and Processes," given as the 1998 Prebisch Lecture at UNCTAD, Geneva, October 19, 1998; emphasis in original.

78. Norgaard, *Development Betrayed*, 1.

79. E. Shils, "Political Development in the New States—The Will to Be Modern," in *Readings in Social Evolution and Development*, ed. S. N. Eisenstadt (Oxford: Pergamon, 1970), 379–82.

80. Francis Fukuyama, "The End of History?" *National Interest* 16 (1989): 4.

81. Fukuyama, *End of History and the Last Man*, xii.

82. R. Wright, *Nonzero*, 3, 6.

83. For more of Clinton's comments, see www.nonzero.org.

84. Nisbet, *History of the Idea of Progress*, 317; emphasis in original.

85. Charles Murray, "The Idea of Progress: Once Again, with Feeling," *Hoover Digest*, 2001, no. 3. See also Murray, *Human Accomplishment*. Murray is the coauthor of the controversial book *The Bell Curve: Intelligence and Class Structure in American Life* (New York: Free Press, 1994).

86. Nisbet, *History of the Idea of Progress*, 7.

87. Iggers, "Idea of Progress in Historiography," 43–44, 59, 53.

88. Gray, *Enlightenment's Wake*, 123, 125; emphasis in original.

4. THE NOTION OF UNIVERSAL CIVILIZATION

1. H. J. Blackburn, *The Future of Our Past: From Ancient Greece to Global Village*, ed. Barbara Smoker (Amherst, NY: Prometheus, 1996), 9.

2. Paul Ricoeur, *History and Truth*, trans. Charles A. Kelbley (Evanston, IL: Northwestern University Press, 1965), 271.

3. Couze Venn, "Altered States: Post-Enlightenment Cosmopolitanism and Transmodern Socialities," *Theory, Culture and Society* 19, nos. 1-2 (2002): 65-68.

4. Ranajit Guha, *History at the Limit of World-History* (New York: Columbia University Press, 2002), 9.

5. Hegel, *Philosophy of History*, 87, 162, 142, 163.

6. Hegel, *Philosophy of Right*, 213, para. 331.

7. Guha, *History*, 10, 44-45.

8. Venn, "Altered States," 68.

9. Ricoeur, *History and Truth*, 273.

10. John Gray, "Global Utopias and Clashing Civilizations: Misunderstanding the Present," *International Affairs* 74, no. 1 (1998): 153, 158. See also J. K. Gibson-Graham, *The End of Capitalism (As We Knew It): A Feminist Critique of Political Economy* (Minneapolis: University of Minnesota Press, 2006).

11. Marx and Engels, "Manifesto of the Communist Party," 1:38.

12. David P. Fidler, "A Kinder, Gentler System of Capitulation? International Law, Structural Adjustment Policies, and the Standard of Liberal, Globalized Civilization," *Texas International Law Journal* 35, no. 3 (2000): 412.

13. Michael Howard, *The Invention of Peace: Reflections on War and International Order* (London: Profile, 2000), 2-6.

14. Norbert Elias, "Violence and Civilization: The State Monopoly of Physical Violence and Its Infringement," in *Civil Society and the State: New European Perspectives*, ed. John Keane (London: Verso, 1988), 180-81.

15. Quoted in Febvre, "*Civilization*," 257n118.

16. For example, US Secretary of State Condoleezza Rice, "The Promise of Democratic Peace: Why Promoting Freedom Is the Only Realistic Path to Security," *Washington Post*, December 11, 2005, B07.

17. Hedley Bull, *The Anarchical Society: A Study of Order in World Politics*, 2nd ed. (London: Macmillan, 1995), 13; emphasis in original.

18. Hedley Bull and Adam Watson, introduction to *The Expansion of International Society*, ed. Hedley Bull and Adam Watson (Oxford: Clarendon, 1984), 1.

19. See Hedley Bull, "The Grotian Conception of International Society," in *Diplomatic Investigations*, ed. Herbert Butterfield and Martin Wight (London: Allen & Unwin, 1966), 51-73; and Martin Wight, "Western Values in International Relations," in *Diplomatic Investigations*, ed. Herbert Butterfield and Martin Wight (London: Allen & Unwin, 1966), 89-131. On the distinction between pluralist and solidarist conceptions of international society, see John M. Hobson and Leonard Seabrooke, "Reimagining Weber: Constructing International Society and the Social Balance of Power," *European Journal of International Relations* 7, no. 2 (2001): 239-74.

20. Compare Shogo Suzuki, "Japan's Socialization into Janus-Faced European International Society," *European Journal of International Relations* 11, no. 1 (2005): 137-64; and Suzuki, *Civilisation and Empire: East Asia's Encounter with the European International Society* (London: Routledge, forth-

coming). For a different approach again, see Paul Keal, *European Conquest and the Rights of Indigenous Peoples: The Moral Backwardness of International Society* (Cambridge: Cambridge University Press, 2003).

21. Friedrich von Schiller, "Nature and Value of Universal History," 327.

22. Michael W. Doyle, "Liberalism and World Politics," *American Political Science Review* 80, no. 4 (1986): 1151.

23. Schapiro, *Condorcet and the Rise of Liberalism*, 260.

24. Condorcet, *Sketch*, 194.

25. Martha C. Nussbaum, "Kant and Stoic Cosmopolitanism," *Journal of Political Philosophy* 5, no. 1 (1997): 3. For a different perspective see Isaiah Berlin, "Kant as an Unfamiliar Source of Nationalism," in *The Sense of Reality: Studies in Ideas and Their History*, by Isaiah Berlin, ed. Henry Hardy (London: Chatto & Windus, 1996), 232–48.

26. See Howard, *Invention of Peace*, 31. That is not to suggest that Kant was the first to consider the idea of perpetual peace, for as he acknowledges, it had already been considered and dismissed by both Abbé de Saint-Pierre and Jean-Jacques Rousseau. See Rousseau, "Abstract and Judgement of Saint-Pierre's Project for Perpetual Peace" [1756], in *Rousseau on International Relations*, ed. Stanley Hoffman and David P. Fidler (Oxford: Clarendon, 1991), 53–100. Jeremy Bentham had also earlier expressed his thoughts on the matter in *Plan for an Universal and Perpetual Peace* (1786–89; London: Peace Book, 1939).

27. Kant, "Idea for a Universal History," 16.

28. Kant, "Perpetual Peace," 93–94. Here (95–96) Kant makes the point "not to confuse the republican constitution with the democratic (as is commonly done) . . . [for] democracy is, properly speaking, necessarily a despotism."

29. These three propositions are referred to by some as the "Kantian Tripod." See Bruce Russett, John R. Oneal, and David R. Davis, "The Third Leg of the Kantian Tripod for Peace: International Organizations and Militarized Disputes, 1950–85," *International Organization* 52, no. 3 (1998): 441–67.

30. Kant, "Idea for a Universal History," 23.

31. Lars-Erik Cederman, "Back to Kant: Reinterpreting the Democratic Peace as a Macrohistorical Learning Process," *American Political Science Review* 95, no. 1 (2001): 16–17.

32. See Andrew Moravcsik, "Taking Preferences Seriously: A Liberal Theory of International Politics," *International Organization* 51, no. 4 (1997): 518. Similarly, Boutros Boutros-Ghali, *An Agenda for Peace* (New York: United Nations, 1992); Commission on Global Governance, *Our Global Neighborhood* (New York: Oxford University Press, 1995); and Gareth Evans, *Cooperating for Peace* (St. Leonards: Unwin & Hyman, 1993). All assume there is a "connection between domestic and international order to justify greater intervention in domestic affairs." See Michael N. Barnett, "Bringing in the New World Order: Liberalism, Legitimacy, and the United Nations," *World Politics* 49, no. 4 (1997): 536.

33. Kant, "Old Question," 151.

34. Bruce Buchan, "Explaining War and Peace: Kant and Liberal IR Theory," *Alternatives: Global, Local, Political* 27, no. 4 (2002): 414.

35. Kant, "Idea for a Universal History," 15.

36. Both quoted in Anthony Pagden, "Stoicism, Cosmopolitanism, and the Legacy of European Imperialism," *Constellations* 7, no. 1 (2000): 8.

37. Montesquieu, *Spirit of the Laws*, book 20, chap. 1, p. 316.

38. David Ricardo, *Principles of Political Economy and Taxation*, ed. E. C. K. Gonner (London: George Bell & Sons, 1891), 114.

39. Kant, "Perpetual Peace," 114.

40. Michael Mosseau, "Market Prosperity, Democratic Consolidation, and Democratic Peace," *Journal of Conflict Resolution* 44, no. 4 (2000): 472–507. See also Robert O. Keohane, *Power and Governance in a Partially Globalized World* (London: Routledge, 2002).

41. Steve Smith, "Is the Truth out There? Eight Questions about International Order," in *International Order and the Future of World Politics*, ed. T. V. Paul and John A. Hall (Cambridge: Cambridge University Press, 1999), 110.

42. John Rawls, *The Law of Peoples* (Cambridge, MA: Harvard University Press, 1999), 21; emphasis in original; and Kant, "Perpetual Peace," 100.

43. Rawls, *Law of Peoples*, 3.

44. Francis Fukuyama, "Second Thoughts: The Last Man in a Bottle," *National Interest* 56 (1999): 17.

45. See Arie M. Kacowicz, "Explaining Zones of Peace: Democracies as Satisfied Powers?" *Journal of Peace Research* 32, no. 5 (1995): 265–76.

46. Jack S. Levy, "Domestic Politics and War," *Journal of Interdisciplinary History* 18, no. 4 (1988): 662. The firmness of this law is questionable given that the parameters of what Levy (662n14) accepts as a democratic or liberal regime, between which he does not distinguish, are particularly wide. That is, democracies incorporate "(1) regular elections and the free participation of opposition parties, (2) at least ten percent of the adult population being able to vote for, (3) a parliament that either control[s] or share[s] parity with the executive branch."

47. Bruce Russett, *Controlling the Sword: The Democratic Governance of National Security* (Cambridge, MA: Harvard University Press, 1990), 123.

48. Michael W. Doyle, "Kant, Liberal Legacies, and Foreign Affairs, Part 2," *Philosophy and Public Affairs* 12, no. 4 (1983): 352.

49. Rawls, *Law of Peoples*, 54.

50. Boutros-Ghali, *Agenda for Peace*, 47.

51. Doyle, "Liberalism and World Politics," 1151.

52. Levy, "Domestic Politics and War," 659.

53. Ido Oren, "The Subjectivity of the 'Democratic' Peace: Changing U.S. Perceptions of Imperial Germany," in *Debating the Democratic Peace: An International Security Reader*, ed. Michael E. Brown, Sean M. Lynn-Jones, and Steven E. Miller (Cambridge, MA: MIT Press, 1996), 263. For a further critique, see also David E. Spiro, "The Insignificance of the Liberal Peace," in the same volume, 202–38.

54. Fukuyama, "Second Thoughts," 17–19.

55. Norbert Elias, *The Civilizing Process*, trans. Edmund Jephcott (Oxford: Basil Blackwell, 1994), 288, 445–48.

56. Mark W. Zacher and Richard A. Matthew, "Liberal International Theory: Common Threads, Divergent Strands," in *Controversies in International*

Relations Theory, ed. Charles W. Kegley (New York: St. Martin's, 1995), 118; emphasis in original.

57. Fukuyama, *End of History and the Last Man*, 201–2; emphasis in original.

58. Zacher and Matthew, "Liberal International Theory," 109–10.

59. Kant, "Idea for a Universal History," 23.

60. Nussbaum, "Kant and Stoic Cosmopolitanism," 4.

61. Kant, "Perpetual Peace," 105.

62. Thomas W. Pogge, "Cosmopolitanism and Sovereignty," *Ethics* 103, no. 1 (1992): 48–49.

63. Ulrich Beck, "The Cosmopolitan Manifesto," *New Statesman*, March 20, 1998, 29. See also Ulrich Beck, "The Cosmopolitan Perspective: Sociology of the Second Age of Modernity," *British Journal of Sociology* 51, no. 1 (2000): 79–106; and Beck, "The Cosmopolitan Society and Its Enemies," *Theory, Culture and Society* 19, nos. 1–2 (2002): 17–44.

64. Pagden, "Stoicism, Cosmopolitanism," 3.

65. Harvey, "Cosmopolitanism," 546. Harvey also thinks that Martin Heidegger might have been on to something "in insisting that Kant's cosmopolitanism inevitably slips into an internationalism rooted in nationalism." As Heidegger put it, "Nationalism is not overcome through mere internationalism; it is rather expanded and elevated into a system." See Martin Heidegger, "Letter on Humanism," in *Martin Heidegger: Basic Writings*, ed. David Farrell Krell, 2nd ed. (London: Routledge, 1993), 244.

66. Stephen Toulmin, *Cosmopolis: The Hidden Agenda of Modernity* (New York: Free Press, 1990), 67

67. See Arnold J. Toynbee, prefaces in *Greek Historical Thought from Homer to the Age of Heraclius*, ed. and trans. Arnold J. Toynbee (New York: Mentor, 1952), 29–31. On the broader debate about the origins of and influences on Greek thought, see Martin Bernal, *Black Athena: The Afroasiatic Roots of Classical Civilization* (London: Free Association, 1987); Mary R. Lefkowitz and Guy MacLean Rogers, eds. *Black Athena Revisited* (Chapel Hill: University of North Carolina Press, 1996); and Martin Bernal, *Black Athena Writes Back: Martin Bernal Responds to His Critics*, ed. David Chioni Moore (Durham, NC: Duke University Press, 2001).

68. Toulmin, *Cosmopolis*, 68.

69. Mike Featherstone, "Cosmopolis: An Introduction," *Theory, Culture and Society* 19, nos. 1–2 (2002): 2.

70. See J. R. Levenson, *Revolution and Cosmopolitanism: The Western Stages and the Chinese Stages* (Berkeley: University of California Press, 1971); P. Werbner, "Global Pathways: Working-Class Cosmopolitans and the Creation of Transnational Ethnic Worlds," *Social Anthropology* 7, no. 1 (1999): 17–35; and S. Pollock, H. K. Bhaba, C. A. Breckenridge, and D. Chakrabarty, "Cosmopolitanisms," *Public Culture* 12, no. 3 (2000): 577–89.

71. Lisa Hill, "The Two *Republicae* of the Roman Stoics: Can a Cosmopolite Be a Patriot?" *Citizenship Studies* 4, no. 1 (2000): 66.

72. Plutarch; quoted in H. C. Baldry, *The Unity of Mankind in Greek Thought* (Cambridge: Cambridge University Press, 1965), 159.

73. Featherstone, "Cosmopolis," 3.

74. See Kant, "Perpetual Peace," 98–100.

75. Charles Beitz, *Political Theory and International Relations* (Princeton, NJ: Princeton University Press, 1979), 183.

76. Hill, "Two *Republicae*," 67–69.

77. Pogge, "Cosmopolitanism and Sovereignty," 58.

78. See Brett Bowden, "The Perils of Global Citizenship," *Citizenship Studies* 7, no. 3 (2003): 349–62. The reluctance to go beyond geographically based organization possibly stems from the range of concerns and problems such collectives—from antiglobalization protesters to loose-knit terrorist networks such as al-Qa'ida—pose to governments of modern nation-states.

79. Martha C. Nussbaum, "Patriotism and Cosmopolitanism," in *For Love of Country: Debating the Limits of Patriotism*, ed. Joshua Cohen (Boston: Beacon, 1996), 9.

80. Pagden, "Stoicism, Cosmopolitanism," 5–6; emphasis in original.

81. Hill, "Two *Republicae*," 72; emphasis in original.

82. Timothy Brennan, *At Home in the World: Cosmopolitanism Now* (Cambridge, MA: Harvard University Press, 1997), 147.

83. Pagden, "Stoicism, Cosmopolitanism," 3–4.

84. Venn, "Altered States," 68.

85. Giuseppe Mazzini, *Life and Writings of Joseph Mazzini*, 2nd ed. (London: Smith, Elder, 1891), 3:10.

86. Pagden, "Stoicism, Cosmopolitanism," 19–20.

87. Featherstone, "Cosmopolis," 3.

88. Inayatullah and Blaney, *International Relations and the Problem of Difference*, 6–7.

89. Mazzini, *Life and Writings*, 3:8.

90. Michael Walzer, "Spheres of Affection," in *For Love of Country: Debating the Limits of Patriotism*, ed. Joshua Cohen (Boston: Beacon, 1996), 126–27.

91. Pogge, "Cosmopolitanism and Sovereignty," 49.

92. Anthony Pagden, "The Genesis of 'Governance' and Enlightenment Conceptions of the Cosmopolitan World Order," *International Social Science Journal* 50, no. 155 (1998): 14.

93. Pagden, "Stoicism, Cosmopolitanism," 19.

94. Gray, *Enlightenment's Wake*, 120–23.

95. John Gray, *False Dawn: The Delusions of Global Capitalism* (London: Granta, 1998), 2.

96. Ricoeur, *History and Truth*, 277. On this, see also John M. Hobson, *The Eastern Origins of Western Civilisation* (Cambridge: Cambridge University Press, 2004).

97. Ricoeur, *History and Truth*, 277.

98. Fidler, "A Kinder, Gentler System of Capitulation?" 406.

99. Huntington, "Clash of Civilizations?" 41; and "The West Unique, Not Universal," 39.

100. Gertrude Himmelfarb, "In Defense of Progress," *Commentary* 69, no. 6 (1980): 57.

5. THE EXPANSION OF EUROPE AND THE CLASSICAL STANDARD
OF CIVILIZATION

1. Gong, *Standard of "Civilization,"* 3.

2. Robert A. Williams Jr., *The American Indian in Western Legal Thought: The Discourses of Conquest* (New York: Oxford University Press, 1990), 6.

3. James Muldoon, introduction to *The Expansion of Europe: The First Phase,* ed. James Muldoon (Philadelphia: University of Pennsylvania Press, 1977), 4–5.

4. Frederic William Maitland, "Moral Personality and Legal Personality," in *The Collected Papers of Frederic William Maitland,* ed. H. A. L. Fisher (Cambridge: Cambridge University Press, 1911), 3:310.

5. Pope Innocent IV, "Document 40: *Commentaria Doctissima in Quinque Libros Decretalium,*" in *The Expansion of Europe: The First Phase,* ed. Muldoon, 191–92.

6. James Muldoon, *Popes, Lawyers, and Infidels* (Philadelphia: University of Pennsylvania Press, 1979), 6.

7. On the Mongol Empire more generally, see Thomas T. Allsen, *Mongol Imperialism: The Policies of the Grand Qan Möngke in China, Russia, and the Islamic Lands, 1251–1259* (Berkeley: University of California Press, 1987).

8. Muldoon, *Popes, Lawyers, and Infidels,* 24–45.

9. Christopher Dawson, introduction to *The Mongol Mission: Narratives and Letters of the Franciscan Missionaries in Mongolia and China in the Thirteenth and Fourteenth Centuries,* ed. Christopher Dawson (London: Sheed & Ward, 1955), xiv–xviii; and Robert Williams, *American Indian in Western Legal Thought,* 3–4.

10. Brother Benedict, "The Narrative of Brother Benedict the Pole," in *Mongol Mission,* ed. Dawson, 79.

11. The two letters are reproduced in "Two Bulls of Pope Innocent IV to the Emperor of the Tartars," in *Mongol Mission,* ed. Dawson, 73–76. All quotes are taken from here.

12. Benedict, "Narrative," 82.

13. "Guyuk Khan's Letter to Pope Innocent IV (1246)," in *Mongol Mission,* ed. Dawson, 85–86.

14. Muldoon, *Popes, Lawyers, and Infidels,* 45.

15. See Igor de Rachewiltz, *Papal Envoys to the Great Khans* (London: Faber & Faber, 1971), 144–59.

16. Martin Wight, *Systems of States,* ed. Hedley Bull (Leicester: Leicester University Press, 1977), 119.

17. Muldoon, commentary on "Document 40: *Commentaria Doctissima in Quinque Libros Decretalium,*" by Innocent IV, in *Expansion of Europe,* 191.

18. Franciscus de Vitoria, *De Indis et de Iure Belli Relectiones,* ed. Ernest Nys (1539; reprint of 1696 ed.; New York: Oceana, 1964).

19. James Brown Scott, *The Spanish Origin of International Law: Francisco de Vitoria and His Law of Nations* (Oxford: Clarendon, 1932), ix.

20. Pagden, "Stoicism, Cosmopolitanism," 7.

21. Antony Anghie, "Francisco de Vitoria and the Colonial Origins of International Law," *Social and Legal Studies* 5, no. 3 (1996): 322; emphasis in original.

22. Gong, *Standard of "Civilization,"* 3.

23. Vitoria, *De Indis*, 116.

24. Acosta, *Natural and Moral History of the Indies*, 359.

25. Vitoria, *De Indis*, 120.

26. Ibid., 120–21. On natural slavery in Aristotle, see *Politics*, book 1, esp. chaps. 2–9.

27. Vitoria, *De Indis*, 127, 125, 127–28. In this final observation, Vitoria was likely also influenced by a similar sentiment expressed in the Bible, Proverbs 11:29, which states, "and the fool shall be servant to the wise of heart."

28. Vitoria, *De Indis*, 160–61.

29. Lewis Henry Morgan later observed that the Hodenosaunee or Iroquois Confederation's system of government "was an aristocracy liberalised, until it stood upon the verge of democracy." See Lewis H. Morgan, *The League of the Iroquois* (1851; North Dighton, MA: JG Press, 1995), 126. Even earlier, James Adair (c. 1709–1783) noted that the "Indian method of government" generally consists of a "fœderal union of the whole society for mutual safety." He further noted that the "power of their chiefs, is an empty sound." For chiefs "can only persuade or dissuade the people" by "force of good-nature and clear reasoning." He continues,

> When any national affair is in debate, you may hear every father of a family speaking in his house on the subject, with rapid, bold language, and the utmost freedom that a people can use. Their voices, to a man, have due weight in every public affair, as it concerns their welfare alike. . . . They are very deliberate in their councils. . . . They reason in a very orderly manner, with much coolness and good-natured language, though they may differ widely in their opinions. . . . In this manner they proceed, till each of the head men hath given his opinion on the point in debate. Then they sit down together, and determine upon the affair.

Adair concluded that the Amerindians' "whole behaviour, on public occasions, is highly worthy of imitation by some of our British senators and lawyers." See James Adair, *Adair's History of the American Indians*, ed. Samuel Cole Williams (1775; New York: Promontory, 1930), 459–60.

30. Anghie, "Francisco de Vitoria," 326–27.

31. Ibid., 332. See also Antony Anghie, *Imperialism, Sovereignty and the Making of International Law* (Cambridge: Cambridge University Press, 2005), esp. chap. 1.

32. Anghie, "Francisco de Vitoria," 333.

33. The eighteenth- and nineteenth-century use of the term *publicist* to describe international lawyers is very different from that which describes modern

public relations professionals. I continue to use the term *publicist* to describe international lawyers of the era, for their active role in formulating international law is considerably more significant in many ways than that of today's jurists.

34. John Westlake, *The Collected Papers of John Westlake on Public International Law*, ed. L. Oppenheim (Cambridge: Cambridge University Press, 1914), 139–40.

35. Henry Wheaton, *Elements of International Law*, 3rd ed. (London: Sampson Low, Son and Co., 1863), xii–xiii, partially quoting Patrick Henry, the Virginia-born American politician who first uttered the famous phrase, "give me liberty or give me death."

36. William A. Robson, *Civilisation and the Growth of Law* (London: Macmillan, 1935), 11.

37. E. Sidney Hartland, "Law (Primitive)," *Encyclopedia of Religion and Ethics*, 7:812–13; quoted in Robson, *Civilisation and the Growth of Law*, 11.

38. Carleton Kemp Allen, *Law in the Making*, 2nd ed. (Oxford: Clarendon, 1930), 26.

39. Christian Wolff, *Jus Gentium Method Scientifica Pertactatum* (1749; New York: Oceana, 1964), 33–36.

40. Gong, *Standard of "Civilization,"* 3.

41. Robert Ward, *An Enquiry into the Foundation and History of the Law of Nations in Europe from the Time of the Greeks and Romans to the Age of Grotius* (reprint of 1795 ed.; New York: Garland, 1973), 1:136–39.

42. Wolff, *Jus Gentium*, 15–17; emphasis added.

43. William Edward Hall, *A Treatise on International Law*, 3rd ed. (Oxford: Clarendon, 1890), 55

44. Wheaton, *Elements of International Law* (1863), 21, 16–17.

45. Westlake, *Collected Papers*, 78–82; emphasis in original.

46. Ward, *Enquiry*, 2:1–4; emphasis in original.

47. Henry Wheaton, *Wheaton's Elements of International Law*, ed. Coleman Phillipson, 5th ed. (London: Stevens & Sons, 1916), 65–66.

48. Montesquieu, *Spirit of the Laws*, book 18, chap. 11, 276.

49. Wheaton, *Wheaton's Elements of International Law* (1916), 107.

50. On the contribution of non-Europeans to the catalog of ideas and innovations more generally, see J. J. Clarke, *Oriental Enlightenment: The Encounter between Asian and Western Thought* (London: Routledge, 1997); Cyriac K. Pullapilly and Edwin J. Van Kley, eds., *Asia and the West: Encounters and Exchanges from the Age of Explorations* (Notre Dame, IN: Cross Cultural, 1986); Lewis A. Maverick, *China: A Model for Europe* (San Antonio, TX: Paul Anderson, 1946); Stanwood Cobb, *Islamic Contributions to Civilisation* (Washington, DC: Avalon, 1963); and Adolf Reichwein, *China and Europe: Intellectual and Artistic Contacts in the Eighteenth Century* (London: Kegan Paul, Trench, Trubner, 1925).

51. Lorimer, *Institutes of the Law of Nations*, 1:93, 1:101.

52. Westlake, *Collected Papers*, 143; emphasis in original.

53. W. Hall, *Treatise on International Law*, 87.

54. Wheaton, *Elements of International Law* (1863), xiv.

55. Georg Schwarzenberger, "The Standard of Civilisation in International Law," in *Current Legal Problems*, ed. George W. Keeton and Georg Schwarzenberger (London: Stevens & Sons, 1955), 220; emphasis added.

56. Pasquale Fiore, *International Law Codified and Its Legal Sanction* (New York: Baker, Voorhis, 1918), 117, 119; emphasis in original.

57. Wheaton, *Elements of International Law* (1863), 33.

58. W. Hall, *Treatise on International Law*, 87–88.

59. Fiore, *International Law Codified*, 362.

60. Wheaton, *Elements of International Law* (1863), 27.

61. Alpheus Henry Snow, *The Question of Aborigines in the Law and Practice of Nations* (New York: Putnam's Sons; Knickerbocker, 1921), 315–16.

62. Schwarzenberger, "Standard of Civilisation in International Law," 218.

63. Gong, *Standard of "Civilization,"* 84.

64. H. Lauterpacht, *Recognition in International Law* (Cambridge: Cambridge University Press, 1947), 31 and note 1.

65. Collingwood, "What 'Civilization' Means," in *New Leviathan*, 486.

66. Schwarzenberger, "Standard of Civilisation in International Law," 227.

67. Anghie, "Francisco de Vitoria," 332–33; see also, Antony Anghie, "Finding the Peripheries: Sovereignty and Colonialism in Nineteenth-Century International Law," *Harvard International Law* 40, no. 1 (1999): 1–80.

68. Anghie, "Francisco de Vitoria," 333.

6. THE BURDEN OF CIVILIZATION AND THE "ART AND SCIENCE OF COLONIZATION"

1. Christopher Columbus, "Letter of 15th February 1493 on the islands newly found by the King of Spain," reproduced in *The Journal of Christopher Columbus*, trans. Cecil Jane (London: Anthony Blond and Orion Press, 1960), 191–202.

2. Bartolomé de la Vega, "Introductory Letter," in *In Defense of the Indians*, by Bartolomé de Las Casas, ed. and trans. Stafford Poole (DeKalb: Northern Illinois University Press, 1974), 5.

3. Barry Hindess, "The Liberal Government of Unfreedom," *Alternatives: Global, Local, Political* 26, no. 2 (2001): 101.

4. Todorov, *Conquest of America*, 5.

5. John Darwin, "Civility and Empire," in *Civil Histories: Essays Presented to Sir Keith Thomas*, ed. Peter Burke, Brian Harrison, and Paul Slack (Oxford: Oxford University Press, 2000), 322.

6. The Statute of Kilkenny of 1366, renewed in 1498 and supplemented in 1536; quoted in Darwin, "Civility and Empire," 322.

7. Darwin, "Civility and Empire," 322.

8. Sir John Davies, *Historical Relations: or, a discovery of the true causes why Ireland was never entirely subdued nor brought under obedience of the Crown of England until the beginning of the Reign of King James of happy memory* (Dublin: Samuel Dancer, 1664), 4–5.

9. See James Muldoon, "The Indian as Irishman," *Essex Institute Historical Collections* 111 (1975): 267–89.

10. Anghie, "Finding the Peripheries," 4–5.

11. Spencer, *Social Statistics*, 248–49.

12. Eduard von Hartmann, *Philosophy of Unconscious*, trans. William Chatterton Coupland (London: Kegan Paul, Trench, Trübner, 1893), 2:11–12.

13. Snow, *Question of Aborigines*, 176.

14. See John R. Stevenson, "South West Africa Cases (Ethiopia v. South Africa; Liberia v. South Africa), Second Phase," *American Journal of International Law* 61, no. 1 (1967): 116–210.

15. Quoted in Charles H. Alexandrowicz, "The Juridical Expression of the Sacred Trust of Civilization," *American Journal of International Law* 65, no. 1 (1971): 65.

16. Las Casas, "Summary of the Defense of the Most Reverend Lord, Fray Bartolomé de Las Casas, Late Bishop of Chiapa, against Ginés Sepúlveda, Theologian of Córdoba," in Las Casas, *In Defense of the Indians*, 7–9.

17. Ginés Sepúlveda, "Summary of Sepúlveda's Position," in Las Casas, *In Defense of the Indians*, 11–13.

18. Las Casas, preface to *In Defense of the Indians*, 18. For a celebration of Las Casas, see Hayward R. Alker Jr., "The Humanistic Moment in International Studies: Reflections on Machiavelli and Las Casas: 1992 Presidential Address," *International Studies Quarterly* 36, no. 4 (1992): 347–71.

19. Las Casas, "Summary of the Defense," 8.

20. Las Casas, *In Defense of the Indians*, 28.

21. Boswell, *Boswell's Life of Johnson*, 1:455.

22. J. L. Brierly, *The Law of Nations*, 4th ed. (Oxford: Clarendon, 1949), 6.

23. Robert Williams, *American Indian in Western Legal Thought*, 96–97.

24. Innocent IV, "Two Bulls of Pope Innocent IV," 73–76.

25. Vitoria, *De Indis*, 150–51.

26. Ernest Nys, introduction to Vitoria, *De Indis*, 100.

27. J. Scott, *Spanish Origin of International Law*, 277.

28. Vitoria, *De Indis*, 158.

29. Pope Alexander VI; quoted in James Muldoon, *The Americas in the Spanish World Order: The Justification for Conquest in the Seventeenth Century* (Philadelphia: University of Pennsylvania Press, 1994), 40.

30. Patent for the Council of New England of 1620; quoted in Muldoon, *The Americas in the Spanish World Order*, 38.

31. Locke, *Two Treatises of Government*, book 2, pp. 438–39, para. 184; emphasis in original; and Barbara Arneil, "Trade, Plantations, and Property: John Locke and the Economic Defense of Colonialism," *Journal of the History of Ideas* 55, no. 4 (1994): 591–609.

32. Locke, *Two Treatises of Government*, book 2, p. 336, para. 37. On the influence of Locke more generally, see James Tully, *An Approach to Political Philosophy: Locke in Contexts* (Cambridge: Cambridge University Press, 1993).

33. Emerich de Vattel, *The Law of Nations; or, The Principles of Natural Law*, trans. Charles G. Fenwick (1758; New York: Oceana, 1964), 85, 37–38, 85.

34. Fiore, *International Law Codified*, 46.

35. See V. I. Lenin, *Imperialism, the Highest Stage of Capitalism: A Popular Outline* (Peking: Foreign Languages, 1965).

36. Fiore, *International Law Codified*, 120.

37. Lorimer, *Institutes of the Law of Nations*, 2:28.

38. Antoine Rougier, "La Théorie de l'Intervention d'Humanité," *Revue Générale de Droit International Public* 17 (1910): 495–96; quoted in Snow, *Question of Aborigines*, 316–17.

39. Westlake, *Collected Paper*, 145.

40. G. W. F. Hegel, *Aesthetics: Lectures on Fine Art*, trans. T. M. Knox (1835–1838; Oxford: Clarendon, 1975), 2:1061–62.

41. Hegel, *Philosophy of Right*, 151, para. 246–48.

42. A. Smith, *Wealth of Nations*, 296–97. For Smith's thoughts on the possible economic advantages of American colonies, see book 4, chap. 7, "Of Colonies," 227–66.

43. See Sankar Muthu, "Enlightenment Anti-Imperialism," *Social Research* 66, no. 4 (1999): 959–1007; and Muthu, *Enlightenment against Empire* (Princeton, NJ: Princeton University Press, 2003).

44. Nussbaum, "Kant and Stoic Cosmopolitanism," 14. Michael Doyle argues that "Kant rejects conquest or imperial intervention as . . . wrong." See Doyle, "Kant, Liberal Legacies," 325.

45. Kant, "Perpetual Peace," 86–87.

46. Nussbaum, "Kant and Stoic Cosmopolitanism," 3.

47. Harvey, "Cosmopolitanism," 534. Kant sought an exemption from university regulations to teach geography and taught the course at least forty-nine times. By way of comparison, he taught logic and metaphysics fifty-four times, ethics on forty-six occasions, and anthropology twenty-eight times.

48. Immanuel Kant, *Geographie (Physiche Geographie)*, trans. M. Cohen-Halimi, M. Marcuzzi, and V. Seroussi (Paris: Bibliotheque Philosophique, 1999); quoted in Harvey, "Cosmopolitanism," 533.

49. George Tatham, "Environmentalism and Possibilism," in *Geography in the Twentieth Century: A Study of Growth, Fields, Techniques, Aims and Trends*, ed. Griffith Taylor, 3rd ed. (New York: Philosophical Library; London: Methuen, 1957), 130–31; and J. A. May, *Kant's Concept of Geography and Its Relation to Recent Geographical Thought* (Toronto: University of Toronto Press, 1970), 66.

50. Kant, "Perpetual Peace," 92n1.

51. Harvey, "Cosmopolitanism," 535.

52. Robert van Krieken, "The Barbarism of Civilization: Cultural Genocide and the 'Stolen Generations,'" *British Journal of Sociology* 50, no. 2 (1999): 309; emphasis in original.

53. John Stuart Mill, "A Few Words on Non-Intervention," in *Essays on Politics and Culture*, ed. Gertrude Himmelfarb (1859; Garden City, NY: Doubleday, 1962), 407.

54. Ibid., 406–7; emphasis in original. For further critical analysis of J. S. Mill and his father, James, on matters of imperialism, see Uday Singh Mehta, *Liberalism and Empire: A Study in Nineteenth-Century British Thought* (Chi-

cago: University of Chicago Press, 1999), esp. chap. 3, "Progress, Civilization, and Consent," 77–114.

55. Arthur James Balfour; quoted in Edward W. Said, *Orientalism* (London: Routledge & Kegan Paul, 1978), 31–33. For an argument that many peoples of the world have a long history of not only self-government, but some form of democratic or quasi-democratic government, see Steven Muhlberger and Phil Paine, "Democracy's Place in World History," *Journal of World History* 4, no. 1 (1993): 23–45.

56. Snow, *Question of Aborigines*, 191.

57. Cecil Rhodes, "Rhodes' 'Confession of Faith' of 1877," appendix to *Cecil Rhodes*, by John Flint (London: Hutchinson, 1976), 249–50.

58. Michael W. Doyle, *Empires* (Ithaca, NY: Cornell University Press, 1986), 143.

59. One of the more comprehensive general studies is Thomas Pakenham, *The Scramble for Africa (1876–1912)* (London: Abacus, 1992). For detailed analysis of the range of motivations, and critiques thereof, behind the "scramble for Africa," see Doyle, *Empires*, part 2.

60. General Act of the Berlin Conference of 1884–1885, February 26, 1885, chap. 1, article 6.

61. See, for instance, Lindqvist, *"Exterminate All the Brutes."* For a graphic account from the late nineteenth century, see E. J. Glave, "Cruelty in the Congo Free State: Concluding Extracts from the Journals of the late E. J. Glave," *The Century Illustrated Monthly Magazine* 54, n.s., 32 (New York: Century; London: Macmillan, May–October 1897); 699–715.

62. Hartmann, *Philosophy of Unconscious*, 2:12.

63. Charles Henry Alexandrowicz, *The European-African Confrontation: A Study in Treaty Making* (Leiden: Sijthoff, 1973), 6.

64. Long before it became a formal colonial power, under the (abused) authority of President James Monroe's Doctrine of 1823, the United States had persistently been intervening militarily in what it saw as its Latin American "sphere of influence." The most notable intervention was the war against Mexico in the mid-1840s, in which the United States annexed part of the country, but there were also interventions in Puerto Rico (1824), in Nicaragua (1850, 1853, 1854, 1857, and 1860), and in Panama (1856 and 1860). The prominent role of the United Fruit Company in Latin America from the late nineteenth century on is also worthy of note. See Charles D. Kepner Jr. and Jay H. Soothill, *The Banana Empire: A Case Study of Economic Imperialism* (New York: Russell & Russell, 1967).

65. See Robert L. Beisner, *Twelve against Empire: The Anti-Imperialists, 1898–1900* (New York: McGraw-Hill, 1968).

66. Snow, *Question of Aborigines*, 175–76.

67. Anders Stephanson, *Manifest Destiny: American Expansion and the Empire of Right* (New York: Hill & Wang, 1995), 19.

68. Snow, *Question of Aborigines*, 190.

69. See, for instance, Veltisezar B. Bautista, *The Filipino Americans (from 1763 to the Present): Their History, Culture, and Traditions*, 2nd ed. (Farmington Hills, MI: Bookhaus, 2002); Daniel B. Schirmer and Stephen Rosskamm

Shalom, eds., *The Philippines Reader: A History of Colonialism, Neocolonialism, Dictatorship, and Resistance* (Cambridge, MA: South End, 1987).

70. John A. Hobson, *Imperialism: A Study*, 3rd ed. (London: Allen & Unwin, 1948), 73–74.

71. Paul Hasluck, "The Native Welfare Conference, 1951," in *Native Welfare in Australia: Speeches and Addresses* (Perth: Paterson Brakensha, 1953), 17.

72. Stiglitz, "Towards a New Paradigm for Development."

73. Dean C. Tipps, "Modernization Theory and the Comparative Study of Societies: A Critical Perspective," *Comparative Studies in Society and History* 15, no. 2 (1973): 210.

74. Jules Harmand; quoted in Edward W. Said, *Culture and Imperialism* (New York: Vintage, 1994), 17.

75. John Stuart Mill, *Utilitarianism, Liberty, and Representative Government* (London: Dent & Sons, 1962), 73–74. See also David Scott, *Refashioning Futures* (Princeton, NJ: Princeton University Press, 1999), 86.

7. NEW BARBARISM AND THE TEST OF MODERNITY

1. Anders Stephanson (*Manifest Destiny*, 19) describes Humphreys as an officer in the Revolutionary Army, a diplomat, and a protégé of George Washington.

2. Collingwood, "What 'Civilization' Means," in *New Leviathan*, 486.

3. Schwarzenberger, "Standard of Civilisation in International Law," 227.

4. Wight, *Systems of States*, 125.

5. See James M. Goldgeier and Michael McFaul, "A Tale of Two Worlds: Core and Periphery in the Post–Cold War Era," *International Organization* 46, no. 2 (1992): 467–91.

6. Ian Clark, *The Hierarchy of States: Reform and Resistance in International Order* (Cambridge: Cambridge University Press, 1989), 2.

7. For example, in the former Yugoslavia, parts of the former Soviet Union, Western Africa, the Horn of Africa, and the Great Lakes region of Central Africa. But not all of these necessarily have direct causal links with the ending of the Cold War.

8. Eric Hobsbawm, "Barbarism: A User's Guide," *New Left Review* 206 (1994): 45; emphasis in original.

9. Clifford S. Poirot Jr., "The Return to Barbarism," *Journal of Economic Issues* 31, no. 1 (1997): 233. See also Clause Offe, "Modern 'Barbarity': A Micro State of Nature," *Constellations* 2, no. 3 (1996): 354–77.

10. Nathan Gardels, "Comment: The New Babel and the Noblest of Pains," *New Perspectives Quarterly* 8, no. 4 (1991): 2–3.

11. Robert D. Kaplan, "The Coming Anarchy," *Atlantic Monthly*, February 1994, 48. See also Robert D. Kaplan, *Balkan Ghosts: A Journey through History* (London: Macmillan, 1993).

12. Kaplan, "Coming Anarchy," 60. See Thomas F. Homer-Dixon, "On the Threshold: Environmental Changes as Causes of Acute Conflict," *International Security* 16, no. 2 (1991): 76–116; Homer-Dixon, "Environmental Scar-

cities and Violent Conflict: Evidence from Cases," *International Security* 19, no. 1 (1994): 5–40; and Homer-Dixon, *Environment, Scarcity, and Violence* (Princeton, NJ: Princeton University Press, 2001).

13. Kaplan, "Coming Anarchy," 62; emphasis in original.

14. Ibid., 71–73. See Francis Fukuyama, "Natural Rights and Human History," *National Interest* 64 (2001): 27.

15. Kaplan, "Coming Anarchy," 60.

16. Paul Richards, *Fighting for the Rainforest: War, Youth and Resources in Sierra Leone* (Oxford: International Africa Institute in association with James Currey; and Portsmouth, NH: Heinemann, 1996). For more on such distinctions in respect to warfare, see Brett Bowden, "Civilization and Savagery in the Crucible of War," *Global Change, Peace and Security* 19, no. 1 (2007): 3–16.

17. Steve Bradshaw, "The Coming Chaos?" *Moving Pictures Bulletin* 25 (1996): 18–19.

18. Gong, *Standard of "Civilization,"* 90–92.

19. Ian Brownlie, *Principles of Public International Law*, 5th ed. (Oxford: Clarendon, 1998), 602. Brownlie's claim is based on the *South West Africa* cases (Second Phase), ICJ Reports, 1966. See chapter 6 above.

20. Compare Bahar Rumelili, *Constructing Regional Community and Order in Europe and Southeast Asia* (Basingstoke: Palgrave, 2007).

21. Gong, *Standard of "Civilization,"* 91–92.

22. Ibid., 92–93; and Gerrit W. Gong, "The Beginning of History: Remembering and Forgetting as Strategic Issues," *Washington Quarterly* 24, no. 2 (2001): 47.

23. See Hedley Bull and Adam Watson, ed. *The Expansion of International Society* (Oxford: Clarendon, 1984), particularly the chapter by Bull, "The Emergence of a Universal International Society," 117–26. A case in point: at the instigation of socialist and nonaligned countries, in 1962 the United Nations established a special committee to come up with a more expansive set of "universal" values than those set out in the charter. The process resulted in the Declaration on Friendly Relations of 1970 (Resolution 2625-XXV). See Antonio Cassese, *International Law in a Divided World* (Oxford: Clarendon, 1986), 127–28.

24. U. Beck, "Cosmopolitan Manifesto," 29.

25. Mehdi Mozaffari, "The Transformationalist Perspective and the Rise of a Global Standard of Civilization," *International Relations of the Asia-Pacific* 1, no. 2 (2001): 253–54.

26. John Rawls, "The Law of Peoples," in *On Human Rights: The Oxford Amnesty Lectures*, ed. Stephen Shute and Susan Hurley (New York: Basic, 1993), 70–71.

27. Jack Donnelly, "Human Rights: A New Standard of Civilization," *International Affairs* 74, no. 1 (1998): 1, 15–16, 21, 15–16.

28. On this point, see Muhlberger and Paine, "Democracy's Place in World History," 23–45; Amy Chua, *World on Fire: How Exporting Market Democracy Breeds Ethnic Hatred and Global Instability* (New York: Doubleday, 2002); Fareed Zakaria, "Culture Is Destiny: A Conversation with Lee Kuan Yew," *Foreign Affairs* 73, no. 2 (1994): 109–25; Anwar Ibrahim, "Universal Values and Muslim Democracy," *Journal of Democracy* 17, no. 3 (2006): 5–12; Kim Dae Jung, "Is Culture Destiny?" *Foreign Affairs* 73, no. 6 (1994):

189–94; Chenyang Li, "Confucian Value and Democratic Value," *Journal of Value Inquiry* 31, no. 2 (1997): 183–93; and Lee Teng-hui, "Chinese Culture and Political Renewal," *Journal of Democracy* 6, no. 4 (1995): 3–8.

29. J. Donnelly, "Human Rights," 16–19.

30. Thomas M. Franck, *Fairness in International Law and Institutions* (Oxford: Clarendon, 1995), 136–38. See also Thomas M Franck, "The Emerging Right to Democratic Governance," *American Journal of International Law* 86 (1992): 46–91.

31. Franck, *Fairness in International Law and Institutions*, 139n253.

32. Amartya Sen, "Democracy as Universal Value," *Journal of Democracy* 10, no. 3 (1999): 4.

33. For the details of Ronald Reagan's speech, see *New York Times*, June 9, 1982; for George Bush Sr.'s statements, see Bruce Russett, *Grasping the Democratic Peace* (Princeton, NJ: Princeton University Press, 1993), 127–29; and for Bill Clinton's comments see *New York Times*, August 14, 1992, and his State of the Union address of January 1994.

34. Gong, *Standard of "Civilization,"* 91–92.

35. Firoze Manji and Carl O'Coill, "The Missionary Position: NGOs and Development in Africa," *International Affairs* 78, no. 3 (2002): 574.

36. David S. Landes, "The Role of Culture in Sustainable Development," in *Culture Counts: Financing, Resources, and the Economics of Culture in Sustainable Development—Proceedings of the Conference, Florence, Italy* (Washington, DC: World Bank, 1999), 30. See also David S. Landes, *The Wealth and Poverty of Nations* (London: Little, Brown, 1998).

37. Franck, *Fairness in International Law and Institutions*, 138. See also Dani Rodrik's discussion of the "political trilemma" in "How Far Will International Economic Integration Go?" *Journal of Economic Perspectives* 14, no. 1 (2000): 177–86.

38. Fukuyama, "Natural Rights and Human History," 29–30. See also Chua, *World on Fire*.

39. Fidler, "Kinder, Gentler System of Capitulations?" 389–401.

40. Ronnie D. Lipschutz, "Reconstructing World Politics: The Emergence of Global Civil Society," *Millennium: Journal of International Studies* 21, no. 3 (1992): 407.

41. See Brett Bowden and Leonard Seabrooke, eds., *Global Standards of Market Civilization* (London: Routledge, 2006).

42. Gong, "Asian Financial Crisis."

43. See www.wto.org; and Deepak Bhattasali, Shantong Li, and William J. Martin, eds., *China and the WTO: Accession, Policy Reform, and Poverty Reduction Strategies* (Washington, DC: World Bank, 2004).

44. See Timothy J. Sinclair, "Passing Judgement: Credit Rating Processes as Regulatory Mechanisms of Governance in the Emerging World Order, *Review of International Political Economy* 1, no. 1 (1994): 133–59; and Gong, "Standards of Civilization Today," 75–96.

45. Pagden, "Genesis of 'Governance,'" 14.

46. Mozaffari, "Transformationalist Perspective," 247, 250–51. In another passage, Mozaffari represents "the conjunction of two pillars of globalization" in the formula "capitalism and liberalism = global civilization" (259).

47. See also Martti Koskenniemi's *The Gentle Civilizer of Nations: The Rise and Fall of International Law 1870–1960* (Cambridge: Cambridge University Press, 2001).

48. US President George W. Bush, "Address to a Joint Session of Congress and the American People," September 20, 2001, www.whitehouse.gov/news/releases/2001/09/20010920-8.html; emphasis added.

49. "NATO Lines Up Russian Support," *New York Times (on the Web)*, September 13, 2001, www.nytimes.com/; and *The Independent*, September 12, 2001.

50. US President George W. Bush, State of the Union address, January 29, 2002; and John R. Bolton, US Under Secretary of State for Arms Control and International Security, "Beyond the Axis of Evil: Additional Threats from Weapons of Mass Destruction," speech delivered at the Heritage Foundation, Washington, DC, May 6, 2002.

51. Quintan Wiktorowicz, "A Genealogy of Radical Islam," *Studies in Conflict and Terrorism* 28, no. 2 (2005): 81. Wiktorowicz includes extracts from al-Zawhiri's pamphlet, *Knight's under the Prophet's Banner.*

52. Mill, "Civilization," 52, 55.

53. Harry Holbert Turney-High, *Primitive War: Its Practice and Concepts*, 2nd ed. (Columbia: University of South Carolina Press, 1971), 23.

54. On this topic generally, see Michael Walzer, *Just and Unjust Wars*, 3rd ed. (New York: Basic, 2000). See also John Kelsay and James Turner Johnson, eds. *Just War and Jihad: Historical and Theoretical Perspectives on War and Peace in Western and Islamic Traditions* (New York: Greenwood, 1991); and James Turner Johnson, *The Holy War Idea in Western and Islamic Traditions* (University Park: Pennsylvania State University Press, 1997).

55. Turney-High, *Primitive War*, 23.

56. Robertson, *History of America*, 2:149–54.

57. Ward, *Enquiry*, 2:3–4; emphasis in original.

58. Quincy Wright, "The Bombardment of Damascus," *American Journal of International Law* 20, no. 2 (1926): 266. The English writer cited by Wright is F. W. Hirst (*The Arbiter in Council*, 230).

59. Eldridge Colby, "How to Fight Savage Tribes," *American Journal of International Law* 21, no. 2 (1927): 279.

60. Ibid., 280; and J. F. C. Fuller, *The Reformation of War* (London: Hutchinson, 1923), 191.

61. Colby, "Savage Tribes," 280; and Great Britain War Office, *Manual of Military Law* (London: HMSO, 1914), 235.

62. Colby, "Savage Tribes," 284.

63. Everett L. Wheeler, "Terrorism and Military Theory: An Historical Perspective," *Terrorism and Political Violence* 3, no. 1 (1991): 15.

64. John Keegan, "Why the West Will Win," *The Age* (Melbourne), October 9, 2001, 19.

65. Sir John Keegan, interviewed on *Foreign Correspondent*, Australian Broadcasting Corporation, October 10, 2001, www.abc.net.au/foreign/stories/s387060.htm.

66. While in Berlin on September 26, 2001, Berlusconi stated: "We should be conscious of the superiority of our civilization, which consists of a value system that has given people widespread prosperity in those countries that embrace it and guarantees respect for human rights and religion. This respect certainly does not exist in Islamic countries." Following the outrage caused by his remarks, Berlusconi later retracted them and claimed he had been misquoted and his remarks taken out of context. The damage had been done.

67. Keegan, "Why the West Will Win." For a more favorable and balanced comparative study, see Roxanne L. Euben, *Enemy in the Mirror: Islamic Fundamentalism and the Limits of Modern Rationalism: A Work of Comparative Political Theory* (Princeton, NJ: Princeton University Press, 1999).

68. George W. Bush, "President Addresses Nation, Discusses Iraq, War on Terror," June 28, 2005, www.whitehouse.gov/news/releases/2005/06/20050628-7.html.

69. For a good account of the persistent feature in American politics of the "inflation, stigmatization, and dehumanization of political foes," from "the Indian cannibal . . . [to] the agents of international terrorism," see Michael Paul Rogin, *Ronald Reagan, the Movie: And Other Episodes in Political Demonology* (Berkeley: University of California Press, 1987).

70. See Quintan Wiktorowicz and John Kaltner, "Killing in the Name of Islam: Al-Qaeda's Justification for September 11," *Middle East Policy* 10, no. 2 (2003): 76–92.

71. Walter Benjamin, *Illuminations*, ed. Hannah Arendt (New York: Schocken, 1969), 256.

72. Schwarzenberger, "Standard of Civilisation in International Law," 218–19.

73. Maria Misra, "The Empire Strikes Back," *New Statesman*, November 12, 2001, 25. Misra is not actually arguing such but is engaging with Niall Ferguson, Martin Wolf, and Philip Hensher, who all make similar cases for the return of imperialism, a topic discussed at length in chapter 8.

74. Benedict Kingsbury, "Sovereignty and Inequality," in *Inequality, Globalization, and World Politics*, ed. Andrew Hurrell and Ngaire Woods (Oxford: Oxford University Press, 1999), 90.

8. THE "NEW REALITIES" OF IMPERIALISM

1. Ron Suskind, "Without a Doubt," *New York Times Magazine*, October 17, 2004, 51.

2. Doyle, *Empires*, 11.

3. A few examples include the essays of Gore Vidal in *Perpetual War for Perpetual Peace* (New York: Nation, 2002); Gore Vidal, *Imperial America: Reflections on the United States of Amnesia* (New York: Nation, 2004); Owen Harries, *Benign or Imperial? Reflections on American Hegemony* (Sydney: ABC Books, 2004); David Harvey, *The New Imperialism* (Oxford: Oxford

University Press, 2003); Niall Ferguson, *Empire: The Rise and Demise of the British World Order and the Lessons for Global Power* (New York: Basic, 2003); Niall Ferguson, *Colossus: The Price of America's Empire* (New York: Penguin, 2004). There are also advocates of the United States's imperial-like status, such as William E. Odom and Robert Dujarric's *America's Inadvertent Empire* (New Haven: Yale University Press, 2004); and Robert Kagan, "The Benevolent Empire," *Foreign Policy* 111 (1998): 24–34. And there are countless polemics, such as Julian Ninio's *The Empire of Ignorance, Hypocrisy and Obedience* (Melbourne: Scribe, 2004).

4. Doyle, *Empires*, 13.

5. Ibid., 13, 20, 45.

6. Herfried Münkler, *Empires: The Logic of World Domination from Ancient Rome to the United States*, trans. Patrick Camiller (Cambridge: Polity Press, 2007), 85.

7. Charles S. Maier, "An American Empire? The Problems of Frontiers and Peace in Twenty-First-Century World Politics," *Harvard Magazine* 105, no. 2 (2002): 31.

8. Michael Ignatieff, "Nation-Building Lite," *New York Times Magazine*, July 28, 2002, 54.

9. Michael Ignatieff, "The Burden," *New York Times Magazine*, January 5, 2003, 54.

10. See Donald R. Wolfsenberger, "The Return of the Imperial Presidency?" *Wilson Quarterly*, Spring 2002, 36–41.

11. George W. Bush, preface to *The National Security Strategy of the United States of America* (Washington, DC: White House, September 2002).

12. Maier, "American Empire?" 31.

13. Inayatullah and Blaney, *International Relations and the Problem of Difference*, 17.

14. Shweder, "Return of the 'Civilizing Project,'" 121.

15. Paul Johnson, "Colonialism's Back—and Not a Moment Too Soon," *New York Times Magazine*, April 18, 1993, 22, 44.

16. On the French intervention in Rwanda, see African Rights, *Rwanda: Death, Despair and Defiance*, 2nd ed. (London: African Rights, 1995), chap. 18, "The International Role: Hear No Evil, See No Evil, Do No Good," 1101–60. On "Operation Turquoise" in particular, see, 1104–9 and 1138–54.

17. P. Johnson, "Colonialism's Back," 44.

18. William Pfaff, *The Wrath of Nations: Civilization and the Furies of Nationalism* (New York: Simon & Schuster, 1993), 155.

19. Ali Mazrui, "The Message of Rwanda: Recolonize Africa?" *New Perspectives Quarterly* 11, no. 4 (1994): 18.

20. Michael Walzer, "The Politics of Rescue," *Social Research* 62, no. 1 (1995): 61.

21. Michael Ignatieff, "The Seductiveness of Moral Disgust," *Social Research* 62, no. 1 (1995): 95; and Ignatieff, *The Warrior's Honor: Ethnic War and the Modern Conscience* (London: Vintage, 1999), 106.

22. Ignatieff, "Burden," 24; and Michael Ignatieff, *Empire Lite* (London: Vintage, 2003).

23. Ignatieff, "Nation-Building Lite," 30.

24. Ignatieff, "Burden," 53.

25. Ellen Meiksins Wood, "Kosovo and the New Imperialism," *Monthly Review* 51, no. 2 (1999), www.monthlyreview.org/699wood.htm.

26. Bill Clinton; quoted in Wood, "Kosovo and the New Imperialism."

27. See, for instance, Michael Hardt and Antonio Negri, *Empire* (Cambridge, MA: Harvard University Press, 2000); Samir Amin, "Imperialism and Globalization," *Monthly Review* 53, no. 2 (2001): 6–24; Robert Hunter Wade, "The Invisible Hand of the American Empire," openDemocracy, March 13, 2003, www.opendemocracy.net; William Finnegan, "The Economics of Empire: Notes on the Washington Consensus," *Harper's Magazine* (May 2003): 41–54; and Leo Panitch and Sam Gindin, "Global Capitalism and American Empire," in *The New Imperial Challenge: Socialist Register 2004*, ed. Leo Panitch and Colin Leys (New York: Monthly Review, 2003).

28. See, for an example, Michel Chossudovsky, *The Globalisation of Poverty* (London: Zed, 1997).

29. Fidler, "Kinder, Gentler System of Capitulations?" 407.

30. Ibid., 403, 405. See also Bowden and Seabrooke, *Global Standards of Market Civilization*.

31. Quoted in Finnegan, "Economics of Empire," 41.

32. United States Federal Reserve Bank Chairman Alan Greenspan; quoted in Wade, "Invisible Hand of the American Empire."

33. Bush, preface to *National Security Strategy*.

34. White House, *The National Security Strategy of the United States of America* (Washington, DC: White House, September 2002), 17.

35. Anatol Lieven, "The Empire Strikes Back," *Nation*, July 7, 2003, 25–30.

36. Maier, "American Empire?" 28.

37. Stephanson, *Manifest Destiny*, 18.

38. Paul Kennedy and Charles Krauthammer; quoted in Emily Eakin, " 'It Takes an Empire,' Say Several U.S. Thinkers," *New York Times*, April 2, 2002.

39. Theodore Roosevelt; quoted in Howard K. Beale, *Theodore Roosevelt and the Rise of America to World Power* (Baltimore: Johns Hopkins Press, 1956), 68.

40. Craig Snyder, "Democracy and the Vitality of Evil," *National Interest* 17 (1989): 84.

41. Krauthammer and Kennedy; quoted in Eakin, "It Takes an Empire." See also Paul Kennedy, *The Rise and Fall of the Great Powers: Economic Change and Military Conflict from 1500 to 2000* (New York: Random House, 1987).

42. Henry Cabot Lodge; quoted in William Appleman Williams, *The Tragedy of American Diplomacy*, 2nd ed. (New York: Delta, 1972), 34.

43. David Rothkopf, "In Praise of Cultural Imperialism?" *Foreign Policy* 107 (1997): 41–42.

44. Sebastian Mallaby, "The Reluctant Imperialist," *Foreign Affairs* 81, no. 2 (2002): 2–7.

45. Stephen Peter Rosen, "The Future of War and the American Military," *Harvard Magazine* 104, no. 5 (2002): 30–31.

46. See Chalmers Johnson, *Nemesis: The Last Days of the American Republic* (New York: Metropolitan, 2006); see also Chalmers Johnson, *The Sorrows of Empire: Militarism, Secrecy, and the End of the Republic* (New York: Metropolitan, 2004).

47. Rosen, "Future of War," 31.

48. See Niall Ferguson, "Hegemony or Empire?" *Foreign Affairs* 82, no. 5 (2003): 160.

49. For an argument that the United States is in decline, see Immanuel Wallerstein, "The Eagle Has Crash Landed," *Foreign Policy* 131 (2002): 60–68; and Wallerstein, *The Decline of American Power: The US in a Chaotic World* (New York: New Press, 2003).

50. Finnegan, "Economics of Empire," 53.

51. Lieven, "Empire Strikes Back," 29. For further analysis of this issue, see Leonard Seabrooke, "The Economic Taproot of U.S. Imperialism: The Bush Rentier Shift," *International Politics* 41, no. 3 (2004): 293–318.

52. Daniel Patrick Moynihan, "Civilization Need Not Die," *Harvard Magazine*, July–August 2002, 67–69.

53. For a comparative study of four centuries of terror in Europe, see Brett Bowden and Michael T. Davis, eds., *Terror: From Tyrannicide to Terrorism* (St. Lucia: University of Queensland Press; London: Routledge, 2008).

54. Rosen, "Future of War," 31.

55. Ignatieff, "Nation-Building Lite," 28.

56. Joseph Nye, "The New Rome Meets the New Barbarians," *Economist*, March 23, 2002, 23–25.

57. Charles Krauthammer, "The Bush Doctrine: In American Foreign Policy, a New Motto: Don't Ask. Tell," *Time*, March 5, 2001, 42.

58. Lieven, "Empire Strikes Back," 25.

59. Max Boot, "Colonise Wayward Nations," *Australian*, October 15, 2001, 13. See also Max Boot, *The Savage Wars of Peace: Small Wars and the Rise of American Power* (New York: Basic, 2002).

60. Robert Cooper, "The New Liberal Imperialism," *Observer*, April 7, 2002, www.observer.co.uk/worldview/story/0,11581,680095,00.html.

61. Tony Blair, "The Power of Community Can Change the World," speech by the prime minister to the Labour Party conference, Brighton, October 3, 2001.

62. The term is used in Larry Diamond, "Winning the New Cold War on Terrorism: The Democratic-Governance Imperative," Institute for Global Democracy, policy paper no. 1, March 2002, 10–11.

63. Bush, "Address to a Joint Session of Congress and the American People."

64. Ignatieff, "Burden," 25.

65. Compare Sally B. Donnelly, "Long-Distance Warrior," *Time*, December 12, 2005.

66. Marx, "Eighteenth Brumaire," 1:247. On the sources of this passage, which is in part Hegel's *Philosophy of History* and in part a letter to Marx from Engels, see Bruce Mazlish, "The Tragic Farce of Marx, Hegel, and Engels: A Note," *History and Theory* 11, no. 3 (1972): 335–37.

67. Seumas Milne, "The Battle for History," *Guardian Weekly*, September 19–25, 2002, 11. When one considers that as many as ten million Congolese are estimated to have perished as a result of Belgian forced labor and mass murder in the early twentieth century alone, the term *holocaust* is not entirely inappropriate.

68. John Lloyd, "The Return of Imperialism," *New Statesman*, April 15, 2002, 22.

9. CONCLUSION

1. Jay Tolson, "A Civilizing Mission?" *Wilson Quarterly* 18, no. 1 (1994): 6–9.

2. See also Bowden, "Civilization and Savagery in the Crucible of War."

3. Todorov, *Conquest of America*, 254; emphasis in original.

4. Stanley Kurtz, "Democratic Imperialism: A Blueprint," *Policy Review* 118 (2003), www.policyreview.org/apro3/kurtz.html.

5. See Jagdish P. Sharma, *Republics in Ancient India, c. 1500 BC–500 BC* (Leiden: Brill, 1968); Anant Sadashiv Altekar, *State and Government in Ancient India*, 2nd ed. (Banaras: Motilal Banarsidass, 1955).

6. Starobinski, "The Word Civilization," 30–31.

7. Nisbet, *History of the Idea of Progress*, 9.

8. On this general issue, see J. M. Hobson, *Eastern Origins of Western Civilisation*.

9. Bernal, *Black Athena*, 1:2. See also the discussion of Charles Murray in chapter 3 above.

10. Eric R. Wolf, *Europe and the People without History* (Berkeley: University of California Press, 1982), 4–5.

11. See, for instance, J. M. Roberts, *Triumph of the West* (London: British Broadcasting Corporation, 1985).

12. See Clarke, *Oriental Enlightenment*; Pullapilly and Van Kley, *Asia and the West*; Maverick, *China*; Cobb, *Islamic Contributions to Civilisation*; and Reichwein, *China and Europe*.

13. John Keane, *The Life and Death of Democracy* (London: Free Press; New York: Norton, forthcoming).

14. Muhlberger and Paine, "Democracy's Place in World History," 27, 32.

15. See Jeffrey Wattles, *The Golden Rule* (New York: Oxford University Press, 1996).

16. Perez Zagorin, *How the Idea of Religious Toleration Came to the West* (Princeton, NJ: Princeton University Press, 2003); Compare John Christian Laursen, ed., *Religious Toleration: The "Variety of Rites" from Cyrus to Defoe* (New York: St. Martin's, 1999); Mehdi Amin Razavi and David Ambuel, eds., *Philosophy, Religion, and the Question of Intolerance* (Albany: SUNY Press, 1997).

17. John Donne, "Meditation 17," from *Devotions upon Emergent Occasions*, 1624.

18. Guizot, *History of Civilization in Europe*, 12.

19. Daniel Lerner, *The Passing of Traditional Society: Modernizing the Middle East* (New York: Free Press, 1964), 46–47.

20. Bush, preface to *National Security Strategy*.

21. George W. Bush, "Securing Freedom's Triumph," *New York Times*, September 11, 2002, A33.

22. Fidler, "Kinder, Gentler System of Capitulations?" 406–7.

23. Herder, *On World History*, 41; emphasis in original.

24. Inayatullah and Blaney, *International Relations and the Problem of Difference*, 6.

25. Ricoeur, *History and Truth*, 283–84.

26. Edward Said, preface to *Orientalism*, 25th anniversary ed. (London: Penguin, 2003), xxii.

27. Will Durant in *Life* magazine, October 18, 1963.

Bibliography

Acosta, José de. *Natural and Moral History of the Indies.* 1590. Edited by Jane E. Mangan. Translated by Frances M. López-Morillas. Durham, NC: Duke University Press, 2002.

Adair, James. *Adair's History of the American Indians.* 1775. Edited by Samuel Cole Williams, New York. Promontory, 1930.

Adler, Hans, and Ernest A. Menze. "Introduction: On the Way to World History: Johann Gottfried Herder." In *On World History: An Anthology,* by Johann Gottfried Herder, edited by Hans Adler and Ernest A. Menze, translated by Ernest A. Menze and Michael Palma, 3–19. Armonk, NY: Sharpe, 1997.

African Rights. *Rwanda: Death, Despair and Defiance.* 2nd ed. London: African Rights, 1995.

Alexandrowicz, Charles H. *The European-African Confrontation: A Study in Treaty Making.* Leiden: Sijthoff, 1973.

———. "The Juridical Expression of the Sacred Trust of Civilization." *American Journal of International Law* 65, no. 1 (1971): 149–59.

Alker, Hayward R., Jr. "The Humanistic Moment in International Studies: Reflections on Machiavelli and Las Casas: 1992 Presidential Address." *International Studies Quarterly* 36, no. 4 (1992): 347–71.

Allen, Carleton Kemp. *Law in the Making.* 2nd ed. Oxford: Clarendon, 1930.

Allsen, Thomas T. *Mongol Imperialism: The Policies of the Grand Qan Möngke in China, Russia, and the Islamic Lands, 1251–1259.* Berkeley: University of California Press, 1987.

Altekar, Anant Sadashiv. *State and Government in Ancient India.* 2nd ed. Banaras: Motilal Banarsidass, 1955.

Amin, Samir. "Imperialism and Globalization." *Monthly Review* 53, no. 2 (2001): 6–24.

Anderson, Walter Truett. *All Connected Now: Life in the First Global Civilization.* Boulder, CO: Westview, 2001.

Anghie, Antony. "Finding the Peripheries: Sovereignty and Colonialism in Nineteenth-Century International Law." *Harvard International Law Journal* 40, no. 1 (1999): 1–80.

———. "Francisco de Vitoria and the Colonial Origins of International Law." *Social & Legal Studies* 5, no. 3 (1996): 321–36.

———. *Imperialism, Sovereignty and the Making of International Law.* Cambridge: Cambridge University Press, 2005.

Anwar Ibrahim. "Universal Values and Muslim Democracy." *Journal of Democracy* 17, no. 3 (2006): 5–12.

Aristotle. *The Politics.* London: Dent & Sons, 1912.

Armitage, David. *The Ideological Origins of the British Empire.* Cambridge: Cambridge University Press, 2000.

Arneil, Barbara. "Trade, Plantations, and Property: John Locke and the Economic Defense of Colonialism." *Journal of the History of Ideas* 55, no. 4 (1994): 591–609.

Bagehot, Walter. *Physics and Politics.* London: Kegan Paul, Trench, Trubner, [1875].

Bain, William. *Between Anarchy and Society.* Oxford: Oxford University Press, 2003.

Baldry, H. C. *The Unity of Mankind in Greek Thought.* Cambridge: Cambridge University Press, 1965.

Ball, Terrence, James Farr, and Russell L. Hanson. Introduction to *Political Innovation and Conceptual Change*, edited by Terence Ball, James Farr, and Russell L. Hanson, 1–5. Cambridge: Cambridge University Press, 1989.

Barnett, Michael N. "Bringing in the New World Order: Liberalism, Legitimacy, and the United Nations." *World Politics* 49, no. 4 (1997): 526–51.

Bateson, Mary Catherine. "Beyond Sovereignty: An Emerging Global Civilization." In *Contending Sovereignties: Redefining Political Community*, edited by R. B. J. Walker and Saul H. Medlovitz, 145–58. Boulder, CO: Lynne Reinner, 1990.

Bauman, Zygmunt. *Legislators and Interpreters: On Modernity, Post-Modernity and Intellectuals.* Ithaca, NY: Cornell University Press, 1987.

Bautista, Veltisezar B. *The Filipino Americans (from 1763 to the Present): Their History, Culture, & Traditions.* 2nd ed. Farmington Hills, MI: Bookhaus, 2002.

Beale, Howard K. *Theodore Roosevelt and the Rise of America to World Power.* Baltimore: Johns Hopkins Press, 1956.

Beck, Lewis White. Editor's introduction to *Kant on History*, vii–xxvi. Indianapolis: Bobbs-Merrill, 1963.

Beck, Ulrich. "The Cosmopolitan Manifesto." *New Statesman*, March 20, 1998, 29–30.

———. "The Cosmopolitan Perspective: Sociology of the Second Age of Modernity." *British Journal of Sociology* 51, no. 1 (2000): 79–106.

———. "The Cosmopolitan Society and Its Enemies." *Theory, Culture & Society* 19, nos. 1–2 (2002): 17–44.

Beisner, Robert L. *Twelve against Empire: The Anti-Imperialists, 1898–1900*. New York: McGraw-Hill, 1968.

Beitz, Charles. *Political Theory and International Relations*. Princeton, NJ: Princeton University Press, 1979.

Bell, Duncan S. A. *The Idea of Greater Britain: Empire and the Future of World Order, 1860–1900*. Princeton, NJ: Princeton University Press, 2007.

———. "Language, Legitimacy, and the Project of Critique." *Alternatives: Global, Local, Political* 27, no. 3 (2002): 327–50.

Benedict, Brother. "The Narrative of Brother Benedict the Pole." In *The Mongol Mission*, edited by Christopher Dawson, 79–84.

Benjamin, Walter. *Illuminations*. Edited by Hannah Arendt. New York: Schocken, 1969.

Bentham, Jeremy. *Plan for an Universal and Perpetual Peace*. 1786–1789. London: Peace Book, 1939.

Benveniste, Emile. "Civilization: A Contribution to the History of the Word." In *Problems in General Linguistics*, translated by Mary Elizabeth Meek, 289–296. Coral Gables, FL: University of Miami Press, 1971.

Berlin, Isaiah. "Kant as an Unfamiliar Source of Nationalism." In *The Sense of Reality: Studies in Ideas and their History*, by Isaiah Berlin, edited by Henry Hardy, 232–48. London: Chatto & Windus, 1996.

Bernal, Martin. *Black Athena: The Afroasiatic Roots of Classical Civilization*. 2 vols. London: Free Association, 1987.

———. *Black Athena Writes Back: Martin Bernal Responds to His Critics*. Edited by David Chioni Moore. Durham, NC: Duke University Press, 2001.

Bhattasali, Deepak, Shantong Li, and William J. Martin, eds. *China and the WTO: Accession, Policy Reform, and Poverty Reduction Strategies*. Washington, DC: World Bank, 2004.

Blackburn, H. J. *The Future of Our Past: From Ancient Greece to Global Village*. Edited by Barbara Smoker. Amherst, NY: Prometheus, 1996.

Blair, Tony. "The Power of Community Can Change the World." Speech by the prime minister to the Labour Party Conference, Brighton, October 3, 2001. At www.ppionline.org/ndol/print.cfm?contentid=3881.

Bolton, John R. "Beyond the Axis of Evil: Additional Threats from Weapons of Mass Destruction." Speech delivered at the Heritage Foundation, Washington, DC, May 6, 2002. At www.state.gov/t/us/rm/9962.htm.

Boot, Max. "Colonise Wayward Nations." *Australian*, October 15, 2001, 13.

———. *The Savage Wars of Peace: Small Wars and the Rise of American Power*. New York: Basic, 2002.

Booth, Ken. "Discussion: A Reply to Wallace." *Review of International Studies* 23, no. 3 (1997): 371–77.

Boswell, James. *Boswell's Life of Johnson.* 1791. 6 vols. Oxford: Clarendon, 1934.

Boutros-Ghali, Boutros. *An Agenda for Peace.* New York: United Nations, 1992.

Bowden, Brett. "Civilization and Savagery in the Crucible of War." *Global Change, Peace & Security* 19, no. 1 (2007): 3–16.

———. "The Colonial Origins of International Law: European Expansion and the Classical Standard of Civilisation." *Journal of the History of International Law/Revue d'histoire du droit international* 7, no. 1 (2005): 1–23.

———. "The Ideal of Civilization: Its Origins and Socio-Political Character." *Critical Review of International Social and Political Philosophy* 7, no. 1 (2004): 25–50.

———. "In the Name of Progress and Peace: The 'Standard of Civilization' and the Universalizing Project." *Alternatives: Global, Local, Political* 29, no. 1 (2004): 43–68.

———. "The Perils of Global Citizenship." *Citizenship Studies* 7, no. 3 (2003): 349–62.

———. "The River of Inter-civilisational Relations: The Ebb and Flow of Peoples, Ideas and Innovations." *Third World Quarterly* 28, no. 7 (2007): 1359–74.

Bowden, Brett, and Leonard Seabrooke, eds. *Global Standards of Market Civilization.* London: Routledge, 2006.

Bowden, Brett, and Michael T. Davis, eds. *Terror: From Tyrannicide to Terrorism.* St. Lucia: University of Queensland Press; London: Routledge, 2008.

Bradshaw, Steve. "The Coming Chaos?" *Moving Pictures Bulletin* 25 (1996): 18–19.

Brandon, William. *New Worlds for Old: Reports from the New World and Their Effect on the Development of Social Thought in Europe, 1500–1800.* Athens: Ohio University Press, 1986.

Braudel, Fernand. *A History of Civilizations.* Translated by Richard Mayne. New York: Allen Lane / Penguin, 1987.

———. *On History.* Translated by Sarah Matthews. London: Weidenfeld & Nicolson, 1980.

Brennan, Timothy. *At Home in the World: Cosmopolitanism Now.* Cambridge, MA: Harvard University Press, 1997.

Brierly, J. L. *The Law of Nations.* 4th ed. Oxford: Clarendon, 1949.

Brown, Chris. "The Construction of a 'Realistic Utopia': John Rawls and International Political Theory." *Review of International Studies* 28, no. 1 (2002): 5–21.

Brownlie, Ian, ed. *Basic Documents in International Law.* 3rd ed. Oxford: Clarendon, 1994.

———. *Principles of Public International Law.* 5th ed. Oxford: Clarendon, 1998.

Buchan, Bruce. "Explaining War and Peace: Kant and Liberal IR Theory." *Alternatives: Global, Local, Political* 27, no. 4 (2002): 407–28.

Bull, Hedley. *The Anarchical Society: A Study of Order in World Politics.* 2nd ed. London: Macmillan, 1995.

———. "The Emergence of a Universal International Society." In *The Expansion of International Society*, edited by Hedley Bull and Adam Watson, 117–26. Oxford: Clarendon, 1984.

———. "The Grotian Conception of International Society." In *Diplomatic Investigations*, edited by Herbert Butterfield and Martin Wight, 51–73. London: Allen & Unwin, 1966.

Bull, Hedley, and Adam Watson, eds. *The Expansion of International Society.* Oxford: Clarendon, 1984.

———. Introduction to *The Expansion of International Society.* Edited by Hedley Bull and Adam Watson, 1–9. Oxford: Clarendon, 1984.

Burke, Edmund. "India." In *Selections: With Essays by Hazlitt, Arnold & Others*, edited by A. M. D. Hughes, 111–27. Oxford: Clarendon, 1921.

Bury, J. B. *The Idea of Progress: An Inquiry into Its Origin and Growth.* New York: Dover, 1960.

Bush, George W. "Address to a Joint Session of Congress and the American People." September 20, 2001. www.whitehouse.gov/news/releases/2001/09/print/20010920-8.html.

———. Preface to *The National Security Strategy of the United States of America.* Washington, DC: White House, September 2002.

———. "President Addresses Nation, Discusses Iraq, War on Terror." June 28, 2005. www.whitehouse.gov/news/releases/2005/06/20050628-7.html.

———. President's State of the Union address, January 29, 2002. www.whitehouse.gov/news/releases/2002/01/20020129-11.html.

———. "Securing Freedom's Triumph." *New York Times*, September 11, 2002, A33.

Cassese, Antonio. *International Law in a Divided World.* Oxford: Clarendon, 1986.

Cederman, Lars-Erik. "Back to Kant: Reinterpreting the Democratic Peace as a Macrohistorical Learning Process." *American Political Science Review* 95, no. 1 (2001): 15–31.

Chenyang Li. "Confucian Value and Democratic Value." *Journal of Value Inquiry* 31, no. 2 (1997): 183–93.

Chossudovsky, Michel. *The Globalisation of Poverty.* London: Zed, 1997.

Chua, Amy. *World on Fire: How Exporting Market Democracy Breeds Ethnic Hatred and Global Instability.* New York: Doubleday, 2002.

Clark, Ian. *The Hierarchy of States: Reform and Resistance in International Order.* Cambridge: Cambridge University Press, 1989.

Clarke, J. J. *Oriental Enlightenment: The Encounter between Asian and Western Thought.* London: Routledge, 1997.

Cobb, Stanwood. *Islamic Contributions to Civilisation.* Washington, DC: Avalon, 1963.

Colby, Eldridge. "How to Fight Savage Tribes." *American Journal of International Law* 21, no. 2 (1927): 279–88.

Collingwood, R. G. *The New Leviathan*. Edited by David Boucher. Oxford: Clarendon, 1992.

Colton, Joel. Foreword to *Progress and Its Discontents*. Edited by Gabriel A. Almond, Marvin Chodorow, and Roy Harvey Pearce, ix–xii. Berkeley: University of California Press, 1982.

Columbus, Christopher. "Letter of 15th February 1493 on the Islands Newly Found by the King of Spain." In *The Journal of Christopher Columbus*, translated by Cecil Jane, 191–202. London: Anthony Blond and Orion Press, 1960.

Commission on Global Governance. *Our Global Neighborhood*. New York: Oxford University Press, 1995.

Condorcet, Antoine-Nicolas de. *Sketch for a Historical Picture of the Progress of the Human Mind*. Translated by June Barraclough. 1795. London: Weidenfeld & Nicolson, 1955.

Conrad, Joseph. *Heart of Darkness and Other Tales*. 1899. Oxford: Oxford University Press, 1998.

Cooper, Robert. "The New Liberal Imperialism." *Observer*, April 7, 2002, www.observer.co.uk/worldview/story/0,11581,680095,00.html.

———. *The Post-Modern State and the World Order*. London: DEMOS, 1996.

Darwin, John. "Civility and Empire." In *Civil Histories: Essays Presented to Sir Keith Thomas*, edited by Peter Burke, Brian Harrison, and Paul Slack, 321–36. Oxford: Oxford University Press, 2000.

Davies, Sir John. *Historical Relations; or, A discovery of the true causes why Ireland was never entirely subdued nor brought under obedience of the Crown of England until the beginning of the Reign of King James of happy memory*. Dublin: Samuel Dancer, 1664.

Dawson, Christopher, ed. *The Mongol Mission: Narratives and Letters of the Franciscan Missionaries in Mongolia and China in the Thirteenth and Fourteenth Centuries*. London: Sheed & Ward, 1955.

Diamond, Jared. *Guns, Germs, and Steel: The Fates of Human Societies*. New York: Norton, 1997.

Diamond, Larry. "Winning the New Cold War on Terrorism: The Democratic-Governance Imperative." Institute for Global Democracy, policy paper no. 1, March 2002.

Donne, John. "Meditation 17," from *Devotions upon Emergent Occasions*, 1624.

Donnelly, Jack. "Human Rights: A New Standard of Civilization." *International Affairs* 74, no. 1 (1998): 1–24.

Donnelly, Sally B. "Long-Distance Warrior." *Time*, December 12, 2005.

Doyle, Michael W. *Empires*. Ithaca, NY: Cornell University Press, 1986.

———. "Kant, Liberal Legacies, and Foreign Affairs, Part 2." *Philosophy and Public Affairs* 12, no. 4 (1983): 323–53.

———. "Liberalism and World Politics." *American Political Science Review* 80, no. 4 (1986): 1151–69.

Dunn, John. "The Identity of the History of Ideas." *Philosophy* 43 (1968): 85–104.

Dunne, Tim. *Inventing International Society: A History of the English School*. London: Palgrave Macmillan, 1998.

Durant, Will. In *Life* magazine, October 18, 1963.

Durkheim, E., and M. Mauss. "Note on the Notion of Civilization." *Social Research* 38, no. 4 (1971): 808–13.

Eakin, Emily. "'It Takes an Empire,' Say Several U.S. Thinkers." *New York Times*, April 2, 2002.

Edelstein, Ludwig. *The Idea of Progress in Classical Antiquity*. Baltimore: Johns Hopkins University Press, 1967.

Elias, Norbert. *The Civilizing Process*. Translated by Edmund Jephcott. Oxford: Basil Blackwell, 1994.

———. *The Civilizing Process*. Translated by Edmund Jephcott. Rev. ed. Oxford: Blackwell, 2000.

———. "Violence and Civilization: The State Monopoly of Physical Violence and Its Infringement." In *Civil Society and the State: New European Perspectives*, edited by John Keane, 177–98. London: Verso, 1988.

Elliot, J. H. *The Old World and the New, 1492–1650*. Cambridge: Cambridge University Press, 1970.

Engels, Frederick. *The Origin of Family, Private Property and the State*. 1884. Moscow: Progress, 1948.

Euben, Roxanne L. *Enemy in the Mirror: Islamic Fundamentalism and the Limits of Modern Rationalism: A Work of Comparative Political Theory*. Princeton, NJ: Princeton University Press, 1999.

Evans, Gareth. *Cooperating for Peace*. St. Leonards, NSW, Australia. Unwin & Hyman, 1993.

Falk, Richard. *Law in an Emerging Global Village: A Post-Westphalian Perspective*. New York: Transnational, 1998.

Farrar, Frederick. "Aptitude of the Races." *Transactions of the Ethnographical Society of London*, 1867.

Featherstone, Mike. "Cosmopolis: An Introduction." *Theory, Culture & Society* 19, nos. 1–2 (2002): 1–16.

Febvre, Lucien. "*Civilization*: Evolution of a Word and a Group of Ideas." In *A New Kind of History: From the Writings of Febvre*, edited by P. Burke, translated by K. Folca, 219–57. London: Routledge & Kegan Paul, 1973.

Fenton, William N., and Elizabeth L. Moore. Introduction to *Customs of the American Indians Compared with the Customs of Primitive Times* [1724], by Joseph Francois Lafitau. Edited and translated by William N. Fenton and Elizabeth L. Moore, xix–xxvii. 2 vols. Toronto: Chaplain Society, 1974.

Ferguson, Adam. *An Essay on the History of Civil Society 1767*. Edited by Duncan Forbes. Edinburgh: Edinburgh University Press, 1966.

———. *Principles of Moral and Political Science*. 1792. 2 vols. Hildesheim, Germany: Georg Olms Verlag, 1975.

Ferguson, Niall. *Colossus: The Price of America's Empire*. New York: Penguin, 2004.

———. *Empire: The Rise and Demise of the British World Order and the Lessons for Global Power*. New York: Basic, 2003.

―――. "Hegemony or Empire?" *Foreign Affairs* 82, no. 5 (2003): 154–61.

Fidler, David P. "A Kinder, Gentler System of Capitulations? International Law, Structural Adjustment Policies, and the Standard of Liberal, Globalized Civilization." *Texas International Law Journal* 35, no. 3 (2000): 387–413.

Finnegan, William. "The Economics of Empire: Notes on the Washington Consensus." *Harper's Magazine*, May 2003, 41–54.

Fiore, Pasquale. *International Law Codified and Its Legal Sanction.* New York: Baker, Voorhis, 1918.

Forbes, Duncan. Introduction to *An Essay on the History of Civil Society 1767,* by Adam Ferguson. Edited by Duncan Forbes, xii–xli. Edinburgh: Edinburgh University Press, 1966.

Franck, Thomas M. "The Emerging Right to Democratic Governance." *American Journal of International Law* 86 (1992): 46–91.

―――. *Fairness in International Law and Institutions.* Oxford: Clarendon, 1995.

Freud, Sigmund. *The Future of an Illusion.* Translated by W. D. Robson-Scott. London: Hogarth Press and the Institute of Psycho-analysis, 1949.

Fukuyama, Francis. "The End of History?" *National Interest* 16 (1989): 3–18.

―――. *The End of History and the Last Man.* London: Penguin, 1992.

―――. "Natural Rights and Human History." *National Interest* 64 (2001): 17–30.

―――. "Second Thoughts: The Last Man in a Bottle." *National Interest* 56 (1999): 16–33.

Fuller, J. F. C. *The Reformation of War.* London: Hutchinson, 1923.

Gardels, Nathan. "Comment: The New Babel and the Noblest of Pains." *New Perspectives Quarterly* 8, no. 4 (1991): 2–3.

General Act of the Berlin Conference of 1884–1885, February 26, 1885.

Gibbon, Edward. *The Decline and Fall of the Roman Empire.* 1776–1788. Harmondsworth: Penguin, with Chatto & Windus, 1963.

Gibson-Graham, J. K. *The End of Capitalism (As We Knew It): A Feminist Critique of Political Economy.* Minneapolis: University of Minnesota Press, 2006.

Glave, E. J. "Cruelty in the Congo Free State: Concluding Extracts from the Journals of the Late E. J. Glave." *The Century Illustrated Monthly Magazine* 54, n.s., 32 (New York: Century; London: Macmillan, May–October 1897): 699–715.

Goddard, E. H., and P. A. Gibbons. *Civilisation or Civilisations: An Essay in the Spenglerian Philosophy of History.* London: Constable, 1926.

Goldgeier, James M., and Michael McFaul. "A Tale of Two Worlds: Core and Periphery in the Post-Cold War Era." *International Organization* 46, no. 2 (1992): 467–91.

Gong, Gerrit W. "Asian Financial Crisis: Culture and Strategy." Paper presented at the ICAS Fall Symposium, University of Pennsylvania, September 29, 1998, www.icasinc.org/f1998/gwgf1998.html.

―――. "The Beginning of History: Remembering and Forgetting as Strategic Issues." *Washington Quarterly* 24, no. 2 (2001): 45–57.

————. *The Standard of "Civilization" in International Society*. Oxford: Clarendon, 1984.

————. "Standards of Civilization Today." In *Globalization and Civilizations*, edited by Mehdi Mozaffari, 75–96. London: Routledge, 2002.

Gray, John. *Enlightenment's Wake: Politics and Culture at the Close of the Modern Age*. London: Routledge, 1995.

————. *False Dawn: The Delusions of Global Capitalism*. London: Granta, 1998.

————. "Global Utopias and Clashing Civilizations: Misunderstanding the Present." *International Affairs* 74, no. 1 (1998): 149–64.

Great Britain War Office. *Manual of Military Law*. London: HMSO, 1914.

Guha, Ranajit. *History at the Limit of World-History*. New York: Columbia University Press, 2002.

Guizot, François. *The History of Civilization in Europe*. Translated by William Hazlitt. 1828. Harmondsworth: Penguin, 1997.

Guyuk Khan. "Guyuk Khan's Letter to Pope Innocent IV (1246)." In *The Mongol Mission*, edited by Christopher Dawson, 85–86.

Haase, Wolfgang, and Meyer Reinhold, eds. *The Classical Tradition and the Americas*. Berlin: W. de Gruyter, 1994.

Hall, Martin, and Patrick Thaddeus Jackson, eds. *The Production and Reproduction of "Civilizations" in International Relations*. New York: Palgrave, 2007.

Hall, William Edward. *A Treatise on International Law*. 3rd ed. Oxford: Clarendon, 1890.

Hampshire, Stuart. Introduction to *Sketch for a Historical Picture of the Progress of the Human Mind* [1795], by Antoine-Nicolas de Condorcet. Translated by June Barraclough, vii–xii. London: Weidenfeld & Nicolson, 1955.

Hankins, Frank H. *The Racial Basis of Civilization*. New York: Knopf, 1926.

Hardt, Michael, and Antonio Negri. *Empire*. Cambridge, MA: Harvard University Press, 2000.

Harries, Owen. *Benign or Imperial? Reflections on American Hegemony*. Sydney: ABC Books, 2004.

Hartmann, Eduard von. *Philosophy of Unconscious*. Translated by William Chatterton Coupland. 3 vols. London: Kegan Paul, Trench, Trübner, 1893.

Harvey, David. "Cosmopolitanism and the Banality of Geographic Evils." *Public Culture* 12, no. 2 (2000): 529–64.

————. *The New Imperialism*. Oxford: Oxford University Press, 2003.

Hasluck, Paul. "The Native Welfare Conference, 1951." In *Native Welfare in Australia: Speeches and Addresses*. Perth: Paterson Brakensha, 1953.

Hegel, G. W. F. *Aesthetics: Lectures on Fine Art*. 1835–1838. Translated by T. M. Knox. 2 vols. Oxford: Clarendon, 1975.

————. *The Philosophy of History*. Translated by J. Sibree. New York: Dover, 1956.

————. *Philosophy of Right*. 1821. Translated by T. M. Knox. Oxford: Clarendon, 1958.

Heidegger, Martin. "Letter on Humanism." In *Martin Heidegger: Basic Writings*, edited by David Farrell Krell. 2nd ed. London: Routledge, 1993.

Herder, Johann Gottfried. *On World History: An Anthology*. Edited by Hans Adler and Ernest A. Menze, translated by Ernest A. Menze and Michael Palma. Armonk, NY: Sharpe, 1997.

———. *Philosophical Writings*. Edited by Michel N. Forster. Cambridge: Cambridge University Press, 2002.

Herf, Jeffrey. *Reactionary Modernism: Technology, Culture, and Politics in Weimar and the Third Reich*. Cambridge: Cambridge University Press, 1984.

Hernstein, Richard J., and Charles Murray. *The Bell Curve: Intelligence and Class Structure in American Life*. New York: Free Press, 1994.

Hill, Lisa. "The Two *Republicae* of the Roman Stoics: Can a Cosmopolite Be a Patriot?" *Citizenship Studies* 4, no. 1 (2000): 65–79.

Himmelfarb, Gertrude. "In Defense of Progress." *Commentary* 69, no. 6 (1980): 53–60.

Hindess, Barry. "The Liberal Government of Unfreedom." *Alternatives: Global, Local, Political* 26, no. 2 (2001): 93–111.

Hobbes, Thomas. *Leviathan*. 1651. Edited by C. B. MacPherson. Harmondsworth: Penguin, 1985.

Hobsbawm, Eric. "Barbarism: A User's Guide." *New Left Review* 206 (1994): 44–54.

Hobson, John A. *Imperialism: A Study*. 3rd ed. London: Allen & Unwin, 1948.

Hobson, John M. *The Eastern Origins of Western Civilisation*. Cambridge: Cambridge University Press, 2004.

Hobson, John M., and Leonard Seabrooke. "Reimagining Weber: Constructing International Society and the Social Balance of Power." *European Journal of International Relations* 7, no. 2 (2001): 239–74.

Homer-Dixon, Thomas F. *Environment, Scarcity, and Violence*. Princeton, NJ: Princeton University Press, 2001.

———. "Environmental Scarcities and Violent Conflict: Evidence from Cases." *International Security* 19, no. 1 (1994): 5–40.

———. "On the Threshold: Environmental Changes as Causes of Acute Conflict." *International Security* 16, no. 2 (1991): 76–116.

Howard, Michael. *The Invention of Peace: Reflections on War and International Order*. London: Profile, 2000.

Humboldt, Alexander von. *Cosmos: A Sketch of a Physical Description of the Universe*. Translated by E. C. Otté. London: Henry G. Bohn, 1864–65.

Humphreys, David. *The Miscellaneous Works of David Humphreys*. New York: T. and J. Swords, 1804.

Huntington, Samuel P. "The Clash of Civilizations?" *Foreign Affairs* 72, no. 3 (1993): 22–49.

———. *The Clash of Civilizations and the Remaking of World Order*. London: Simon & Schuster, 1997.

———. *Political Order in Changing Societies*. New Haven, CT: Yale University Press, 1968.

———. *The Soldier and the State: The Theory and Politics of Civil-Military Relations*. Cambridge, MA: Belknap Press / Harvard University Press, 1957.

————. "The West Unique, Not Universal." *Foreign Affairs* 75, no. 6 (1996): 28–46.

Iggers, Georg G. "The Idea of Progress in Historiography and Social Thought since the Enlightenment." In *Progress and Its Discontents*, edited by Gabriel A. Almond, Marvin Chodorow, and Roy Harvey Pearce, 41–66. Berkeley: University of California Press, 1982.

Ignatieff, Michael. "The Burden." *New York Times Magazine*, January 5, 2003, 22–27 and 50–54.

————. *Empire Lite*. London: Vintage, 2003.

————. "Nation-Building Lite." *New York Times Magazine*, July 28, 2002, 26–31 and 54–56.

————. "The Seductiveness of Moral Disgust." *Social Research* 62, no. 1 (1995): 77–97.

————. *The Warrior's Honor: Ethnic War and the Modern Conscience*. London: Vintage, 1999.

Inayatullah, Naeem, and David L. Blaney. *International Relations and the Problem of Difference*. New York: Routledge, 2004.

Innocent IV, Pope. "Document 40: *Commentaria Doctissima in Quinque Libros Decretalium*." In *The Expansion of Europe: The First Phase*, edited by James Muldoon, 191. Philadelphia: University of Pennsylvania Press, 1977.

————. "Two Bulls of Pope Innocent IV to the Emperor of the Tartars." In *The Mongol Mission*, edited by Christopher Dawson, 73–76.

Jackson, Patrick Thaddeus. *Civilizing the Enemy: German Reconstruction and the Invention of the West*. Ann Arbor: University of Michigan Press, 2006.

Jahn, Beate. *The Cultural Construction of International Relations: The Invention of the State of Nature*. Basingstoke: Palgrave, 2000.

Johnson, Chalmers. *Nemesis: The Last Days of the American Republic*. New York: Metropolitan, 2006.

————. *The Sorrows of Empire: Militarism, Secrecy, and the End of the Republic*. New York: Metropolitan, 2004.

Johnson, James Turner. *The Holy War Idea in Western and Islamic Traditions*. University Park: Pennsylvania State University Press, 1997.

Johnson, Paul. "Colonialism's Back—and Not a Moment Too Soon." *New York Times Magazine*, April 18, 1993, 22 and 43–44.

Kacowicz, Arie M. "Explaining Zones of Peace: Democracies as Satisfied Powers? *Journal of Peace Research* 32, no. 5 (1995): 265–76.

Kagan, Robert. "The Benevolent Empire." *Foreign Policy* 111 (1998): 24–34.

Kant, Immanuel. *Kant: On History*. Edited by Lewis White Beck. Indianapolis: Bobbs-Merrill, 1963.

————. "Idea for a Universal History from a Cosmopolitan Point of View." 1784. In *Kant: On History*, 11–26.

————. "An Old Question Raised Again: Is The Human Race Constantly Progressing?" 1798. In *Kant: On History*, 137–54.

————. "Perpetual Peace." 1795. In *Kant: On History*, 85–135.

————. "Reviews of Herder's *Ideas for a Philosophy of the History of Mankind*." 1785. In *Kant: On History*, 27–39.

Kaplan, Robert D. *Balkan Ghosts: A Journey through History*. London: Macmillan, 1993.

———. "The Coming Anarchy." *Atlantic Monthly*, February 1994, 44–76.

Keal, Paul. *European Conquest and the Rights of Indigenous Peoples: The Moral Backwardness of International Society*. Cambridge: Cambridge University Press, 2003.

Keane, John. *The Life and Death of Democracy*. London: Free Press; New York: Norton, forthcoming.

———. *Reflections on Violence*. London: Verso, 1996.

Keegan, Sir John. Interviewed on *Foreign Correspondent*. Australian Broadcasting Corporation, October, 10 2001, www.abc.net.au/foreign/stories/s387060.htm.

———. "Why the West Will Win." *The Age* (Melbourne), October 9, 2001, 19.

Keene, Edward. *Beyond the Anarchical Society: Grotius, Colonialism and Order in World Politics*. Cambridge: Cambridge University Pres, 2002.

Kelsay, John, and James Turner Johnson, eds. *Just War and Jihad: Historical and Theoretical Perspectives on War and Peace in Western and Islamic Traditions*. New York: Greenwood, 1991.

Kennedy, Paul. *The Rise and Fall of the Great Powers: Economic Change and Military Conflict from 1500 to 2000*. New York: Random House, 1987.

Keohane, Nannerl O. "The Enlightenment Idea of Progress Revisited." In *Progress and Its Discontents*, edited by Gabriel A. Almond, Marvin Chodorow, and Roy Harvey Pearce, 21–40. Berkeley: University of California Press, 1982.

Keohane, Robert O. *Power and Governance in a Partially Globalized World*. London: Routledge, 2002.

Kepner, Charles D., Jr., and Jay H. Soothill. *The Banana Empire: A Case Study of Economic Imperialism*. New York: Russell & Russell, 1967.

Keynes, John Maynard. *The General Theory of Employment, Interest and Money*. London: MacMillan, 1936.

Kim Dae Jung. "Is Culture Destiny?" *Foreign Affairs* 73, no. 6 (1994): 189–94.

Kingsbury, Benedict. "Sovereignty and Inequality." In *Inequality, Globalization, and World Politics*, edited by Andrew Hurrell and Ngaire Woods, 66–94. Oxford: Oxford University Press, 1999.

Knox, Robert. *The Races of Men: A Philosophical Inquiry into the Influence of Race over the Destinies of Nations*. 2nd ed. London: Henry Renshaw, 1862.

Koselleck, Reinhart. *Futures Past: On the Semantics of Historical Time*. Translated by Keith Tribe. Cambridge, MA: MIT Press, 1985.

Koskenniemi, Martti. *The Gentle Civilizer of Nations: The Rise and Fall of International Law 1870–1960*. Cambridge: Cambridge University Press, 2001.

Krauthammer, Charles. "The Bush Doctrine: In American Foreign Policy, a New Motto: Don't Ask. Tell." *Time*, March 5, 2001, 42.

Kraynak, Robert P. "Hobbes on Barbarism and Civilization." *Journal of Politics* 45, no. 1 (1983): 86–109.

Kuper, Adam. *Culture: The Anthropologists' Account.* Cambridge, MA: Harvard University Press, 1999.

Kurtz, Stanley. "Democratic Imperialism: A Blueprint." *Policy Review* 118 (2003), www.policyreview.org/apr03/kurtz.html.

Landes, David S. "The Role of Culture in Sustainable Development." In *Culture Counts: Financing, Resources, and the Economics of Culture in Sustainable Development—Proceedings of the Conference.* Florence, Italy. Washington, DC: World Bank, 1999, 27–30.

———. *The Wealth and Poverty of Nations.* London: Little, Brown, 1998.

Lapham, Edward J. "Liberalism, Civic Humanism, and the Case of Adam Smith." *American Political Science Review* 78, no. 3 (1984): 764–74.

Las Casas, Bartolomé de. *In Defense of the Indians.* Edited and translated by Stafford Poole. DeKalb: Northern Illinois University Press, 1974.

Laursen, John Christian, ed. *Religious Toleration: The "Variety of Rites" from Cyrus to Defoe.* New York: St. Martin's, 1999.

Lauterpacht, H. *Recognition in International Law.* Cambridge: Cambridge University Press, 1947.

Lee Teng-hui. "Chinese Culture and Political Renewal." *Journal of Democracy* 6, no. 4 (1995): 3–8.

Lefkowitz, Mary R., and Guy MacLean Rogers, eds. *Black Athena Revisited.* Chapel Hill: University of North Carolina Press, 1996.

Lenin, V. I. *Imperialism, the Highest Stage of Capitalism: A Popular Outline.* Peking: Foreign Languages, 1965.

Lerner, Daniel. *The Passing of Traditional Society: Modernizing the Middle East.* New York: Free Press, 1964.

Levenson, J. R. *Revolution and Cosmopolitanism: The Western Stages and the Chinese Stages.* Berkeley: University of California Press, 1971.

Levy, Jack S. "Domestic Politics and War." *Journal of Interdisciplinary History* 18, no. 4 (1988): 653–73.

Lieven, Anatol. "The Empire Strikes Back." *Nation,* July 7, 2003, 25–30.

Lindqvist, Sven. *"Exterminate All the Brutes."* Translated by Joan Tate. London: Granta, 1998.

Lipschutz, Ronnie D. "Reconstructing World Politics: The Emergence of Global Civil Society." *Millennium: Journal of International Studies* 21, no. 3 (1992): 389–420.

Lloyd, John. "The Return of Imperialism." *New Statesman,* April 15, 2002, 21–22.

Locke, John. *Two Treatises of Government.* 1690. New York: New American Library, 1965.

Lorimer, James. *The Institutes of the Law of Nations.* 2 vols. Edinburgh: William Blackwood & Sons, 1883.

Lubbock, Sir John. *The Origin of Civilisation and the Primitive Condition of Man: Mental and Social Condition of Savages.* New York: Appleton, 1870.

Macklin, Ruth. "Moral Progress." *Ethics* 87, no. 4 (1977): 370–82.

Maier, Charles S. "An American Empire? The Problems of Frontiers and Peace in Twenty-First-Century World Politics." *Harvard Magazine* 105, no. 2 (2002): 28–31.

Maitland, Frederic William. *The Collected Papers of Frederic William Mait-land*. Edited by H. A. L. Fisher. Cambridge: Cambridge University Press, 1911.

Mallaby, Sebastian. "The Reluctant Imperialist." *Foreign Affairs* 81, no. 2 (2002): 2–7.

Manji, Firoze, and Carl O'Coill. "The Missionary Position: NGOs and Development in Africa." *International Affairs* 78, no. 3 (2002): 567–83.

Marx, Karl. "The Eighteenth Brumaire of Louis Bonaparte" [3rd ed., 1885]. In *Selected Works*, by Karl Marx and Frederick Engels, 1:243–344. Moscow: Foreign Languages, 1958.

Marx, Karl, and Frederick Engels. "Manifesto of the Communist Party." In *Selected Works*, by Karl Marx and Frederick Engels, 1:21–65. Moscow: Foreign Languages, 1958.

Maverick, Lewis A. *China: A Model for Europe*. San Antonio, TX: Paul Anderson, 1946.

May, J. A. *Kant's Concept of Geography and Its Relation to Recent Geographical Thought*. Toronto: University of Toronto Press, 1970.

Mazlish, Bruce. *Civilization and Its Contents*. Stanford, CA: Stanford University Press, 2004.

———. "The Tragic Farce of Marx, Hegel, and Engels: A Note." *History and Theory* 11, no. 3 (1972): 335–37.

Mazrui, Ali. "The Message of Rwanda: Recolonize Africa?" *New Perspectives Quarterly* 11, no. 4 (1994): 18–20.

Mazzini, Giuseppe. *Life and Writings of Joseph Mazzini*, 2nd ed., 6 vols. London: Smith, Elder, 1891.

McMahon, Darrin M. *Enemies of the Enlightenment: The French Counter-Enlightenment and the Making of Modernity*. New York: Oxford University Press, 2001.

Meek, Ronald L. *Social Science and the Ignoble Savage*. Cambridge: Cambridge University Press, 1976.

Mehta, Uday Singh. *Liberalism and Empire: A Study in Nineteenth-Century British Thought*. Chicago: University of Chicago Press, 1999.

Melko, Matthew. *The Nature of Civilizations*. Boston: Porter Sargent, 1969.

Mertens, Thomas. "From 'Perpetual Peace' to 'The Law of Peoples': Kant, Habermas and Rawls on International Relations." *Kantian Review* 6 (2002): 60–84.

Merton, Robert K. "Civilization and Culture." *Sociology and Social Research* 21, no. 2 (1936): 103–13.

Mignolo, Walter D. Introduction to *Natural and Moral History of the Indies* [1590], by José de Acosta. Edited by Jane E. Mangan, translated by Frances M. López-Morillas, xvii–xxviii. Durham, NC: Duke University Press, 2002.

Mill, John Stuart. "Civilization." 1836. In *Essays on Politics and Culture*, edited by Gertrude Himmelfarb, 51–84. Garden City, NY: Doubleday, 1962.

———. "A Few Words on Non-Intervention." 1859. In *Essays on Politics and Culture*, edited by Gertrude Himmelfarb, 396–413. Garden City, NY: Doubleday, 1962.

————. *Utilitarianism, Liberty, and Representative Government.* 1859–1861.
London: Dent & Sons, 1962.

Milne, Seumas. "The Battle for History." *Guardian Weekly*, September 19–25,
2002, 11.

Misra, Maria. "The Empire Strikes Back." *New Statesman*, November 12,
2001, 25–27.

Montesquieu. *The Spirit of the Laws.* 1748. Translated by Thomas Nugent.
New York: Hafner, 1949.

Moravcsik, Andrew. "Taking Preferences Seriously: A Liberal Theory of
International Politics." *International Organization* 51, no. 4 (1997):
513–33.

Morgan, Lewis H. *Ancient Society; or, Researches in the Lines of Human Progress from Savagery through Barbarism to Civilization.* 1877. Chicago:
Kerr, 1907.

————. *The League of the Iroquois.* 1851. North Dighton, MA: JG Press,
1995.

Mosseau, Michael. "Market Prosperity, Democratic Consolidation, and Democratic Peace." *Journal of Conflict Resolution* 44, no. 4 (2000): 472–507.

Moynihan, Daniel Patrick. "Civilization Need Not Die." *Harvard Magazine*,
July–August 2002, 67–69.

Mozaffari, Mehdi. "The Transformationalist Perspective and the Rise of a
Global Standard of Civilization." *International Relations of the Asia-
Pacific* 1, no. 2 (2001): 247–64.

Muhlberger, Steven, and Phil Paine. "Democracy's Place in World History."
Journal of World History 4, no. 1 (1993): 23–45.

Muldoon, James. *The Americas in the Spanish World Order: The Justification
for Conquest in the Seventeenth Century.* Philadelphia: University of Pennsylvania Press, 1994.

————, ed. *The Expansion of Europe: The First Phase.* Philadelphia: University of Pennsylvania Press, 1977.

————. "The Indian as Irishman." *Essex Institute Historical Collections* 111
(1975): 267–89.

————. *Popes, Lawyers, and Infidels.* Philadelphia: University of Pennsylvania
Press, 1979.

Münkler, Herfried. *Empires: The Logic of World Domination from Ancient
Rome to the United States.* Translated by Patrick Camiller. Cambridge:
Polity Press, 2007.

Murray, Charles. *Human Accomplishment: The Pursuit of Excellence in the
Arts and Sciences, 800 B.C. to 1950.* New York: Harper Collins, 2003.

————. "The Idea of Progress: Once Again, with Feeling." *Hoover Digest*,
2001, no. 3. www-hoover.org/publications/digest/3467936.html.

Muthu, Sankar. *Enlightenment against Empire.* Princeton, NJ: Princeton
University Press, 2003.

————. "Enlightenment Anti-Imperialism." *Social Research* 66, no. 4 (1999):
959–1007.

"NATO Lines Up Russian Support." *New York Times (on the Web)*, September
13, 2001.

Neumann, Iver B. *Uses of the Other: "The East" in European Identity Formation*. Minneapolis: University of Minnesota Press, 1998.

Nietzsche, Friedrich. "Aus dem Nachlass der Achtzigerjahre." In *Werke*, 3:837. Munich: Carl Hanser Verlag, 1966.

Ninio, Julian. *The Empire of Ignorance, Hypocrisy and Obedience*. Melbourne: Scribe, 2004.

Nisbet, Robert. *History of the Idea of Progress*. London: Heinemann, 1980.

Norgaard, Richard B. *Development Betrayed: The End of Progress and a Coevolutionary Revisioning of the Future*. London: Routledge, 1994.

Nussbaum, Martha C. "Kant and Stoic Cosmopolitanism." *Journal of Political Philosophy* 5, no. 1 (1997): 1–25.

———. "Patriotism and Cosmopolitanism." In *For Love of Country: Debating the Limits of Patriotism*, edited by Joshua Cohen, 2–17. Boston: Beacon, 1996.

Nye, Joseph. "The New Rome Meets the New Barbarians." *Economist*, March 23, 2002, 23–25.

Nys, Ernest. Introduction to *De Indis et de Iure Belli Relectiones*, by Franciscus de Vitoria. Edited by Ernest Nys, 9–53. Reprint of 1696 ed. New York: Oceana for the Carnegie Institution, 1964.

O'Hagan, Jacinta. *Conceptualizing the West in International Relations: From Spengler to Said*. Basingstoke: Palgrave, 2002.

Odom, William E, and Robert Dujarric. *America's Inadvertent Empire*. New Haven, CT: Yale University Press, 2004.

Offe, Clause. "Modern 'Barbarity': A Micro State of Nature." *Constellations* 2, no. 3 (1996): 354–77.

Onuf, Nicholas Greenwood. *The Republican Legacy in International Thought*. Cambridge: Cambridge University Press, 1998.

Oren, Ido. "The Subjectivity of the 'Democratic' Peace: Changing U.S. Perceptions of Imperial Germany." In *Debating the Democratic Peace: An International Security Reader*, edited by Michael E. Brown, Sean M. Lynn-Jones, and Steven E. Miller, 263–300. Cambridge, MA,: MIT Press, 1996.

Pagden, Anthony. "The 'Defence of Civilization' in Eighteenth-Century Social Theory." *History of the Human Sciences* 1, no. 1 (1988): 33–45.

———. *The Fall of Natural Man: The American Indian and the Origins of Comparative Ethnology*. Cambridge: Cambridge University Press, 1982.

———. "The Genesis of 'Governance' and Enlightenment Conceptions of the Cosmopolitan World Order." *International Social Science Journal* 50, no. 155 (1998): 7–15.

———. *Lords of All the World: Ideologies of Empire in Spain, Britain and France c.1500–c.1800*. New Haven, CT: Yale University Press, 1995.

———. *Peoples and Empires*. London: Weidenfeld & Nicholson, 2001.

———. "Stoicism, Cosmopolitanism, and the Legacy of European Imperialism." *Constellations* 7, no. 1 (2000): 3–22.

Pakenham, Thomas. *The Scramble for Africa (1876–1912)*. London: Abacus, 1992.

Palonen, Kari. "Rhetorical and Temporal Perspectives on Conceptual Change." *Finnish Yearbook of Political Thought* 3 (1999): 41–59.

Panitch, Leo, and Sam Gindin. "Global Capitalism and American Empire." In *The New Imperial Challenge: Socialist Register 2004*, edited by Leo Panitch and Colin Leys. New York: Monthly Review, 2003.

Pfaff, William. *The Wrath of Nations: Civilization and the Furies of Nationalism.* New York: Simon & Schuster, 1993.

Pitts, Jennifer. *A Turn to Empire: The Rise of Imperial Liberalism in Britain and France.* Princeton, NJ: Princeton University Press, 2006.

Pocock, J. G. A. "The History of Political Thought: A Methodological Enquiry." In *Philosophy, Politics, and Society*, 2nd ser., edited by Peter Laslett and W. C. Runicman, 183–202. Oxford: Blackwell, 1962.

Pogge, Thomas W. "Cosmopolitanism and Sovereignty." *Ethics* 103, no. 1 (1992): 48–75.

Poirot, Clifford S., Jr. "The Return to Barbarism." *Journal of Economic Issues* 31, no. 1 (1997): 233–44.

Pollock, S., H. K. Bhaba, C. A. Breckenridge, and D. Chakrabarty. "Cosmopolitanisms." *Public Culture* 12, no. 3 (2000): 577–89.

Prichard, J. C. "On the Extinction of Human Races." *Edinburgh New Philosophical Journal* 28 (1839): 166–70.

Pullapilly, Cyriac K., and Edwin J. Van Kley, eds. *Asia and the West: Encounters and Exchanges from the Age of Explorations.* Notre Dame, IN: Cross Cultural, 1986.

Rachewiltz, Igor de. *Papal Envoys to the Great Khans.* London: Faber & Faber, 1971.

Rawls, John. "The Law of Peoples." In *On Human Rights: The Oxford Amnesty Lectures*, edited by Stephen Shute and Susan Hurley, 41–82. New York: Basic, 1993.

———. *The Law of Peoples.* Cambridge, MA: Harvard University Press, 1999.

Razavi, Mehdi Amin, and David Ambuel, eds. *Philosophy, Religion, and the Question of Intolerance.* Albany: State University of New York Press, 1997.

Rée, Jonathon. "Cosmopolitanism and the Experience of Nationality." In *Cosmopolitics: Thinking and Feeling beyond the Nation*, edited by Pheng Cheah and Bruce Robbins, 77–90. Minneapolis: University of Minnesota Press, 1998.

Reichwein, Adolf. *China and Europe: Intellectual and Artistic Contacts in the Eighteenth Century.* London: Kegan Paul, Trench, Trubner, 1925.

Rhodes, Cecil. "Rhodes' 'Confession of Faith' of 1877." Appendix to *Cecil Rhodes*, by John Flint, 249–52. London: Hutchinson, 1976.

Ricardo, David. *Principles of Political Economy and Taxation.* Edited by E. C. K. Gonner. London: George Bell & Sons, 1891.

Rice, Condoleezza. "The Promise of Democratic Peace: Why Promoting Freedom Is the Only Realistic Path to Security." *Washington Post*, December 11, 2005, B07.

Richards, Paul. *Fighting for the Rainforest: War, Youth & Resources in Sierra Leone.* Oxford: International Africa Institute in association with James Currey; Portsmouth, NH: Heinemann, 1996.

Richter, Melvin. *The History of Political and Social Concepts: A Critical Introduction.* Cambridge: Cambridge University Press, 1995.

Ricoeur, Paul. *History and Truth*. Translated by Charles A. Kelbley. Evanston, IL: Northwestern University Press, 1965.

Roberts, J. M. *Triumph of the West*. London: British Broadcasting Corporation, 1985.

Robertson, William. *The History of America*. 12th ed. 4 vols. London: Cadell & Davies, 1812.

Robson, William A. *Civilisation and the Growth of Law*. London: Macmillan, 1935.

Rodrik, Dani. "How Far Will International Economic Integration Go?" *Journal of Economic Perspectives* 14, no. 1 (2000): 177–86.

Rogin, Michael Paul. *Ronald Reagan, the Movie: And Other Episodes in Political Demonology*. Berkeley: University of California Press, 1987.

Roosevelt, Theodore. "The Roosevelt Corollary to the Monroe Doctrine." United States' President Theodore Roosevelt's Annual Address to Congress, December 6, 1904.

Rosen, Stephen Peter. "The Future of War and the American Military." *Harvard Magazine* 104, no. 5 (2002): 29–31.

Rostow, W. W. *The Stages of Economic Growth: A Non-Communist Manifesto*. New York: Cambridge University Press, 1961.

Rothkopf, David. "In Praise of Cultural Imperialism?" *Foreign Policy* 107 (1997): 38–53.

Rousseau, Jean-Jacques. "Abstract and Judgement of Saint-Pierre's Project for Perpetual Peace." In *Rousseau on International Relations*, edited by Stanley Hoffman and David P. Fidler, 53–100. Oxford: Clarendon, 1991.

Rumelili, Bahar. *Constructing Regional Community and Order in Europe and Southeast Asia*. Basingstoke: Palgrave, 2007.

Russett, Bruce. *Controlling the Sword: The Democratic Governance of National Security*. Cambridge, MA: Harvard University Press, 1990.

———. *Grasping the Democratic Peace*. Princeton, NJ: Princeton University Press, 1993.

Russett, Bruce, John R. Oneal, and David R. Davis. "The Third Leg of the Kantian Tripod for Peace: International Organizations and Militarized Disputes, 1950–85." *International Organization* 52, no. 3 (1998): 441–67.

Ryan, Michael T. "Assimilating New Worlds in the Sixteenth and Seventeenth Centuries." *Comparative Studies in Society and History* 23, no. 4 (1981): 519–53.

Said, Edward W. *Culture and Imperialism*. New York: Vintage, 1994.

———. *Orientalism*. London: Routledge & Kegan Paul, 1978.

———. Preface to *Orientalism*. 25th anniversary ed. London: Penguin, 2003.

Salter, Mark B. *Barbarians & Civilization in International Relations*. London: Pluto, 2002.

Schäfer, Wolf. "Global Civilization and Local Cultures: A Crude Look at the Whole." *International Sociology* 16, no. 3 (2001): 301–19.

Schapiro, J. Salwyn. *Condorcet and the Rise of Liberalism*. New York: Octagon, 1963.

Schiller, F. C. S. Introduction to *Civilisation or Civilisations: An Essay in the Spenglerian Philosophy of History*. Edited by E. H. Goddard and P. A. Gibbons, vii–xvi. London: Constable, 1926.

Schiller, Friedrich von. "The Nature and Value of Universal History: An Inaugural Lecture [1789]." *History and Theory* 11, no. 3 (1972): 321–34.

Schirmer, Daniel B., and Stephen Rosskamm Shalom, eds. *The Philippines Reader: A History of Colonialism, Neocolonialism, Dictatorship, and Resistance*. Cambridge, MA: South End, 1987.

Schmidt, Brian. *The Political Discourse of Anarchy*. Albany: State University of New York Press, 1998.

Schwarzenberger, Georg. "The Standard of Civilisation in International Law." In *Current Legal Problems*, edited by George W. Keeton and Georg Schwarzenberger, 212–34. London: Stevens & Sons, 1955.

Schweitzer, Albert. *The Decay and the Restoration of Civilization*. Translated by C. T. Campion. 2nd ed. London: A. & C. Black, 1947.

Scott, David. *Refashioning Futures*. Princeton, NJ: Princeton University Press, 1999.

Scott, James Brown. *The Spanish Origin of International Law: Francisco de Vitoria and His Law of Nations*. Oxford: Clarendon, 1932.

Scruton, Roger. *The West and the Rest: Globalization and the Terrorist Threat*. London: Continuum, 2002.

Seabrooke, Leonard. "The Economic Taproot of U.S. Imperialism: The Bush Rentier Shift." *International Politics* 41, no. 3 (2004): 293–318.

Sen, Amartya. "Democracy as Universal Value." *Journal of Democracy* 10, no. 3 (1999): 3–17.

Sepúlveda, Ginés. "Summary of Sepúlveda's Position." In *In Defense of the Indians*, by Bartolomé de Las Casas, edited and translated by Stafford Poole, 11–13. DeKalb: Northern Illinois University Press, 1974.

Sharma, Jagdish P. *Republics in Ancient India, c. 1500 BC–500 BC*. Leiden: Brill, 1968.

Shils, E. "Political Development in the New States—The Will to Be Modern." In *Readings in Social Evolution and Development*, edited by S. N. Eisenstadt, 379–419. Oxford: Pergamon, 1970.

Shweder, Richard A. "On the Return of the 'Civilizing Project.'" *Dædalus* 131, no. 3 (2002): 117–21.

Sinclair, Timothy J. "Passing Judgement: Credit Rating Processes as Regulatory Mechanisms of Governance in the Emerging World Order." *Review of International Political Economy* 1, no. 1 (1994): 133–59.

Skinner, Quentin. "Language and Social Change." In *Meaning and Context: Quentin Skinner and His Critics*, edited by James Tully, 119–32. Cambridge: Polity, 1988.

———. "Meaning and Understanding in the History of Ideas." *History and Theory* 8, no. 1 (1969): 3–53.

———. "Rhetoric and Conceptual Change." *Finnish Yearbook of Political Thought* 3 (1999): 60–72.

Smith, Adam. *An Inquiry into the Nature and Causes of the Wealth of Nations*. 1776. London: Nelson & Sons, 1869.

Smith, Steve. "Is the Truth out There? Eight Questions about International
    Order." In *International Order and the Future of World Politics*, edited by
    T. V. Paul and John A. Hall, 99–119. Cambridge: Cambridge University
    Press, 1999.
Snow, Alpheus Henry. *The Question of Aborigines in the Law and Practice of
    Nations*. New York: Putnam's Sons; Knickerbocker, 1921.
Snyder, Craig. "Democracy and the Vitality of Evil." *National Interest* 17
    (1989): 81–84.
Spencer, Herbert. *Social Statistics*. Rev. ed. London: Williams & Norgate,
    1892.
Spengler, Oswald. *The Decline of the West*. Edited by Helmut Werner, trans-
    lated by Charles Francis Atkinson. New York: Knopf, 1962.
Spiro, David E. "The Insignificance of the Liberal Peace." In *Debating the
    Democratic Peace: An* International Security *Reader*, edited by Michael E.
    Brown, Sean M. Lynn-Jones, and Steven E. Miller, 202–38. Cambridge,
    MA: MIT Press, 1996.
Starobinski, Jean. "The Word Civilization." In *Blessings in Disguise; or, The
    Morality of Evil*. Translated by Arthur Goldhammer, 1–35. Cambridge,
    MA: Harvard University Press, 1993.
Stephanson, Anders. *Manifest Destiny: American Expansionism and the Em-
    pire of Right*. New York: Hill & Wang, 1995.
Stevenson, John R. "South West Africa Cases (Ethiopia v. South Africa; Liberia
    v. South Africa), Second Phase." *American Journal of International Law*
    61, no. 1 (1967): 116–210.
Stiglitz, Joseph E. "Towards a New Paradigm for Development: Strategies, Pol-
    icies, and Processes." 1998 Prebisch Lecture at UNCTAD, Geneva, October
    19, 1998.
Suskind, Ron. "Without a Doubt." *New York Times Magazine*, October 17,
    2004, 44–51, 64, 102, 106.
Suzuki, Shogo. *Civilisation and Empire: East Asia's Encounter with the Euro-
    pean International Society*. London: Routledge, forthcoming.
———. "Japan's Socialization into Janus-Faced European International Soci-
    ety." *European Journal of International Relations* 11, no. 1 (2005):
    137–64.
Tatham, George. "Environmentalism and Possibilism." In *Geography in the
    Twentieth Century: A Study of Growth, Fields, Techniques, Aims and
    Trends*, edited by Griffith Taylor, 3rd ed., 128–62. New York: Philosophi-
    cal Library; London: Methuen, 1957.
Tipps, Dean C. "Modernization Theory and the Comparative Study of Socie-
    ties: A Critical Perspective." *Comparative Studies in Society and History*
    15, no. 2 (1973): 199–226.
Todorov, Tzvetan. *The Conquest of America: The Question of the Other*.
    Translated by Richard Howard. New York: HarperPerennial, 1984.
Tolson, Jay. "A Civilizing Mission?" *Wilson Quarterly* 18, no. 1 (1994): 6–9.
Toulmin, Stephen. *Cosmopolis: The Hidden Agenda of Modernity*. New York:
    Free Press, 1990.

Toynbee, Arnold J. *Civilization on Trial*. New York: Oxford University Press, 1948.

—, ed. and trans. *Greek Historical Thought from Homer to the Age of Heraclius*. New York: Mentor, 1952.

—. *A Study of History*. Rev. and abr. ed. London: Thames & Hudson and Oxford University Press, 1972.

—. *The World and the West*. London: Oxford University Press, 1953.

Tribe, Keith. Translator's introduction to *Futures Past: On the Semantics of Historical Time*, by Reinhart Koselleck. Translated by Keith Tribe, vii–xvii. Cambridge, MA: MIT Press, 1985.

Tuck, Richard. *The Rights of War and Peace: Political Thought and the International Order from Grotius to Kant*. Oxford: Oxford University Press, 2001.

Tully, James. *An Approach to Political Philosophy: Locke in Contexts*. Cambridge: Cambridge University Press, 1993.

—. *Strange Multiplicity: Constitutionalism in an Age of Diversity*. Cambridge: Cambridge University Press, 1995.

Turgot, Anne Robert Jacques. "A Philosophical Review of the Successive Advances of the Human Mind." In *Turgot on Progress, Sociology and Economics*, edited and translated by Ronald L. Meek, 41–62. Cambridge: Cambridge University Press, 1973.

Turney-High, Harry Holbert. *Primitive War: Its Practice and Concepts*. 2nd ed. Columbia: University of South Carolina Press, 1971.

Van Doren, Charles. *The Idea of Progress*. New York: Praeger, 1967.

van Krieken, Robert. "The Barbarism of Civilization: Cultural Genocide and the 'Stolen Generations.'" *British Journal of Sociology* 50, no. 2 (1999): 297–315.

Vattel, Emerich de. *The Law of Nations; or, The Principles of Natural Law*. 1758. Translated by Charles G. Fenwick. New York: Oceana Publications for the Carnegie Institution, 1964.

Vega, Bartolomé de la. "Introductory Letter." In *In Defense of the Indians*, by Bartolomé de Las Casas, edited and translated by Stafford Poole, 3–5. DeKalb: Northern Illinois University Press, 1974.

Venn, Couze. "Altered States: Post-Enlightenment Cosmopolitanism and Transmodern Socialities." *Theory, Culture & Society* 19, nos. 1–2 (2002): 65–80.

Vidal, Gore. *Imperial America: Reflections on the United States of Amnesia*. New York: Nation, 2004.

—. *Perpetual War for Perpetual Peace*. New York: Nation, 2002.

Virgil. *The Aeneid*. Translated by Robert Fitzgerald. New York: Random House, 1983.

Vitoria, Franciscus de. *De Indis et de Iure Belli Relectiones*. 1539. Edited by Ernest Nys. Reprint of 1696 ed. New York: Oceana Publications for the Carnegie Institution, 1964.

Voltaire. *The Philosophy of History*. Reprint of 1766 ed. London: Vision, 1965.

von Hippel, Karin. "Democracy by Force: A Renewed Commitment to Nation Building." *Washington Quarterly* 23, no. 1 (2000): 95–112.

———. *Democracy by Force: US Military Intervention in the Post-Cold War World*. Cambridge: Cambridge University Press, 2000.

Wade, Robert Hunter. "The Invisible Hand of the American Empire." openDemocracy, www.opendemocracy.net, March 13, 2003.

Walker, R. B. J. *Inside/Outside: International Relations as Political Theory*. Cambridge: Cambridge University Press, 1993.

Wallerstein, Immanuel. *The Decline of American Power: The US in a Chaotic World*. New York: New Press, 2003.

———. "The Eagle Has Crash Landed." *Foreign Policy* 131 (2002): 60–68.

Walzer, Michael. *Just and Unjust Wars*. 3rd ed. New York: Basic, 2000.

———. "The Politics of Rescue." *Social Research* 62, no. 1 (1995): 53–66.

———. "Spheres of Affection." In *For Love of Country: Debating the Limits of Patriotism*, edited by Joshua Cohen, 126–27. Boston: Beacon, 1996.

Ward, Robert. *An Enquiry into the Foundation and History of the Law of Nations in Europe from the Time of the Greeks and Romans to the Age of Grotius*. Reprint of 1795 ed. 2 vols. New York: Garland, 1973.

Wattles, Jeffrey. *The Golden Rule*. New York: Oxford University Press, 1996.

Welsh, Jennifer M. *Edmund Burke and International Relations: The Commonwealth of Europe and the Crusade against the French Revolution*. New York: St. Martin's, 1995.

Werbner, P. "Global Pathways: Working-Class Cosmopolitans and the Creation of Transnational Ethnic Worlds." *Social Anthropology* 7, no. 1 (1999): 17–35.

Westlake, John. *The Collected Papers of John Westlake on Public International Law*. Edited by L. Oppenheim. Cambridge: Cambridge University Press, 1914.

Wheaton, Henry. *Elements of International Law*. 3rd ed. London: Sampson Low, Son and Co., 1863.

———. *Wheaton's Elements of International Law*. Edited by Coleman Phillipson. 5th ed. London: Stevens & Sons, 1916.

Wheeler, Everett L. "Terrorism and Military Theory: An Historical Perspective." *Terrorism and Political Violence* 3, no. 1 (1991): 6–33.

Wheeler, Nicholas J. "Guardian Angel or Global Gangster: A Review of the Ethical Claims of International Society." *Political Studies* 44, no. 1 (1996): 123–35.

White House. *The National Security Strategy of the United States of America*. Washington, DC: White House, September 2002.

Whitney, William Dwight. *Oriental and Linguistic Studies*. Reprint of 1872 ed. 2 vols. Freeport, NY: Books for Libraries, 1972.

Wight, Martin. *Systems of States*. Edited by Hedley Bull. Leicester: Leicester University Press, 1977.

———. "Western Values in International Relations." In *Diplomatic Investigations*, edited by Herbert Butterfield and Martin Wight, 89–131. London: Allen & Unwin, 1966.

———. "Why Is There No International Theory?" In *Diplomatic Investigations: Essays in the Theory of International Politics*, edited by Herbert Butterfield and Martin Wight, 17–34. London: Allen & Unwin, 1966.

Wiktorowicz, Quintan, and John Kaltner. "Killing in the Name of Islam: Al-Qaeda's Justification for September 11." *Middle East Policy* 10, no. 2 (2003): 76–92.

Wiktorowicz, Quintan. "A Genealogy of Radical Islam." *Studies in Conflict & Terrorism* 28, no. 2 (2005): 75–97.

Williams, Raymond. *Keywords: A Vocabulary of Culture and Society*. Rev. ed. New York: Oxford University Press, 1985.

Williams, Robert A., Jr. *The American Indian in Western Legal Thought: The Discourses of Conquest*. New York: Oxford University Press, 1990.

Williams, William Appleman. *The Tragedy of American Diplomacy*. 2nd ed. New York: Delta, 1972.

Wolf, Eric R. *Europe and the People without History*. Berkeley: University of California Press, 1982.

Wolff, Christian. *Jus Gentium Method Scientifica Pertactatum*. 1749. New York: Oceana, 1964.

Wolfsenberger, Donald R. "The Return of the Imperial Presidency? *Wilson Quarterly*, Spring 2002, 36–41.

Wood, Ellen Meiksins. "Kosovo and the New Imperialism." *Monthly Review* 51, no. 2 (1999), www.monthlyreview.org/699wood.htm.

Wright, Quincy. "The Bombardment of Damascus." *American Journal of International Law* 20, no. 2 (1926): 263–89.

Wright, Robert. *Nonzero: The Logic of Human Destiny*. New York: Vintage, 2001.

Wright, Robert, Paul Davies, Samantha Power, Eric J. Hobsbawm, Francis Fukuyama, Martha Nussbaum, Alice M. Rivlin, and Fareed Zakaria. "The World's Most Dangerous Ideas." *Foreign Policy* 144 (2004): 32–49.

Zacher, Mark W., and Richard A. Matthew. "Liberal International Theory: Common Threads, Divergent Strands." In *Controversies in International Relations Theory*, edited by Charles W. Kegley, 107–50. New York: St. Martin's, 1995.

Zagorin, Perez. *How the Idea of Religious Toleration Came to the West*. Princeton, NJ: Princeton University Press, 2003.

Zakaria, Fareed. "Culture Is Destiny: A Conversation with Lee Kuan Yew." *Foreign Affairs* 73, no. 2 (1994): 109–25.

Index

aborigines, 55, 113–15, 117, 124, 134. *See also* American Indians; Australian Aborigines
Abu Ghraib prison, Iraq, 185, 212
Acosta, José de, 54–55, 180
Adair, James, 250n29
Afghanistan, 186; British occupation of, 133, 210; conflict in, 222, 231; and democracy, 171; Soviet occupation of, 210; and United Nations, 197–98; United Sates–led intervention in, 192, 195, 198, 206, 209–10, 218–19
Africa, 58, 124, 145, 155, 181, 194–96, 256n7; as dark continent, 149, 164; and democracy, 171; intervention in, 194–96; scramble for 17, 149–50, 255n59; sub-Saharan Africa, 150, 155, 186; as uncivilized, 121, 172, 194; warfare of, 183; West Africa, 164–65, 195, 214,

256n7. *See also* South West Africa Cases; *individual countries of Africa*
African Rights, 261n16
Agenda for Peace, 88, 245n32
Alexander IV (pope), 112
Alexander VI (pope), 136, 141
Alexander the Great, 91–92, 242n53
Alexandrowicz, Charles Henry, 150
algebra, 221
Algeria, 122, 148
al-Jazari, 221
al-Khwārizmī, 221
Allen, Carleton Kemp, 118
al-Qa'ida (al Qaeda), 178, 183–84, 248n78
al-Razi, Zakariyya, 221
al-Zahrawi, 221
al-Zawhiri, Ayman, 178, 259n51
American Indians: conquest of, 54, 86, 112–17, 124–25, 130–47 passim, 218; customs and culture of, 54–55, 79; discovery